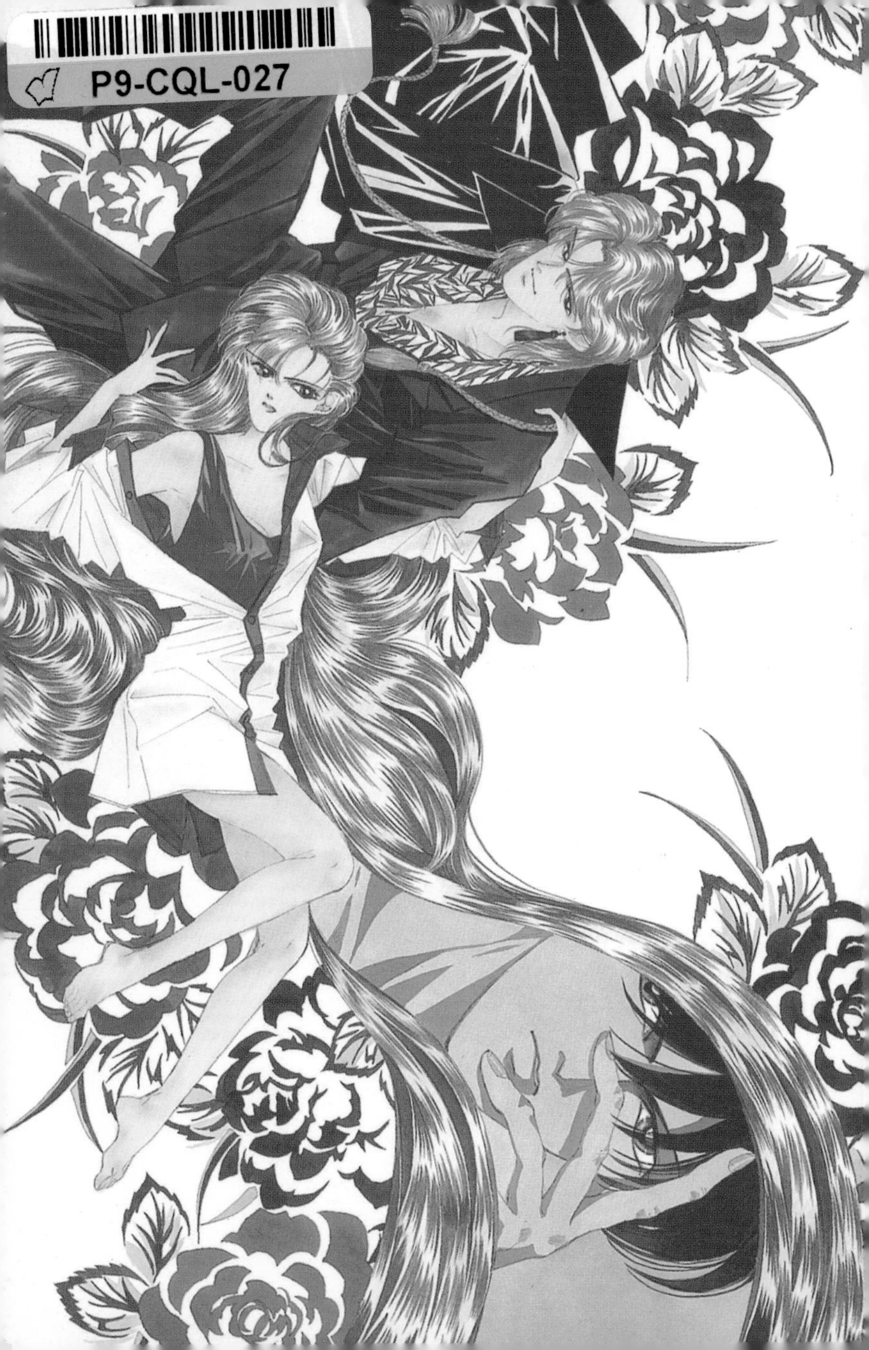

Other titles available from Broccoli Books

Until the Full Moon

1

by Sanami Matoh

brought to you by
BROCCOLI BOOKS
A DIVISION OF BROCCOLI INTERNATIONAL USA

Until the Full Moon Volume 1

English Adaptation Staff
Translation: Rie Hagihara
English Adaptation: Elizabeth Hanel
Touch-Up & Lettering: Fawn "tails" Lau
Cover & Graphic Supervision: Chris McDougall

Editor: Satsuki Yamashita, Dietrich Seto
Sales Manager: Ardith D. Santiago
Managing Editor: Shizuki Yamashita
Publisher: Hideki Uchino

Email: editor@broccolibooks.com
Website: www.bro-usa.com

A ![BROCCOLI BOOKS] Manga
Broccoli Books is a division of Broccoli International USA, Inc.
12211 W. Washington Blvd, Suite 110, Los Angeles CA 90066

FULLMOON ni sasayaite I © Sanami Matoh 1998
Originally published in Japan in 1998 by BIBLOS Co, Ltd.

ISBN: 1-932480-88-9

Published by Broccoli International USA, Inc.
First printing, October 2004

www.bro-usa.com

10 9 8 7 6 5 4 3 2 1
Printed in the United States

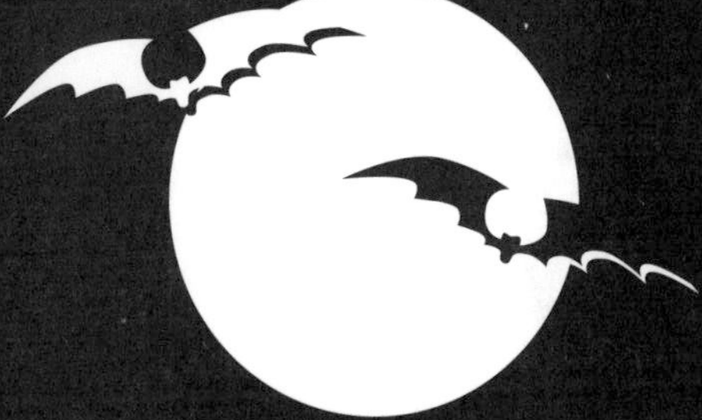

TABLE OF CONTENTS

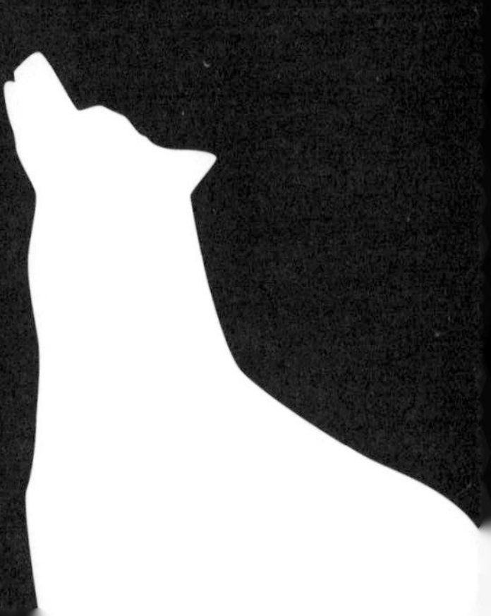

CHARACTERS

Marlo Vincent
Half-werewolf, half-vampire.
Changes into a woman during
the full moon.

Marlo Vincent
Marlo's female form.

David Vincent
Marlo's childhood friend. He's
also a vampire and a womanizer.

Arnet Vincent
David's father. A vampire
and famous doctor.

Kim
Arnet and David's servant.
He's a lower level demon.

Georgio Vincent

Marlo's father. He's a vampire who married a werewolf.

Mira

Marlo's mother. She's a were-wolf who married Georgio, a vampire.

Erik

A vampire. Belicia was adopted into his family as his sister.

Belicia

A werewolf. She was adopted into Erik's family.

Ira

Marlo's ex-girlfriend from America.

Kyle

A werewolf that is betrothed to "Marlo" in the old folk tale.

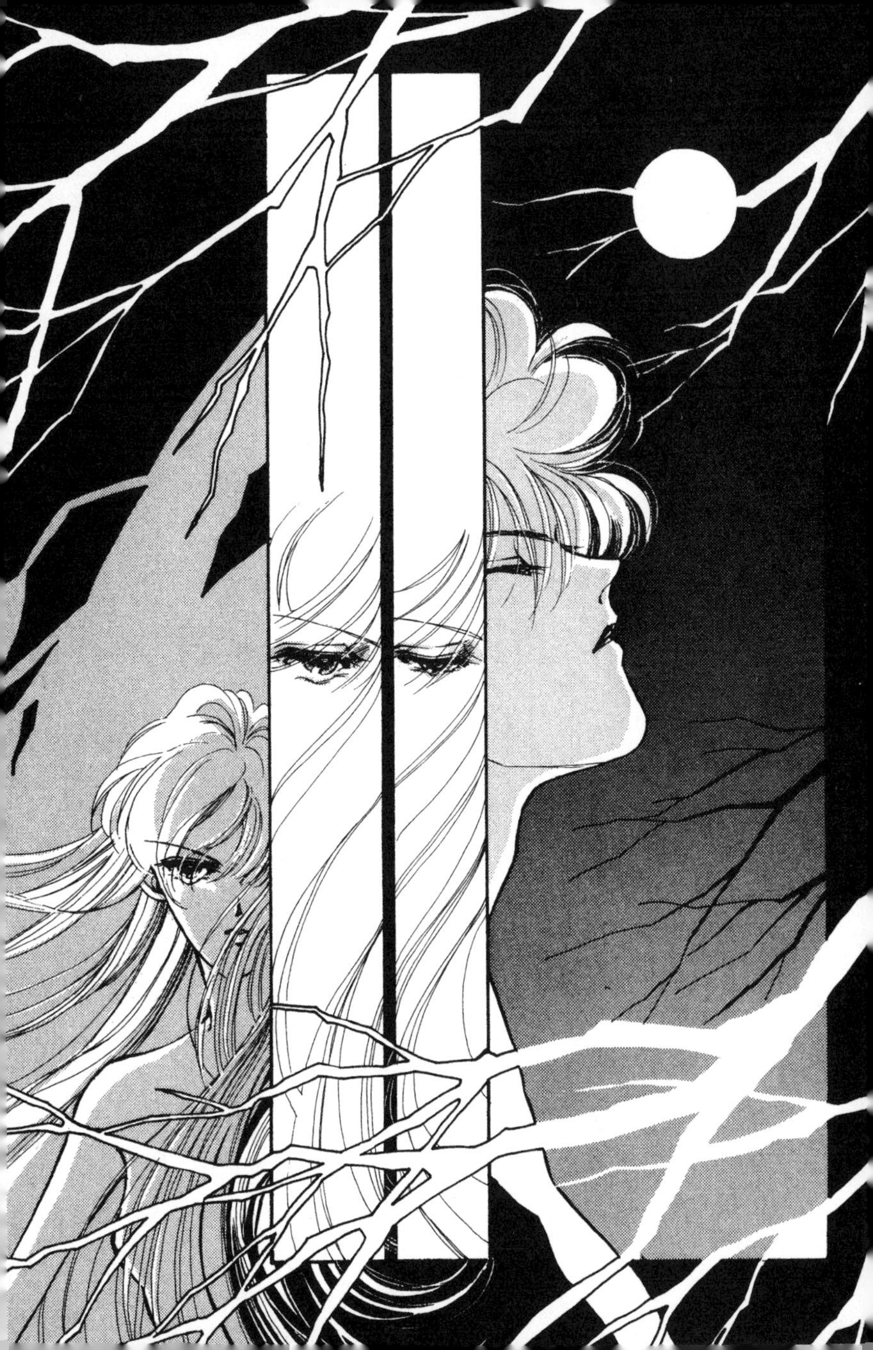

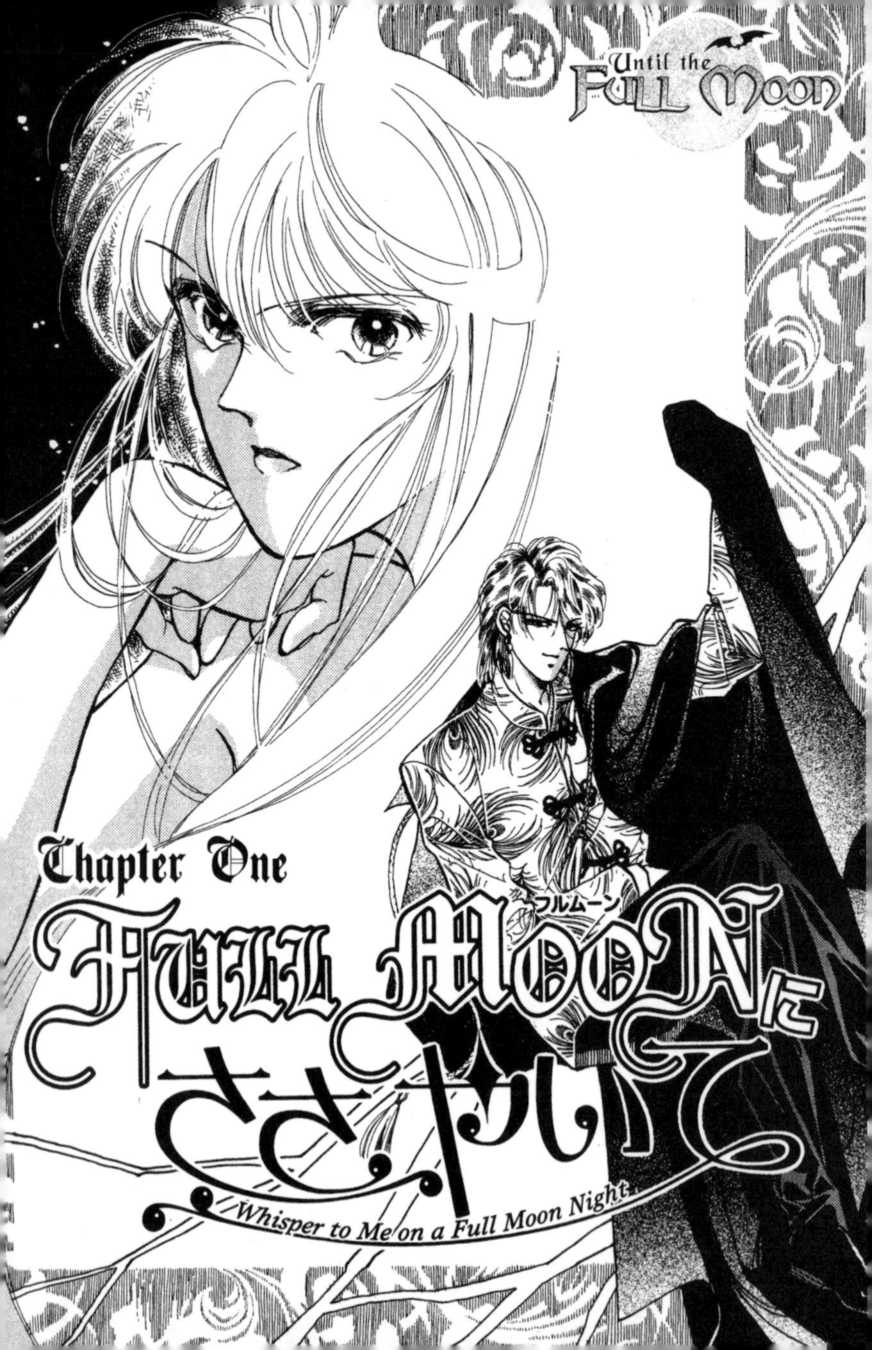
Until the FULL MOON
Chapter One
フルムーン
FULL MOONにささやいて
Whisper to Me on a Full Moon Night

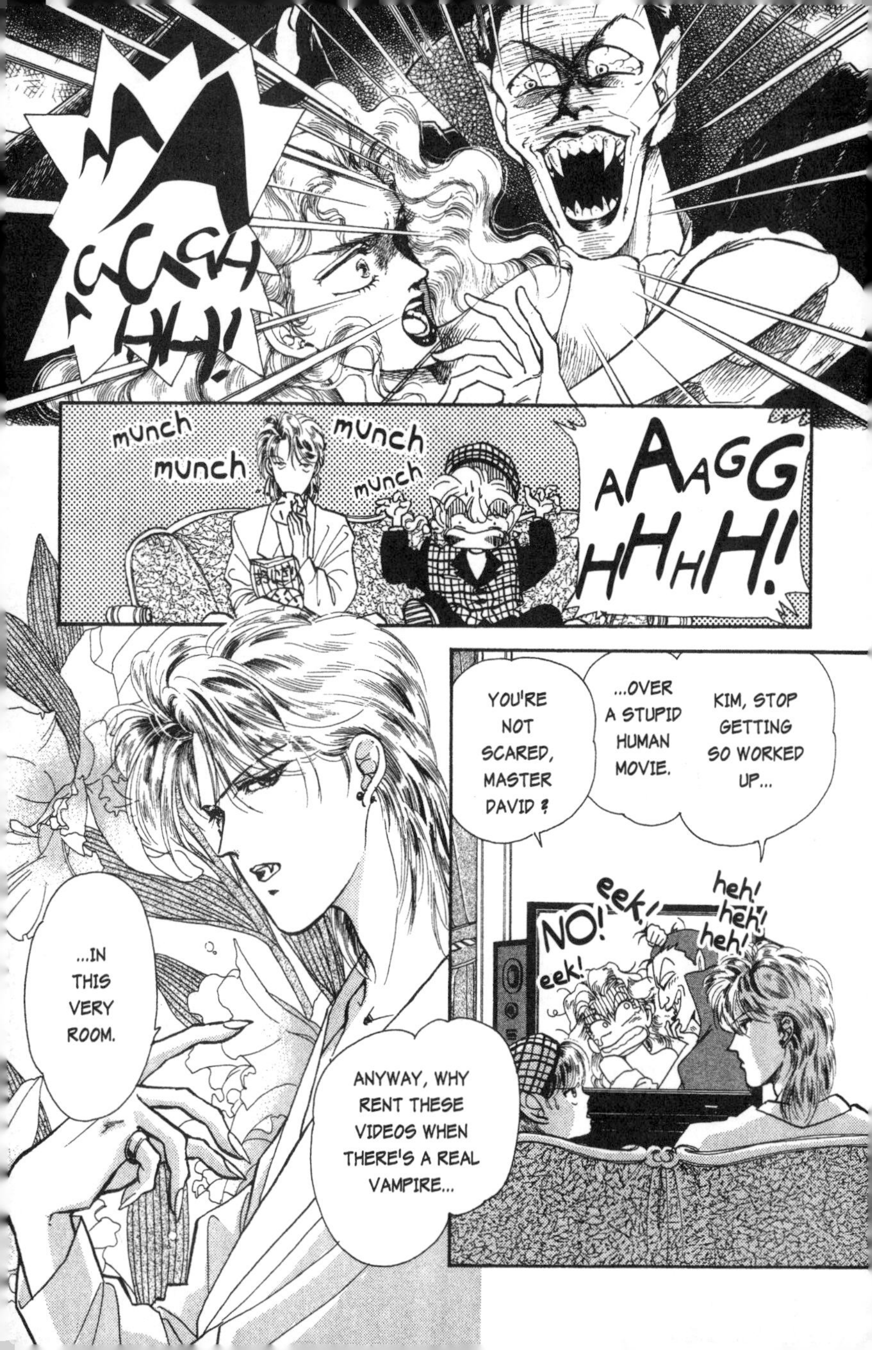
AAAGGGHHH!
AAAGGHHHH!
munch munch
munch munch
KIM, STOP GETTING SO WORKED UP...
...OVER A STUPID HUMAN MOVIE.
YOU'RE NOT SCARED, MASTER DAVID?
heh! heh! heh!
eek!
NO!
eek!
ANYWAY, WHY RENT THESE VIDEOS WHEN THERE'S A REAL VAMPIRE...
...IN THIS VERY ROOM.

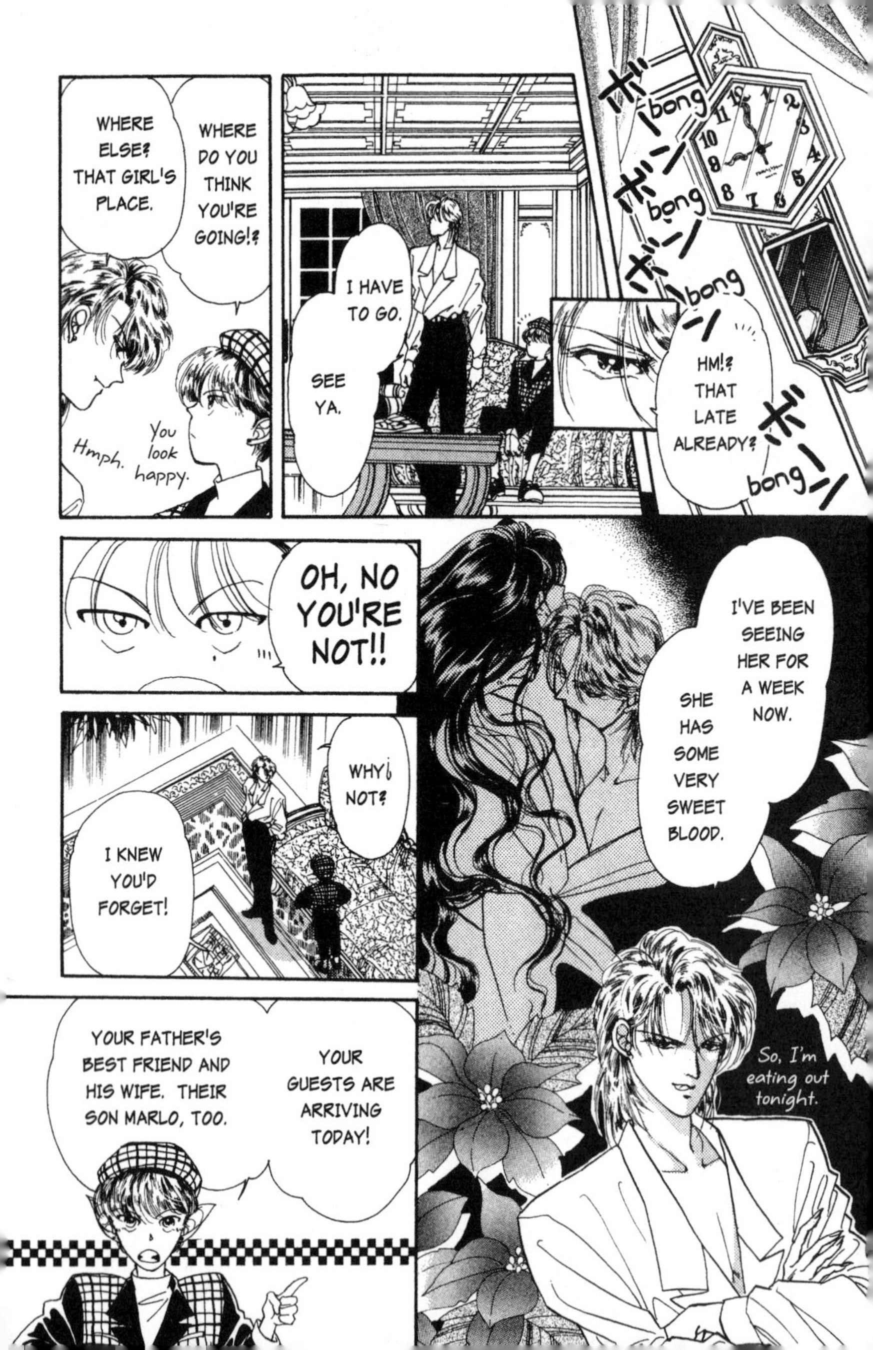
bong
bong
bong
bong
HM!? THAT LATE ALREADY?
I HAVE TO GO.
SEE YA.
WHERE DO YOU THINK YOU'RE GOING!?
WHERE ELSE? THAT GIRL'S PLACE.
Hmph.
You look happy.
I'VE BEEN SEEING HER FOR A WEEK NOW.
SHE HAS SOME VERY SWEET BLOOD.
So, I'm eating out tonight.
OH, NO YOU'RE NOT!!
WHY!? NOT?
I KNEW YOU'D FORGET!
YOUR GUESTS ARE ARRIVING TODAY!
YOUR FATHER'S BEST FRIEND AND HIS WIFE. THEIR SON MARLO, TOO.

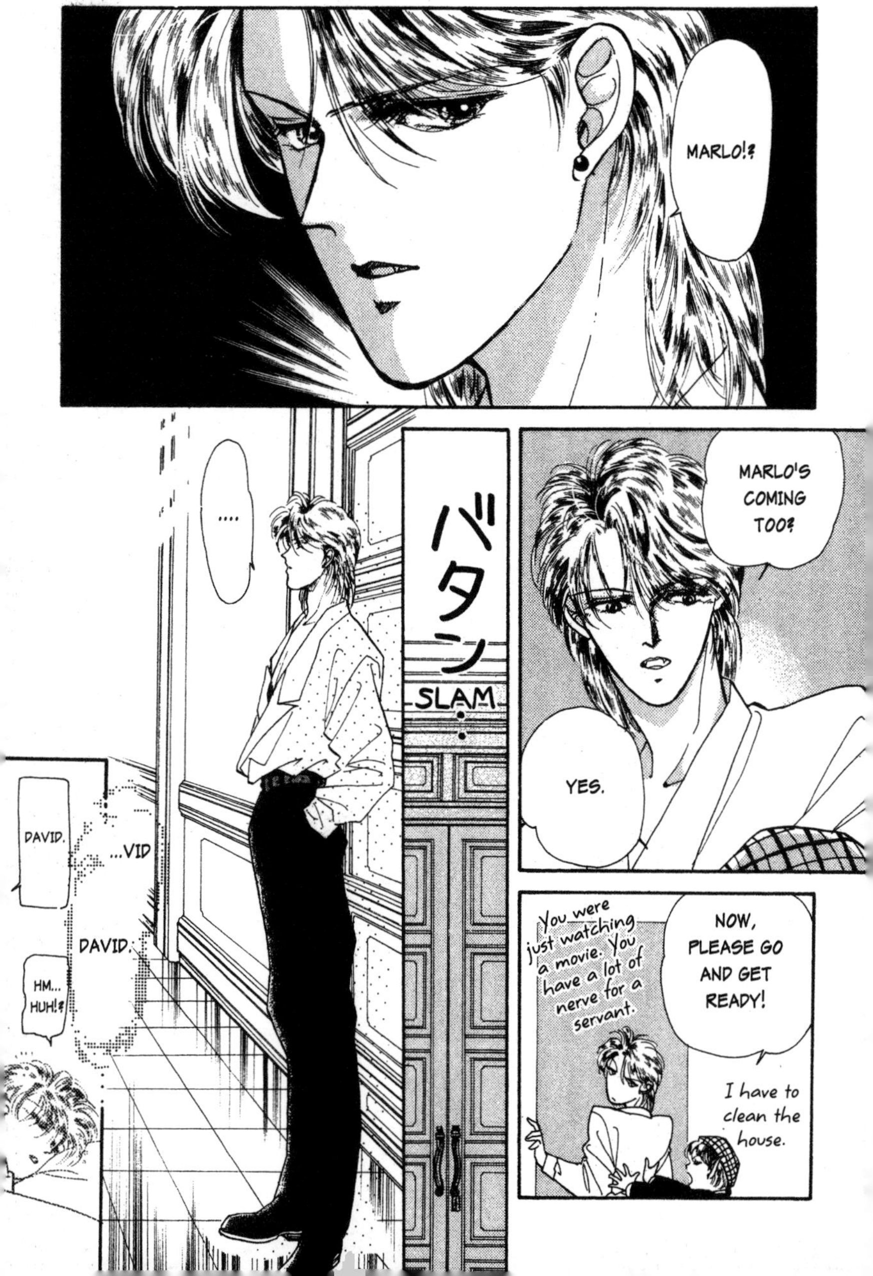
MARLO!?
MARLO'S COMING TOO?
YES.
NOW, PLEASE GO AND GET READY!
You were just watching a movie. You have a lot of nerve for a servant.
I have to clean the house.
バタン
SLAM
....
DAVID.
...VID
DAVID.
HM... HUH!?

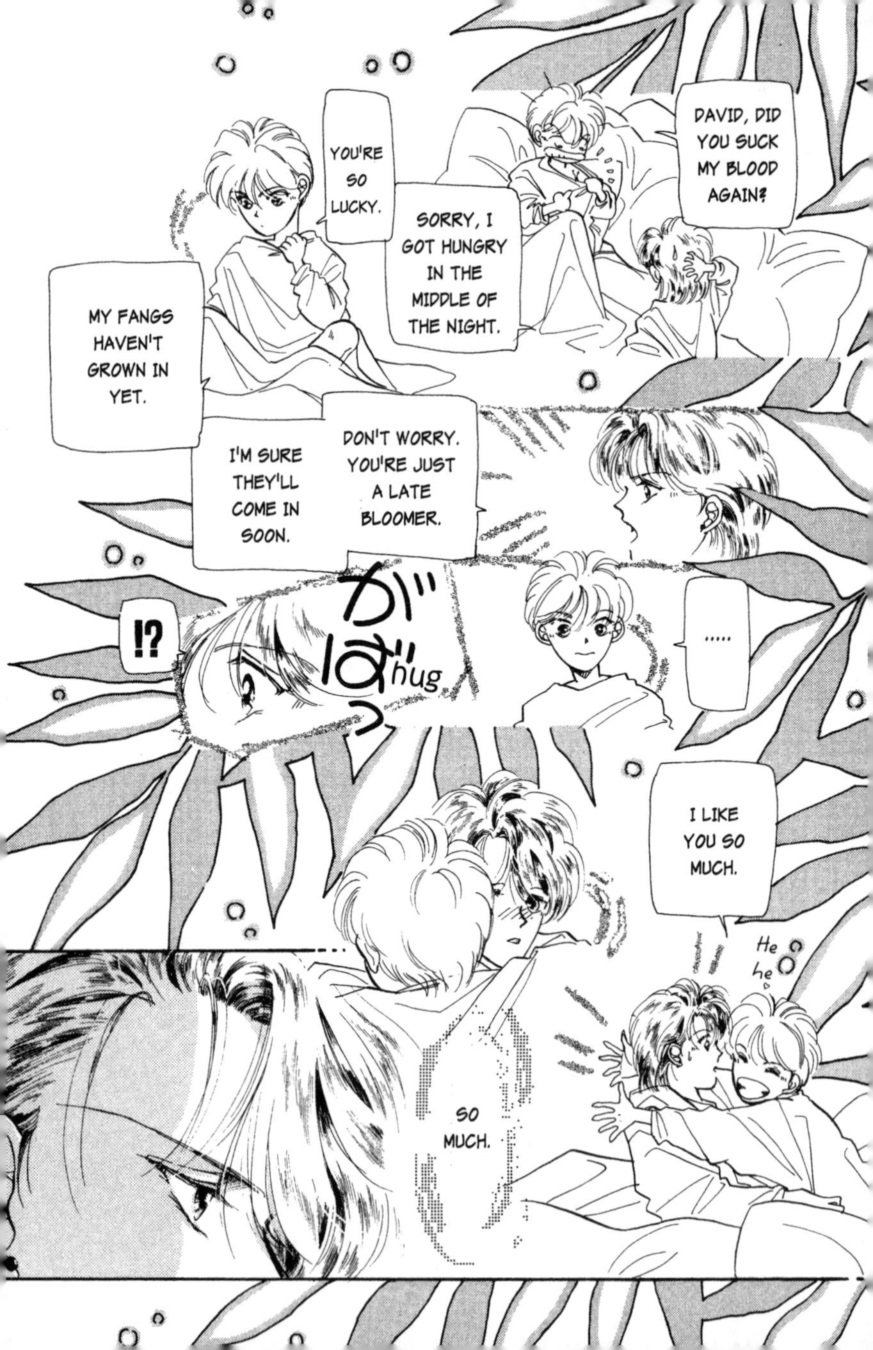
DAVID, DID YOU SUCK MY BLOOD AGAIN?
SORRY, I GOT HUNGRY IN THE MIDDLE OF THE NIGHT.
YOU'RE SO LUCKY.
MY FANGS HAVEN'T GROWN IN YET.
DON'T WORRY. YOU'RE JUST A LATE BLOOMER.
I'M SURE THEY'LL COME IN SOON.
.....
がばっ
hug
!?
I LIKE YOU SO MUCH.
He he
SO MUCH.

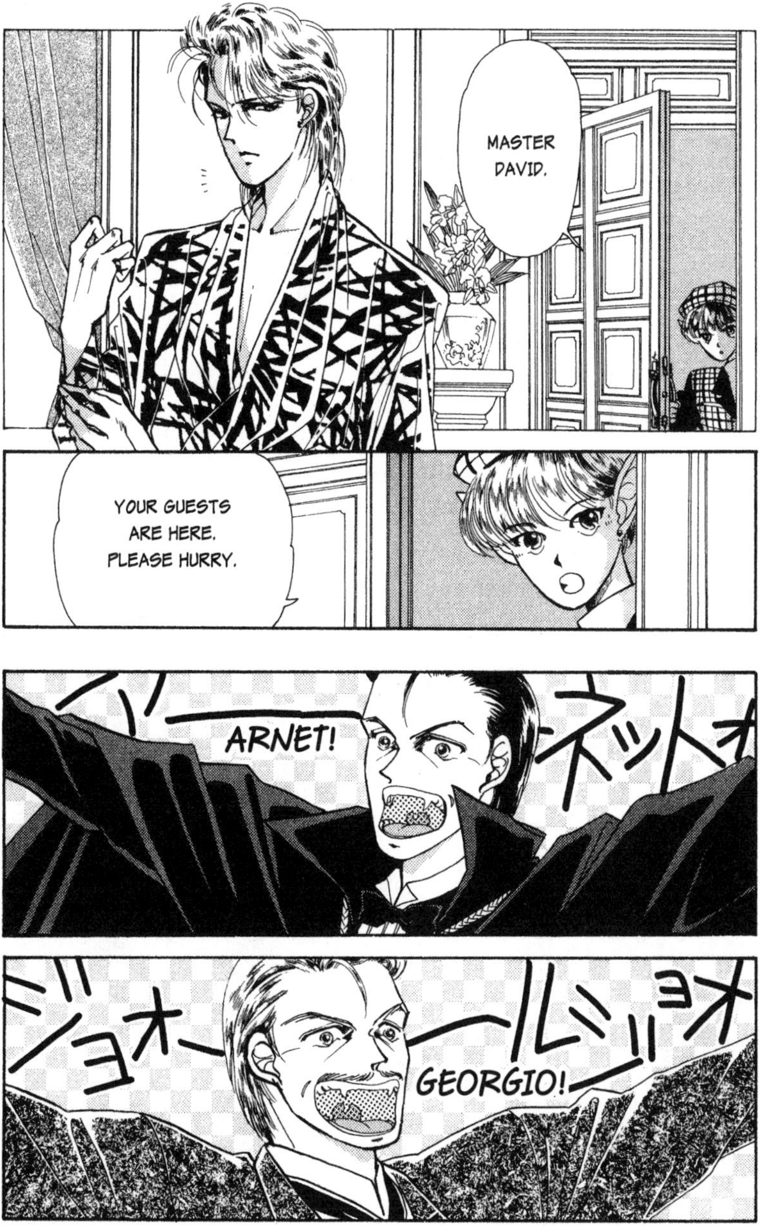
MASTER DAVID.
YOUR GUESTS ARE HERE. PLEASE HURRY.
ARNET!
GEORGIO!

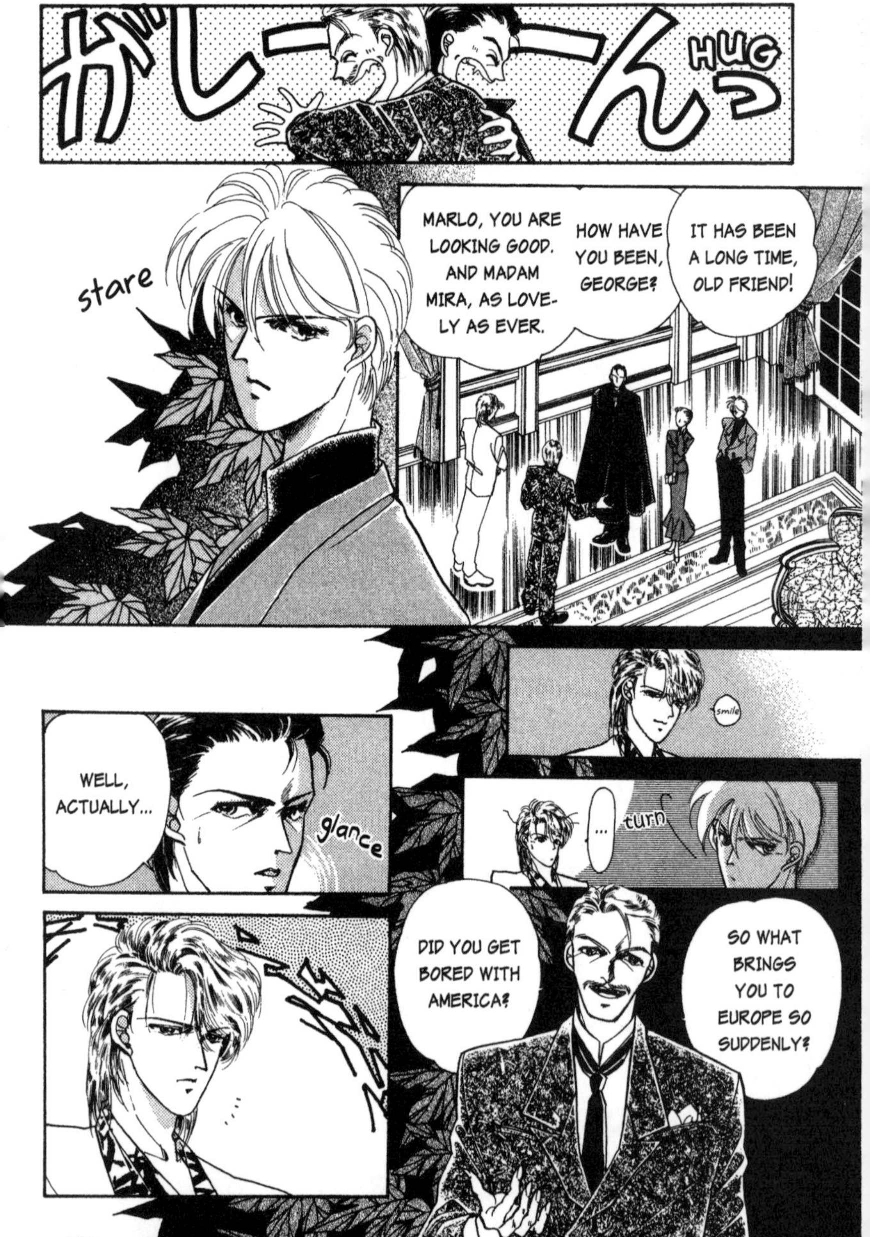
がしーーんっ
HUG
IT HAS BEEN A LONG TIME, OLD FRIEND!
HOW HAVE YOU BEEN, GEORGE?
MARLO, YOU ARE LOOKING GOOD. AND MADAM MIRA, AS LOVE-LY AS EVER.
stare
smile
turn
...
WELL, ACTUALLY...
glance
SO WHAT BRINGS YOU TO EUROPE SO SUDDENLY?
DID YOU GET BORED WITH AMERICA?
...

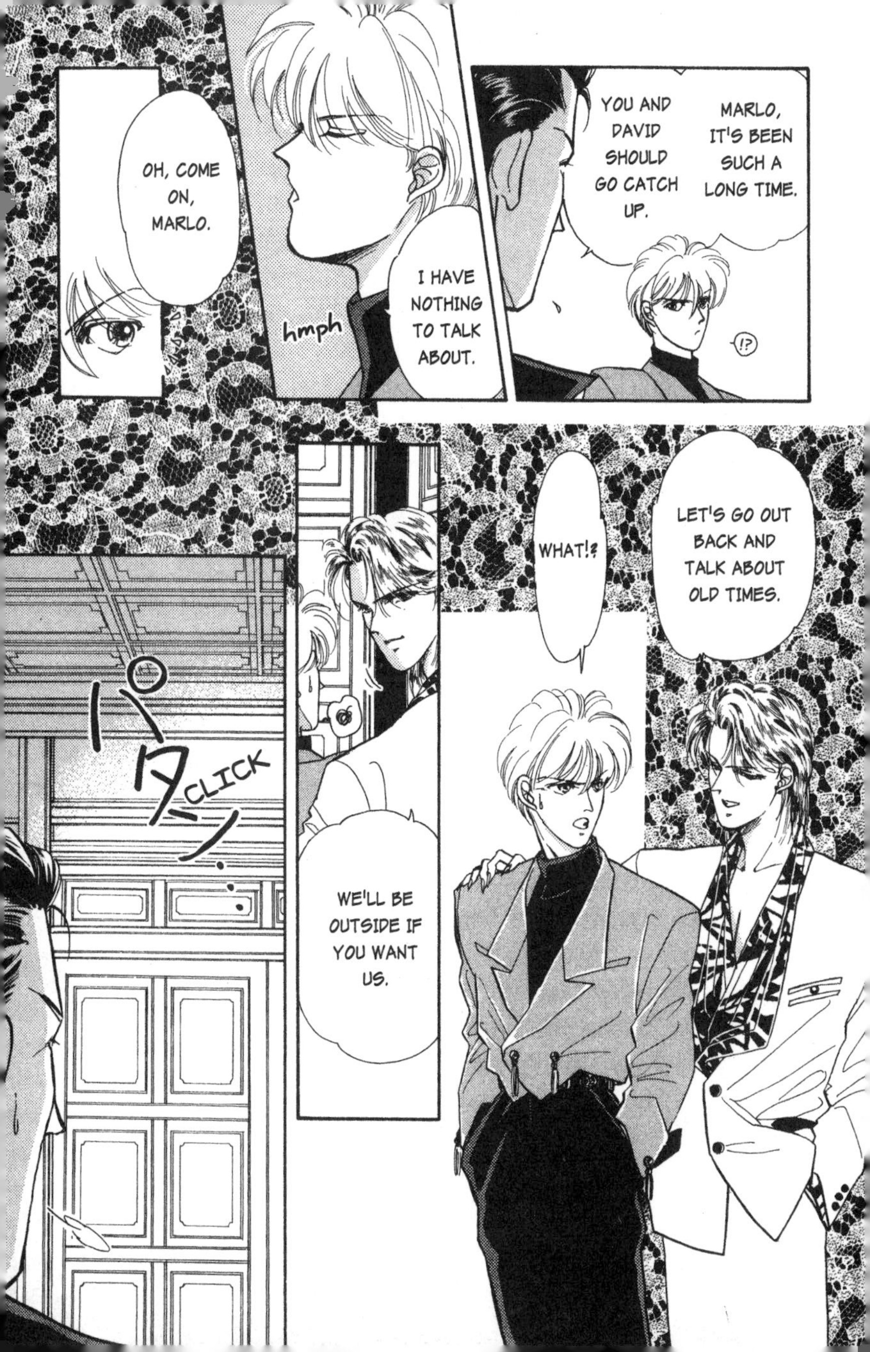
MARLO, IT'S BEEN SUCH A LONG TIME.
YOU AND DAVID SHOULD GO CATCH UP.
!?
I HAVE NOTHING TO TALK ABOUT.
hmph
OH, COME ON, MARLO.
LET'S GO OUT BACK AND TALK ABOUT OLD TIMES.
WHAT!?
WE'LL BE OUTSIDE IF YOU WANT US.
パタン
CLICK

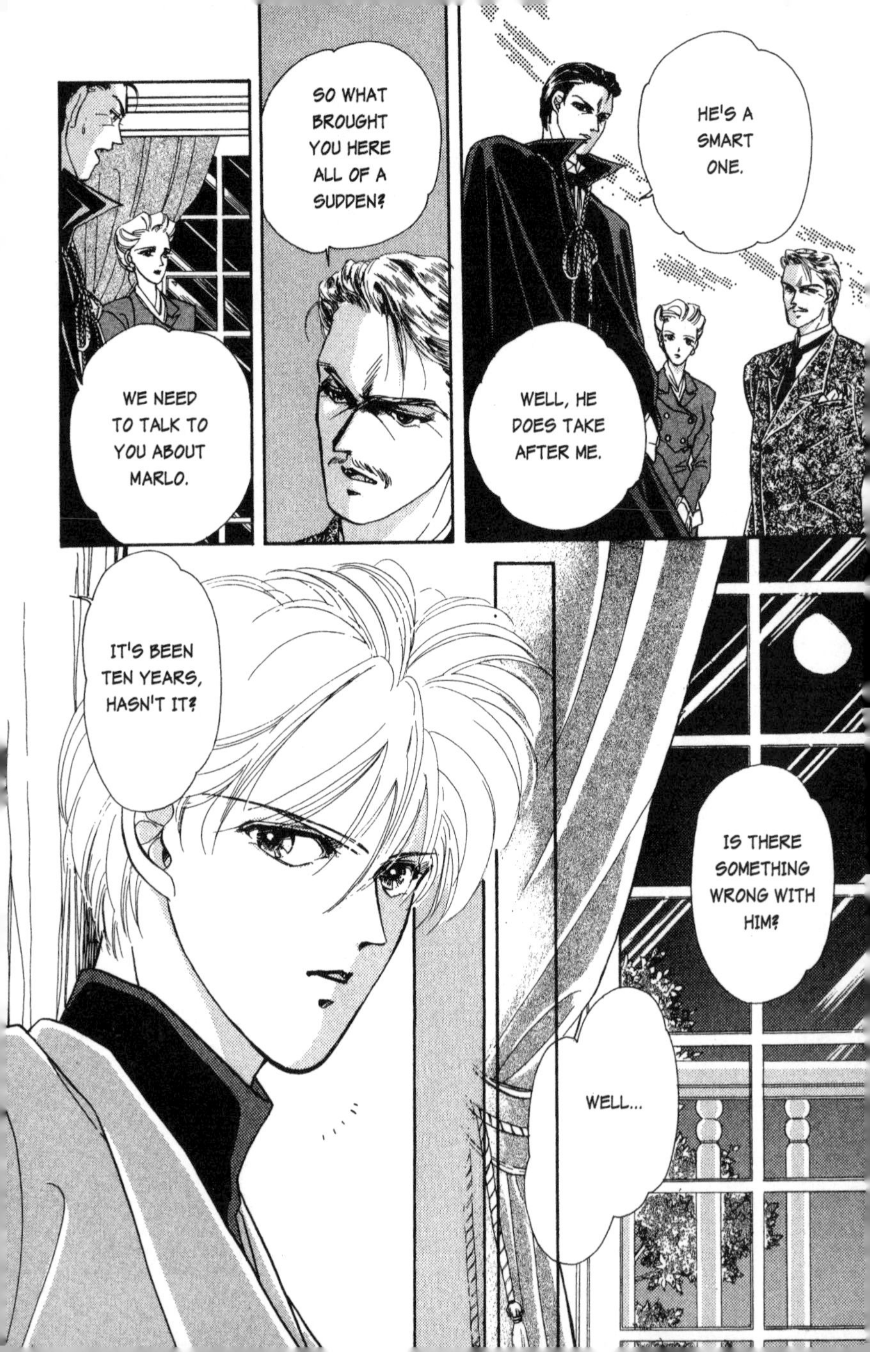
HE'S A SMART ONE.
WELL, HE DOES TAKE AFTER ME.
SO WHAT BROUGHT YOU HERE ALL OF A SUDDEN?
WE NEED TO TALK TO YOU ABOUT MARLO.
IT'S BEEN TEN YEARS, HASN'T IT?
IS THERE SOMETHING WRONG WITH HIM?
WELL...

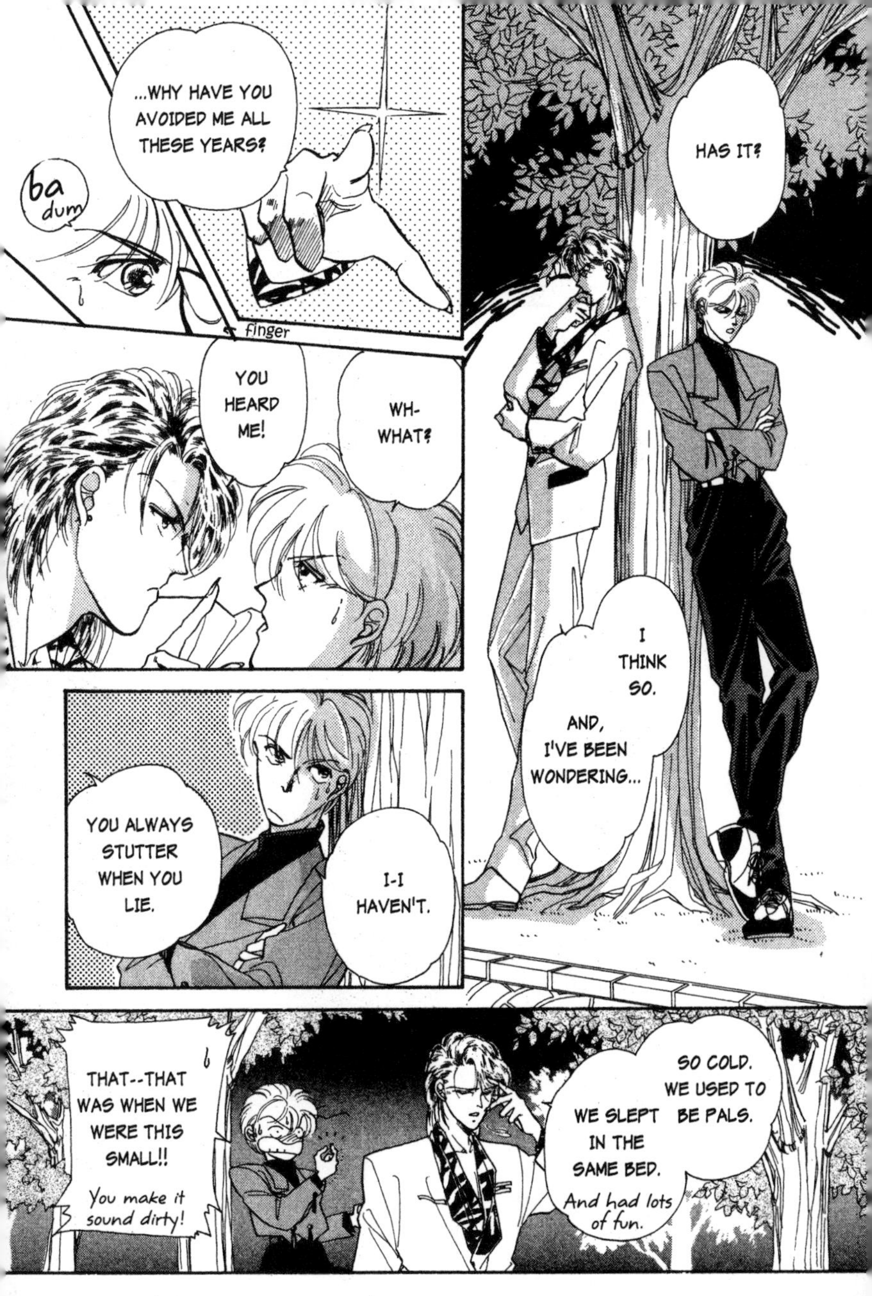
HAS IT?
I THINK SO.
AND, I'VE BEEN WONDERING...
...WHY HAVE YOU AVOIDED ME ALL THESE YEARS?
ba dum
finger
WH- WHAT?
YOU HEARD ME!
I-I HAVEN'T.
YOU ALWAYS STUTTER WHEN YOU LIE.
SO COLD. WE USED TO BE PALS.
WE SLEPT IN THE SAME BED.
And had lots of fun.
THAT--THAT WAS WHEN WE WERE THIS SMALL!!
You make it sound dirty!

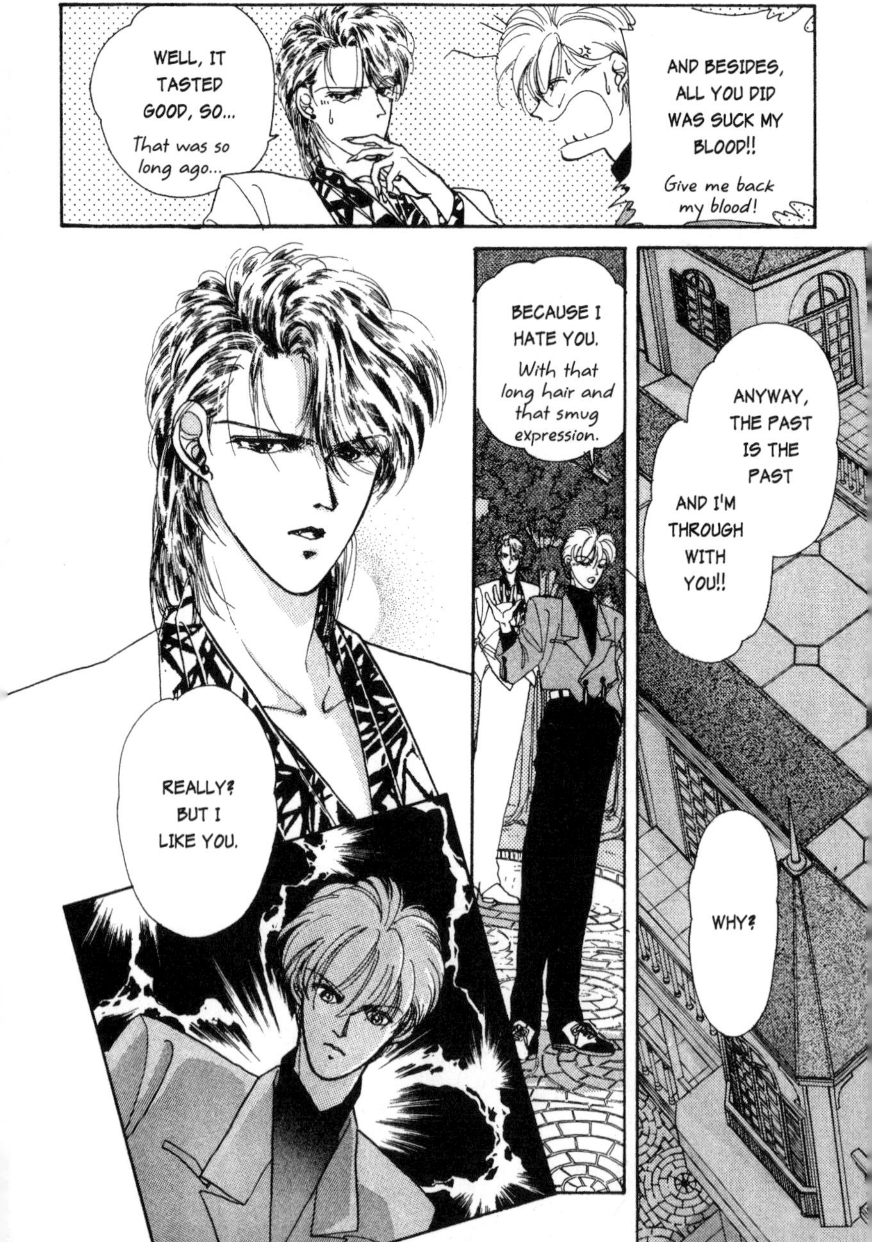
AND BESIDES, ALL YOU DID WAS SUCK MY BLOOD!!
Give me back my blood!
WELL, IT TASTED GOOD, SO...
That was so long ago...
ANYWAY, THE PAST IS THE PAST
AND I'M THROUGH WITH YOU!!
WHY?
BECAUSE I HATE YOU.
With that long hair and that smug expression.
REALLY? BUT I LIKE YOU.

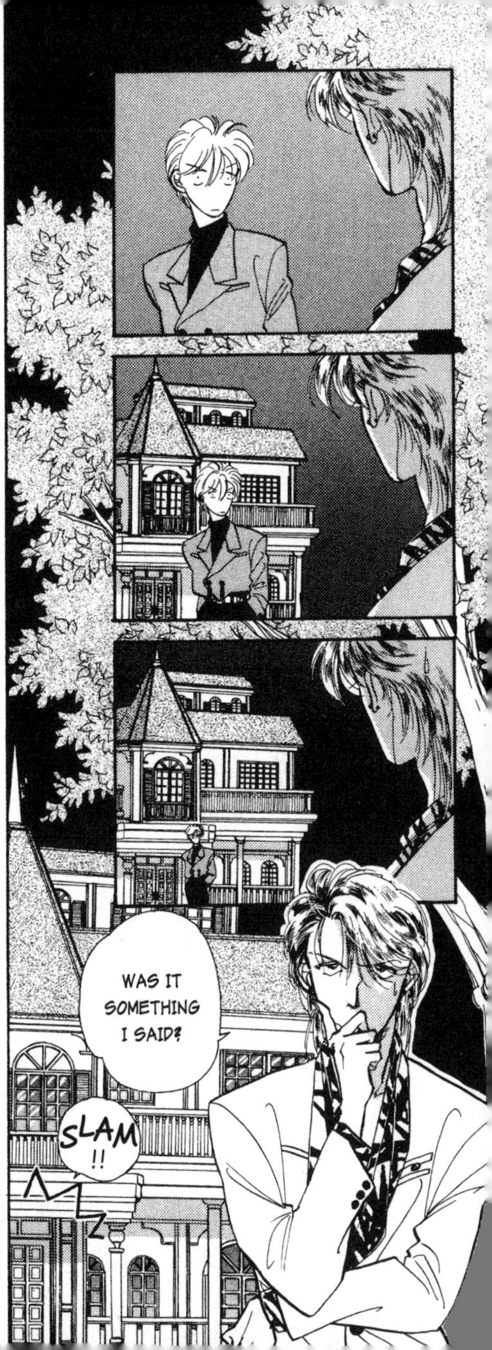
WAS IT SOMETHING I SAID?
SLAM!!
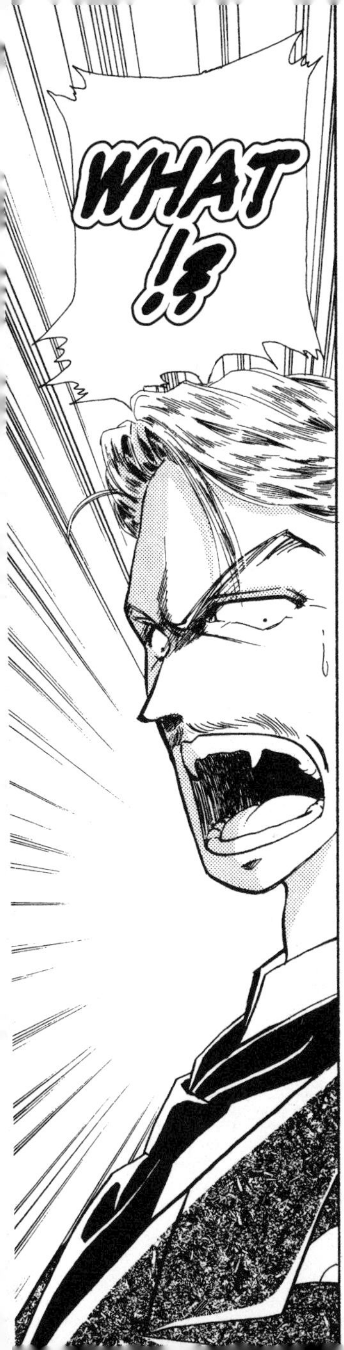
WHAT!?

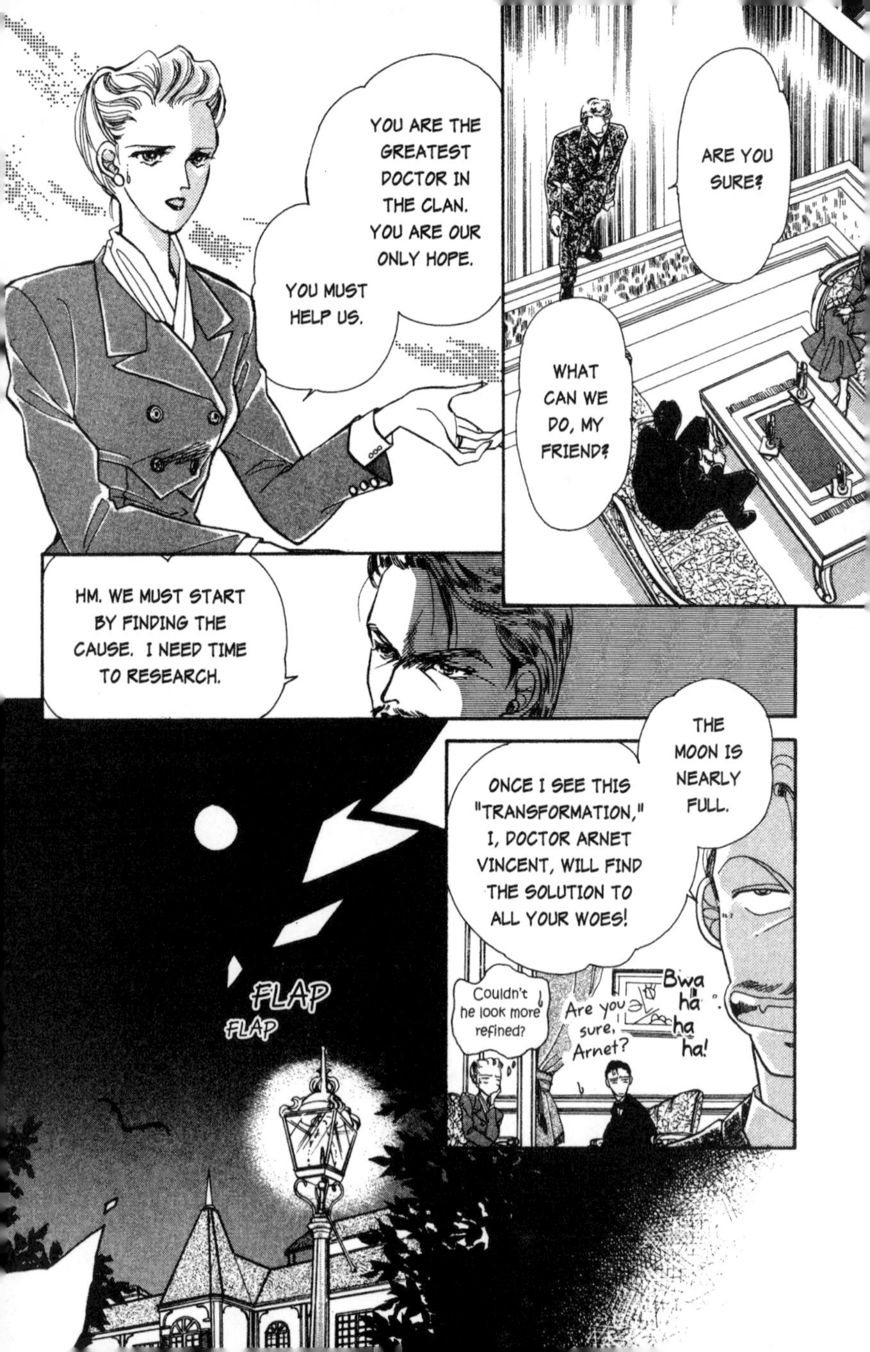
ARE YOU SURE?
WHAT CAN WE DO, MY FRIEND?
YOU ARE THE GREATEST DOCTOR IN THE CLAN. YOU ARE OUR ONLY HOPE.
YOU MUST HELP US.
HM. WE MUST START BY FINDING THE CAUSE. I NEED TIME TO RESEARCH.
THE MOON IS NEARLY FULL.
ONCE I SEE THIS "TRANSFORMATION," I, DOCTOR ARNET VINCENT, WILL FIND THE SOLUTION TO ALL YOUR WOES!
Bwa ha ha ha!
Are you sure, Arnet?
Couldn't he look more refined?
FLAP
FLAP

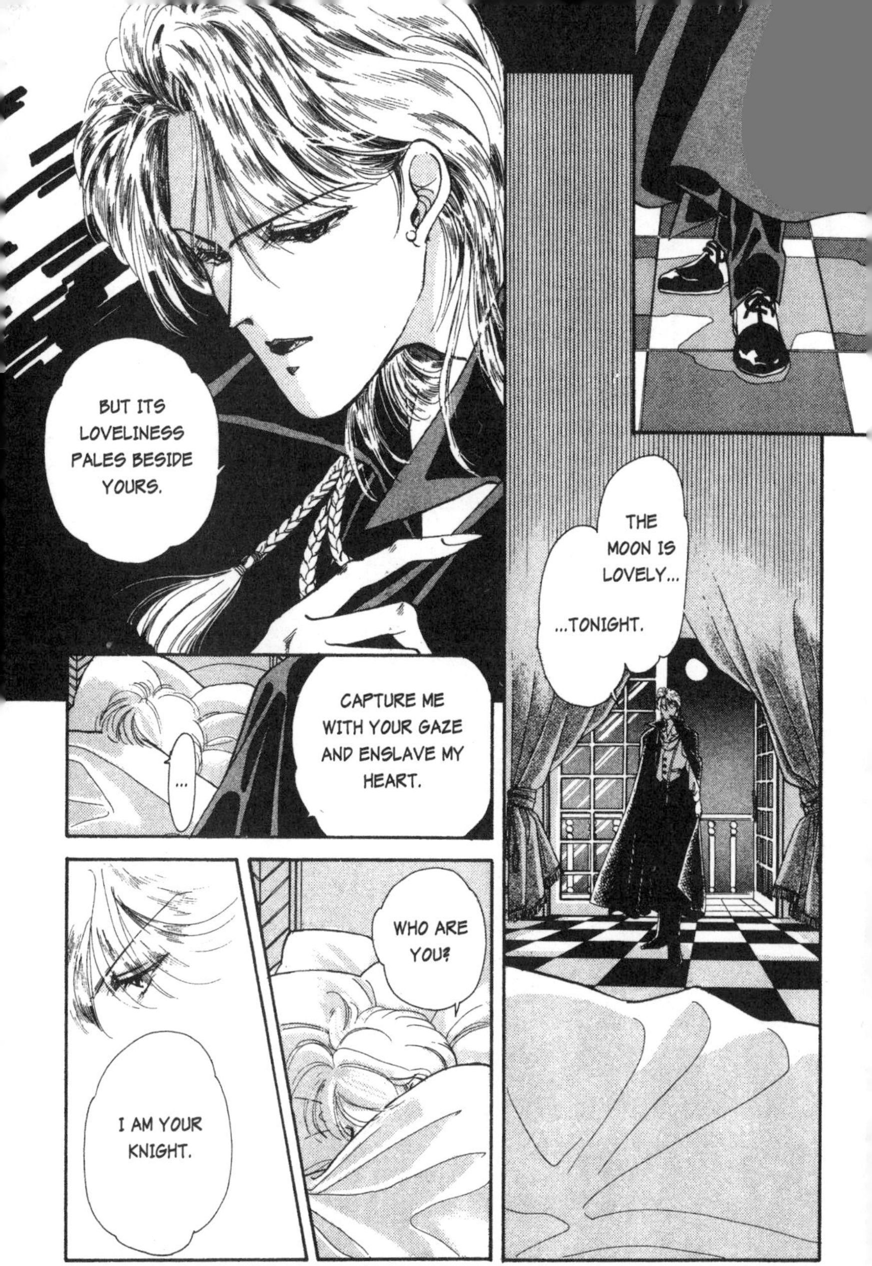
THE MOON IS LOVELY...
...TONIGHT.
BUT ITS LOVELINESS PALES BESIDE YOURS.
CAPTURE ME WITH YOUR GAZE AND ENSLAVE MY HEART.
...
WHO ARE YOU?
I AM YOUR KNIGHT.

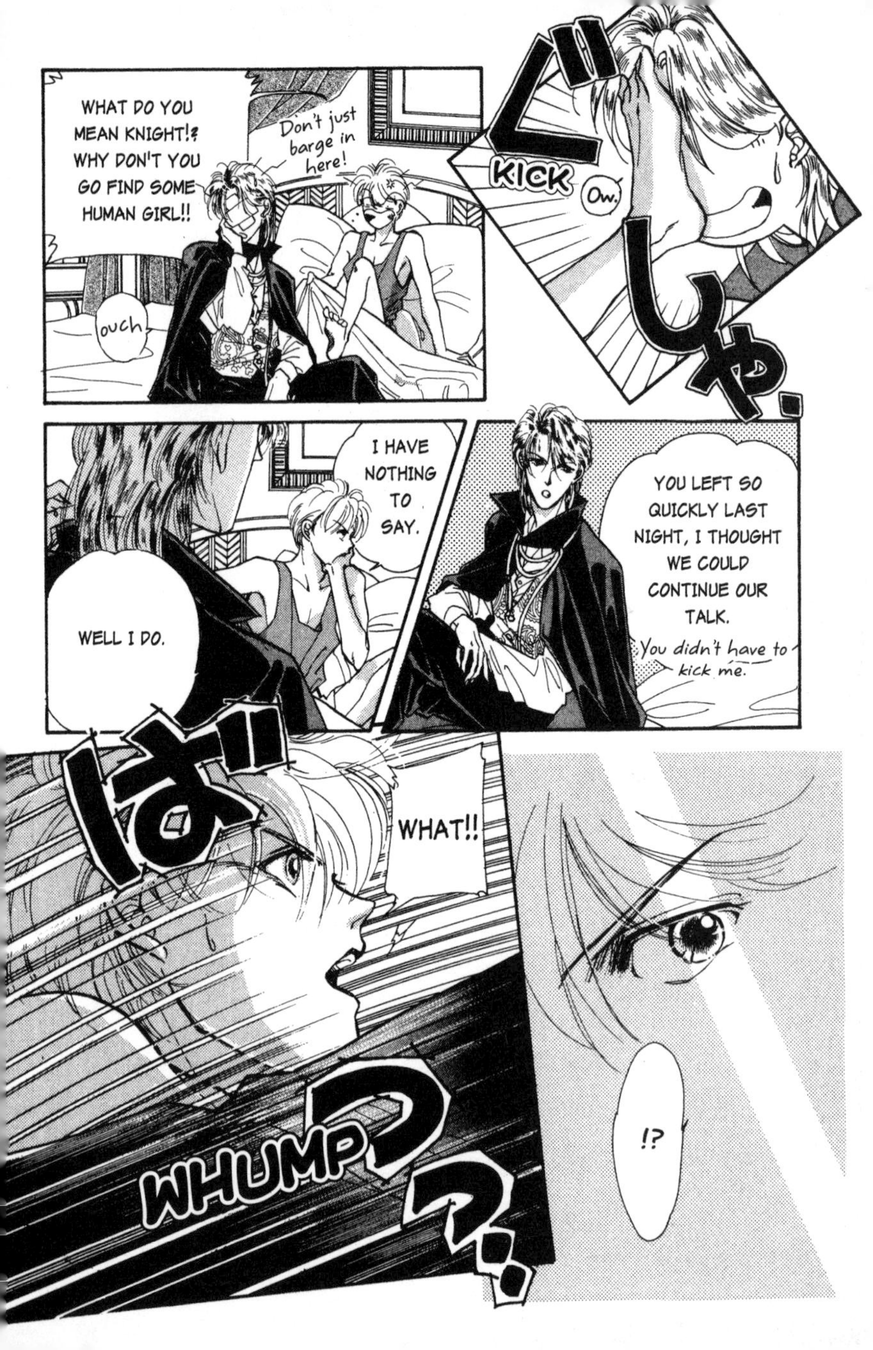
ぐしゃ.
KICK
Ow.
Don't just barge in here!
WHAT DO YOU MEAN KNIGHT!? WHY DON'T YOU GO FIND SOME HUMAN GIRL!!
ouch
YOU LEFT SO QUICKLY LAST NIGHT, I THOUGHT WE COULD CONTINUE OUR TALK.
You didn't have to kick me.
I HAVE NOTHING TO SAY.
WELL I DO.
!?
WHAT!!
ばっ
WHUMP
つつ..

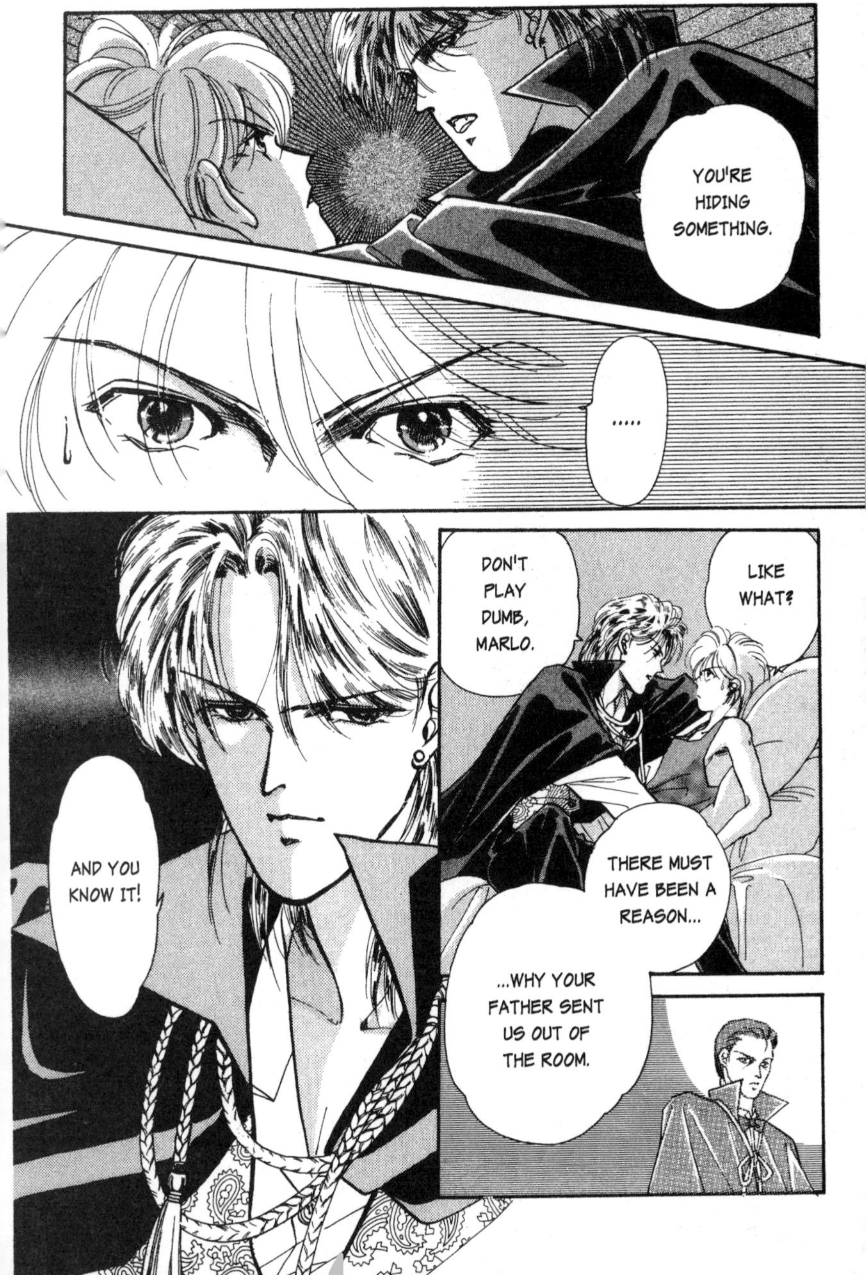
YOU'RE HIDING SOMETHING.
.....
LIKE WHAT?
DON'T PLAY DUMB, MARLO.
THERE MUST HAVE BEEN A REASON...
...WHY YOUR FATHER SENT US OUT OF THE ROOM.
AND YOU KNOW IT!

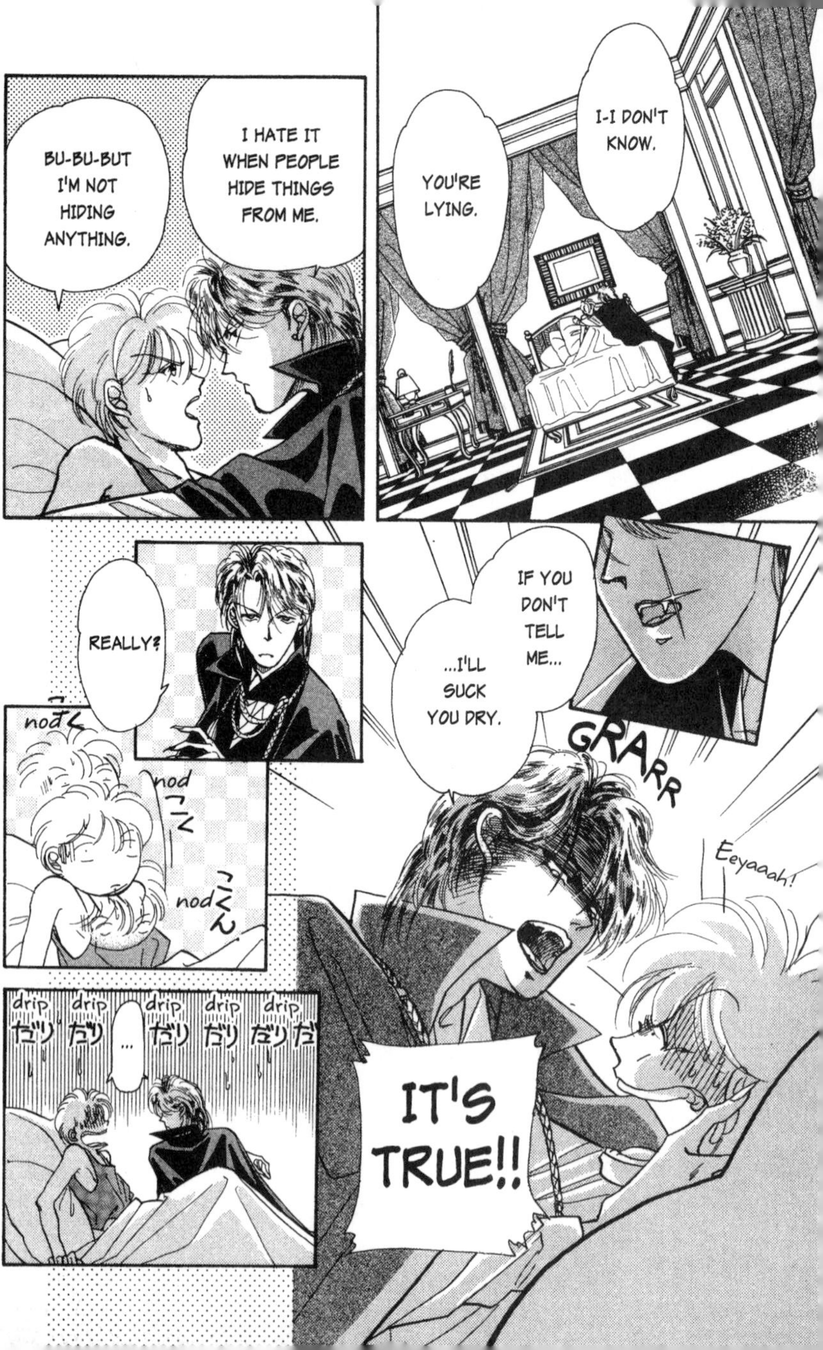
I-I DON'T KNOW.
YOU'RE LYING.
I HATE IT WHEN PEOPLE HIDE THINGS FROM ME.
BU-BU-BUT I'M NOT HIDING ANYTHING.
IF YOU DON'T TELL ME...
...I'LL SUCK YOU DRY.
GRARR
Eeyaaah!
IT'S TRUE!!
REALLY?
nod こく
nod こく
nod こくん
drip drip drip drip drip
だり だり だり だり だりだ
...

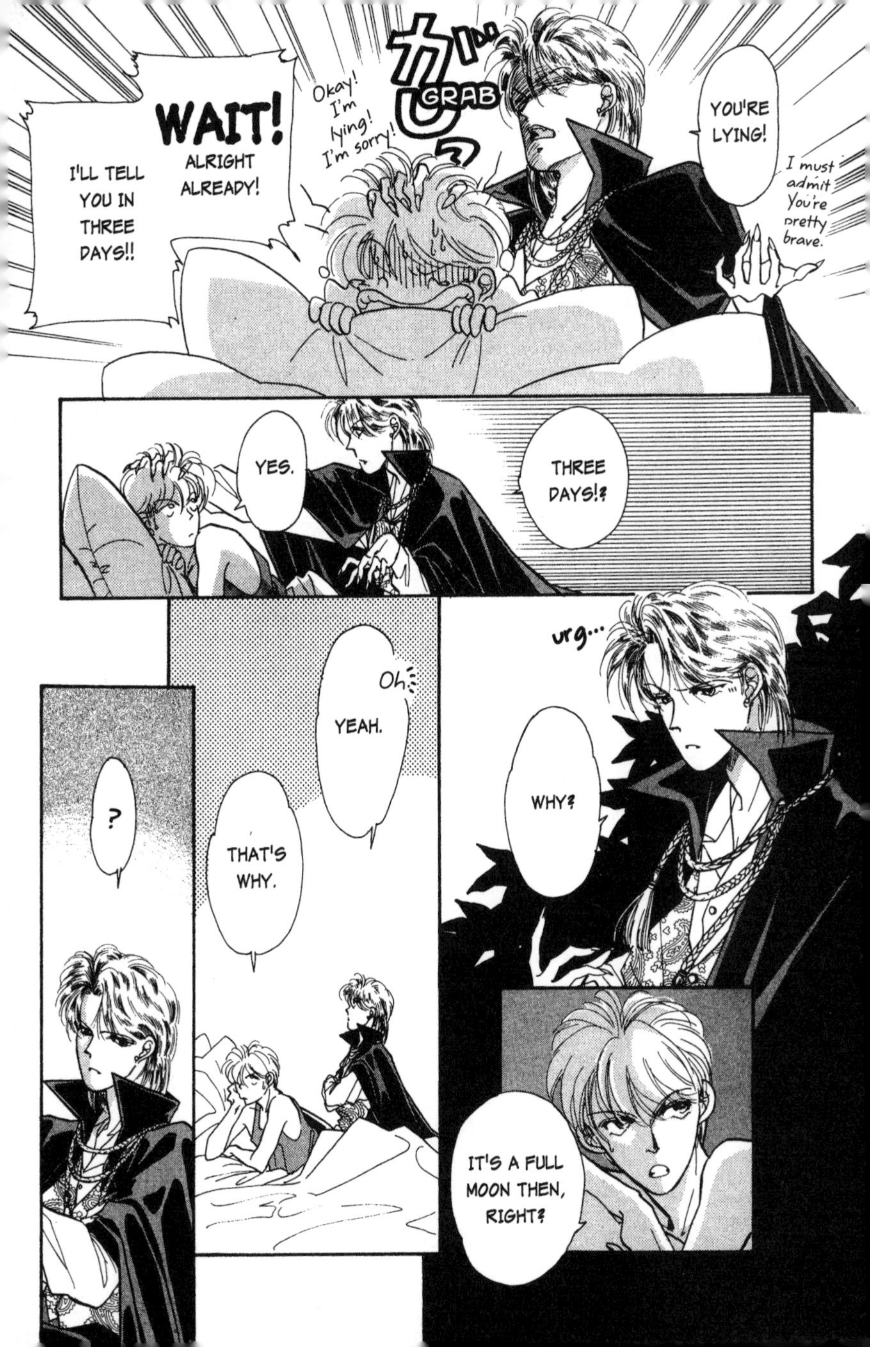
YOU'RE LYING!
I must admit You're pretty brave.
GRAB
Okay! I'm lying! I'm sorry!
WAIT!
ALRIGHT ALREADY!
I'LL TELL YOU IN THREE DAYS!!
THREE DAYS!?
YES.
urg...
WHY?
IT'S A FULL MOON THEN, RIGHT?
Oh
YEAH.
THAT'S WHY.
?

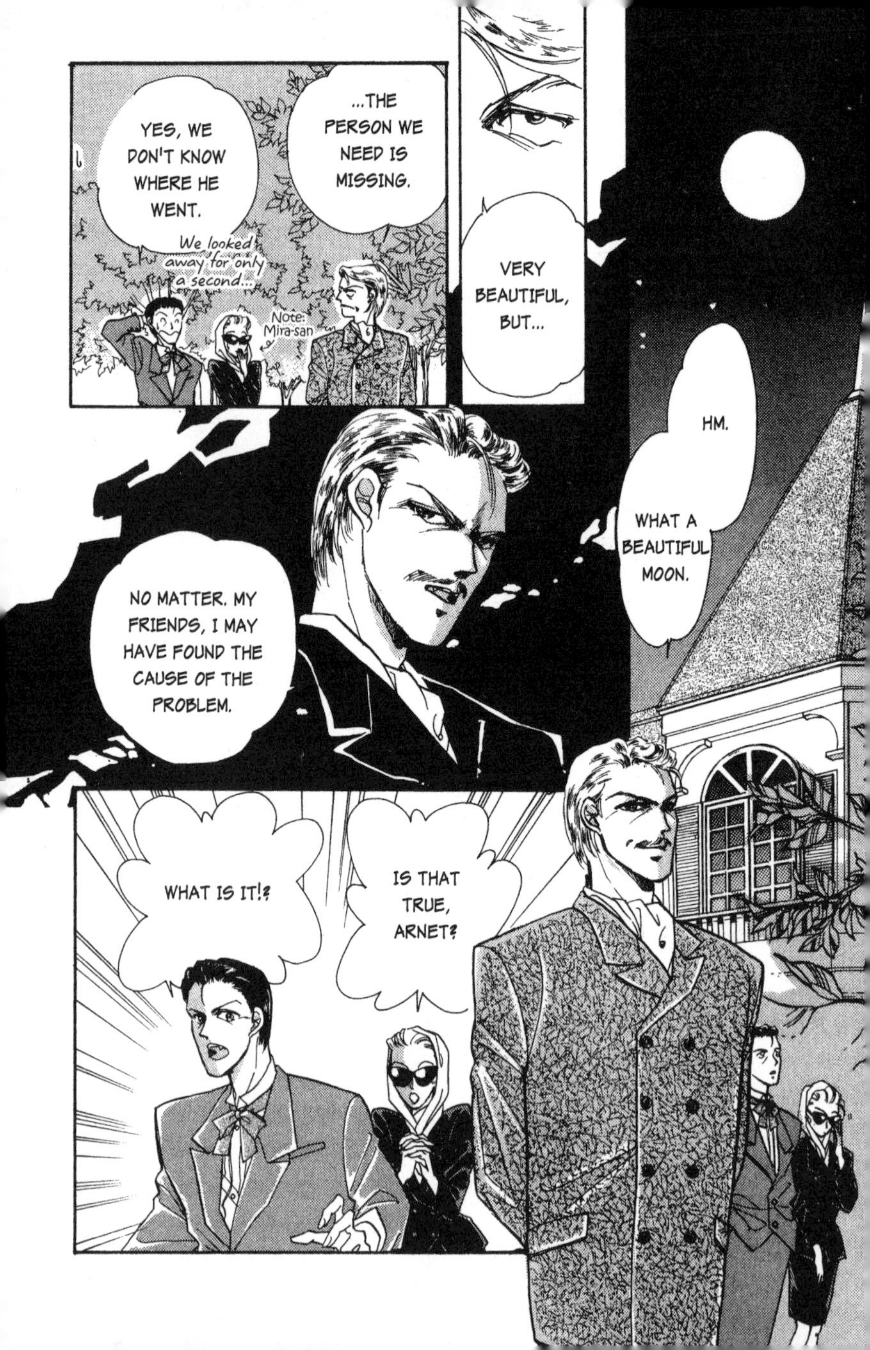
HM.
WHAT A BEAUTIFUL MOON.
VERY BEAUTIFUL, BUT...
...THE PERSON WE NEED IS MISSING.
YES, WE DON'T KNOW WHERE HE WENT.
We looked away for only a second...
Note: Mira-san
NO MATTER. MY FRIENDS, I MAY HAVE FOUND THE CAUSE OF THE PROBLEM.
IS THAT TRUE, ARNET?
WHAT IS IT!?

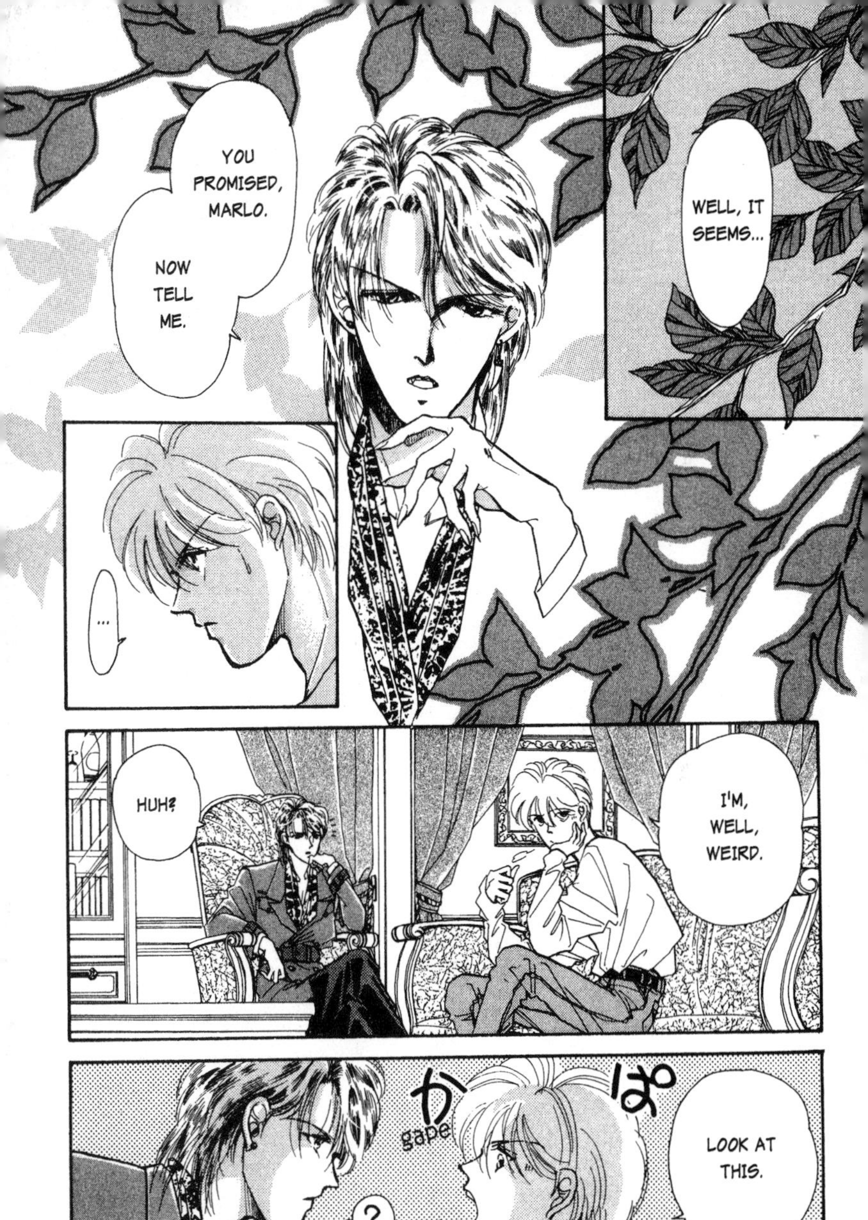
YOU PROMISED, MARLO.
NOW TELL ME.
WELL, IT SEEMS...
...
I'M, WELL, WEIRD.
HUH?
LOOK AT THIS.
かぱ
gape
?

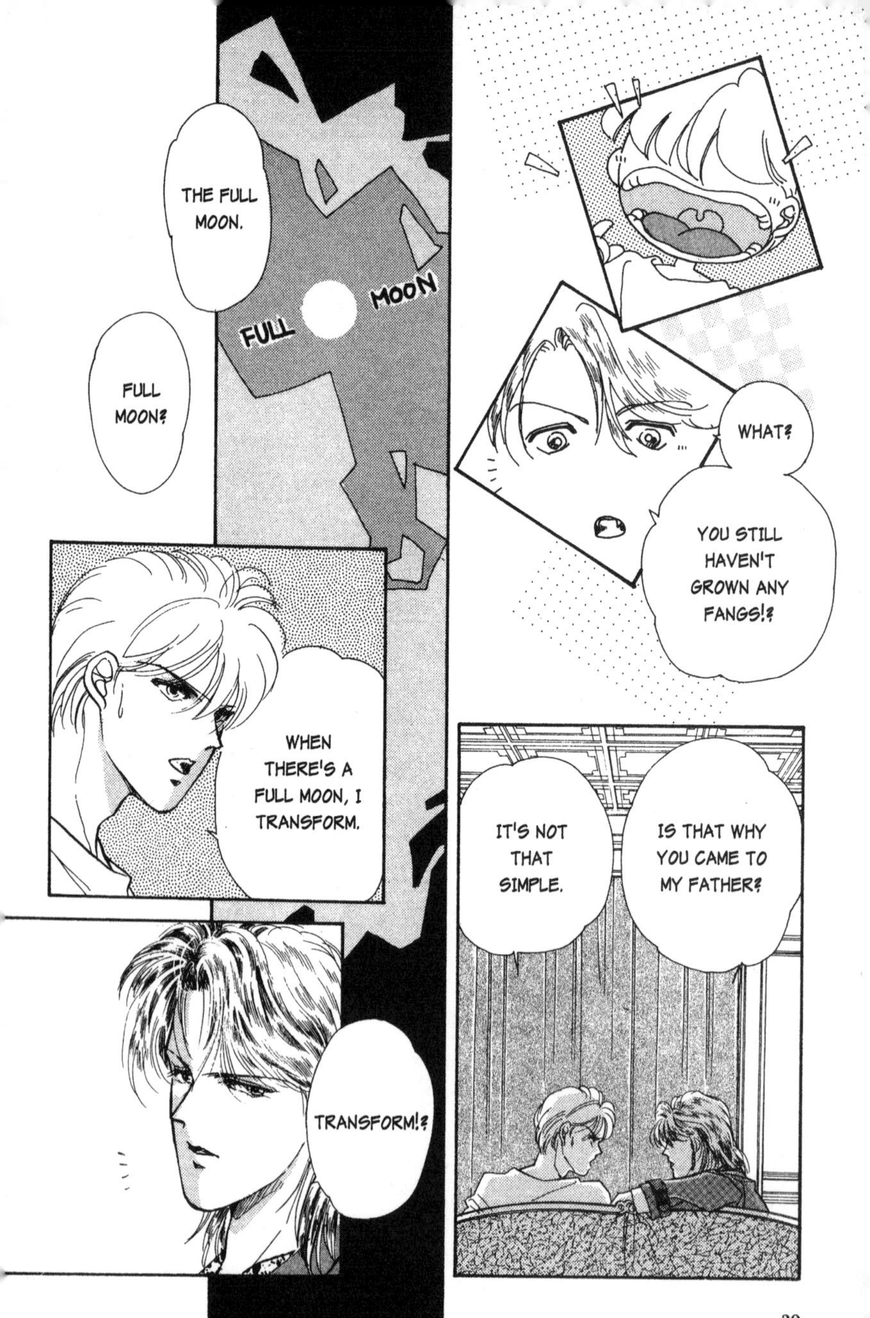
WHAT?
YOU STILL HAVEN'T GROWN ANY FANGS!?
IS THAT WHY YOU CAME TO MY FATHER?
IT'S NOT THAT SIMPLE.
THE FULL MOON.
FULL MOON
FULL MOON?
WHEN THERE'S A FULL MOON, I TRANSFORM.
TRANSFORM!?

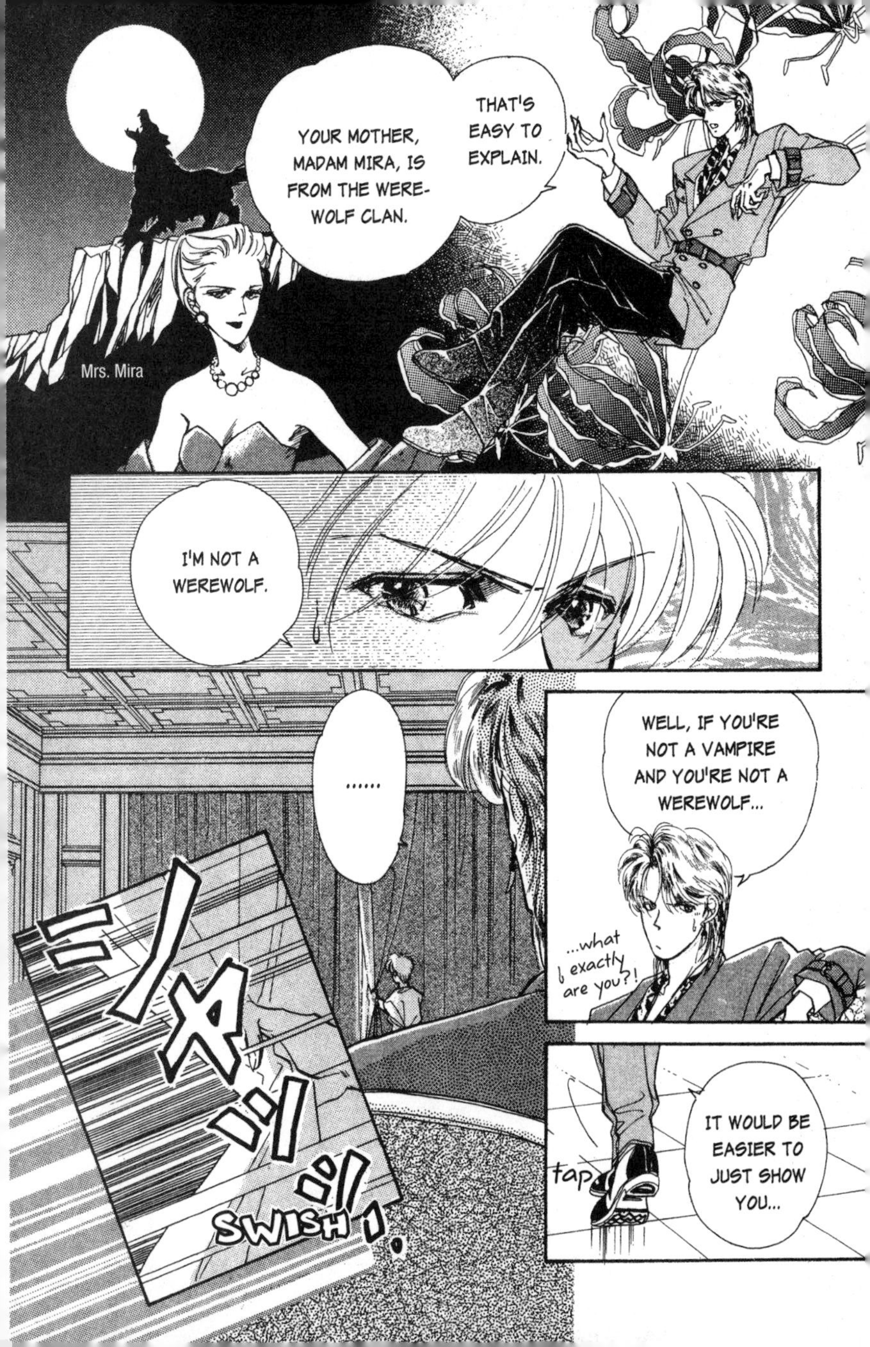
THAT'S EASY TO EXPLAIN.
YOUR MOTHER, MADAM MIRA, IS FROM THE WERE-WOLF CLAN.
Mrs. Mira
I'M NOT A WEREWOLF.
WELL, IF YOU'RE NOT A VAMPIRE AND YOU'RE NOT A WEREWOLF...
...what exactly are you?!
tap
IT WOULD BE EASIER TO JUST SHOW YOU...
......
SWISH!

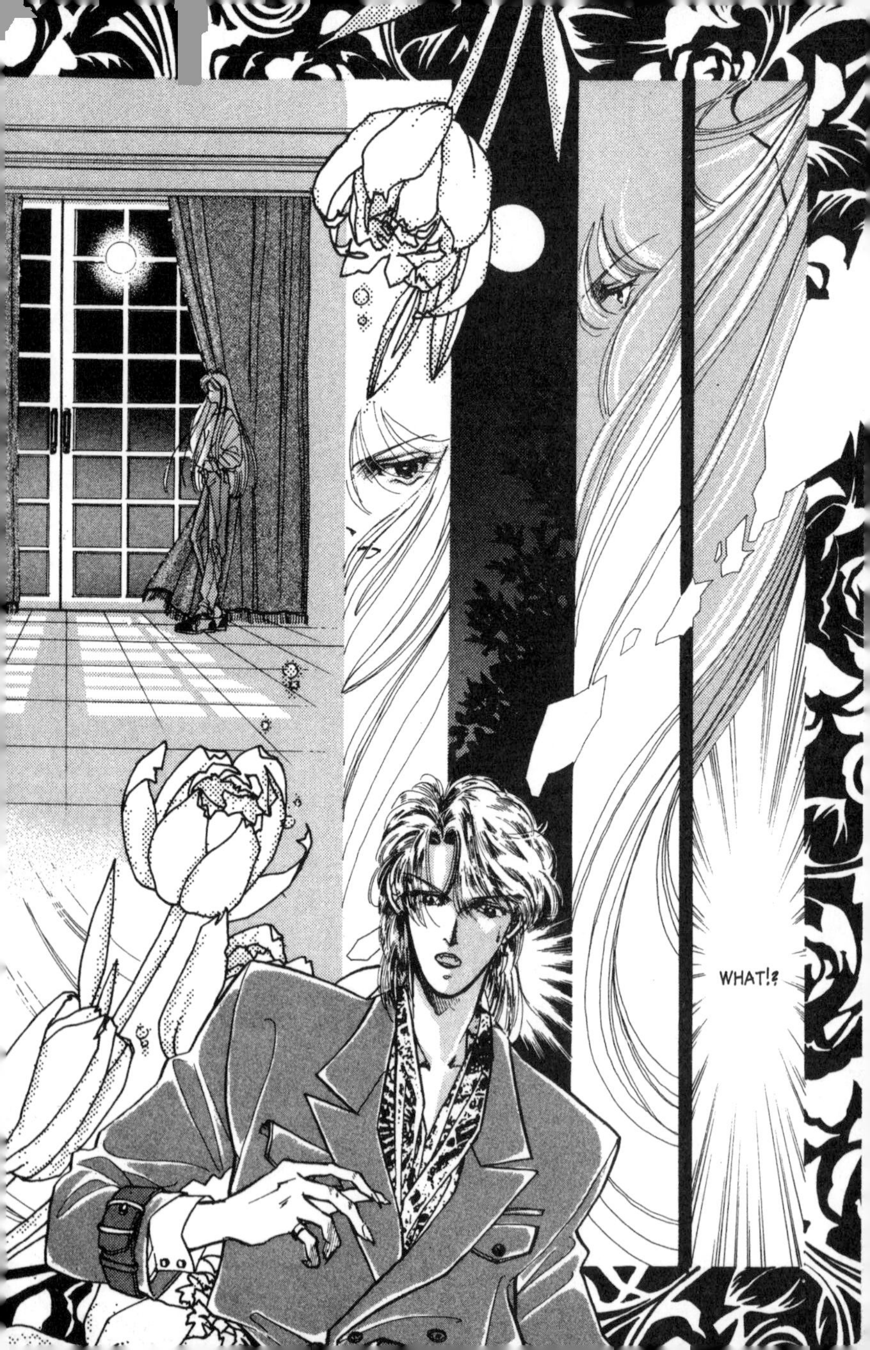
WHAT!?

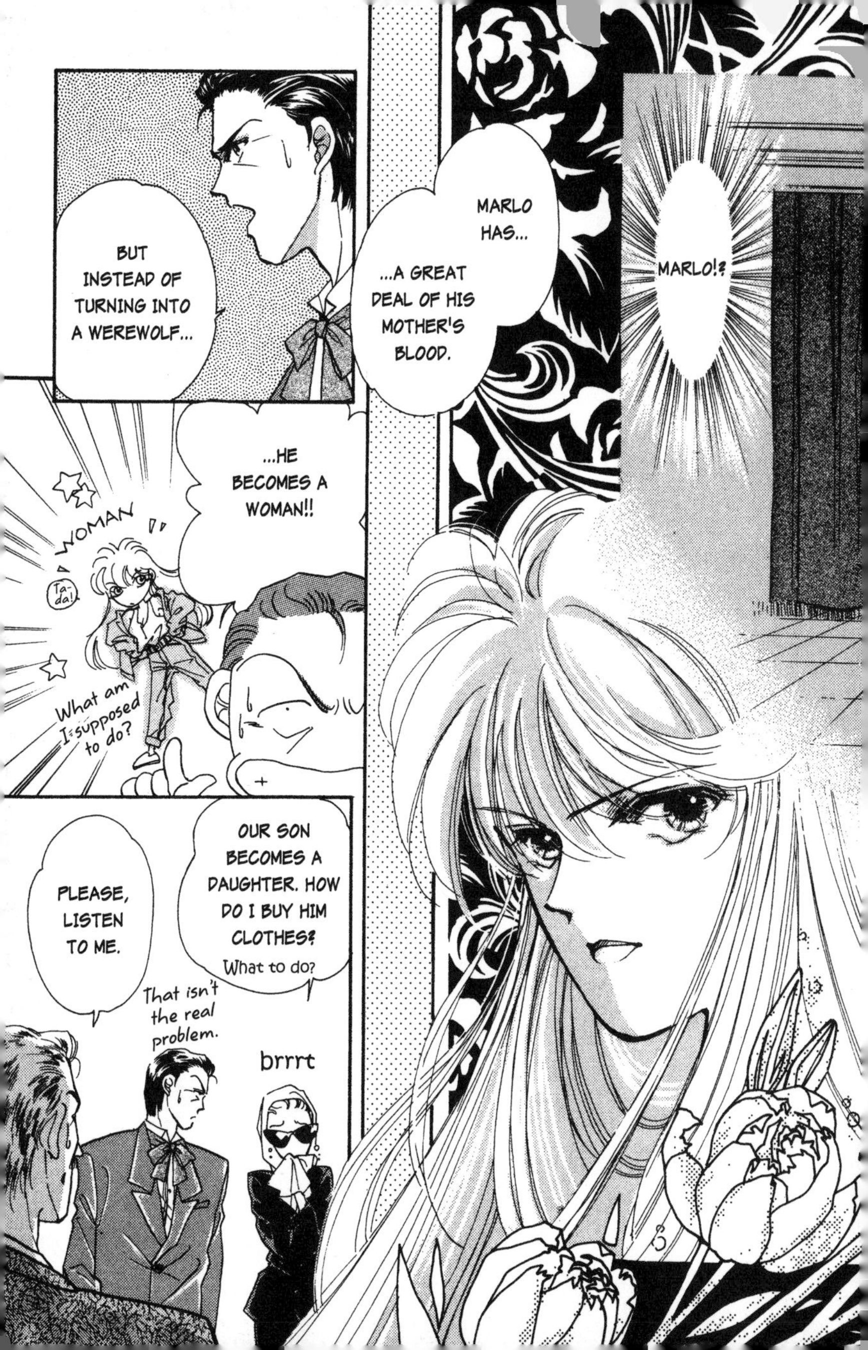
MARLO!?
MARLO HAS...
...A GREAT DEAL OF HIS MOTHER'S BLOOD.
BUT INSTEAD OF TURNING INTO A WEREWOLF...
...HE BECOMES A WOMAN!!
WOMAN
Ta-da!
What am I supposed to do?
OUR SON BECOMES A DAUGHTER. HOW DO I BUY HIM CLOTHES?
What to do?
PLEASE, LISTEN TO ME.
That isn't the real problem.
brrrt

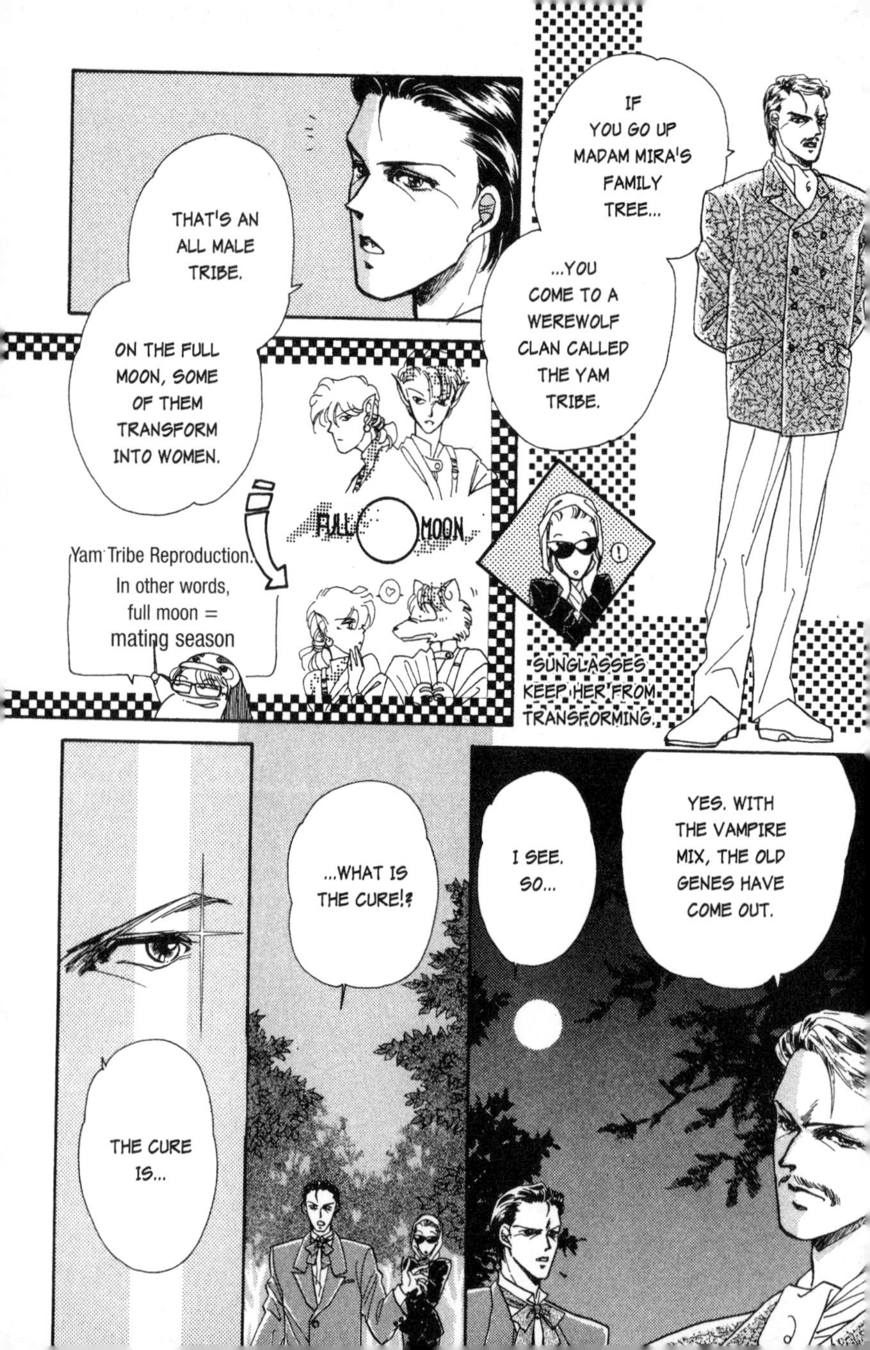
IF YOU GO UP MADAM MIRA'S FAMILY TREE...
...YOU COME TO A WEREWOLF CLAN CALLED THE YAM TRIBE.
SUNGLASSES KEEP HER FROM TRANSFORMING.
THAT'S AN ALL MALE TRIBE.
ON THE FULL MOON, SOME OF THEM TRANSFORM INTO WOMEN.
FULL MOON
Yam Tribe Reproduction. In other words, full moon = mating season
YES. WITH THE VAMPIRE MIX, THE OLD GENES HAVE COME OUT.
I SEE. SO...
...WHAT IS THE CURE!?
THE CURE IS...

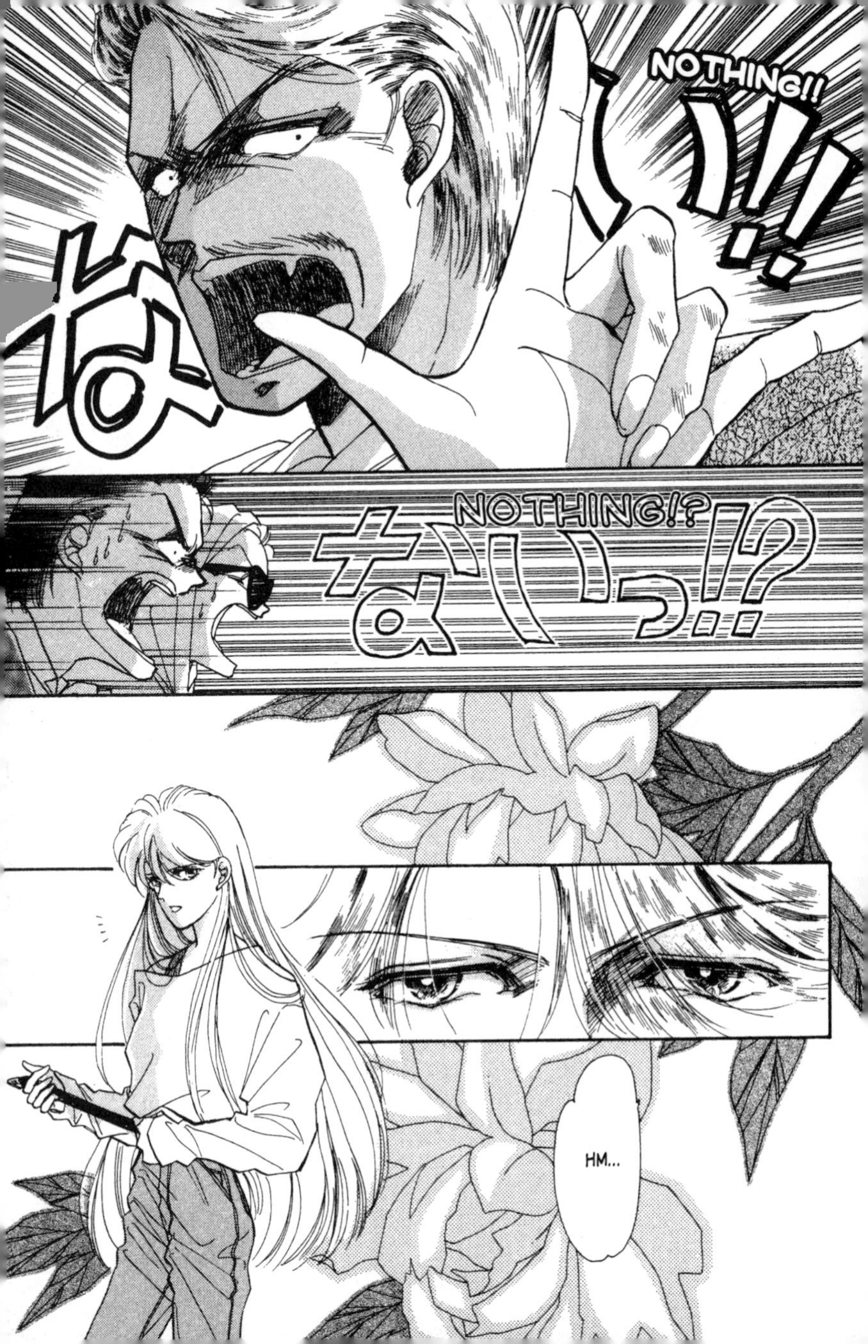
NOTHING!!
NOTHING!?
HM...

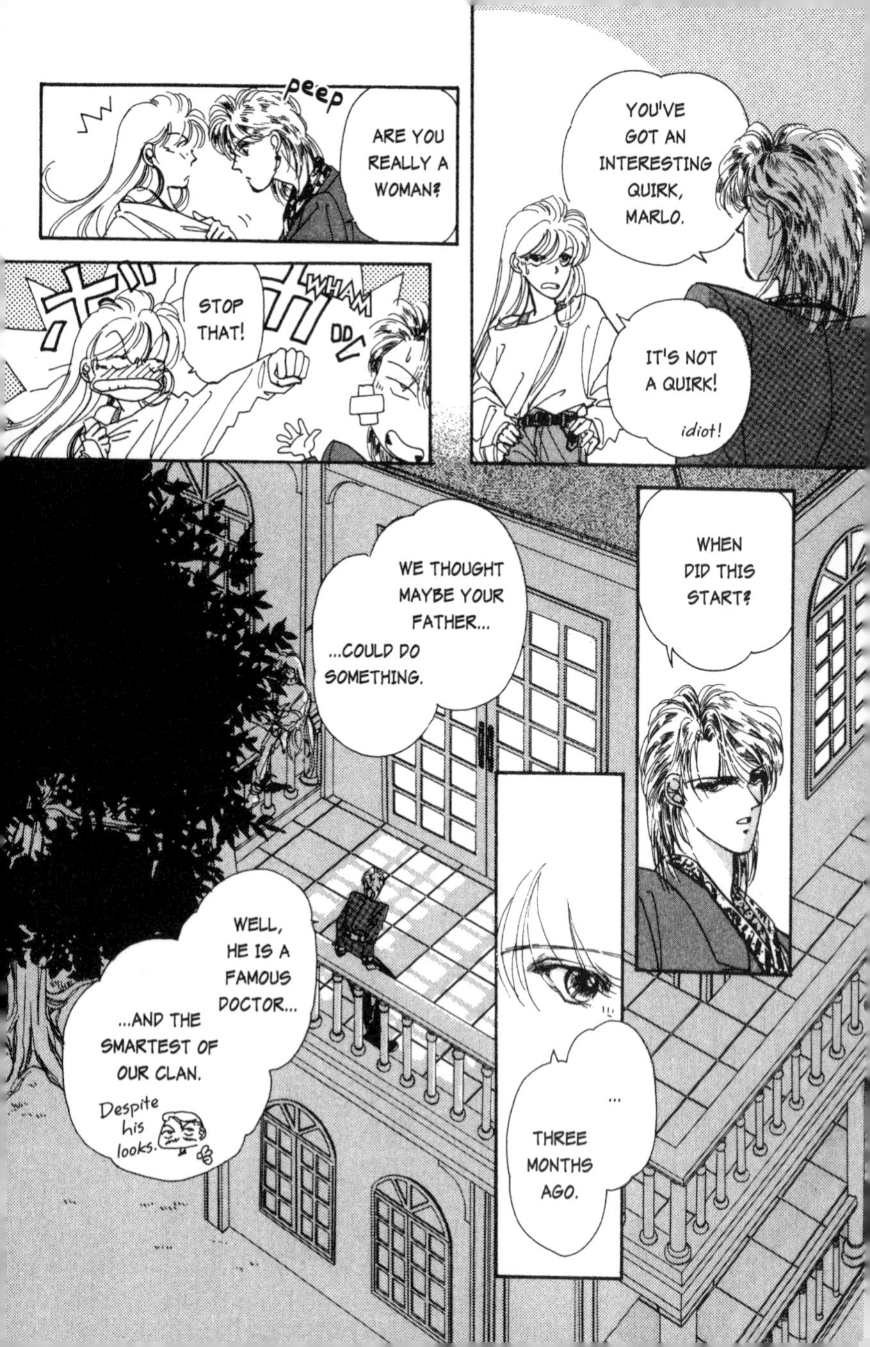
YOU'VE GOT AN INTERESTING QUIRK, MARLO.
IT'S NOT A QUIRK!
idiot!
peep
ARE YOU REALLY A WOMAN?
WHAM
STOP THAT!
WHEN DID THIS START?
...
THREE MONTHS AGO.
WE THOUGHT MAYBE YOUR FATHER...
...COULD DO SOMETHING.
WELL, HE IS A FAMOUS DOCTOR...
...AND THE SMARTEST OF OUR CLAN.
Despite his looks.

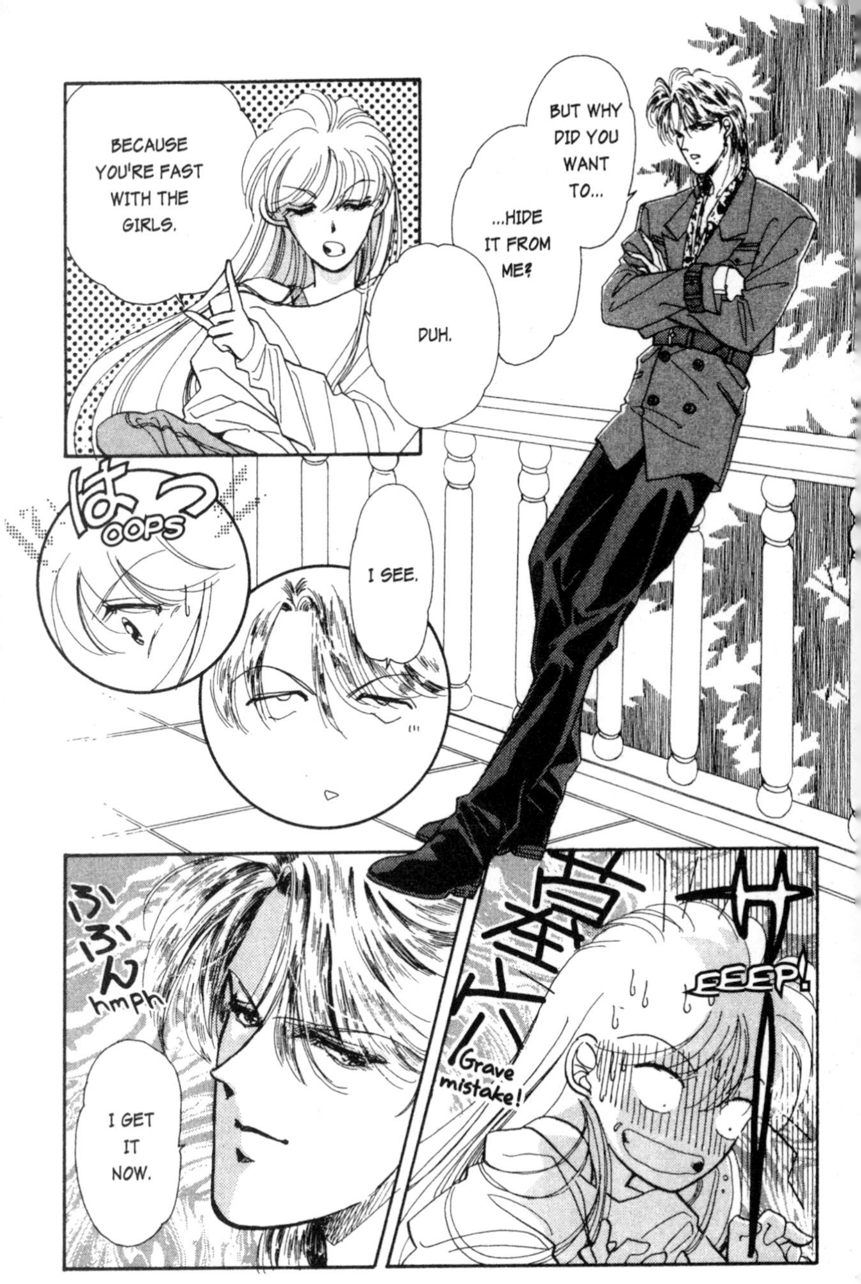
BUT WHY DID YOU WANT TO...
...HIDE IT FROM ME?
BECAUSE YOU'RE FAST WITH THE GIRLS.
DUH.
I SEE.
はっ OOPS
EEEP!
Grave mistake!
ふふん hmph
I GET IT NOW.

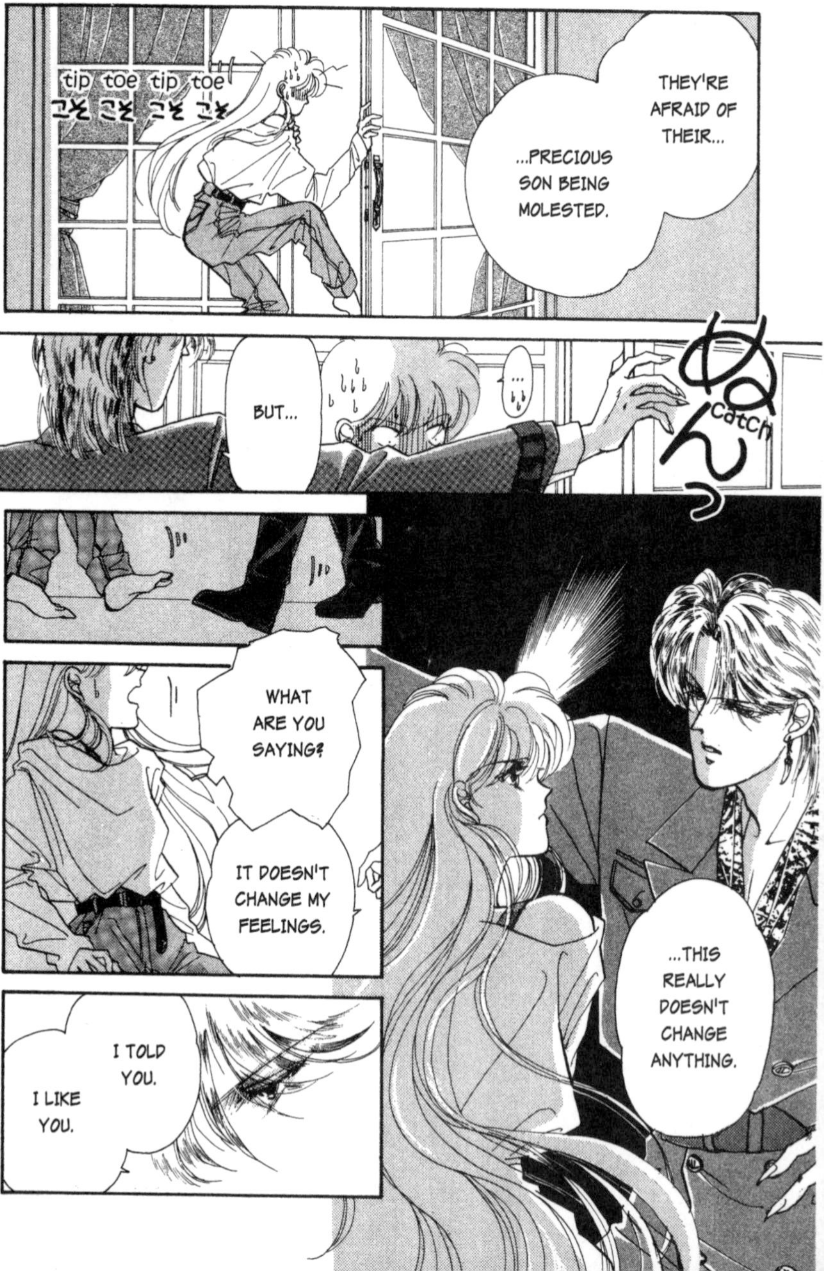
THEY'RE AFRAID OF THEIR...
...PRECIOUS SON BEING MOLESTED.
tip toe tip toe
こそ こそ こそ こそ
ぬんっ
catch
...
BUT...
...THIS REALLY DOESN'T CHANGE ANYTHING.
WHAT ARE YOU SAYING?
IT DOESN'T CHANGE MY FEELINGS.
I TOLD YOU.
I LIKE YOU.

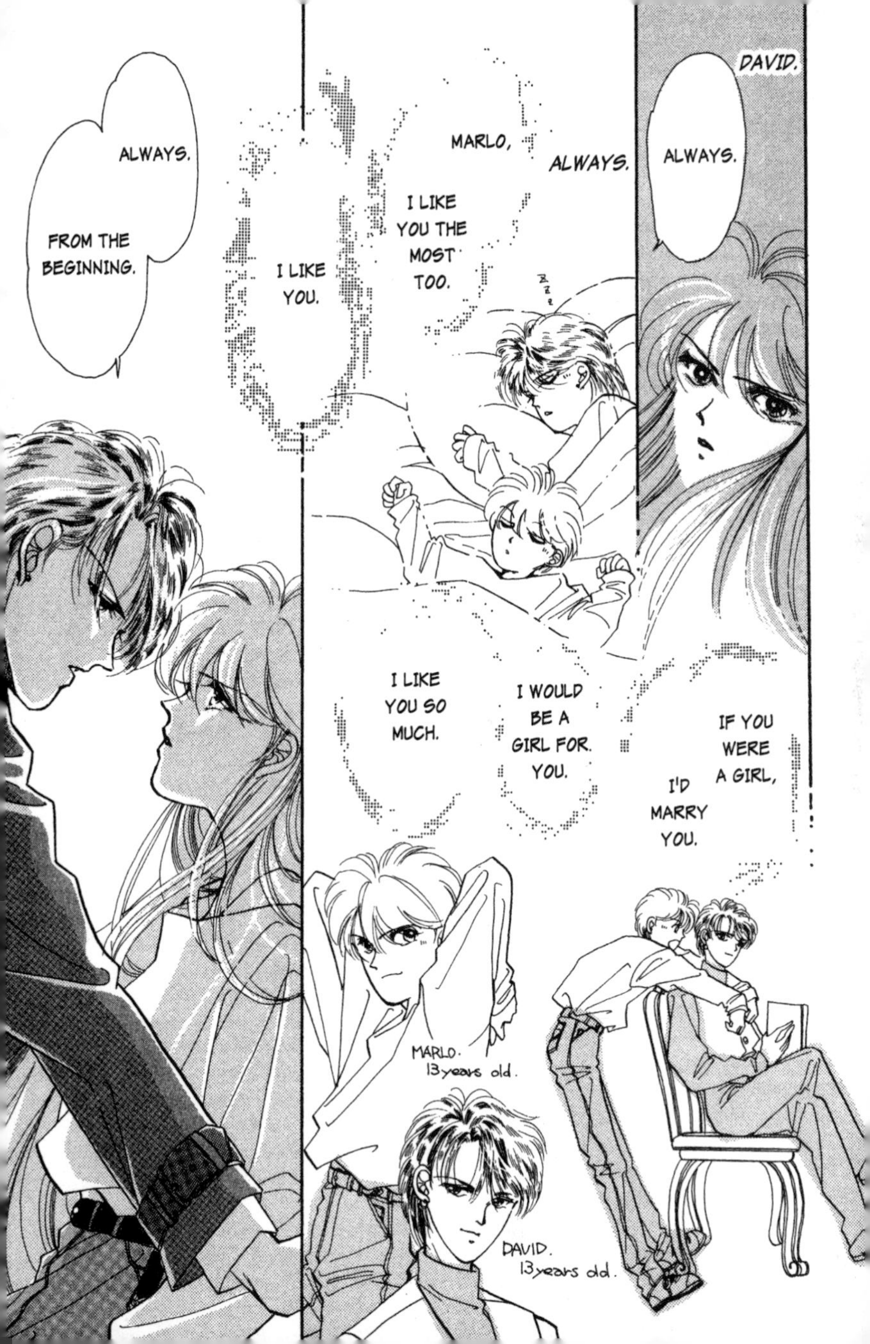
DAVID.
ALWAYS.
ALWAYS.
MARLO,
I LIKE YOU THE MOST TOO.
I LIKE YOU.
IF YOU WERE A GIRL,
I'D MARRY YOU.
I WOULD BE A GIRL FOR YOU.
I LIKE YOU SO MUCH.
MARLO. 13years old.
DAVID. 13years old.
ALWAYS.
FROM THE BEGINNING.

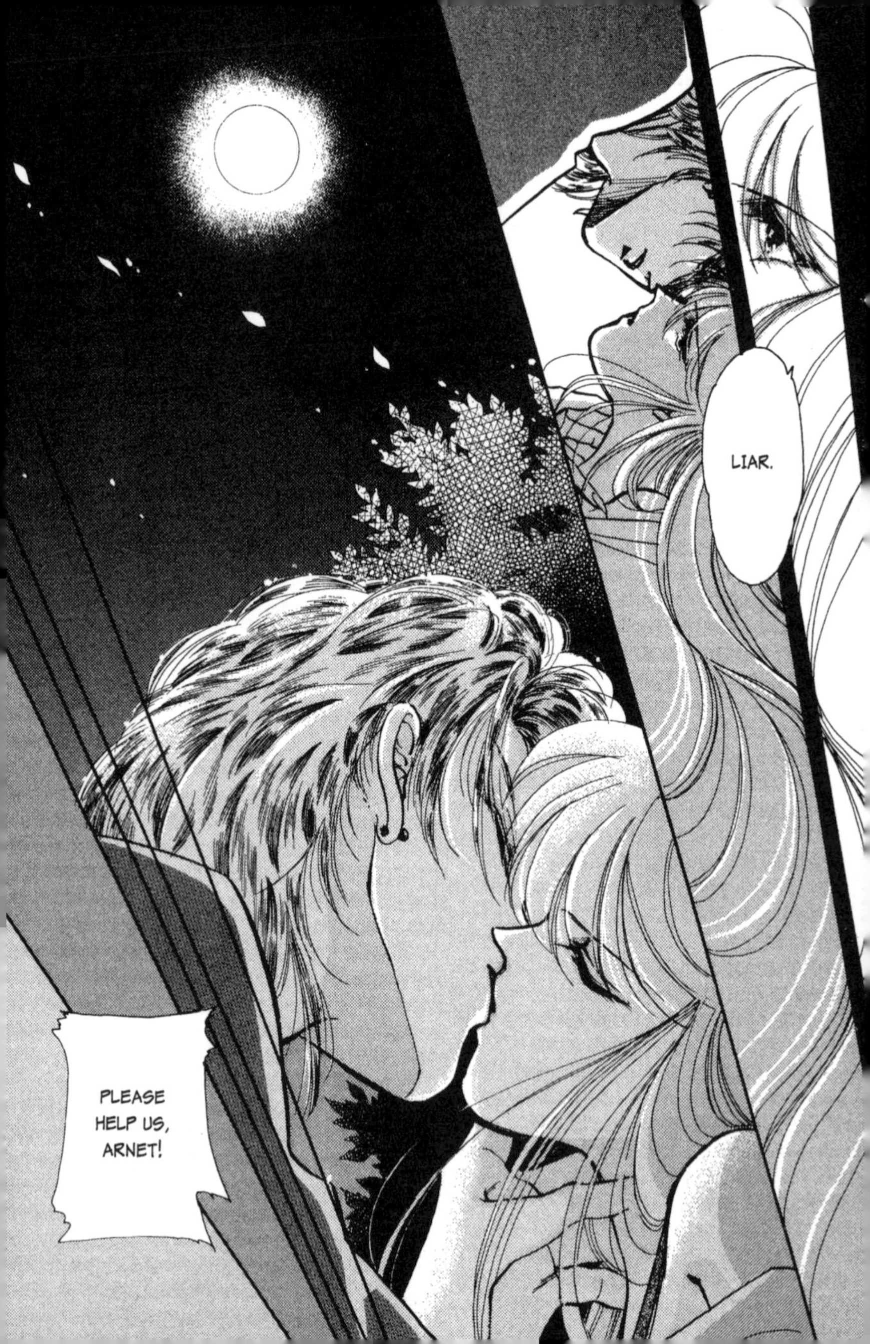
LIAR.
PLEASE HELP US, ARNET!

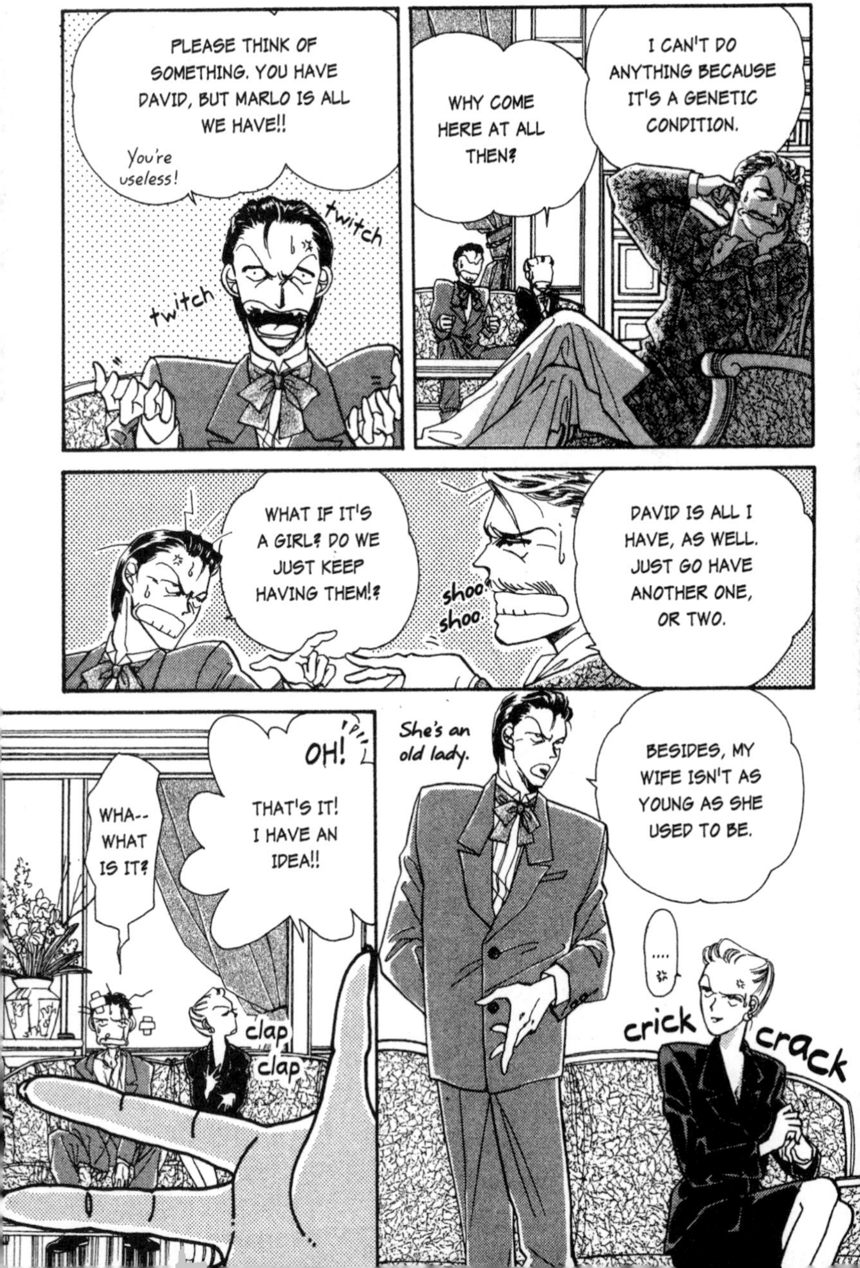
I CAN'T DO ANYTHING BECAUSE IT'S A GENETIC CONDITION.
WHY COME HERE AT ALL THEN?
PLEASE THINK OF SOMETHING. YOU HAVE DAVID, BUT MARLO IS ALL WE HAVE!!
You're useless!
twitch
twitch
DAVID IS ALL I HAVE, AS WELL. JUST GO HAVE ANOTHER ONE, OR TWO.
shoo shoo
WHAT IF IT'S A GIRL? DO WE JUST KEEP HAVING THEM!?
BESIDES, MY WIFE ISN'T AS YOUNG AS SHE USED TO BE.
She's an old lady.
.....
crick
crack
OH!
THAT'S IT! I HAVE AN IDEA!!
WHA-- WHAT IS IT?
clap
clap

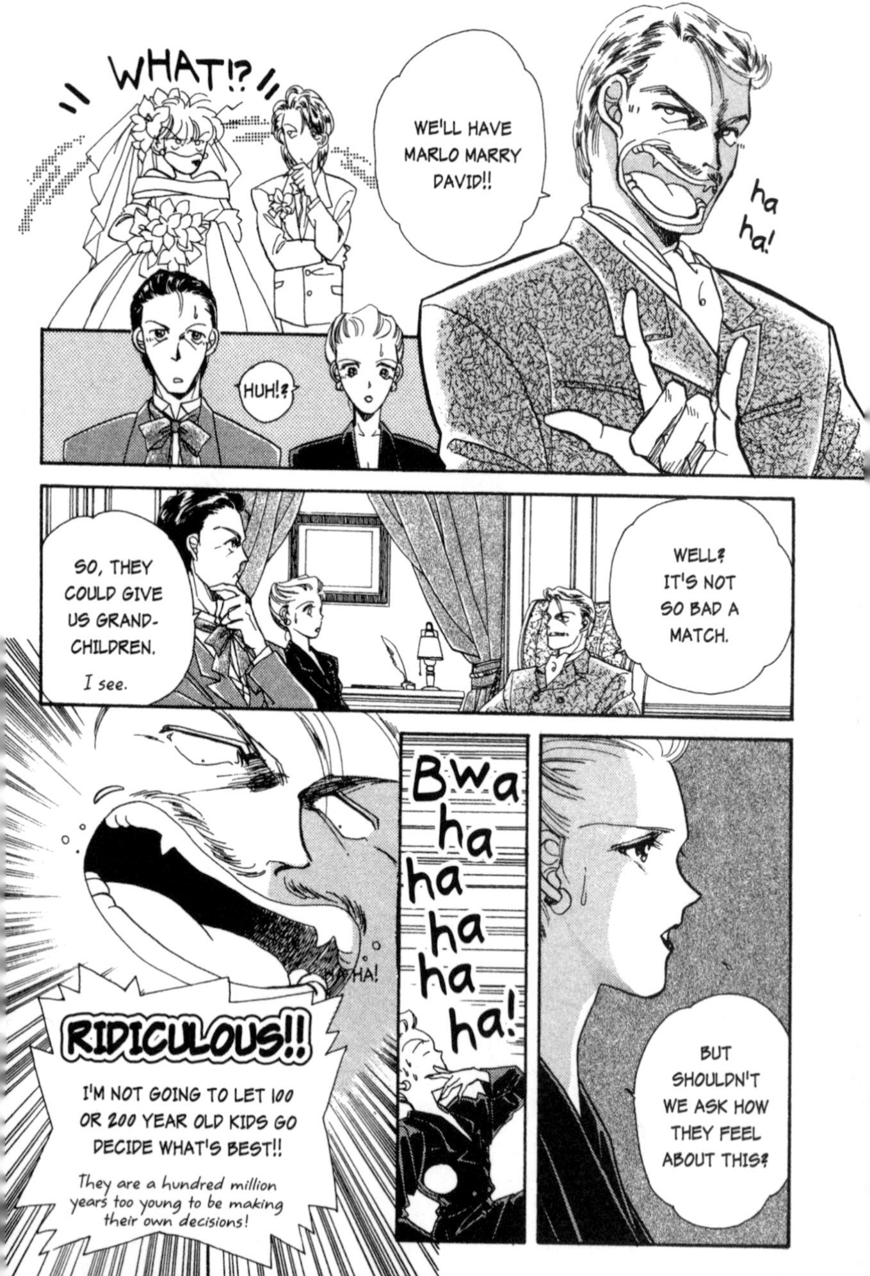
WE'LL HAVE MARLO MARRY DAVID!!
ha ha!
WHAT!?
HUH!?
WELL? IT'S NOT SO BAD A MATCH.
SO, THEY COULD GIVE US GRAND-CHILDREN.
I see.
BUT SHOULDN'T WE ASK HOW THEY FEEL ABOUT THIS?
Bwa ha ha ha ha ha ha!
HA HA!
RIDICULOUS!!
I'M NOT GOING TO LET 100 OR 200 YEAR OLD KIDS GO DECIDE WHAT'S BEST!!
They are a hundred million years too young to be making their own decisions!

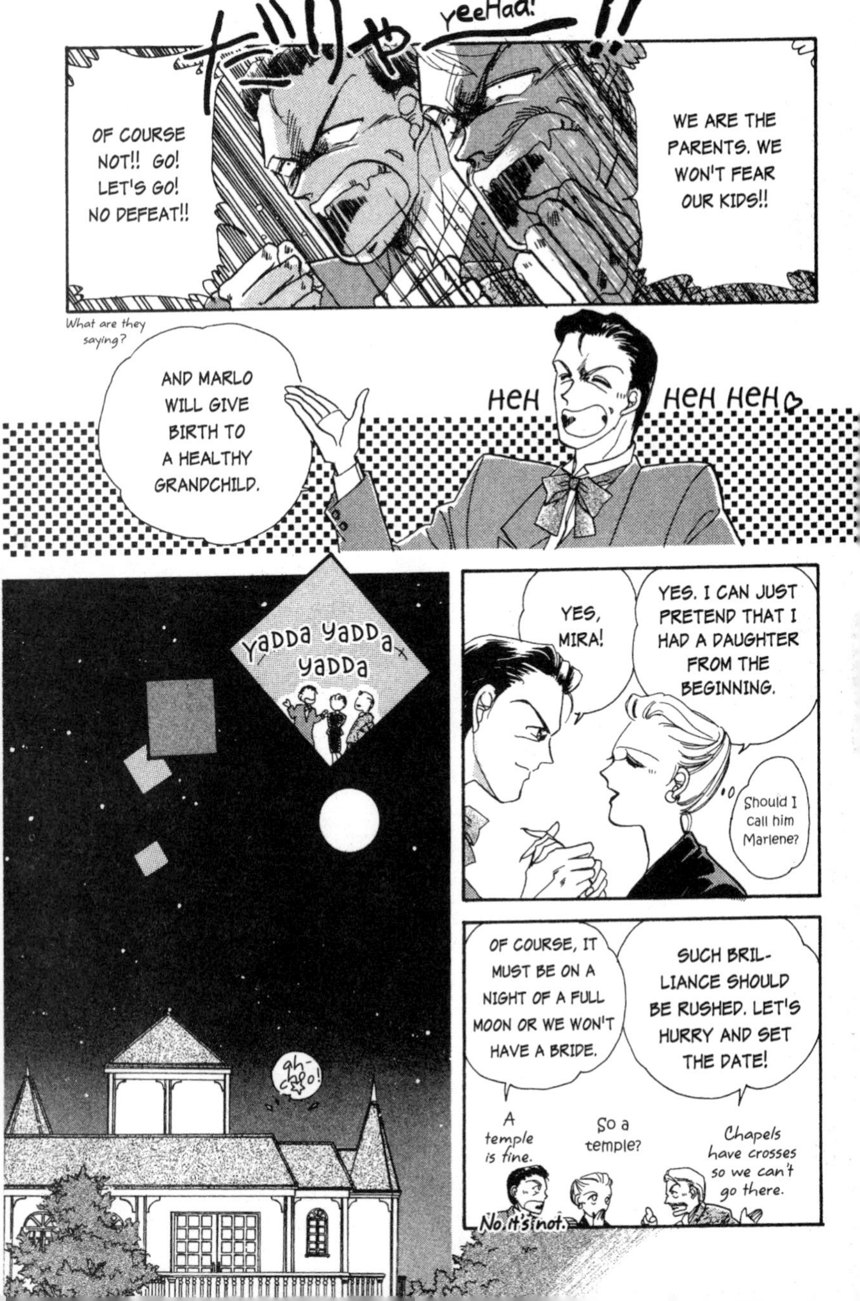
yeeHaa!
WE ARE THE PARENTS. WE WON'T FEAR OUR KIDS!!
OF COURSE NOT!! GO! LET'S GO! NO DEFEAT!!
HEH HEH HEH♡
AND MARLO WILL GIVE BIRTH TO A HEALTHY GRANDCHILD.
What are they saying?
YES. I CAN JUST PRETEND THAT I HAD A DAUGHTER FROM THE BEGINNING.
YES, MIRA!
Should I call him Marlene?
SUCH BRIL-LIANCE SHOULD BE RUSHED. LET'S HURRY AND SET THE DATE!
OF COURSE, IT MUST BE ON A NIGHT OF A FULL MOON OR WE WON'T HAVE A BRIDE.
Chapels have crosses so we can't go there.
So a temple?
A temple is fine.
No, it's not.
yadda yadda yadda
ah-choo!

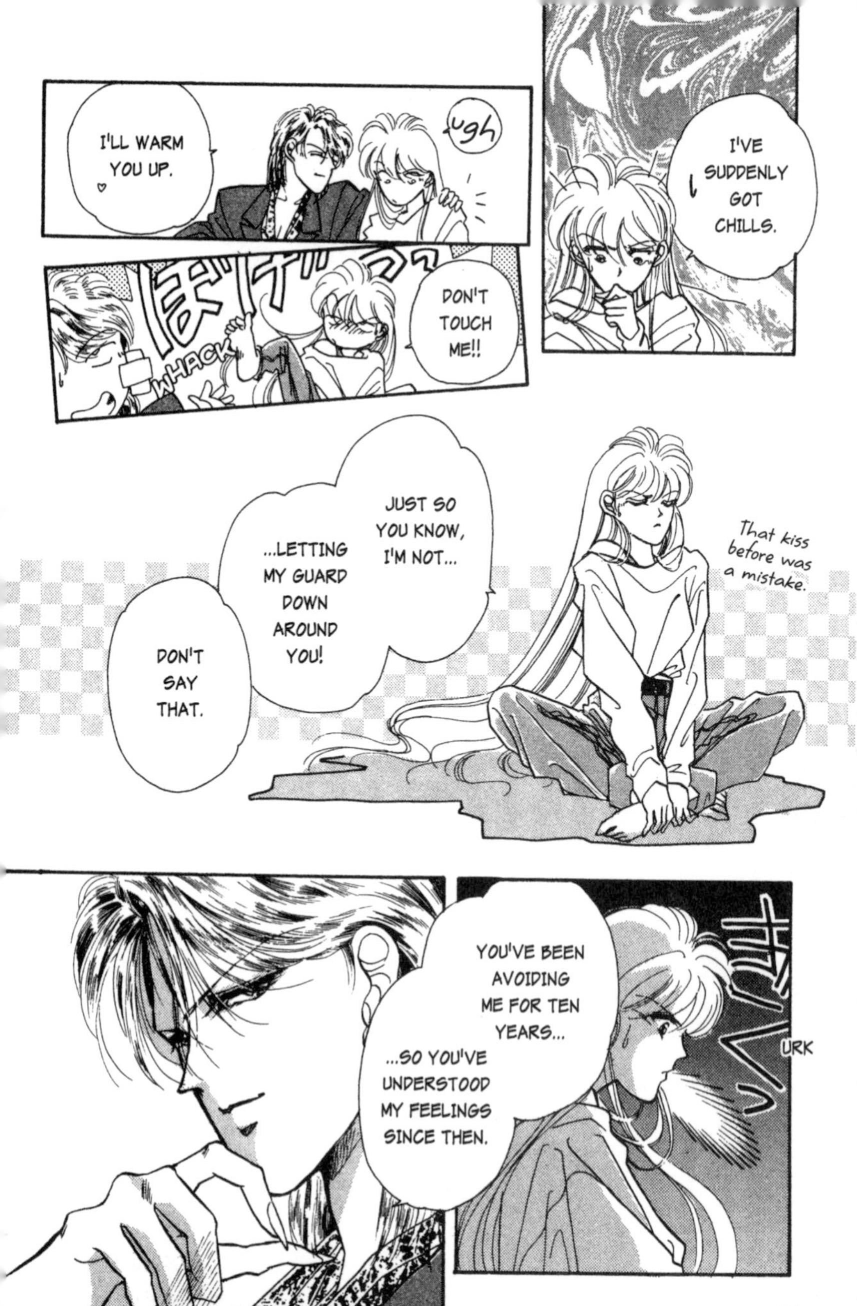
I'VE SUDDENLY GOT CHILLS.
I'LL WARM YOU UP.
ugh
WHACK
DON'T TOUCH ME!!
That kiss before was a mistake.
JUST SO YOU KNOW, I'M NOT...
...LETTING MY GUARD DOWN AROUND YOU!
DON'T SAY THAT.
YOU'VE BEEN AVOIDING ME FOR TEN YEARS...
URK
...SO YOU'VE UNDERSTOOD MY FEELINGS SINCE THEN.

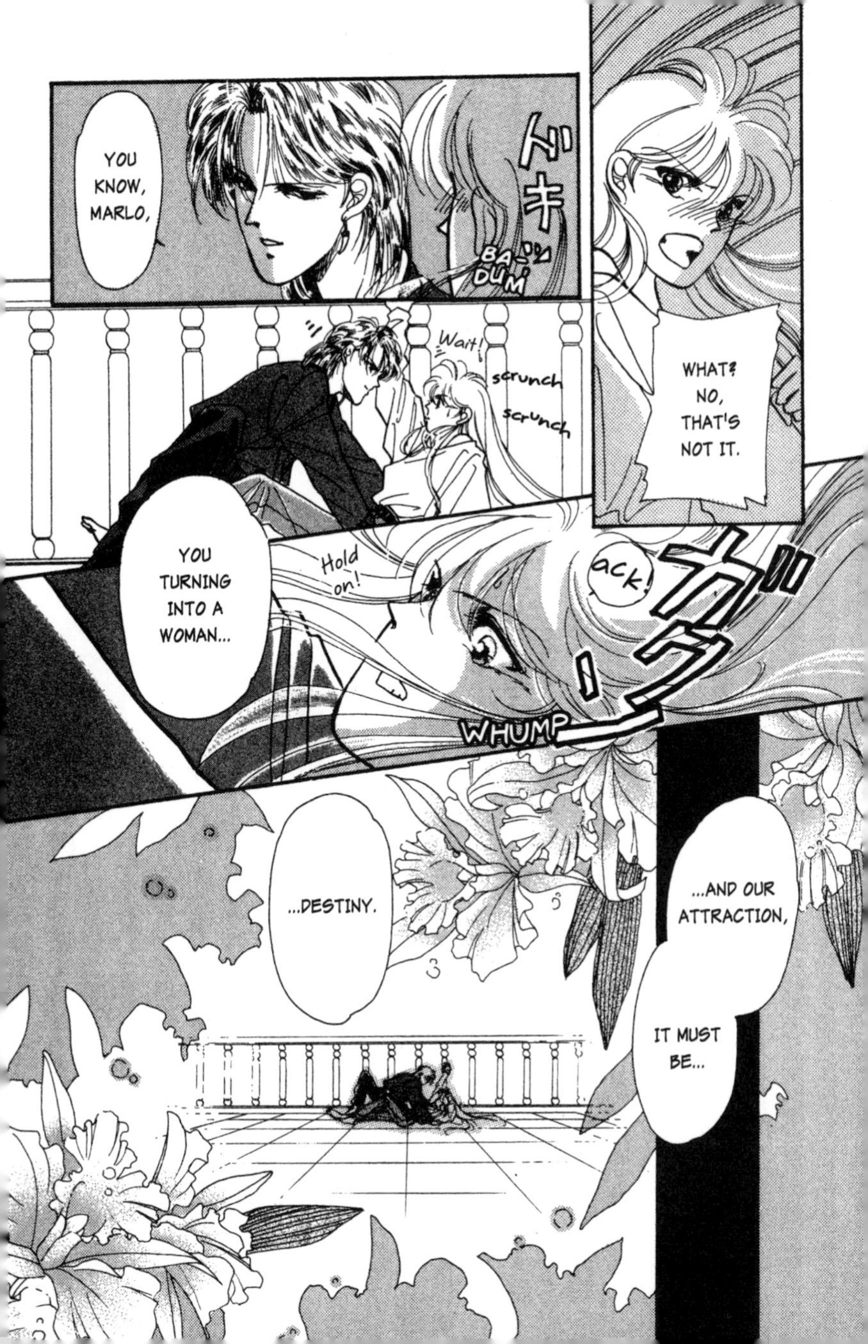
WHAT? NO, THAT'S NOT IT.
YOU KNOW, MARLO,
ドキ
BA-DUM
Wait!
scrunch
scrunch
ガクッ
ack!
WHUMP
Hold on!
YOU TURNING INTO A WOMAN...
...AND OUR ATTRACTION,
IT MUST BE...
...DESTINY.

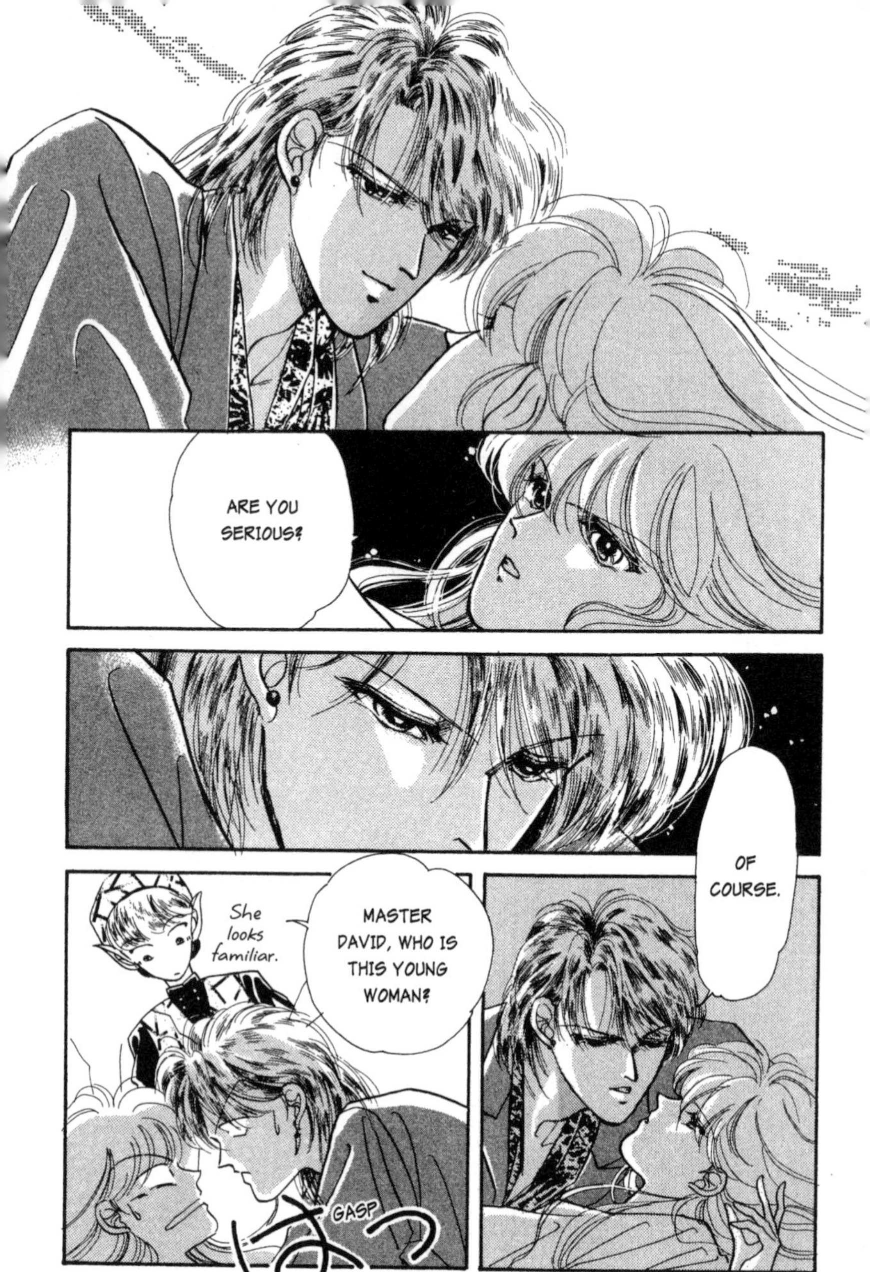
ARE YOU SERIOUS?
OF COURSE.
MASTER DAVID, WHO IS THIS YOUNG WOMAN?
She looks familiar.
GASP

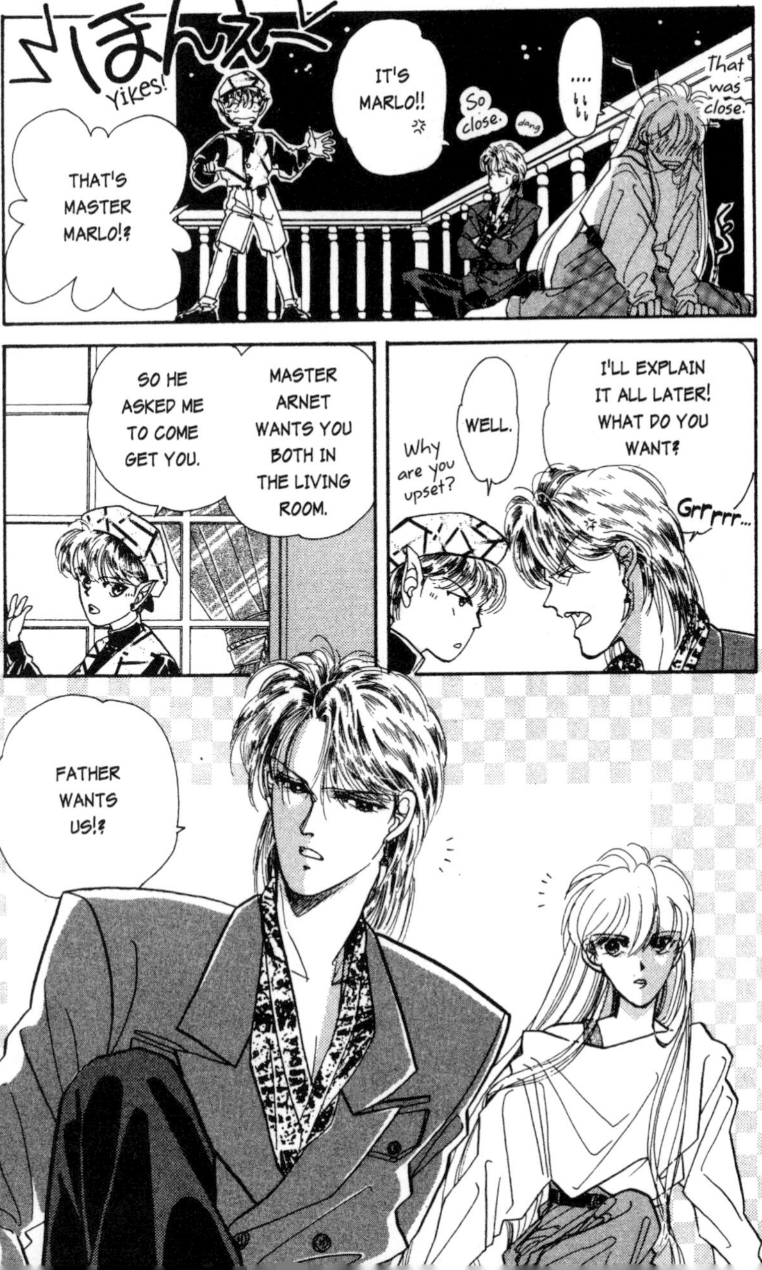
That was close.
....
dang
So close.
IT'S MARLO!!
Yikes!
THAT'S MASTER MARLO!?
I'LL EXPLAIN IT ALL LATER! WHAT DO YOU WANT?
Grrrrr...
WELL.
Why are you upset?
MASTER ARNET WANTS YOU BOTH IN THE LIVING ROOM.
SO HE ASKED ME TO COME GET YOU.
FATHER WANTS US!?

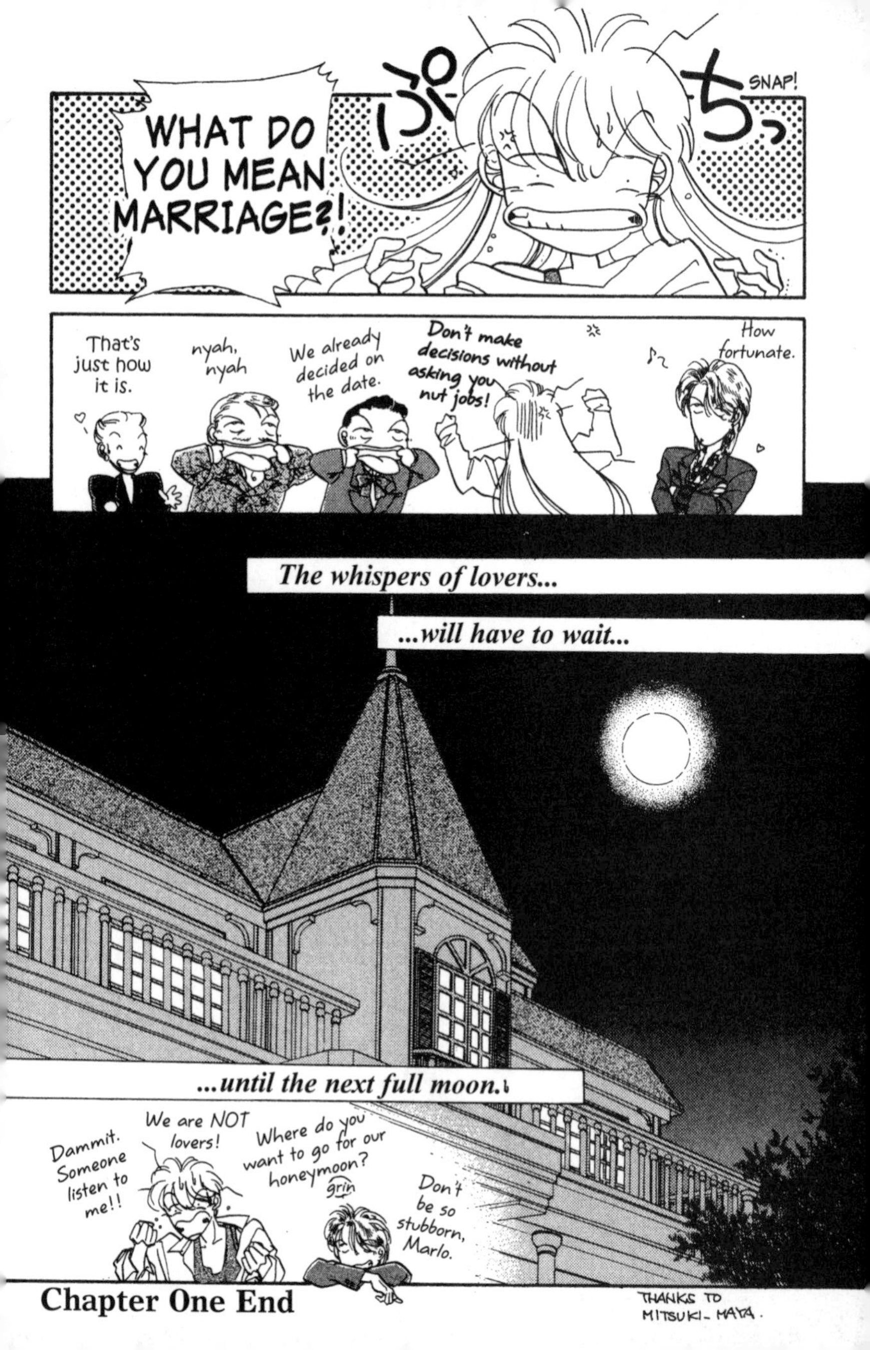
SNAP!
ぷちっ
WHAT DO YOU MEAN MARRIAGE?!
How fortunate.
Don't make decisions without asking you nut jobs!
We already decided on the date.
nyah, nyah
That's just how it is.
The whispers of lovers...
...will have to wait...
...until the next full moon.
Don't be so stubborn, Marlo.
Where do you want to go for our honeymoon?
grin
We are NOT lovers!
Dammit. Someone listen to me!!
Chapter One End
THANKS TO MITSUKI-MAYA.

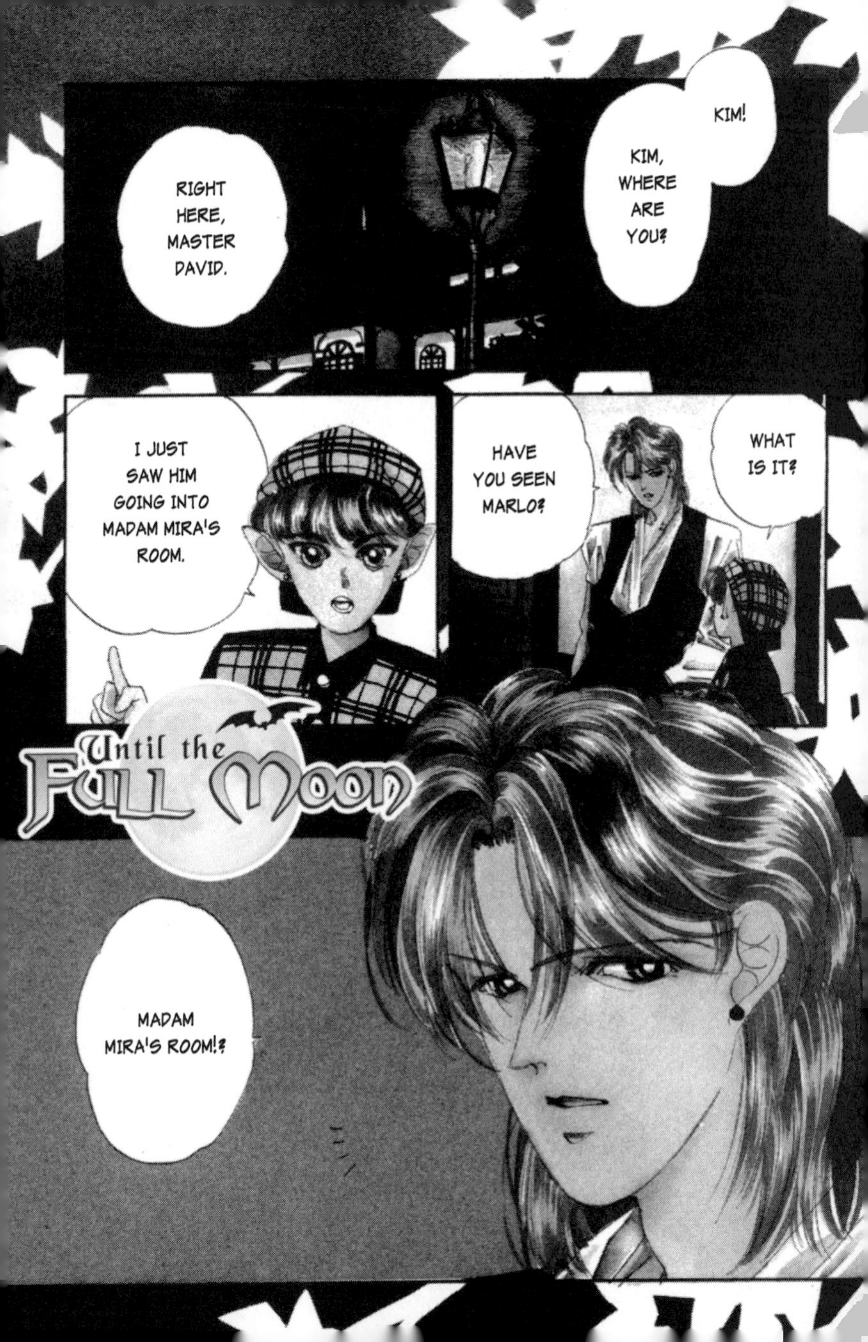
KIM!
KIM, WHERE ARE YOU?
RIGHT HERE, MASTER DAVID.
WHAT IS IT?
HAVE YOU SEEN MARLO?
I JUST SAW HIM GOING INTO MADAM MIRA'S ROOM.
Until the FULL MOON
MADAM MIRA'S ROOM!?

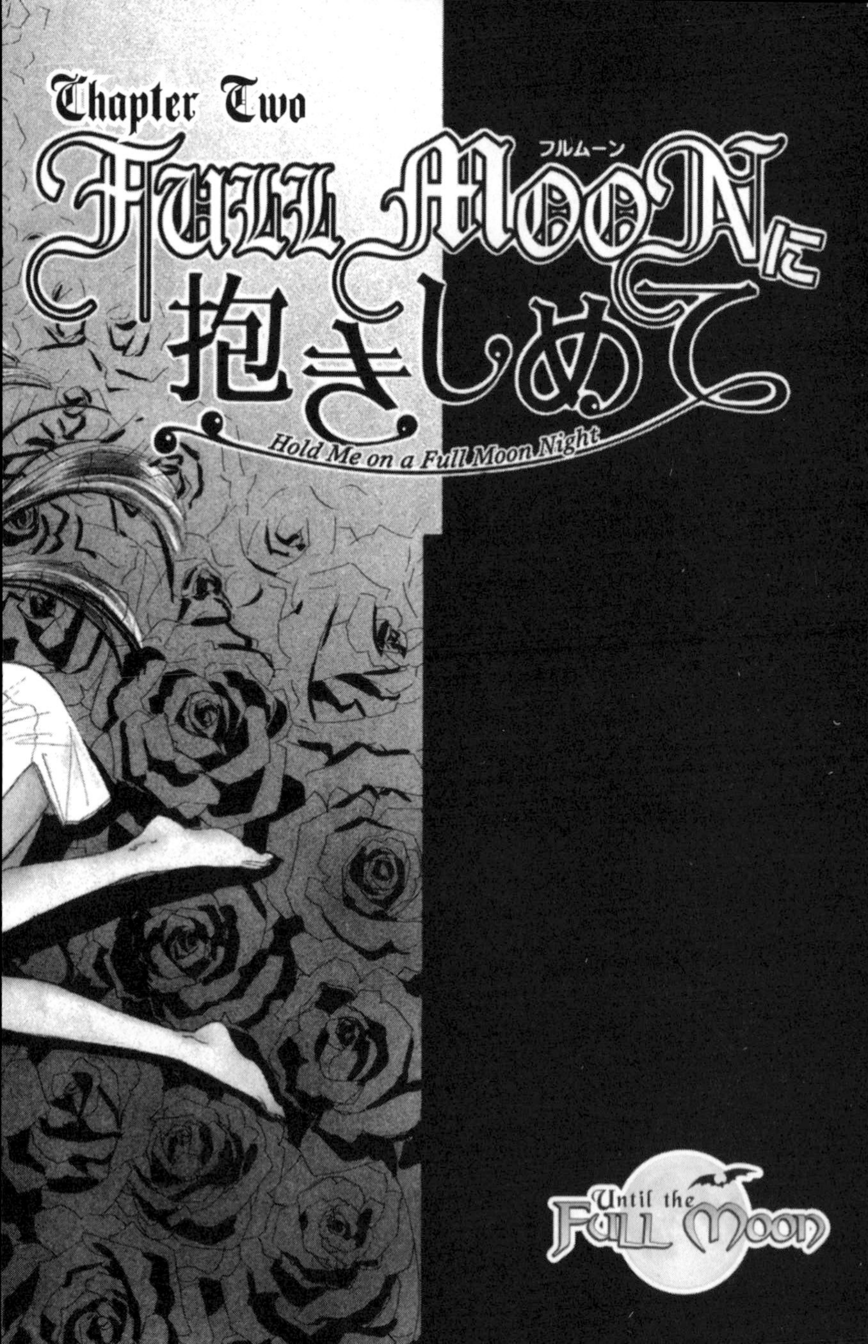
Chapter Two
FULL MOONに抱きしめて
フルムーン
Hold Me on a Full Moon Night
Until the FULL MOON

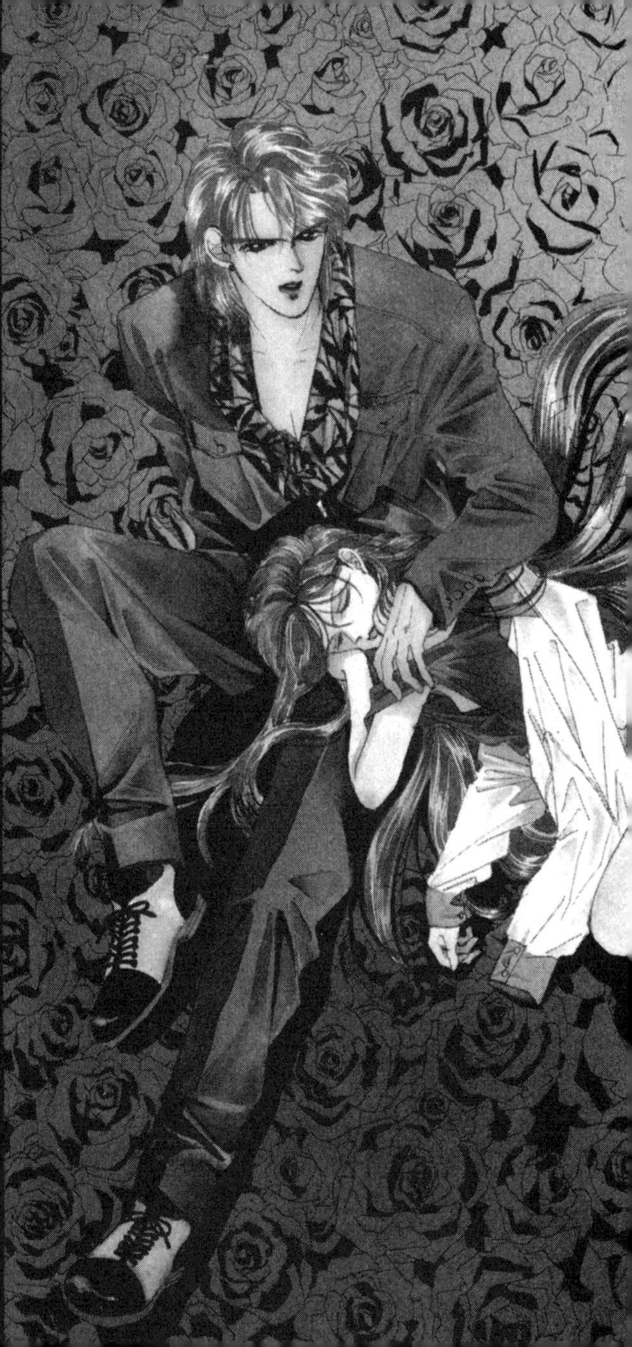

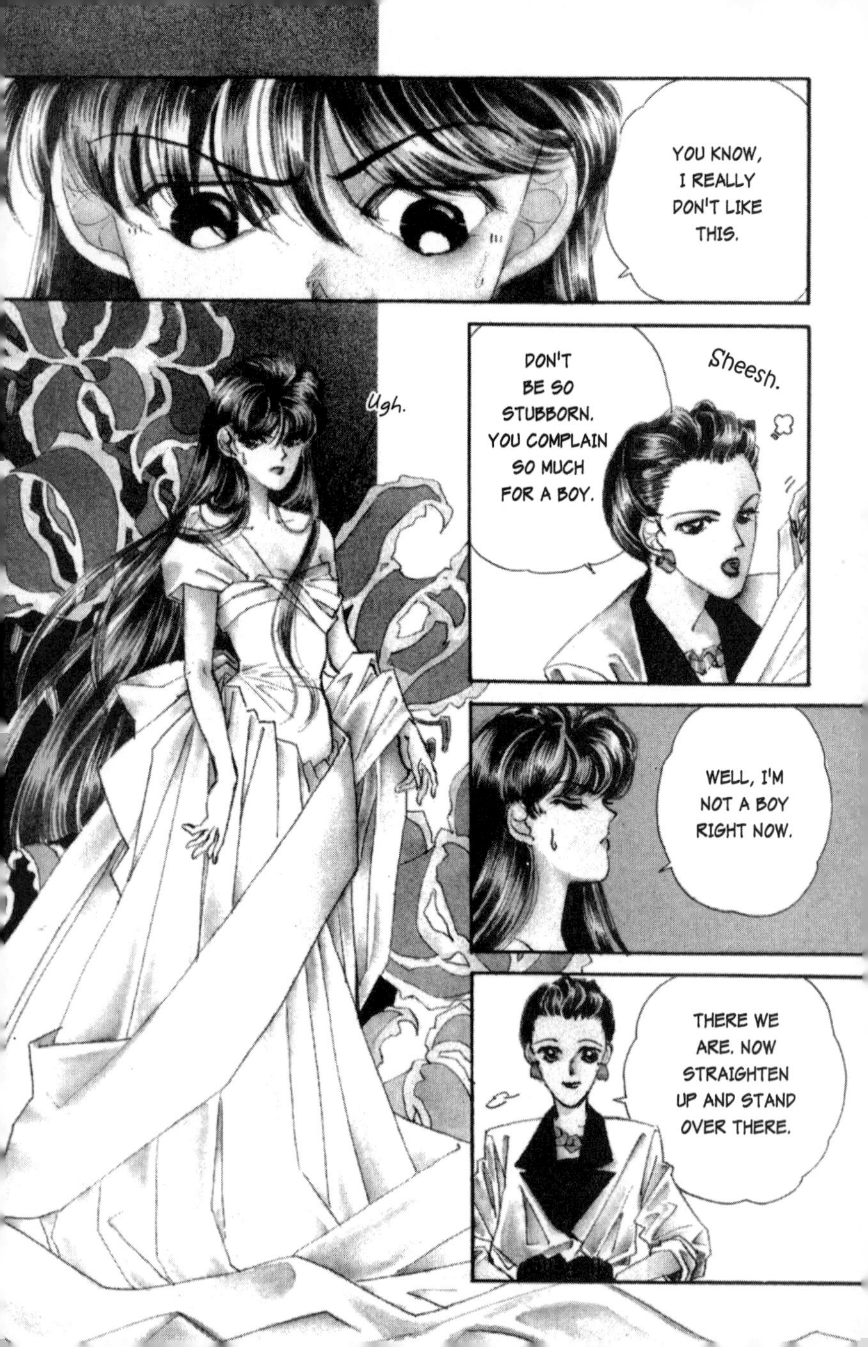
YOU KNOW, I REALLY DON'T LIKE THIS.
Sheesh.
DON'T BE SO STUBBORN. YOU COMPLAIN SO MUCH FOR A BOY.
WELL, I'M NOT A BOY RIGHT NOW.
THERE WE ARE. NOW STRAIGHTEN UP AND STAND OVER THERE.
Ugh.

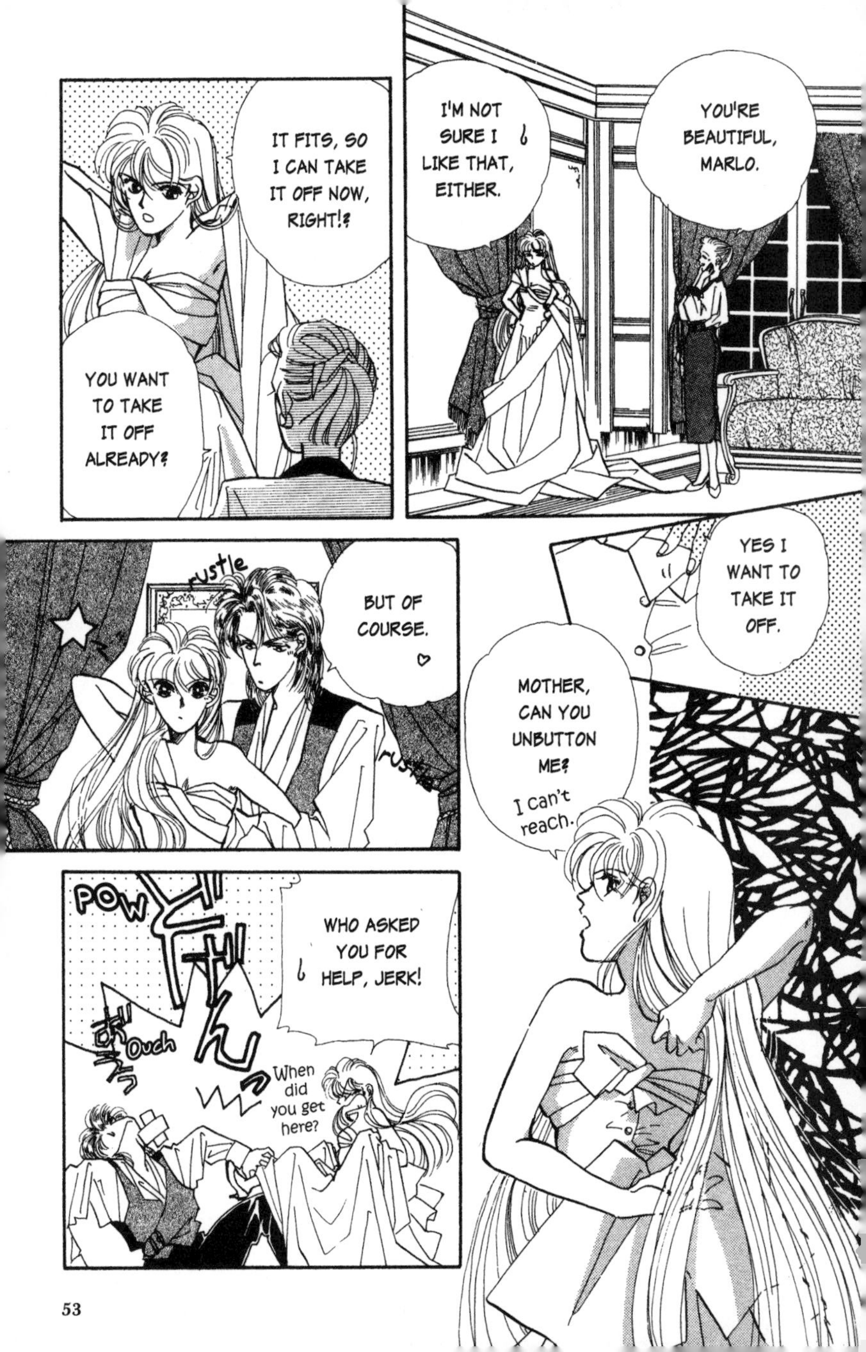

YOU'RE BEAUTIFUL, MARLO.
I'M NOT SURE I LIKE THAT, EITHER.
IT FITS, SO I CAN TAKE IT OFF NOW, RIGHT!?
YOU WANT TO TAKE IT OFF ALREADY?
YES I WANT TO TAKE IT OFF.
MOTHER, CAN YOU UNBUTTON ME?
I can't reach.
rustle
BUT OF COURSE. ♡
rustle
WHO ASKED YOU FOR HELP, JERK!
POW
Ouch
When did you get here?

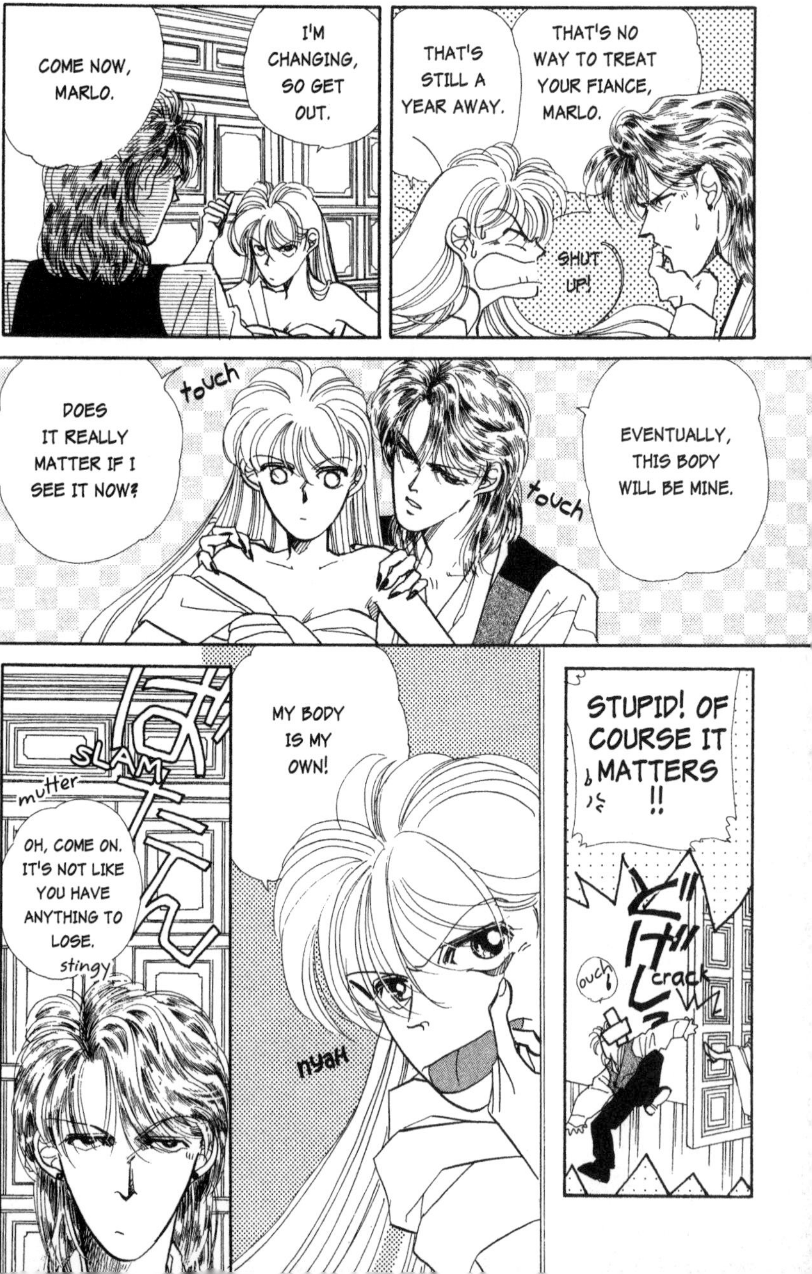
THAT'S NO WAY TO TREAT YOUR FIANCE, MARLO.
THAT'S STILL A YEAR AWAY.
SHUT UP!
I'M CHANGING, SO GET OUT.
COME NOW, MARLO.
EVENTUALLY, THIS BODY WILL BE MINE.
touch
touch
DOES IT REALLY MATTER IF I SEE IT NOW?
STUPID! OF COURSE IT MATTERS !!
ouch
crack
MY BODY IS MY OWN!
nyaH
SLAM
mutter
OH, COME ON. IT'S NOT LIKE YOU HAVE ANYTHING TO LOSE.
stingy

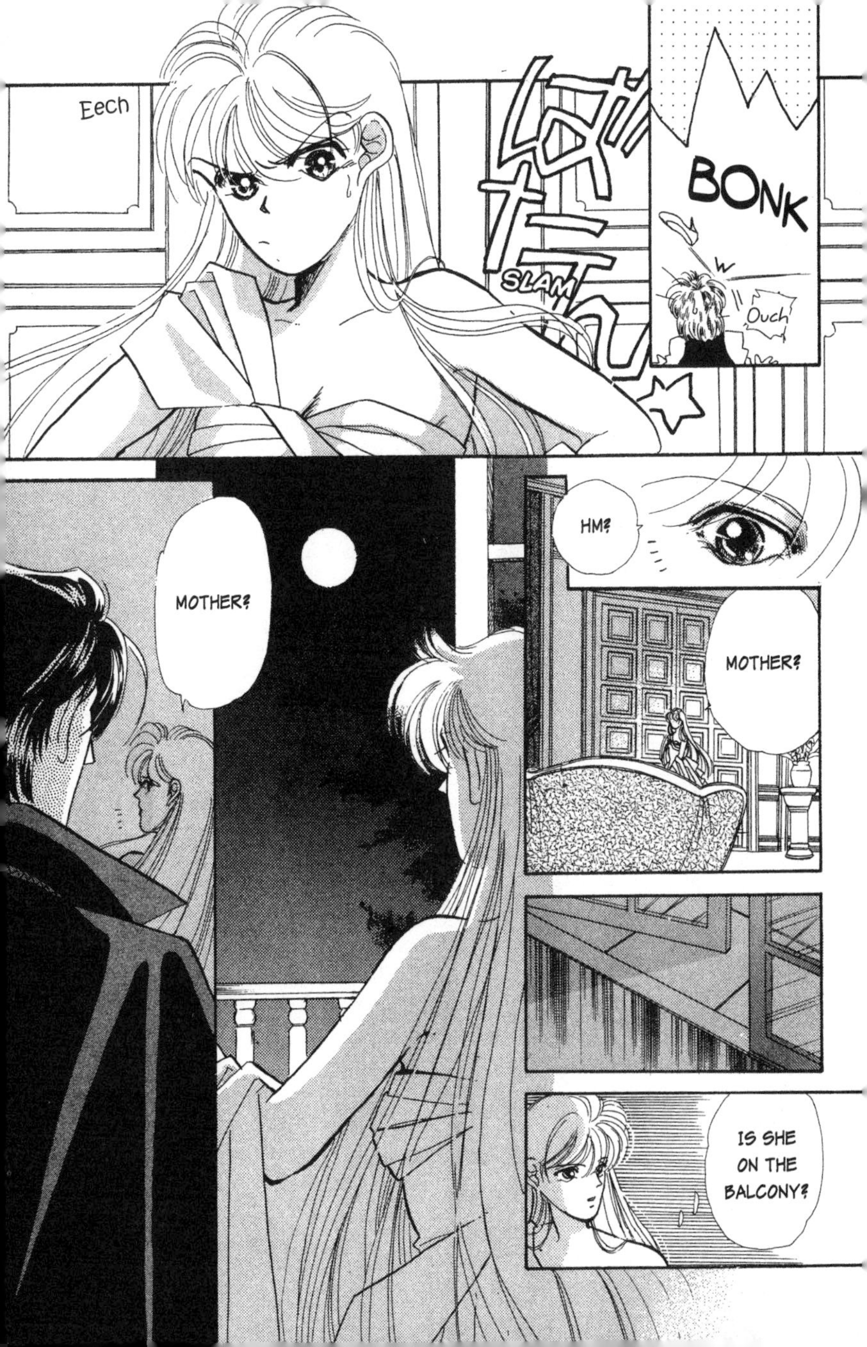
BONK
Ouch
SLAM
Eech
HM?
MOTHER?
IS SHE ON THE BALCONY?
MOTHER?

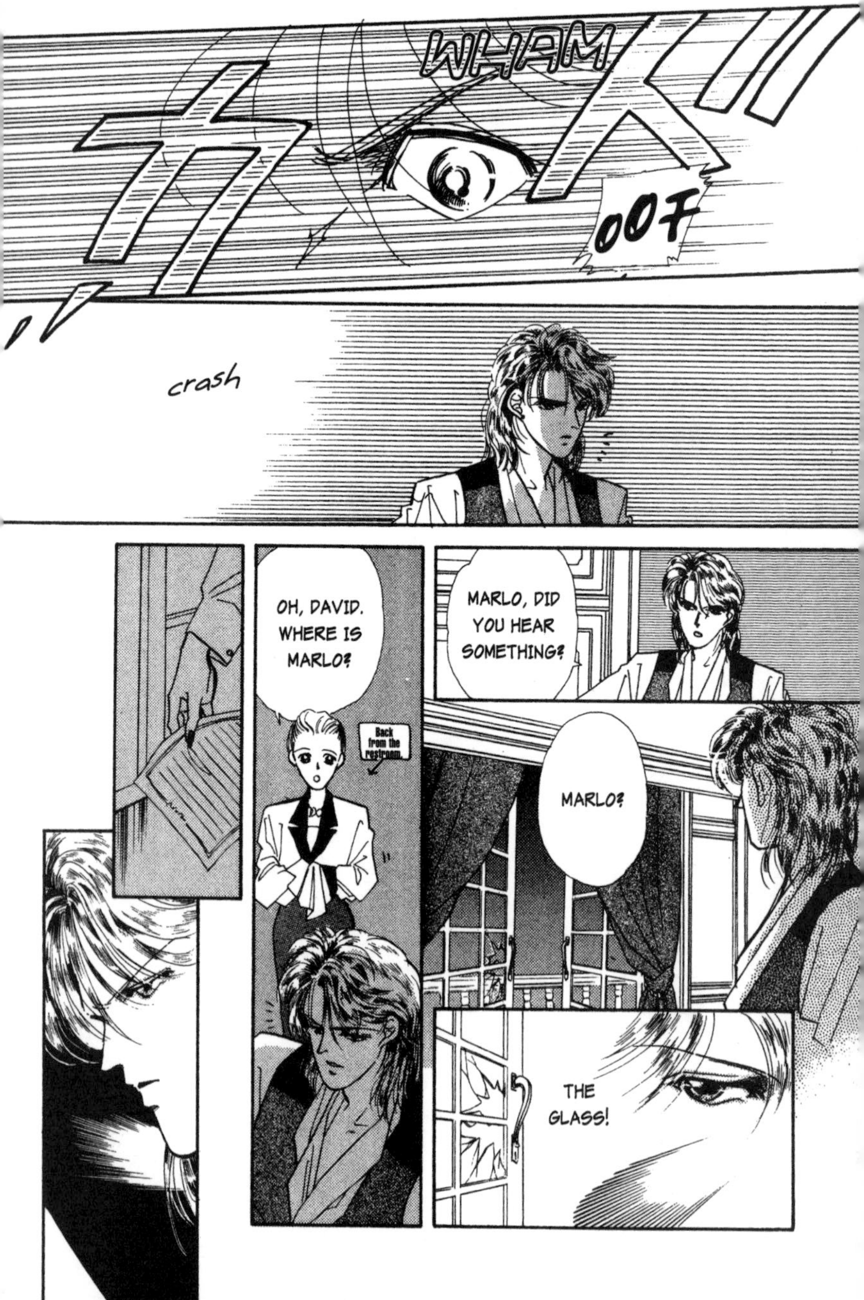
WHAM
OOF
crash
MARLO, DID YOU HEAR SOMETHING?
MARLO?
THE GLASS!
OH, DAVID. WHERE IS MARLO?
Back from the restroom.

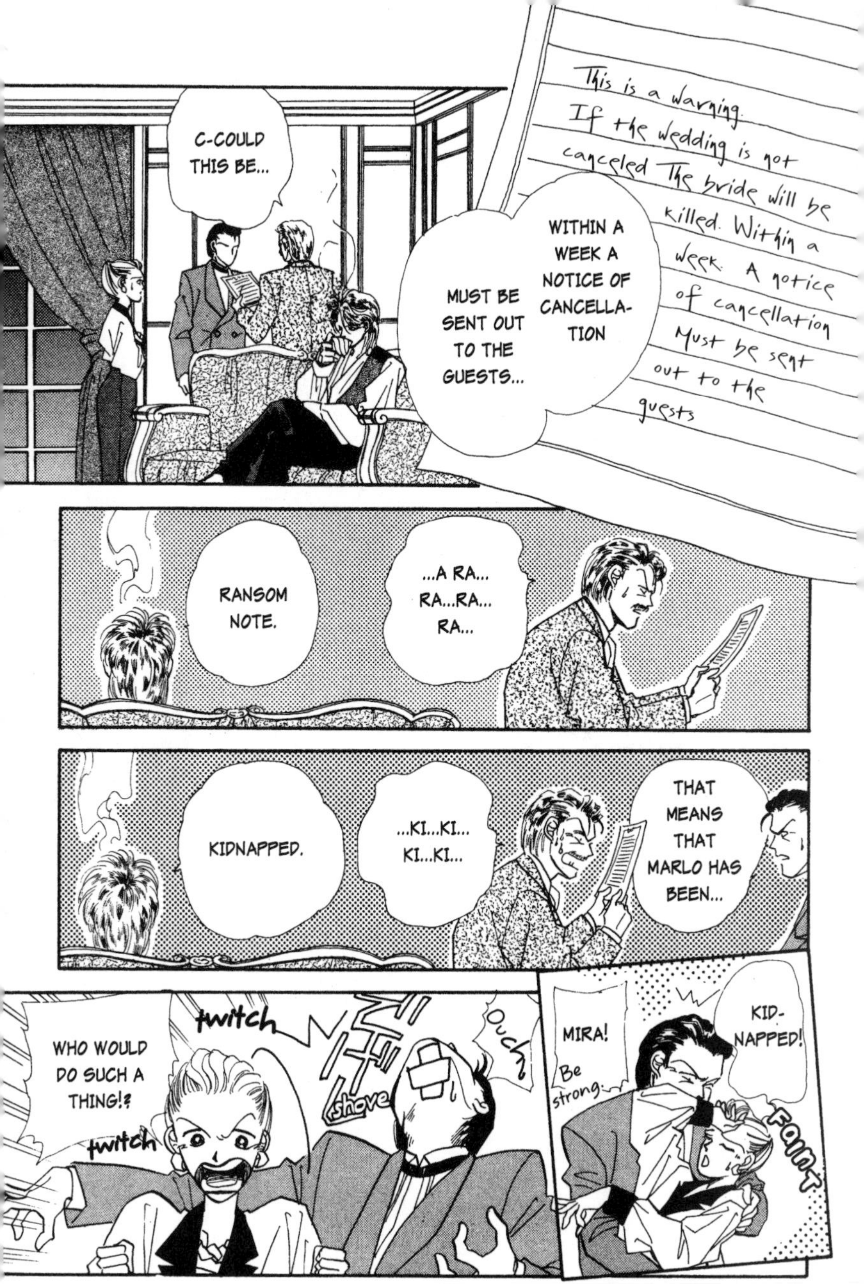
This is a warning. If the wedding is not canceled The bride will be killed. Within a week. A notice of cancellation Must be sent out to the guests
WITHIN A WEEK A NOTICE OF CANCELLA-TION MUST BE SENT OUT TO THE GUESTS...
C-COULD THIS BE...
...A RA... RA...RA... RA...
RANSOM NOTE.
THAT MEANS THAT MARLO HAS BEEN...
...KI...KI... KI...KI...
KIDNAPPED.
KID-NAPPED!
FAINT
MIRA!
Be strong.
Ouch
shove
twitch
WHO WOULD DO SUCH A THING!?
twitch

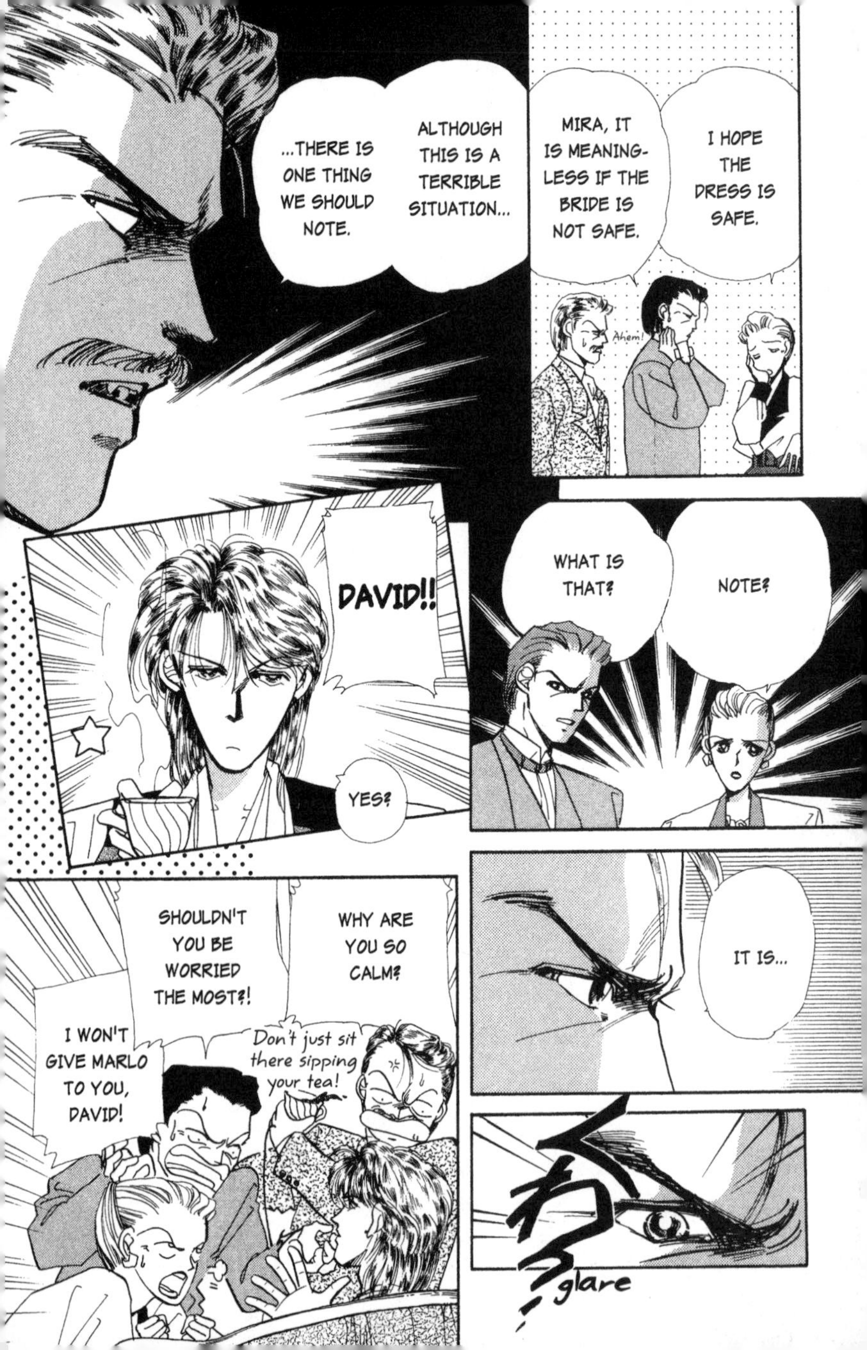
I HOPE THE DRESS IS SAFE.
MIRA, IT IS MEANING-LESS IF THE BRIDE IS NOT SAFE.
Ahem!
ALTHOUGH THIS IS A TERRIBLE SITUATION...
...THERE IS ONE THING WE SHOULD NOTE.
NOTE?
WHAT IS THAT?
DAVID!!
YES?
IT IS...
glare
WHY ARE YOU SO CALM?
SHOULDN'T YOU BE WORRIED THE MOST?!
Don't just sit there sipping your tea!
I WON'T GIVE MARLO TO YOU, DAVID!

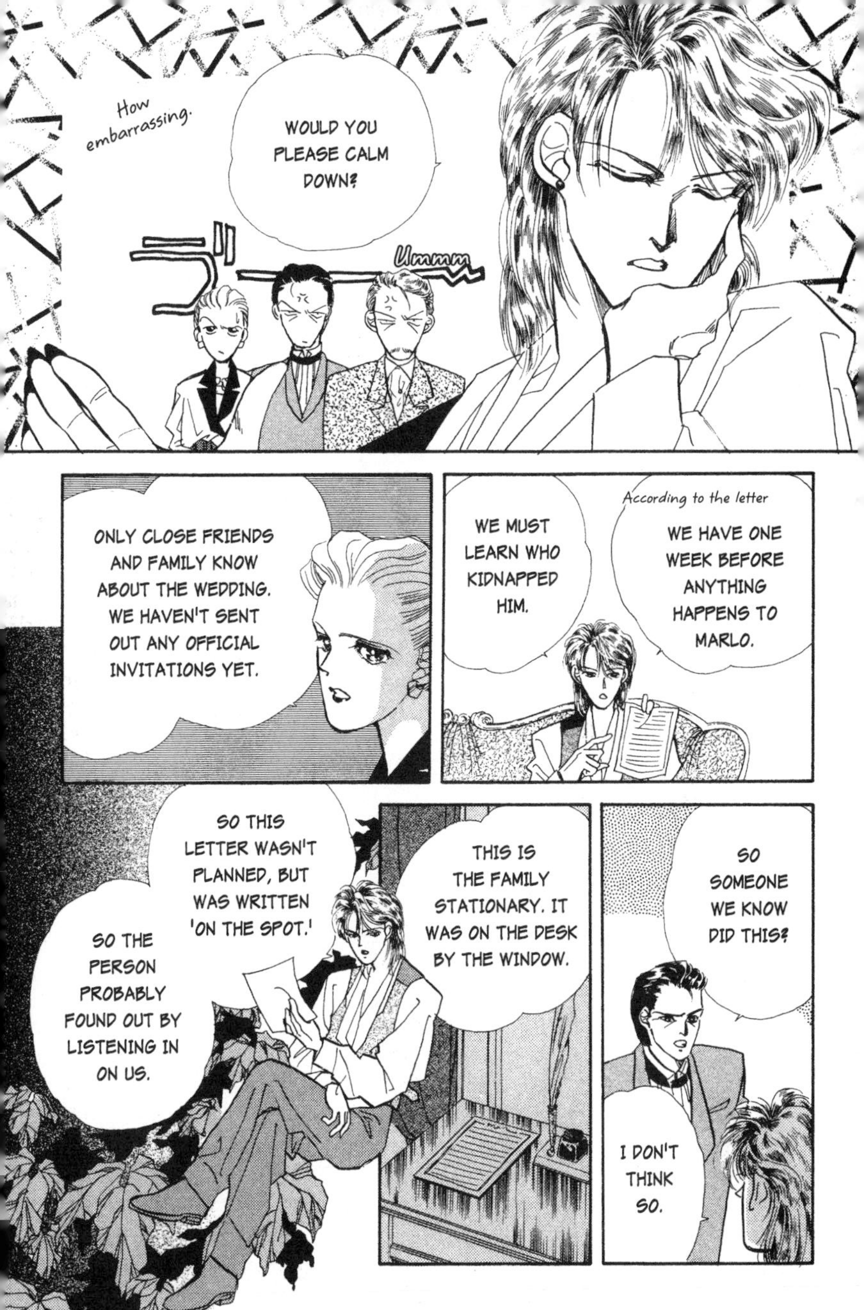
WOULD YOU PLEASE CALM DOWN?
How embarrassing.
Ummm
According to the letter
WE HAVE ONE WEEK BEFORE ANYTHING HAPPENS TO MARLO.
WE MUST LEARN WHO KIDNAPPED HIM.
ONLY CLOSE FRIENDS AND FAMILY KNOW ABOUT THE WEDDING. WE HAVEN'T SENT OUT ANY OFFICIAL INVITATIONS YET.
SO SOMEONE WE KNOW DID THIS?
I DON'T THINK SO.
THIS IS THE FAMILY STATIONARY. IT WAS ON THE DESK BY THE WINDOW.
SO THIS LETTER WASN'T PLANNED, BUT WAS WRITTEN 'ON THE SPOT.'
SO THE PERSON PROBABLY FOUND OUT BY LISTENING IN ON US.

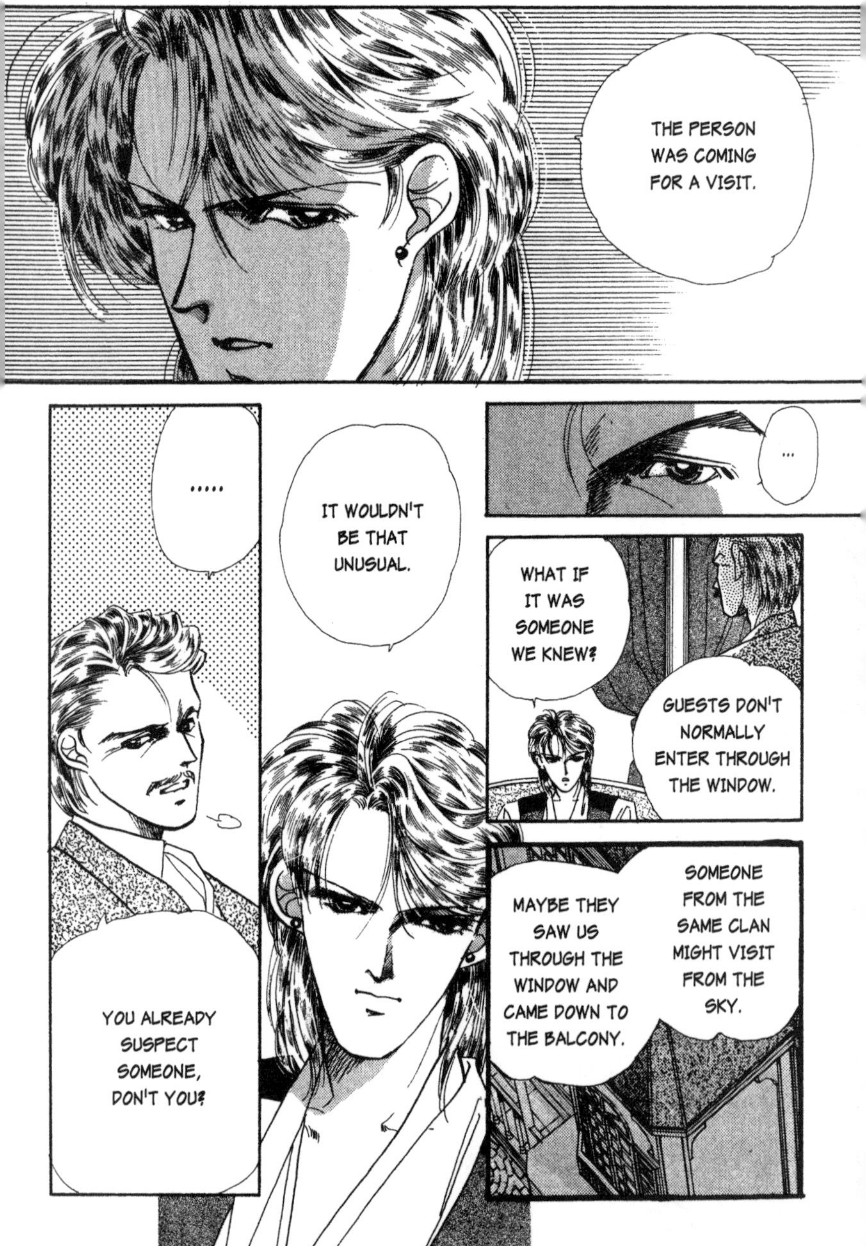
THE PERSON WAS COMING FOR A VISIT.
...
GUESTS DON'T NORMALLY ENTER THROUGH THE WINDOW.
WHAT IF IT WAS SOMEONE WE KNEW?
SOMEONE FROM THE SAME CLAN MIGHT VISIT FROM THE SKY.
MAYBE THEY SAW US THROUGH THE WINDOW AND CAME DOWN TO THE BALCONY.
IT WOULDN'T BE THAT UNUSUAL.
.....
YOU ALREADY SUSPECT SOMEONE, DON'T YOU?

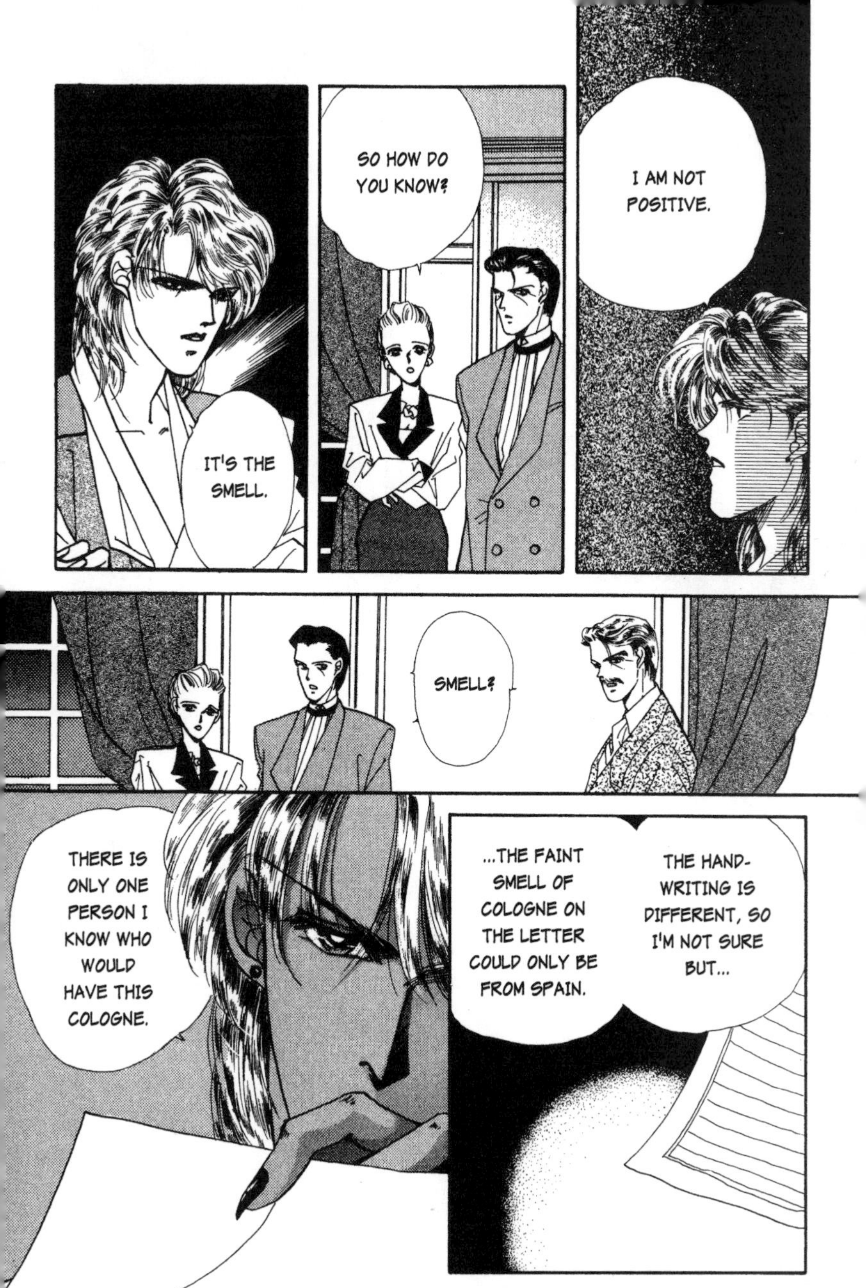
I AM NOT POSITIVE.
SO HOW DO YOU KNOW?
IT'S THE SMELL.
SMELL?
THE HAND-WRITING IS DIFFERENT, SO I'M NOT SURE BUT...
...THE FAINT SMELL OF COLOGNE ON THE LETTER COULD ONLY BE FROM SPAIN.
THERE IS ONLY ONE PERSON I KNOW WHO WOULD HAVE THIS COLOGNE.

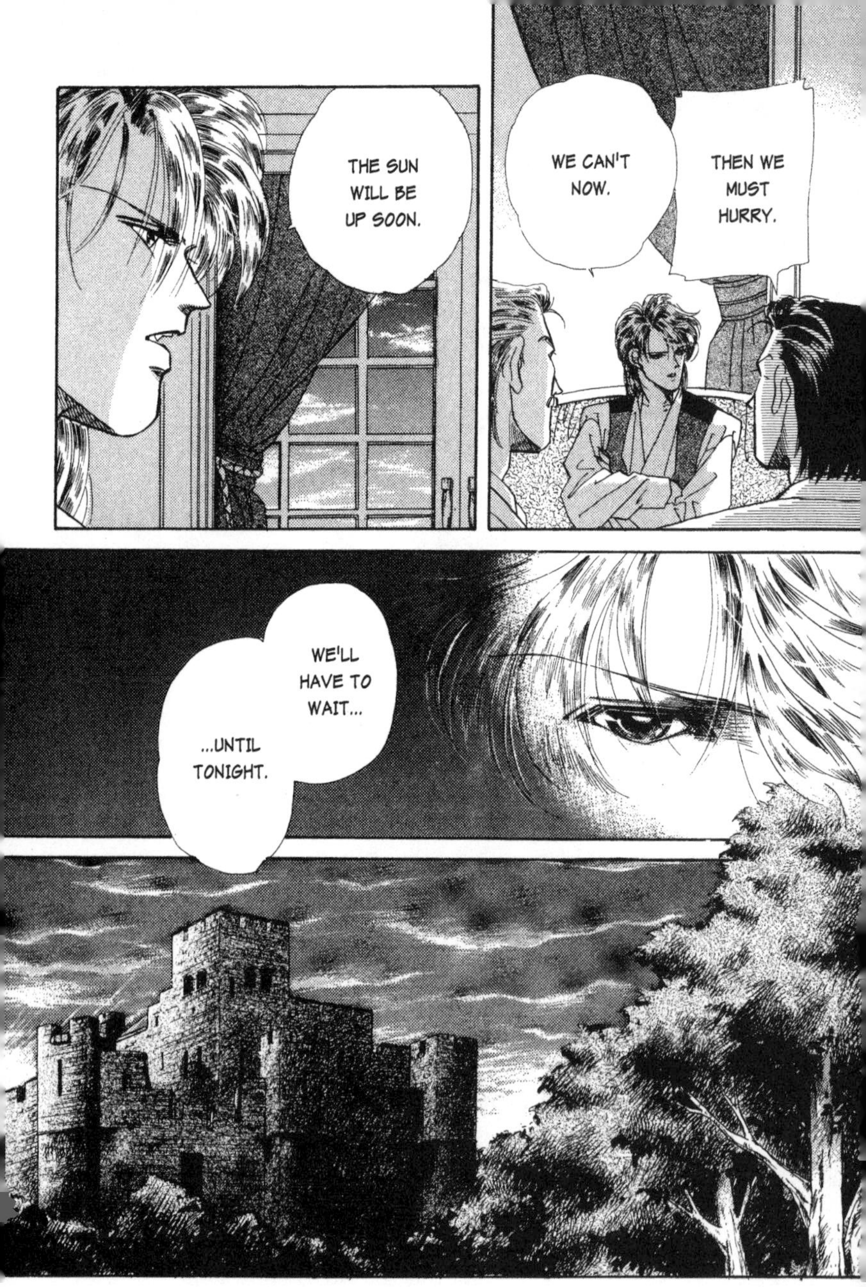
THEN WE MUST HURRY.
WE CAN'T NOW.
THE SUN WILL BE UP SOON.
WE'LL HAVE TO WAIT...
...UNTIL TONIGHT.

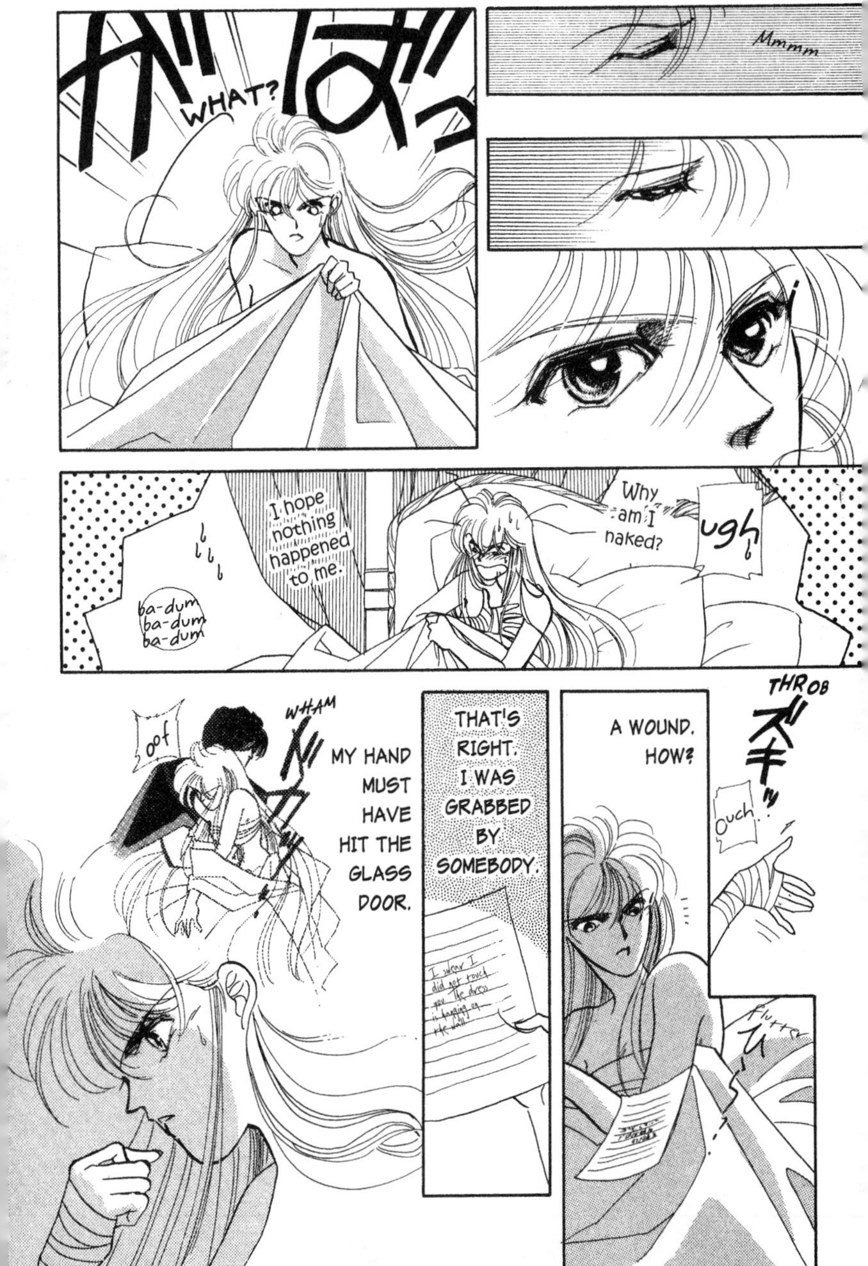
Mmmm
がばっ
WHAT?
ugh
Why am I naked?
I hope nothing happened to me.
ba-dum ba-dum ba-dum
THROB
ズキッ
A WOUND. HOW?
Ouch
Flutter
THAT'S RIGHT. I WAS GRABBED BY SOMEBODY.
I swear I did not touch you. The dress is hanging on the wall
MY HAND MUST HAVE HIT THE GLASS DOOR.
WHAM
oof

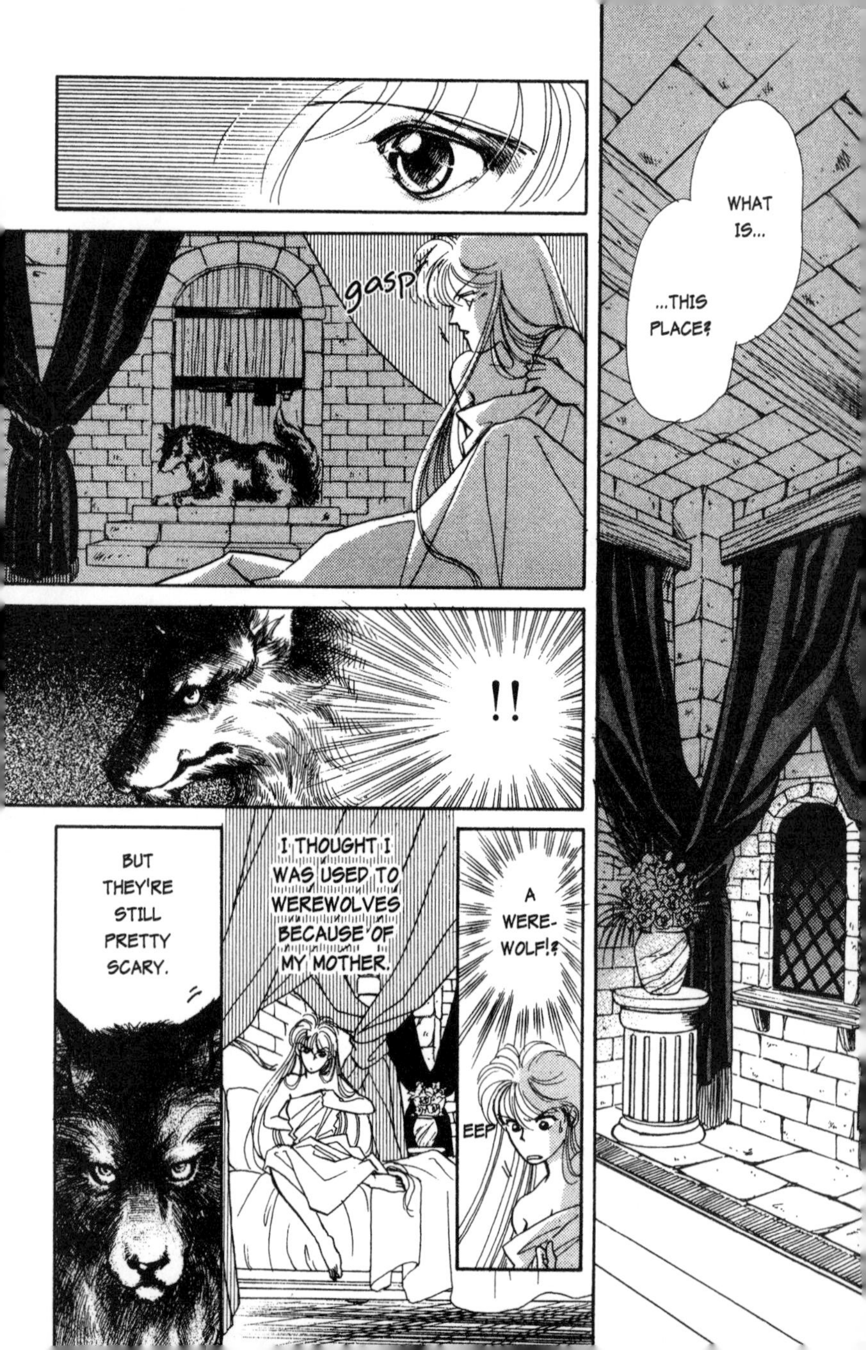
WHAT IS...
...THIS PLACE?
gasp
!!
A WERE-WOLF!?
EEP
I THOUGHT I WAS USED TO WEREWOLVES BECAUSE OF MY MOTHER.
BUT THEY'RE STILL PRETTY SCARY.

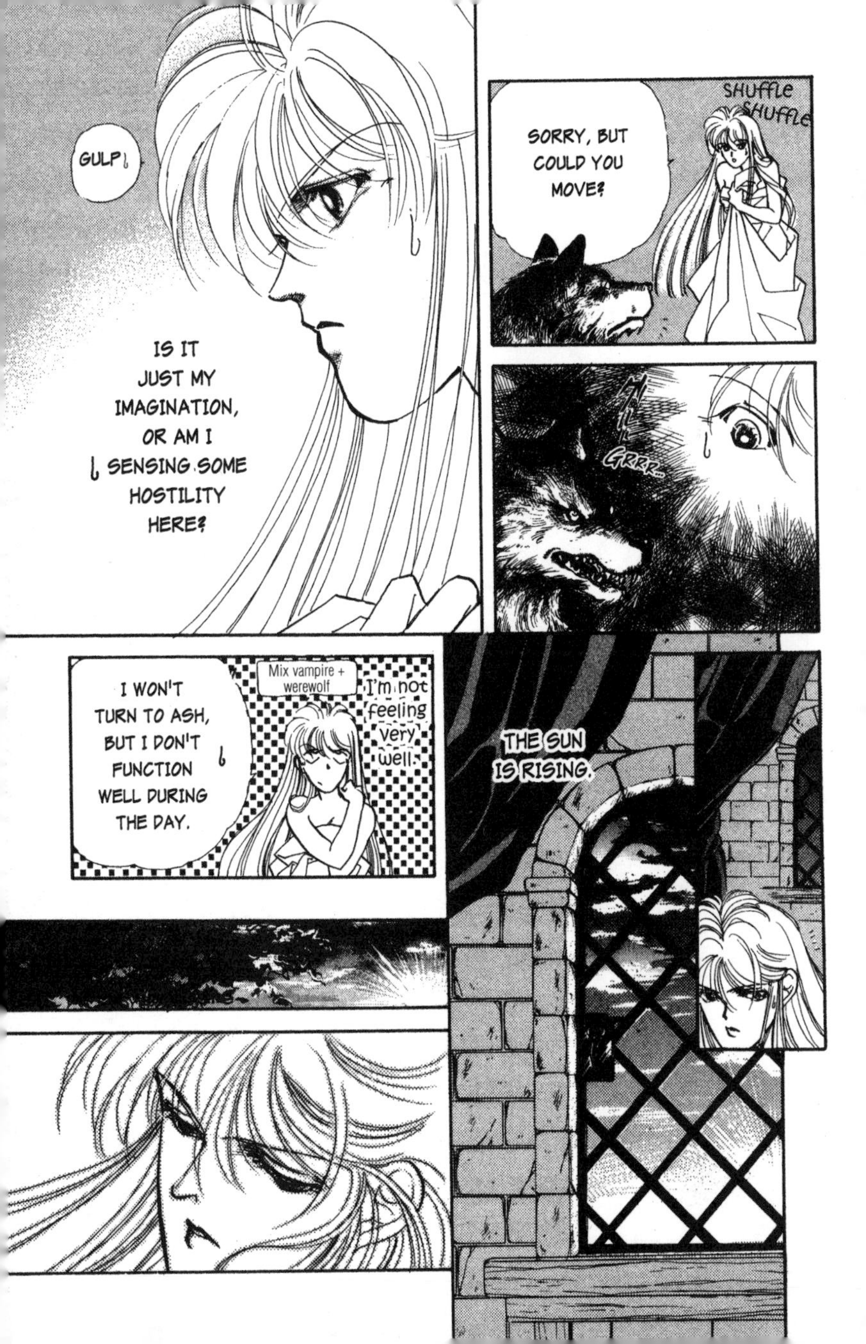
SHUFFLE SHUFFLE
SORRY, BUT COULD YOU MOVE?
GRRR...
GULP
IS IT JUST MY IMAGINATION, OR AM I SENSING SOME HOSTILITY HERE?
THE SUN IS RISING.
Mix vampire + werewolf
I'm not feeling very well.
I WON'T TURN TO ASH, BUT I DON'T FUNCTION WELL DURING THE DAY.

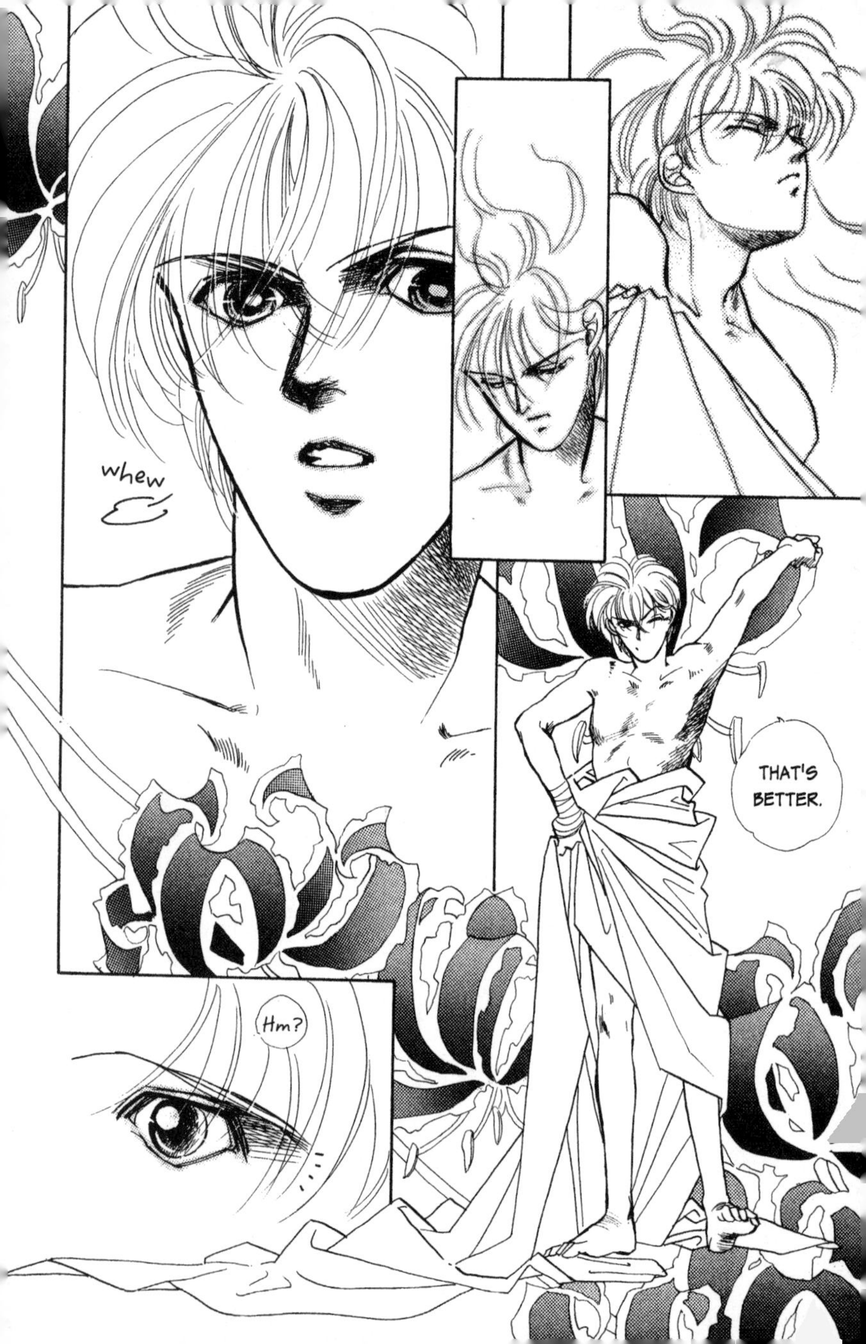
THAT'S BETTER.
whew
Hm?

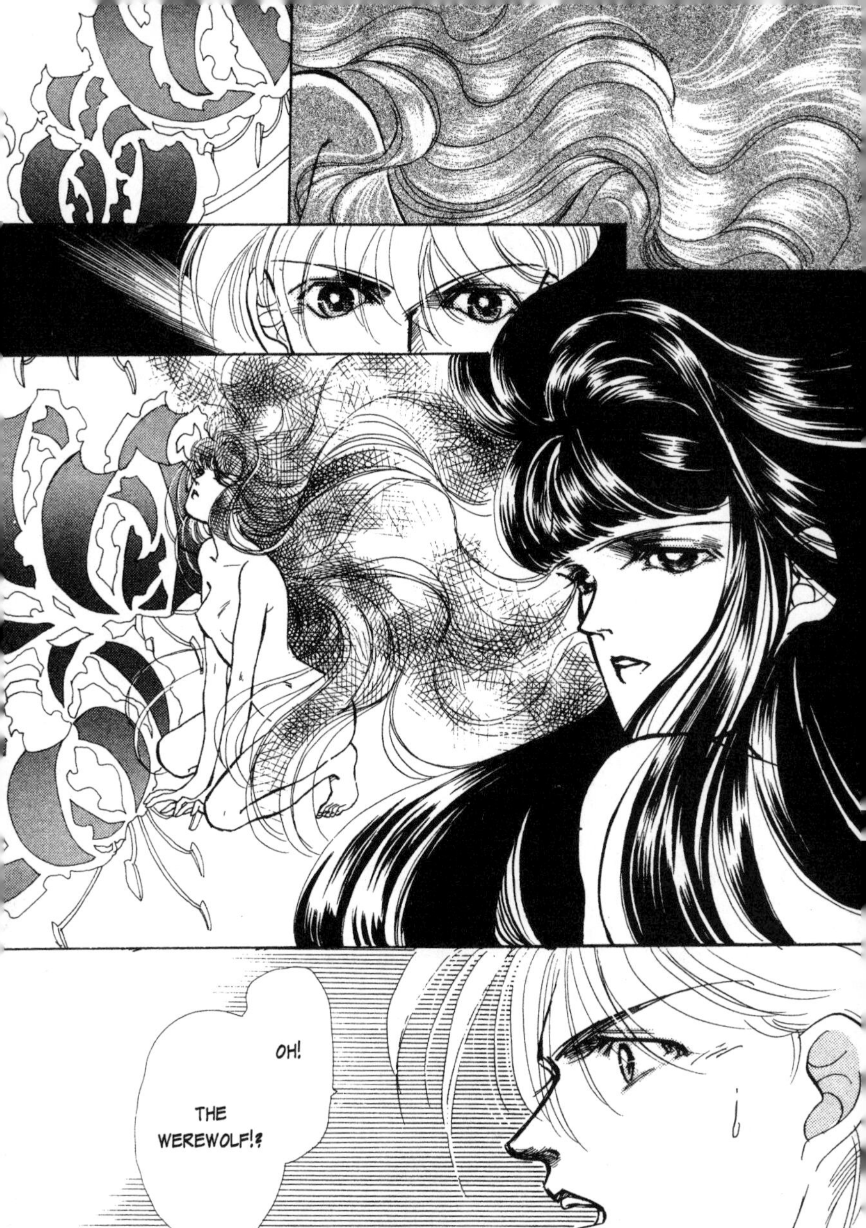
OH!
THE WEREWOLF!?

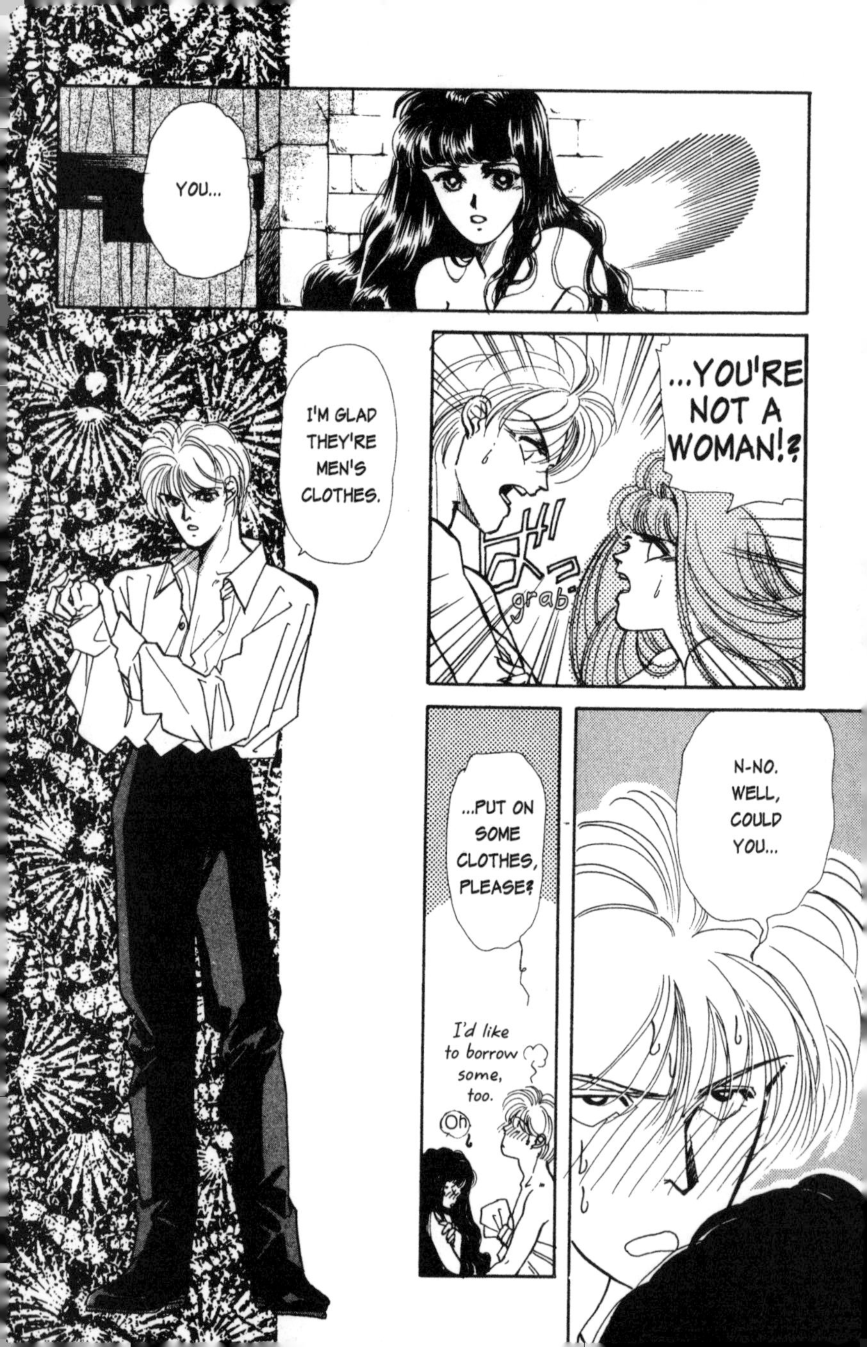
YOU...
...YOU'RE NOT A WOMAN!?
grab
N-NO. WELL, COULD YOU...
...PUT ON SOME CLOTHES, PLEASE?
I'd like to borrow some, too.
Oh
I'M GLAD THEY'RE MEN'S CLOTHES.

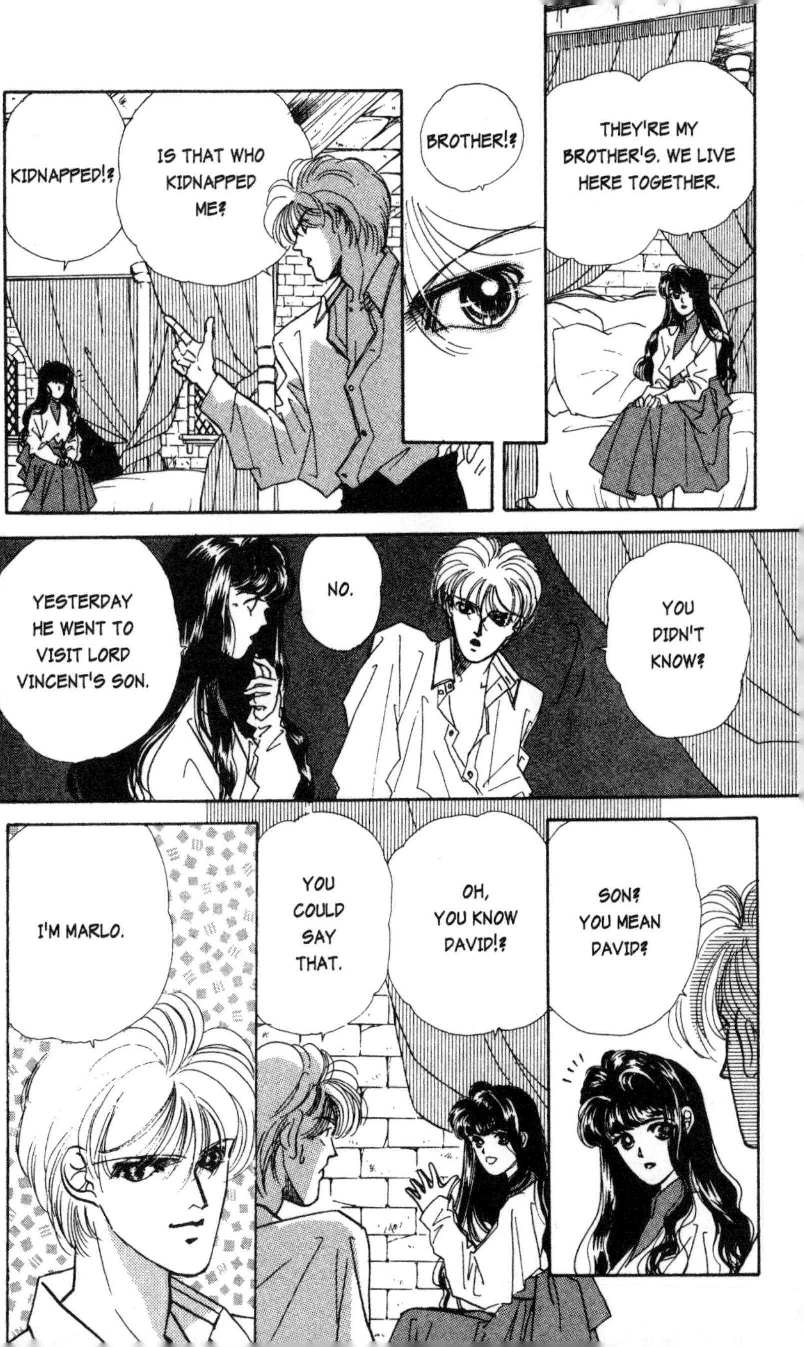
THEY'RE MY BROTHER'S. WE LIVE HERE TOGETHER.
BROTHER!?
IS THAT WHO KIDNAPPED ME?
KIDNAPPED!?
YOU DIDN'T KNOW?
NO.
YESTERDAY HE WENT TO VISIT LORD VINCENT'S SON.
SON? YOU MEAN DAVID?
OH, YOU KNOW DAVID!?
YOU COULD SAY THAT.
I'M MARLO.

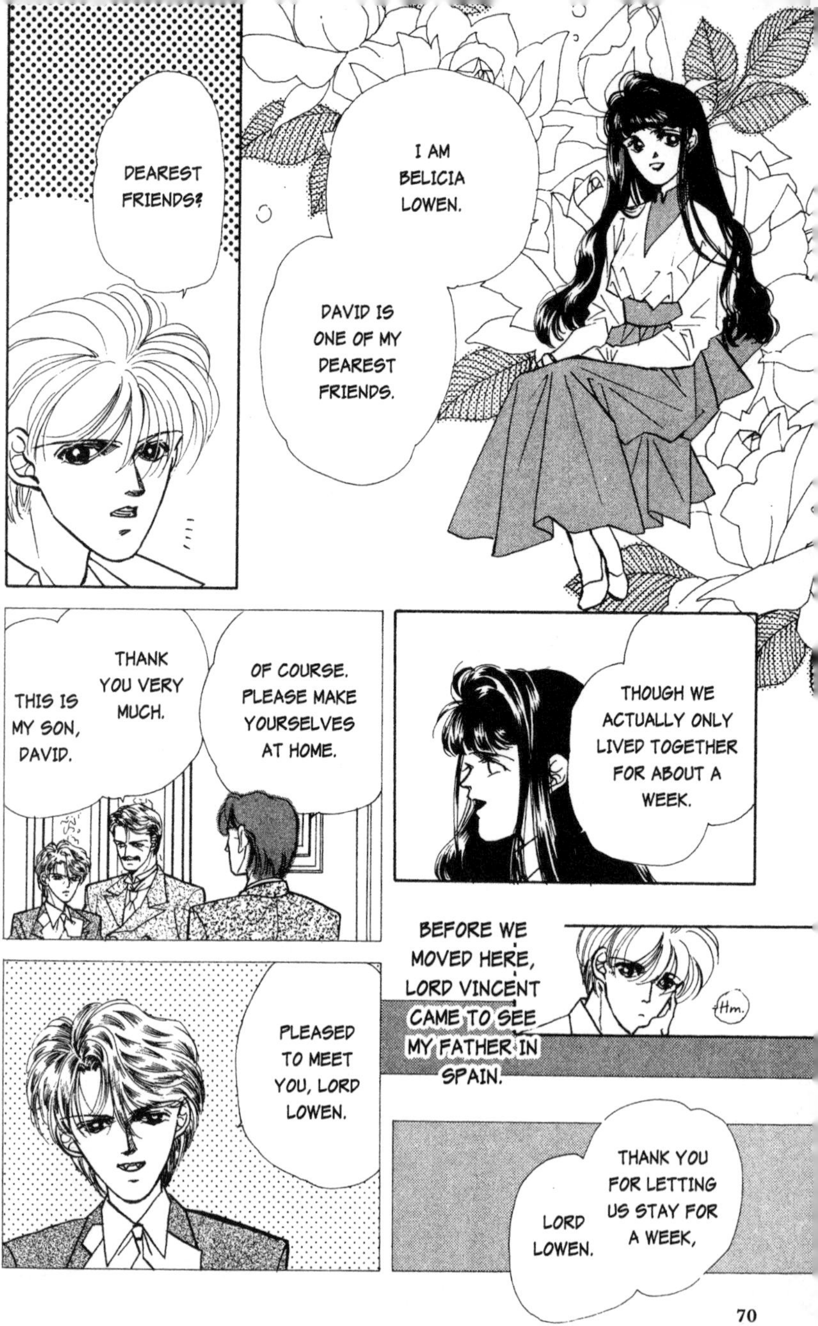
I AM BELICIA LOWEN.
DAVID IS ONE OF MY DEAREST FRIENDS.
DEAREST FRIENDS?
THOUGH WE ACTUALLY ONLY LIVED TOGETHER FOR ABOUT A WEEK.
OF COURSE. PLEASE MAKE YOURSELVES AT HOME.
THANK YOU VERY MUCH.
THIS IS MY SON, DAVID.
BEFORE WE MOVED HERE, LORD VINCENT CAME TO SEE MY FATHER IN SPAIN.
Hm.
THANK YOU FOR LETTING US STAY FOR A WEEK,
LORD LOWEN.
PLEASED TO MEET YOU, LORD LOWEN.

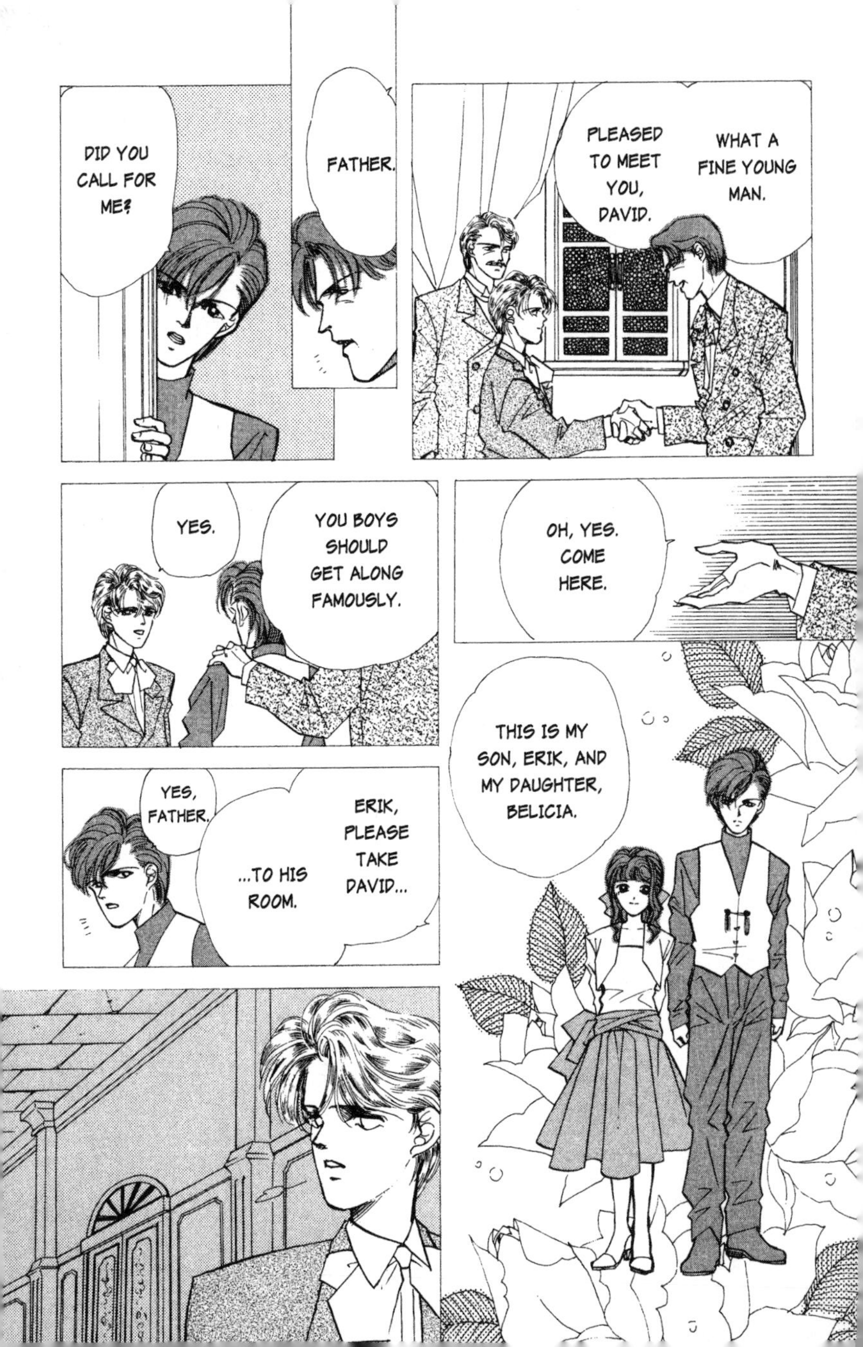
PLEASED TO MEET YOU, DAVID. WHAT A FINE YOUNG MAN.
FATHER.
DID YOU CALL FOR ME?
OH, YES. COME HERE.
THIS IS MY SON, ERIK, AND MY DAUGHTER, BELICIA.
YOU BOYS SHOULD GET ALONG FAMOUSLY.
YES.
ERIK, PLEASE TAKE DAVID...
...TO HIS ROOM.
YES, FATHER.

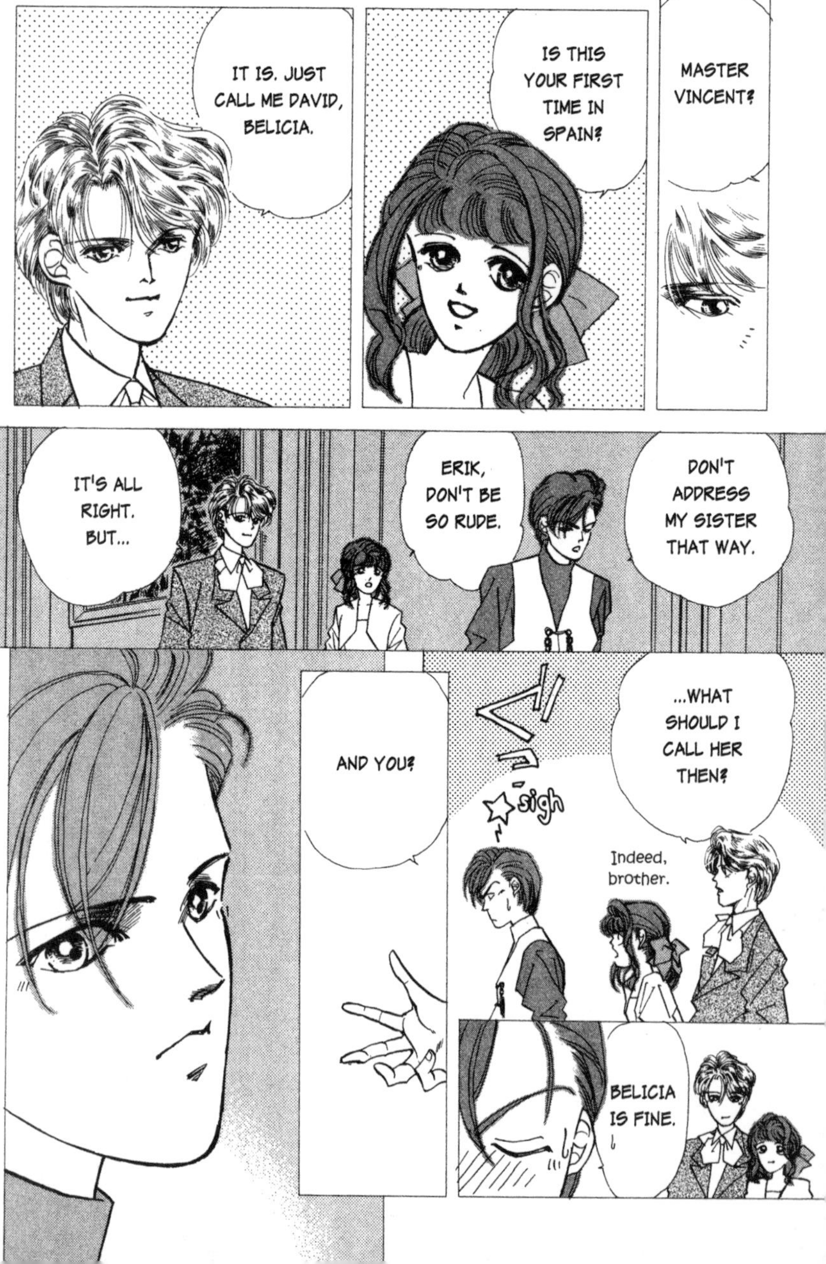
MASTER VINCENT?
IS THIS YOUR FIRST TIME IN SPAIN?
IT IS. JUST CALL ME DAVID, BELICIA.
DON'T ADDRESS MY SISTER THAT WAY.
ERIK, DON'T BE SO RUDE.
IT'S ALL RIGHT. BUT...
...WHAT SHOULD I CALL HER THEN?
sigh
Indeed, brother.
BELICIA IS FINE.
AND YOU?

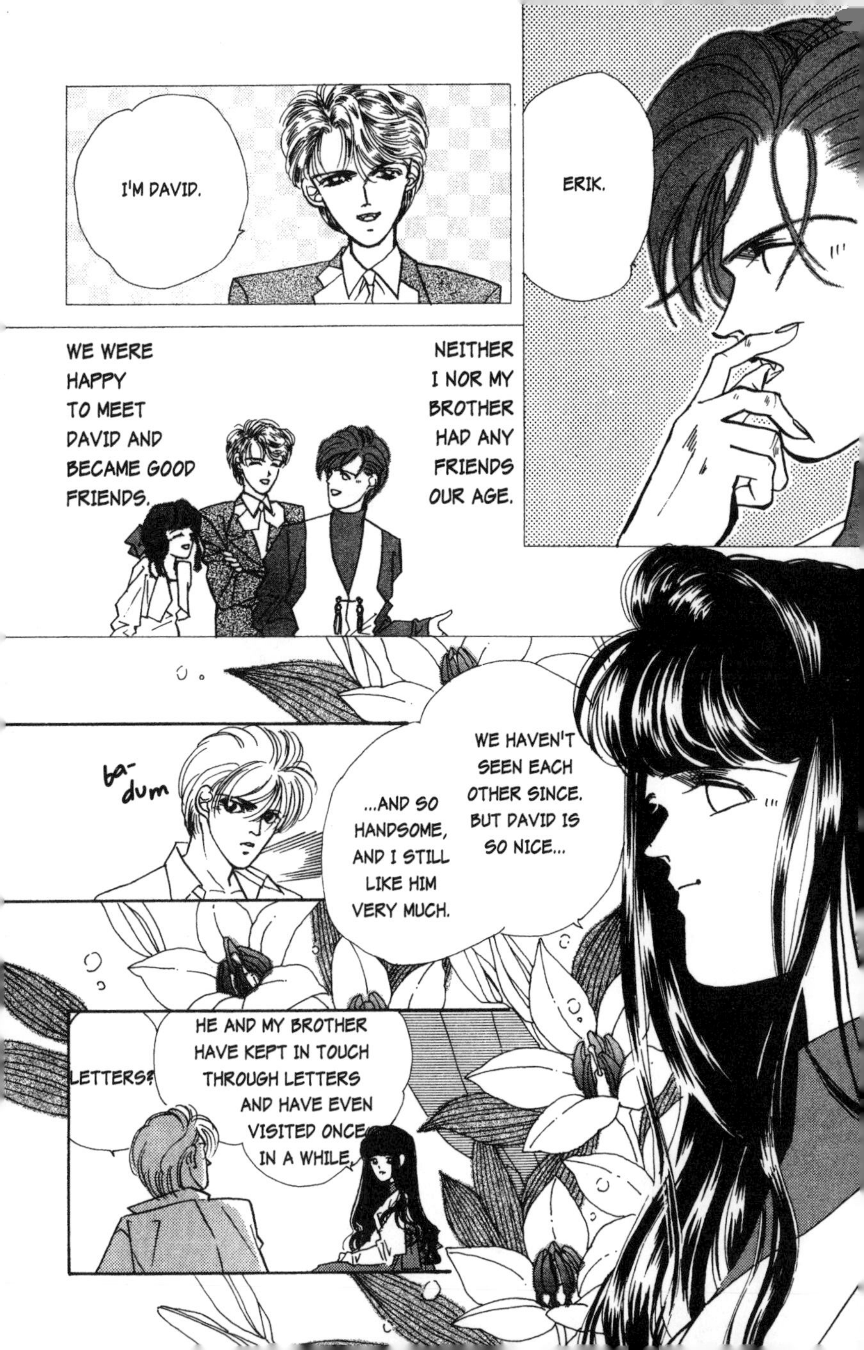
ERIK.
I'M DAVID.
NEITHER I NOR MY BROTHER HAD ANY FRIENDS OUR AGE.
WE WERE HAPPY TO MEET DAVID AND BECAME GOOD FRIENDS.
WE HAVEN'T SEEN EACH OTHER SINCE. BUT DAVID IS SO NICE...
...AND SO HANDSOME, AND I STILL LIKE HIM VERY MUCH.
ba-dum
HE AND MY BROTHER HAVE KEPT IN TOUCH THROUGH LETTERS AND HAVE EVEN VISITED ONCE IN A WHILE.
LETTERS?

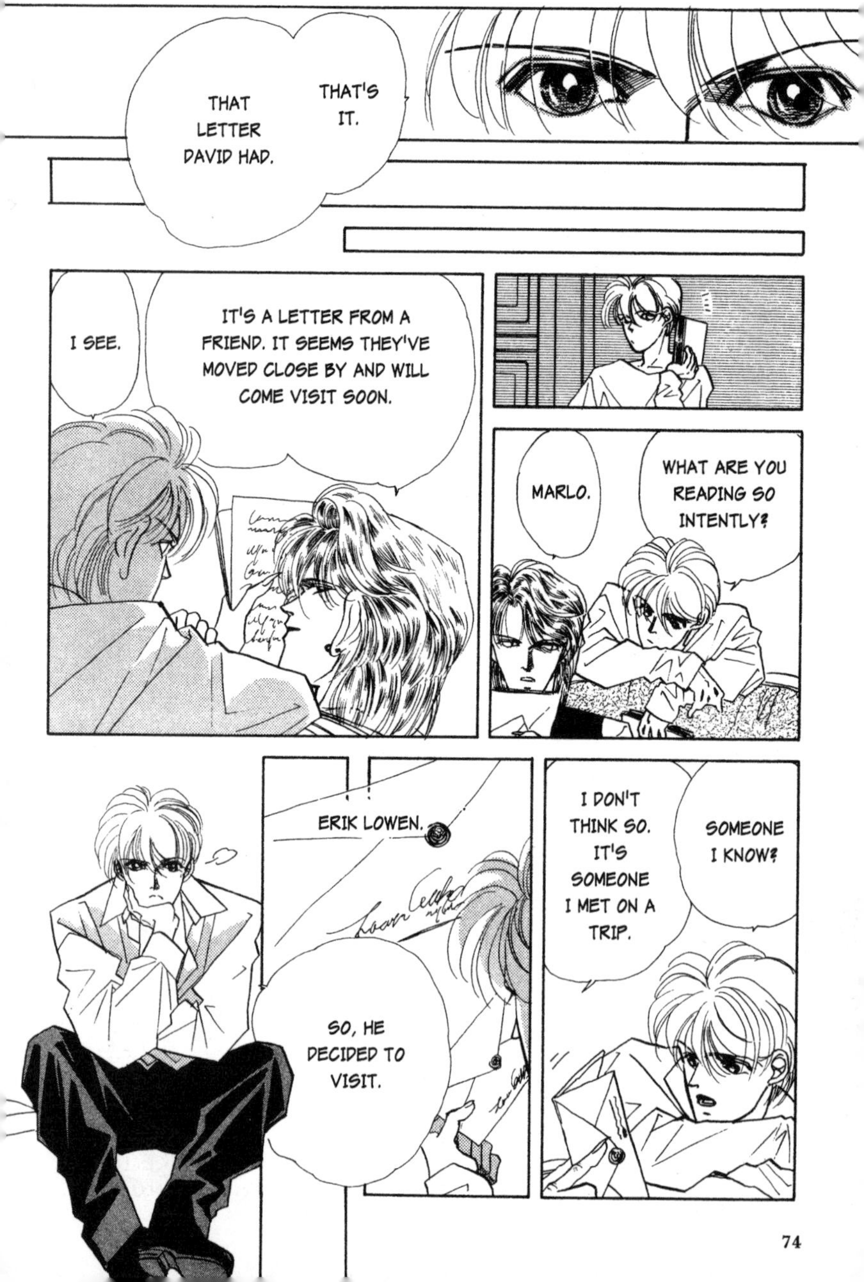
THAT'S IT.
THAT LETTER DAVID HAD.
WHAT ARE YOU READING SO INTENTLY?
MARLO.
IT'S A LETTER FROM A FRIEND. IT SEEMS THEY'VE MOVED CLOSE BY AND WILL COME VISIT SOON.
I SEE.
SOMEONE I KNOW?
I DON'T THINK SO. IT'S SOMEONE I MET ON A TRIP.
ERIK LOWEN.
SO, HE DECIDED TO VISIT.

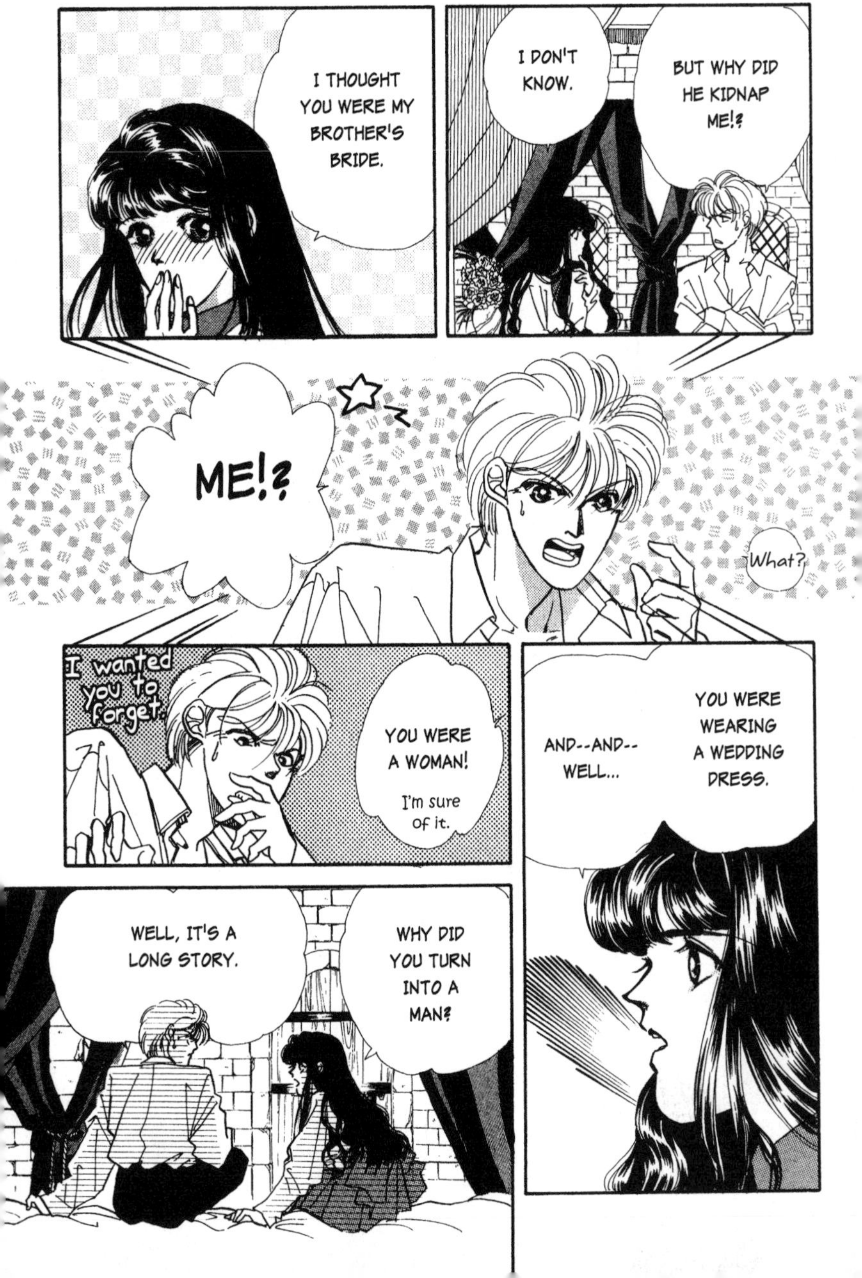
BUT WHY DID HE KIDNAP ME!?
I DON'T KNOW.
I THOUGHT YOU WERE MY BROTHER'S BRIDE.
What?
ME!?
YOU WERE WEARING A WEDDING DRESS.
AND--AND-- WELL...
YOU WERE A WOMAN!
I'm sure of it.
I wanted you to forget.
WHY DID YOU TURN INTO A MAN?
WELL, IT'S A LONG STORY.

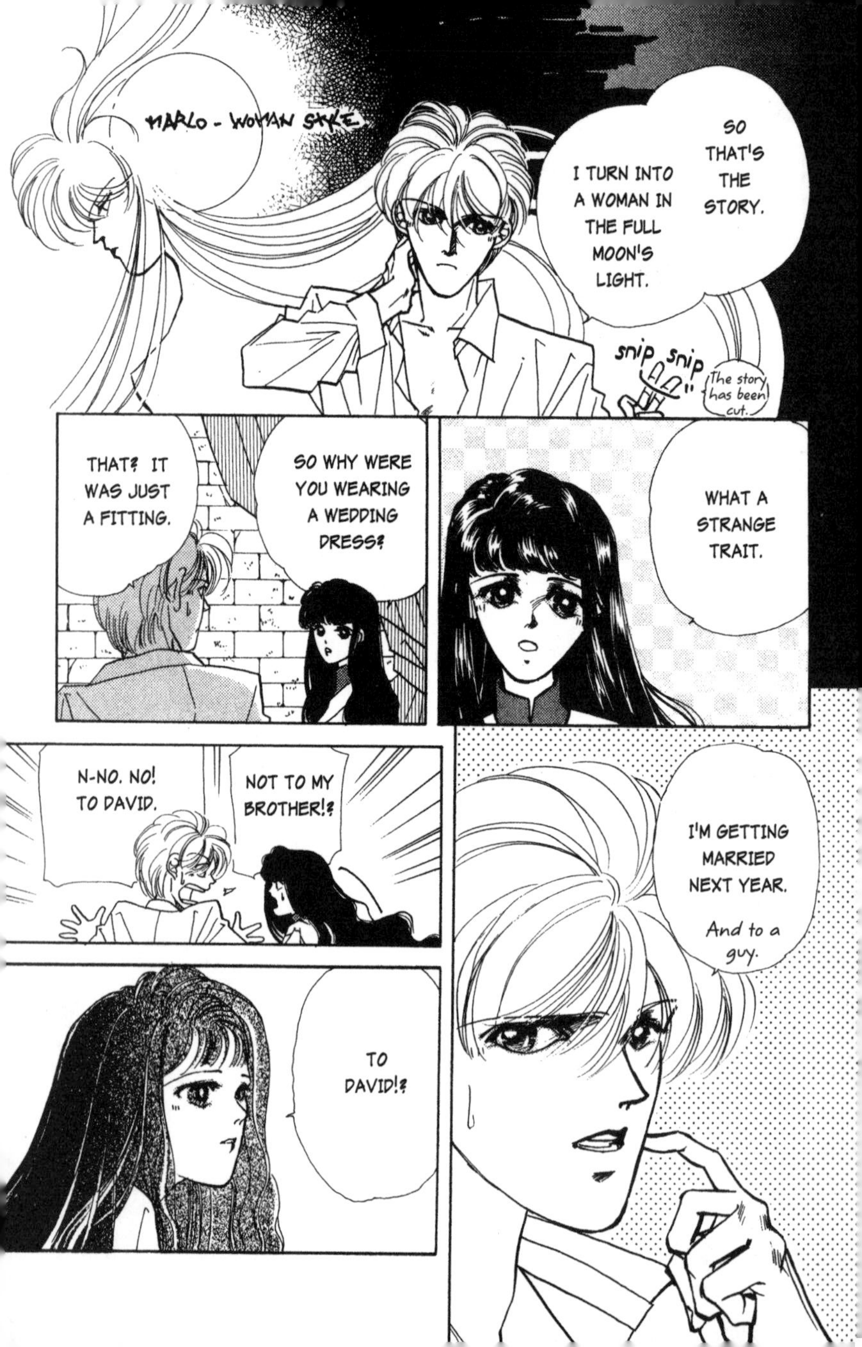
SO THAT'S THE STORY.
I TURN INTO A WOMAN IN THE FULL MOON'S LIGHT.
MARLO - WOMAN STYLE
snip snip
The story has been cut.
WHAT A STRANGE TRAIT.
SO WHY WERE YOU WEARING A WEDDING DRESS?
THAT? IT WAS JUST A FITTING.
I'M GETTING MARRIED NEXT YEAR.
And to a guy.
NOT TO MY BROTHER!?
N-NO. NO! TO DAVID.
TO DAVID!?

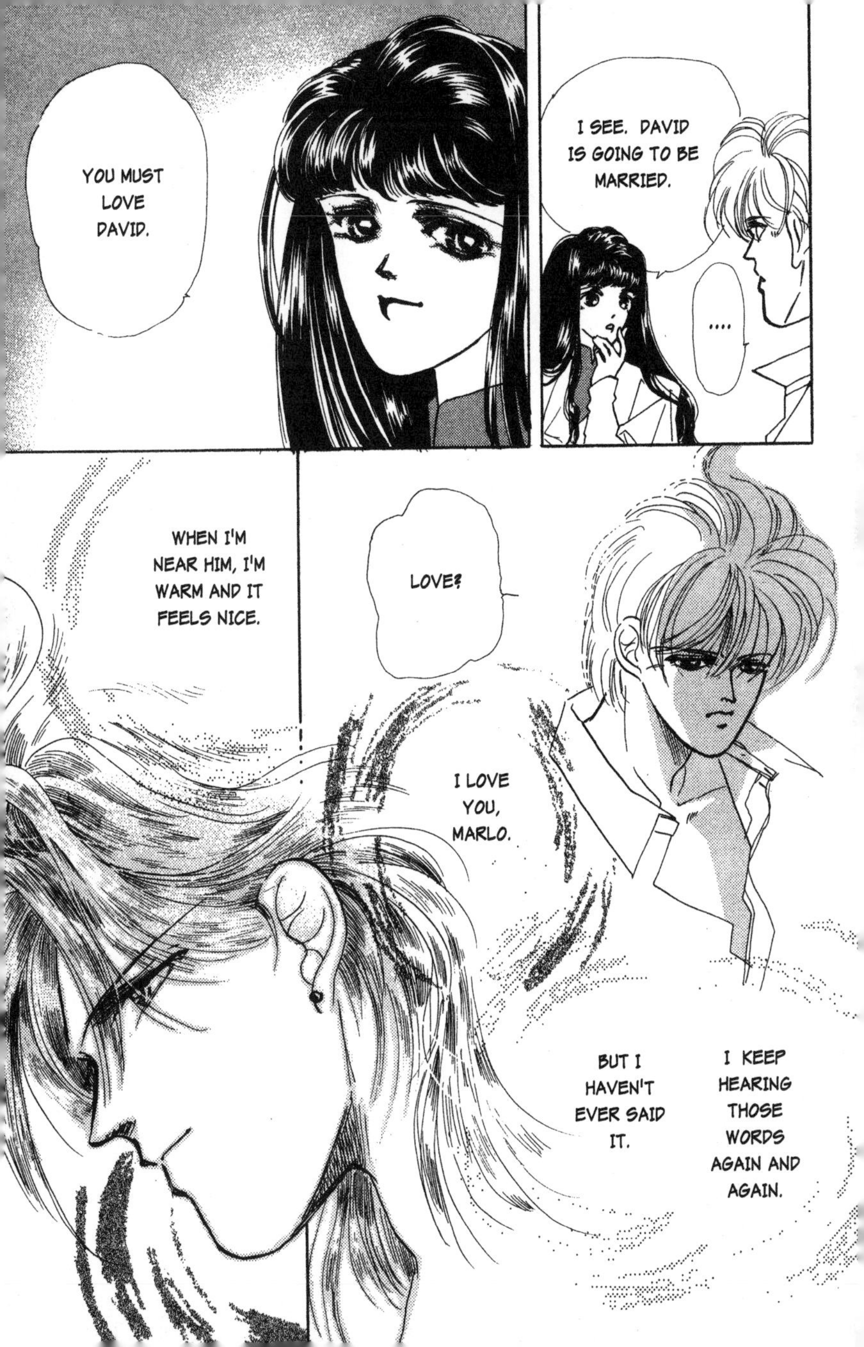
I SEE. DAVID IS GOING TO BE MARRIED.
....
YOU MUST LOVE DAVID.
LOVE?
I LOVE YOU, MARLO.
I KEEP HEARING THOSE WORDS AGAIN AND AGAIN.
BUT I HAVEN'T EVER SAID IT.
WHEN I'M NEAR HIM, I'M WARM AND IT FEELS NICE.

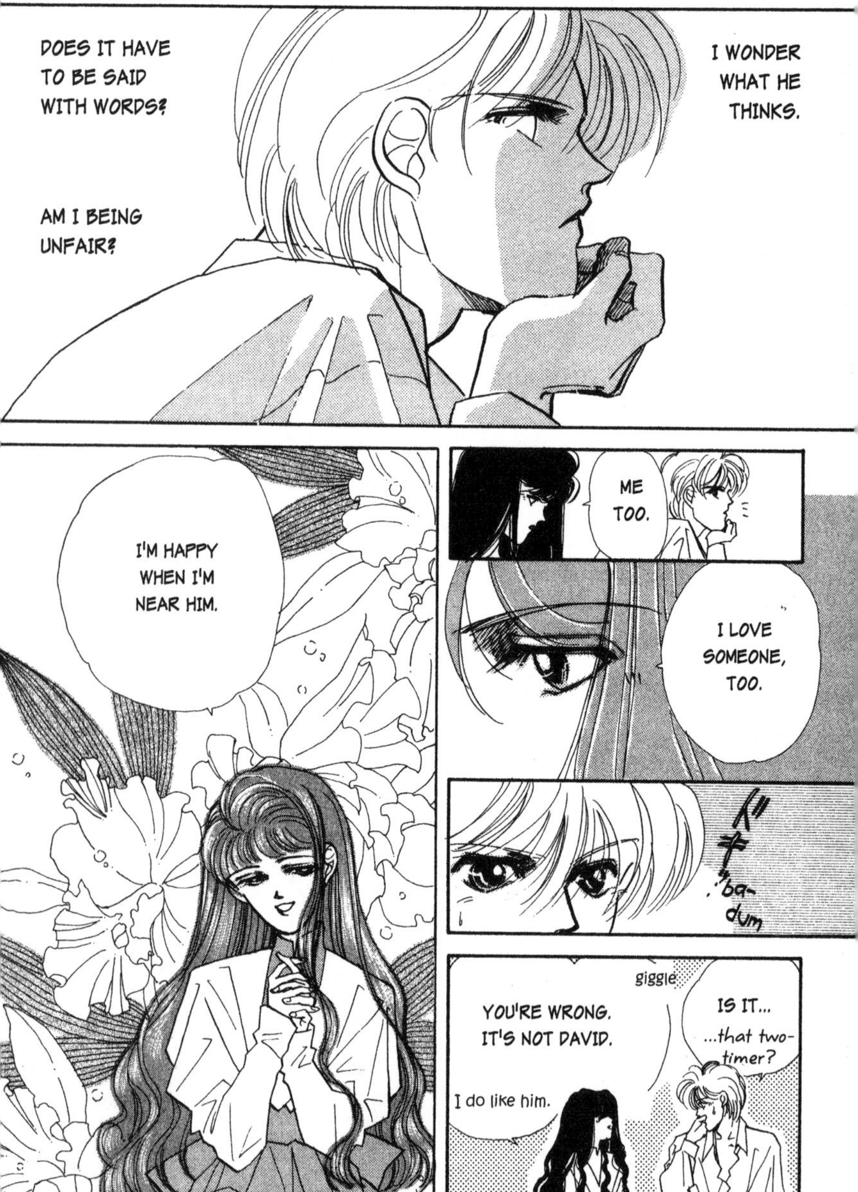
I WONDER WHAT HE THINKS.
DOES IT HAVE TO BE SAID WITH WORDS?
AM I BEING UNFAIR?
ME TOO.
I LOVE SOMEONE, TOO.
ba-dum
IS IT... ...that two-timer?
giggle
YOU'RE WRONG. IT'S NOT DAVID.
I do like him.
I'M HAPPY WHEN I'M NEAR HIM.

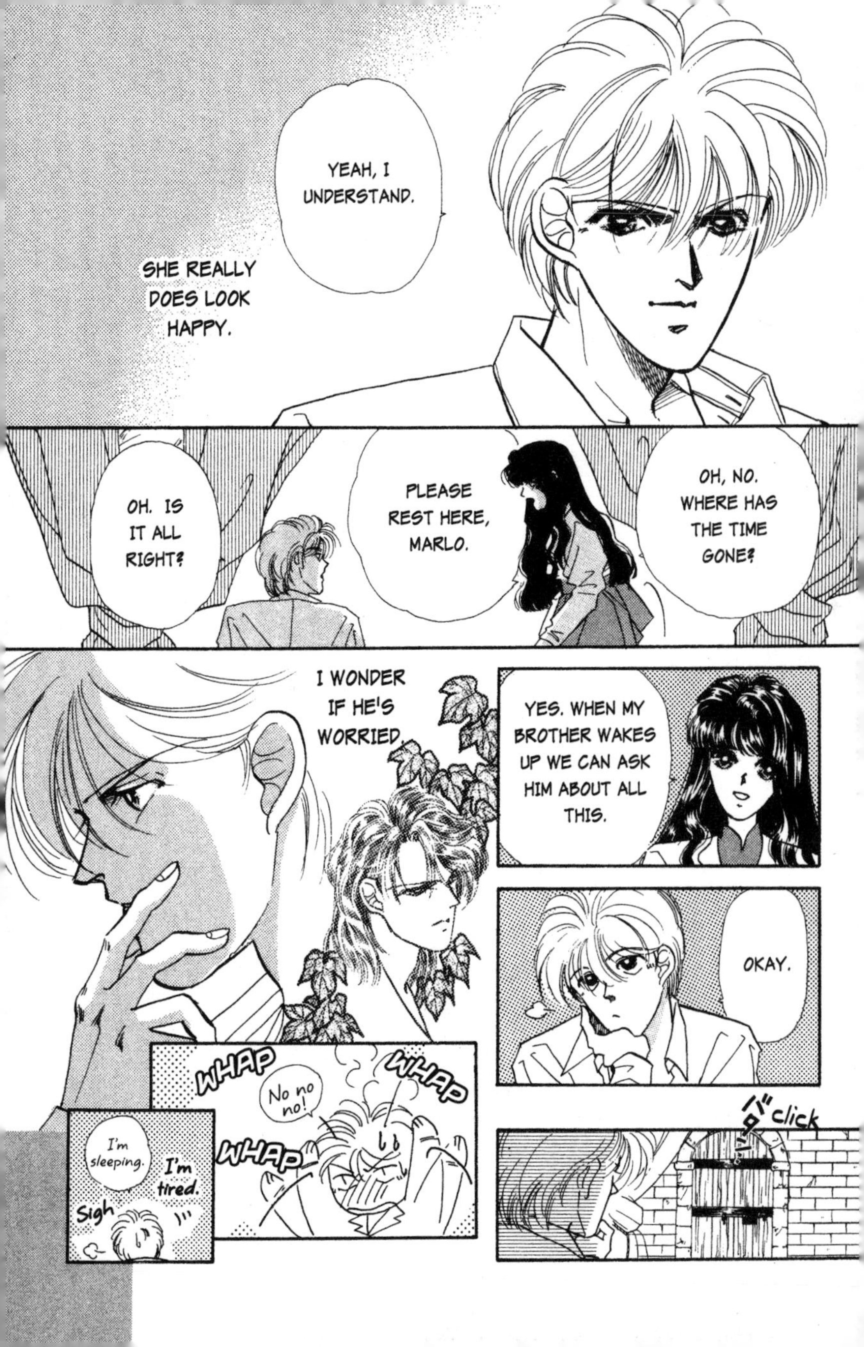
YEAH, I UNDERSTAND.
SHE REALLY DOES LOOK HAPPY.
OH, NO. WHERE HAS THE TIME GONE?
PLEASE REST HERE, MARLO.
OH. IS IT ALL RIGHT?
YES. WHEN MY BROTHER WAKES UP WE CAN ASK HIM ABOUT ALL THIS.
OKAY.
click
I WONDER IF HE'S WORRIED.
WHAP
WHAP
No no no!
WHAP
I'm sleeping.
I'm tired.
Sigh

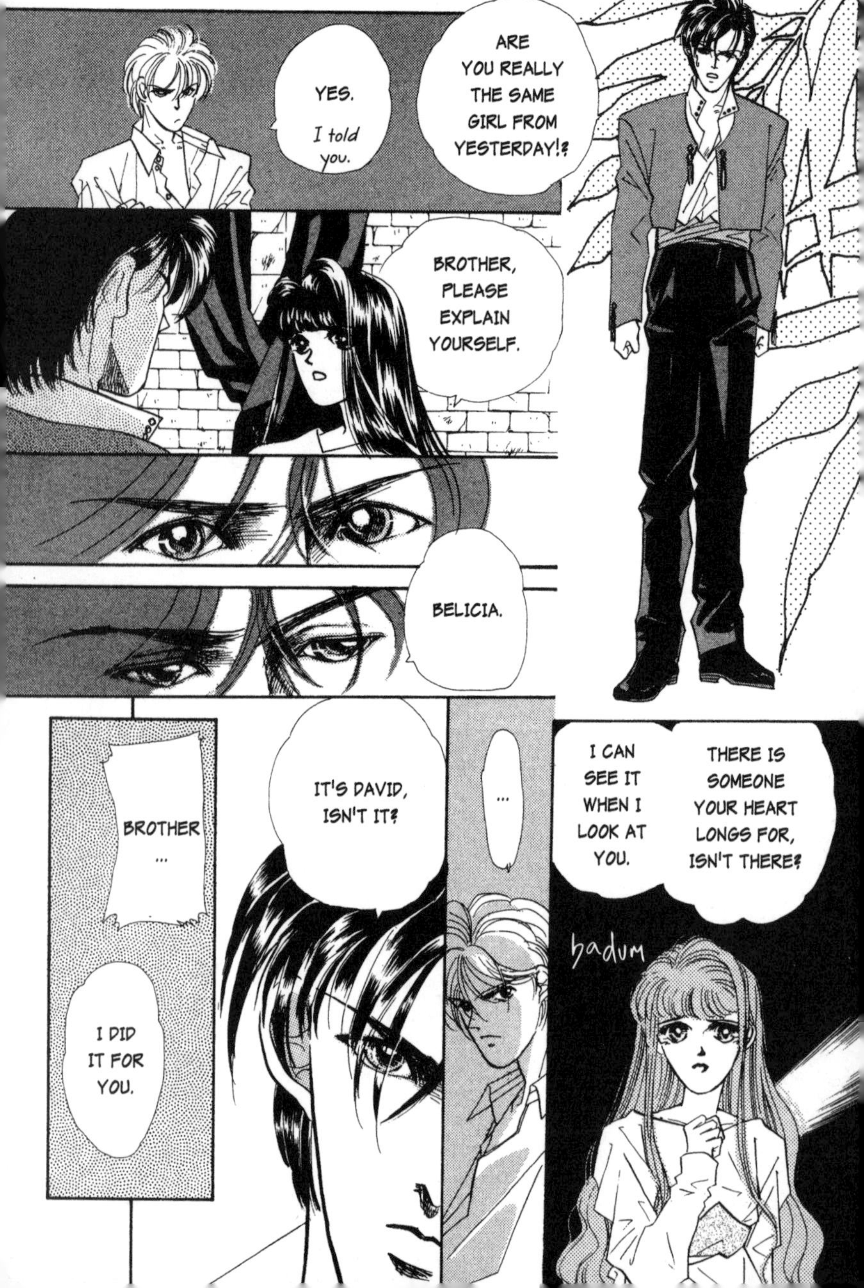
ARE YOU REALLY THE SAME GIRL FROM YESTERDAY!?
YES. I told you.
BROTHER, PLEASE EXPLAIN YOURSELF.
BELICIA.
THERE IS SOMEONE YOUR HEART LONGS FOR, ISN'T THERE?
I CAN SEE IT WHEN I LOOK AT YOU.
badum
...
IT'S DAVID, ISN'T IT?
BROTHER ...
I DID IT FOR YOU.

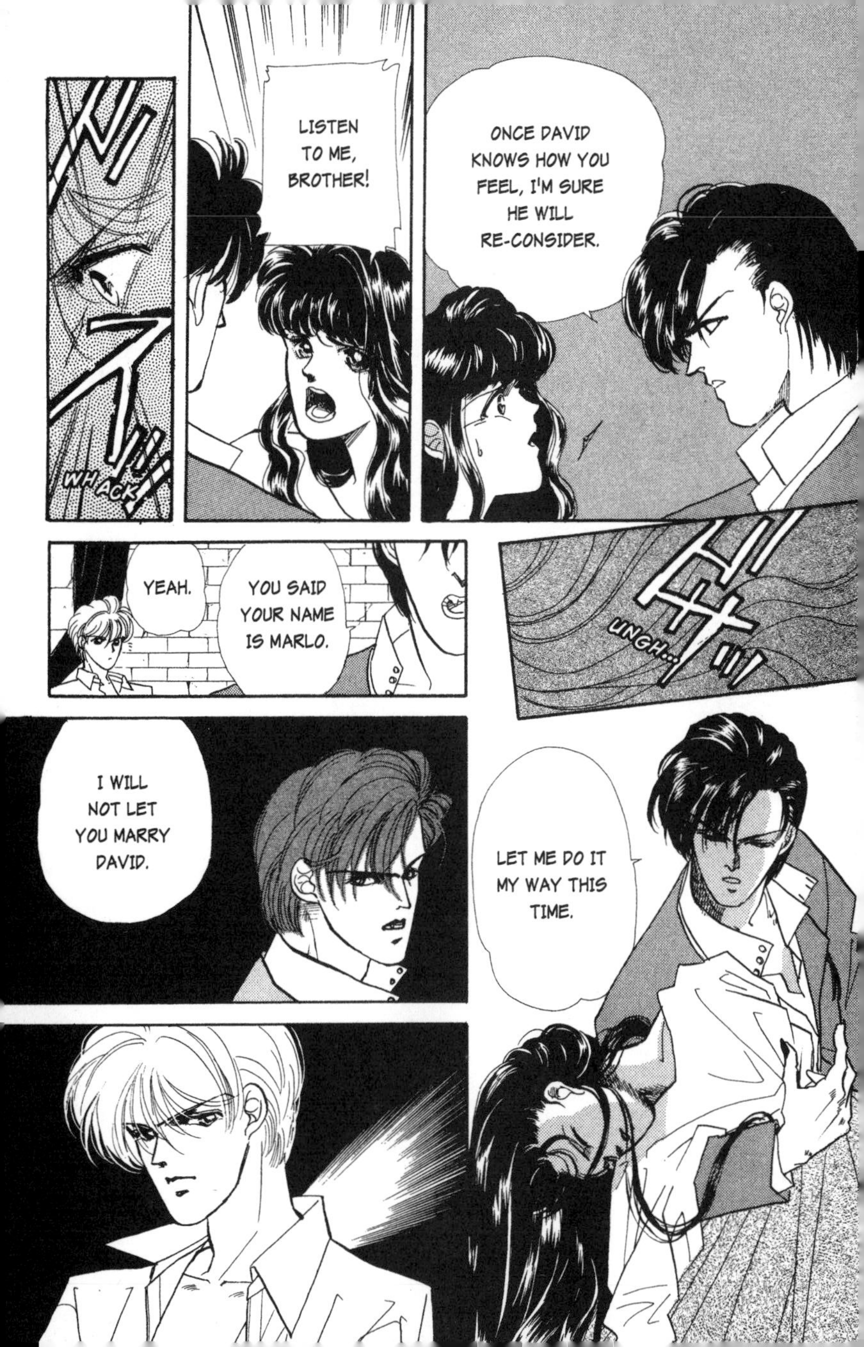
ONCE DAVID KNOWS HOW YOU FEEL, I'M SURE HE WILL RE-CONSIDER.
LISTEN TO ME, BROTHER!
WHACK
UNGH...
YOU SAID YOUR NAME IS MARLO.
YEAH.
LET ME DO IT MY WAY THIS TIME.
I WILL NOT LET YOU MARRY DAVID.

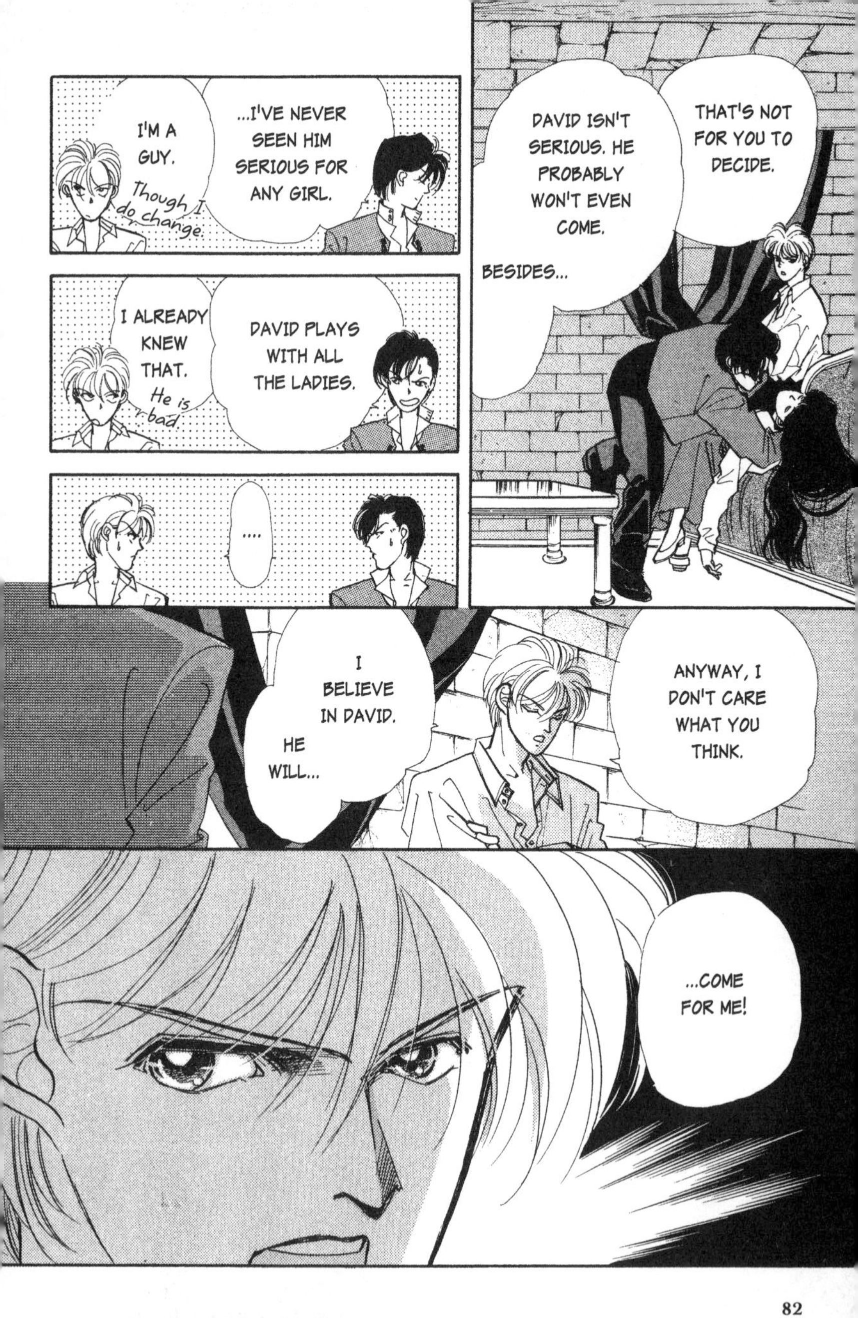
THAT'S NOT FOR YOU TO DECIDE.
DAVID ISN'T SERIOUS. HE PROBABLY WON'T EVEN COME.
BESIDES...
...I'VE NEVER SEEN HIM SERIOUS FOR ANY GIRL.
I'M A GUY.
Though I do change.
DAVID PLAYS WITH ALL THE LADIES.
I ALREADY KNEW THAT.
He is bad.
....
ANYWAY, I DON'T CARE WHAT YOU THINK.
I BELIEVE IN DAVID.
HE WILL...
...COME FOR ME!

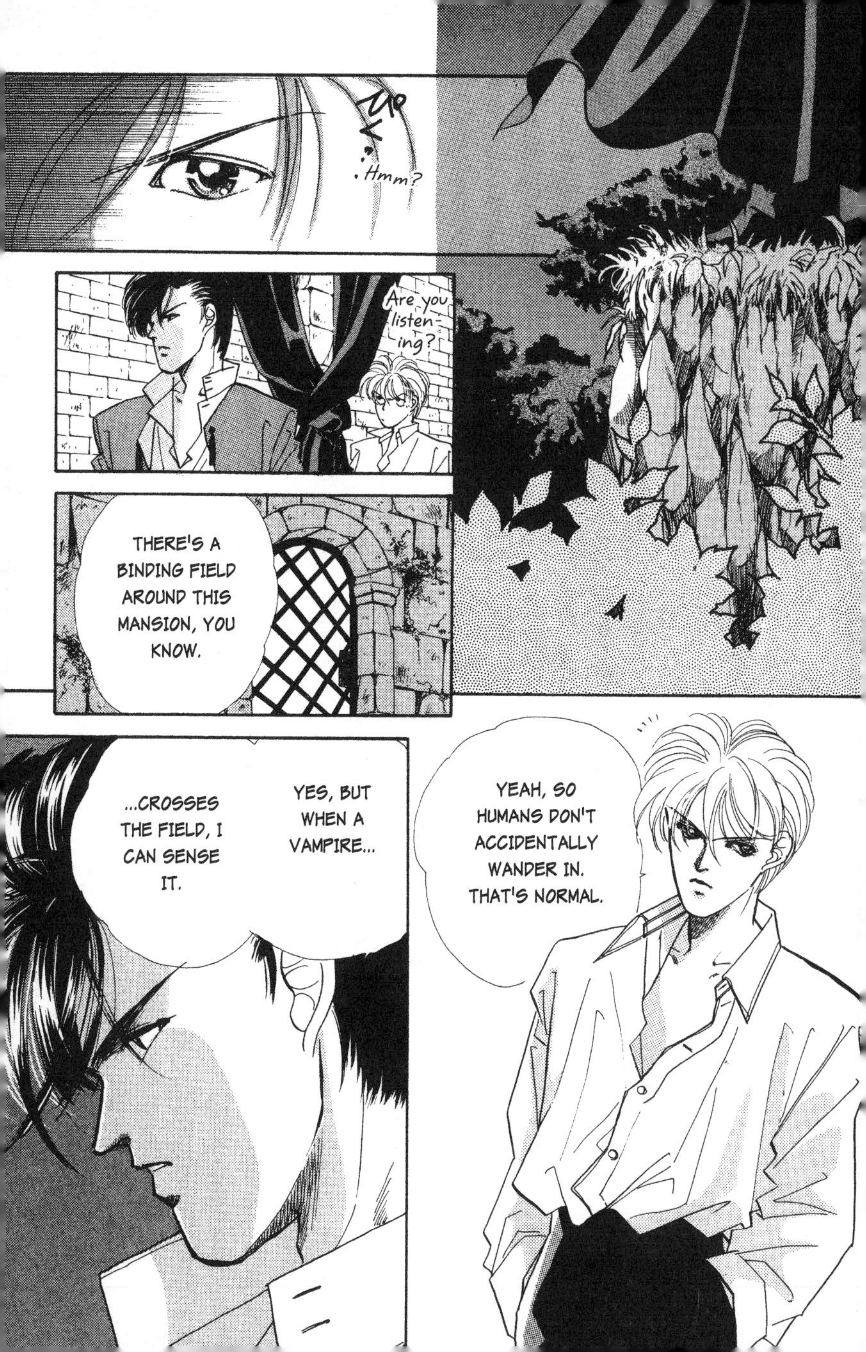

...Hmm?
Are you listen-ing?
THERE'S A BINDING FIELD AROUND THIS MANSION, YOU KNOW.
YEAH, SO HUMANS DON'T ACCIDENTALLY WANDER IN. THAT'S NORMAL.
YES, BUT WHEN A VAMPIRE...
...CROSSES THE FIELD, I CAN SENSE IT.

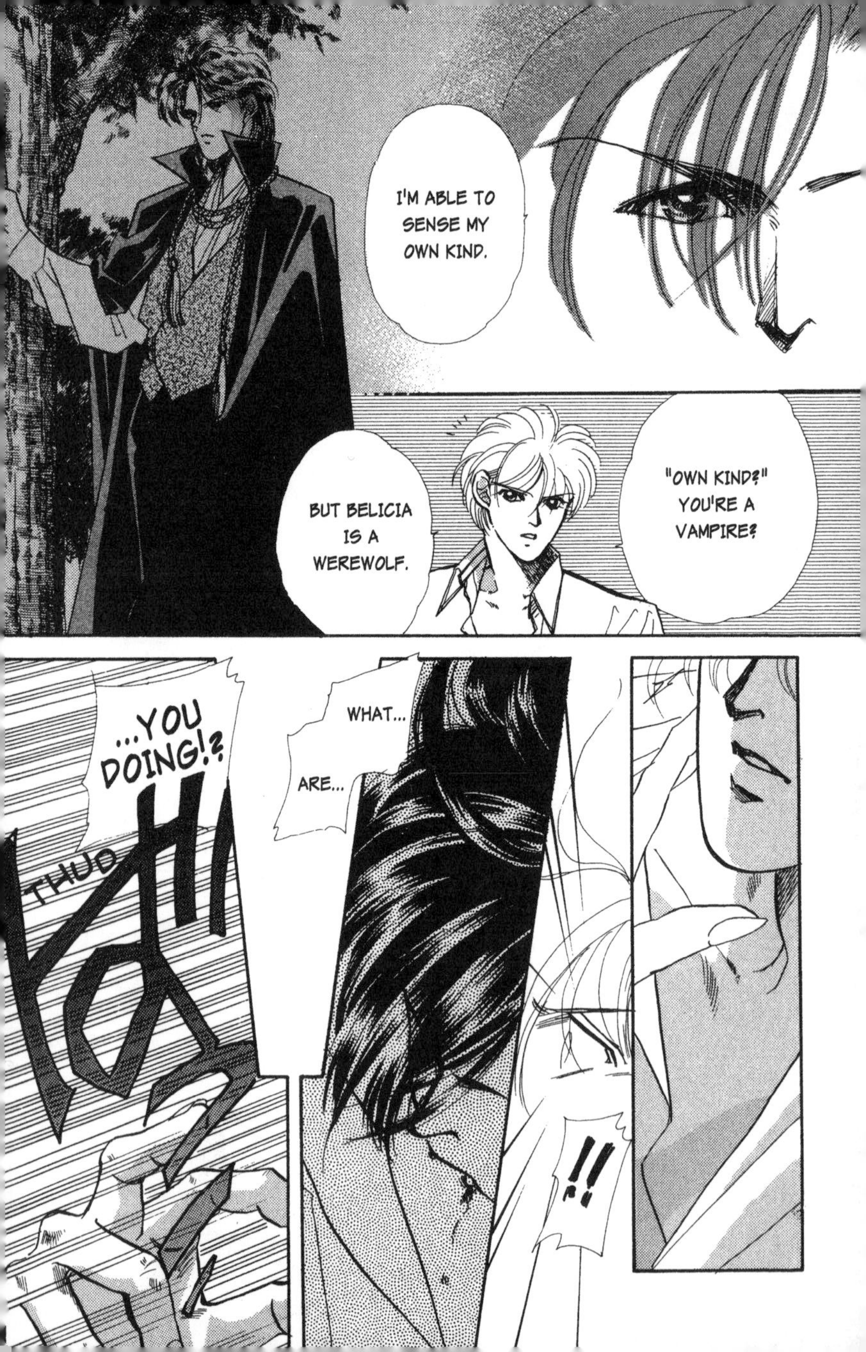
I'M ABLE TO SENSE MY OWN KIND.
"OWN KIND?" YOU'RE A VAMPIRE?
BUT BELICIA IS A WEREWOLF.
!!
WHAT...
ARE...
...YOU DOING!?
THUD

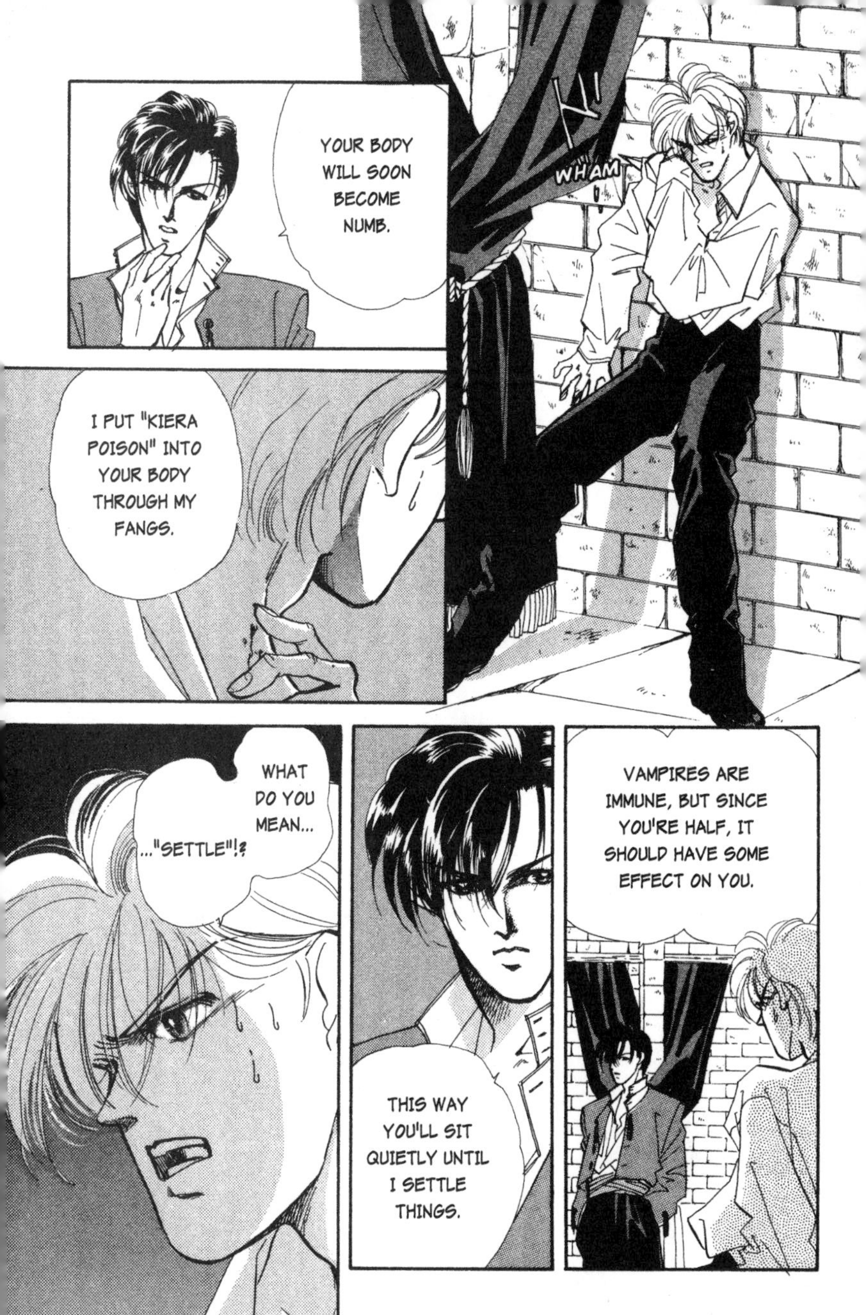
WHAM
YOUR BODY WILL SOON BECOME NUMB.
I PUT "KIERA POISON" INTO YOUR BODY THROUGH MY FANGS.
VAMPIRES ARE IMMUNE, BUT SINCE YOU'RE HALF, IT SHOULD HAVE SOME EFFECT ON YOU.
THIS WAY YOU'LL SIT QUIETLY UNTIL I SETTLE THINGS.
WHAT DO YOU MEAN...
..."SETTLE"!?

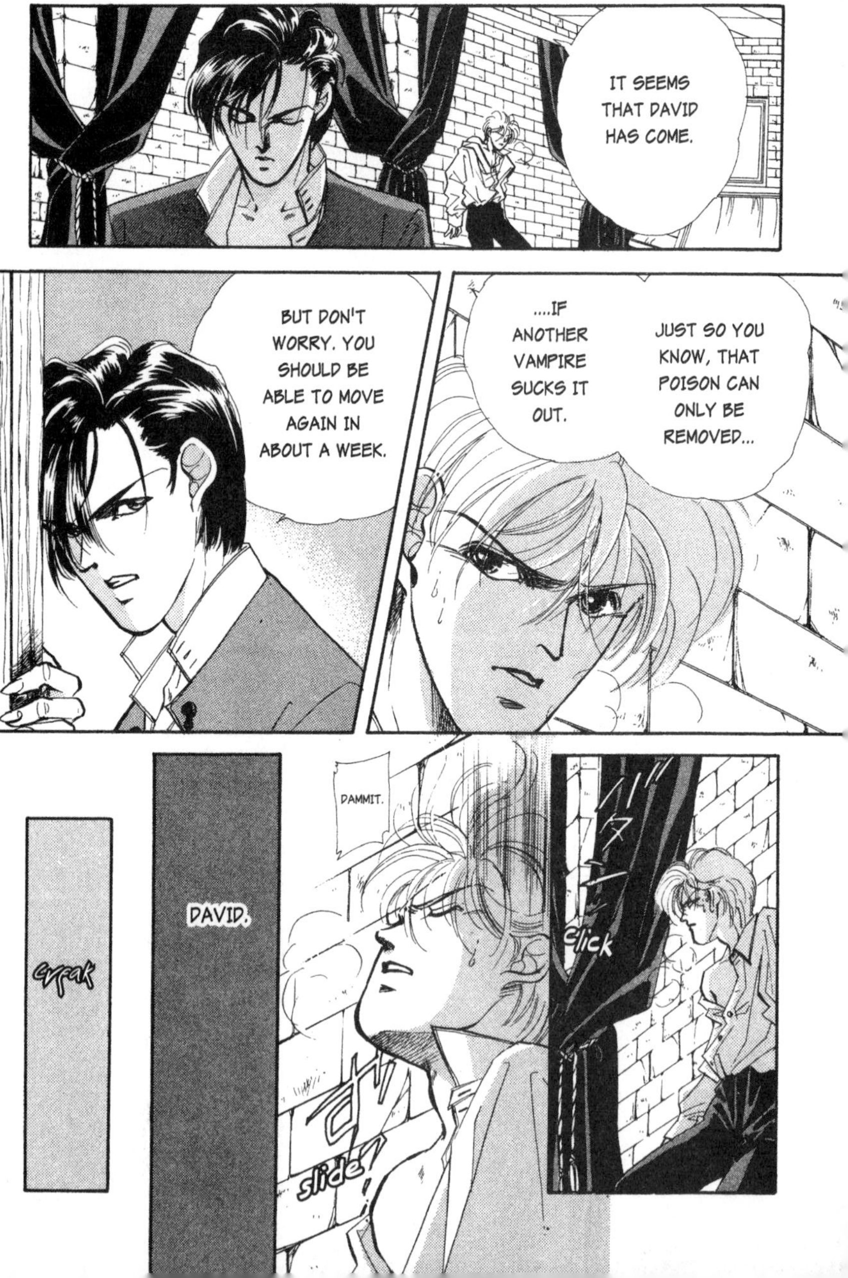
IT SEEMS THAT DAVID HAS COME.
JUST SO YOU KNOW, THAT POISON CAN ONLY BE REMOVED...
....IF ANOTHER VAMPIRE SUCKS IT OUT.
BUT DON'T WORRY. YOU SHOULD BE ABLE TO MOVE AGAIN IN ABOUT A WEEK.
click
DAMMIT.
slide
DAVID.
creak

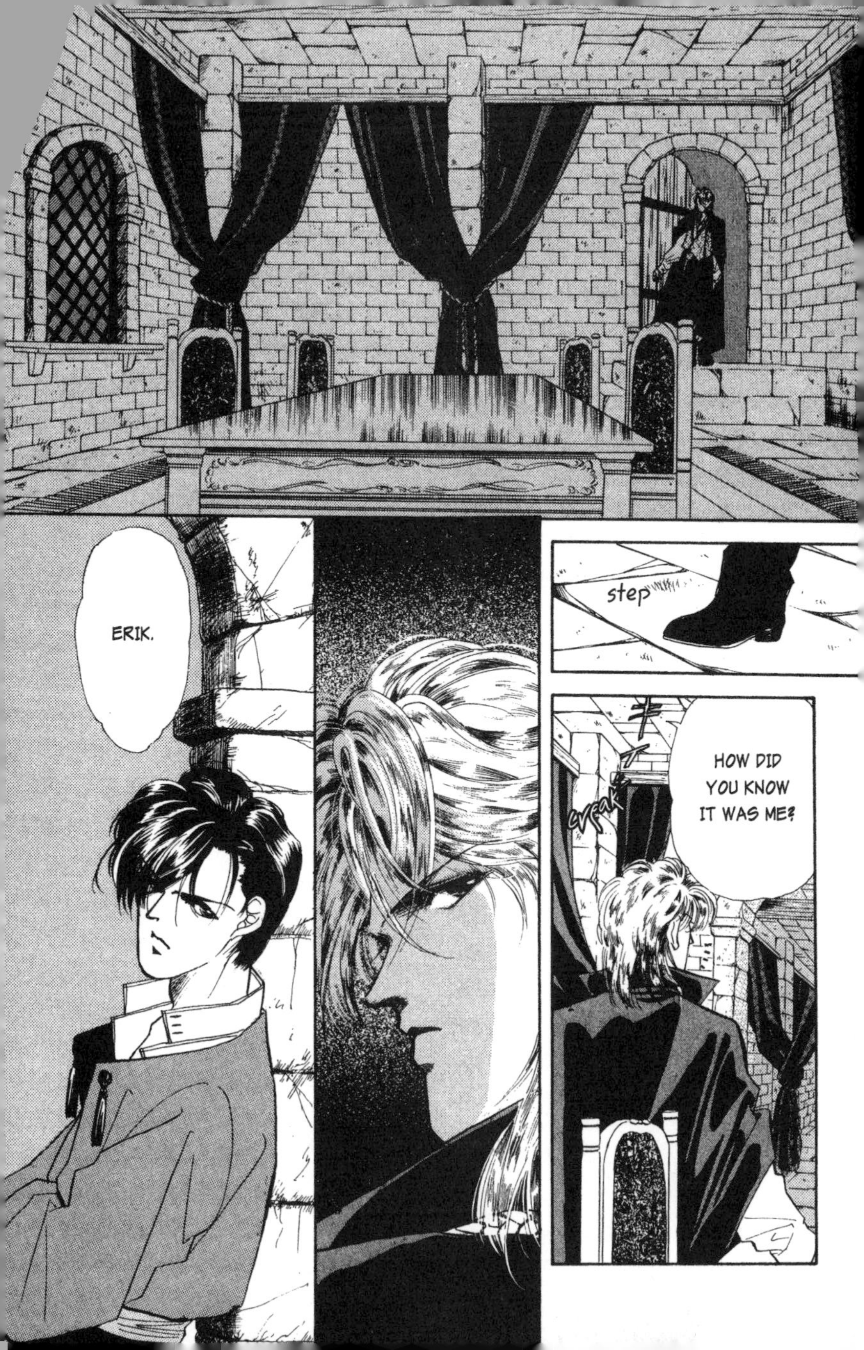
step
HOW DID YOU KNOW IT WAS ME?
creak
ERIK.

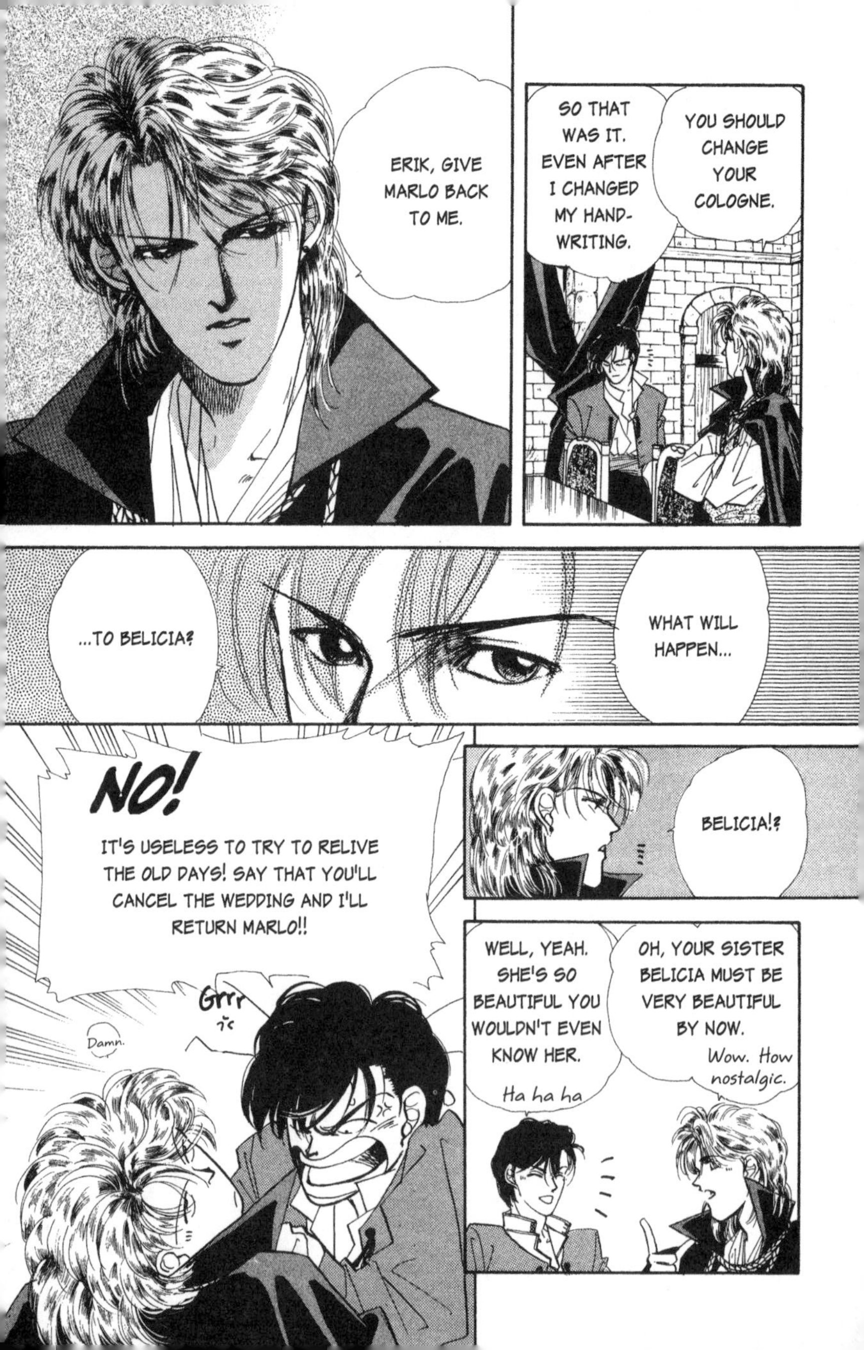
YOU SHOULD CHANGE YOUR COLOGNE.
SO THAT WAS IT. EVEN AFTER I CHANGED MY HAND-WRITING.
ERIK, GIVE MARLO BACK TO ME.
WHAT WILL HAPPEN...
...TO BELICIA?
BELICIA!?
OH, YOUR SISTER BELICIA MUST BE VERY BEAUTIFUL BY NOW.
Wow. How nostalgic.
WELL, YEAH. SHE'S SO BEAUTIFUL YOU WOULDN'T EVEN KNOW HER.
Ha ha ha
NO!
IT'S USELESS TO TRY TO RELIVE THE OLD DAYS! SAY THAT YOU'LL CANCEL THE WEDDING AND I'LL RETURN MARLO!!
Grrr
Damn.

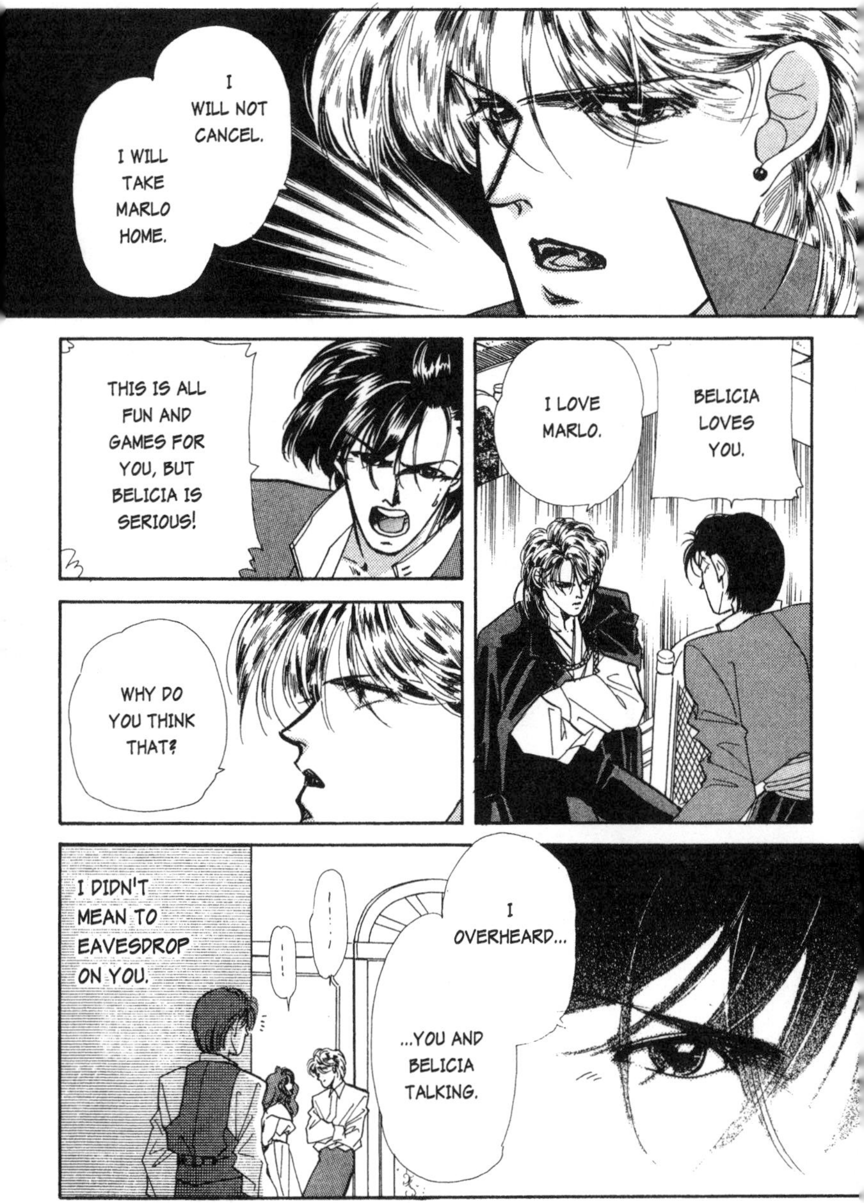
I WILL NOT CANCEL.
I WILL TAKE MARLO HOME.
BELICIA LOVES YOU.
I LOVE MARLO.
THIS IS ALL FUN AND GAMES FOR YOU, BUT BELICIA IS SERIOUS!
WHY DO YOU THINK THAT?
I OVERHEARD...
...YOU AND BELICIA TALKING.
!
!
I DIDN'T MEAN TO EAVESDROP ON YOU.

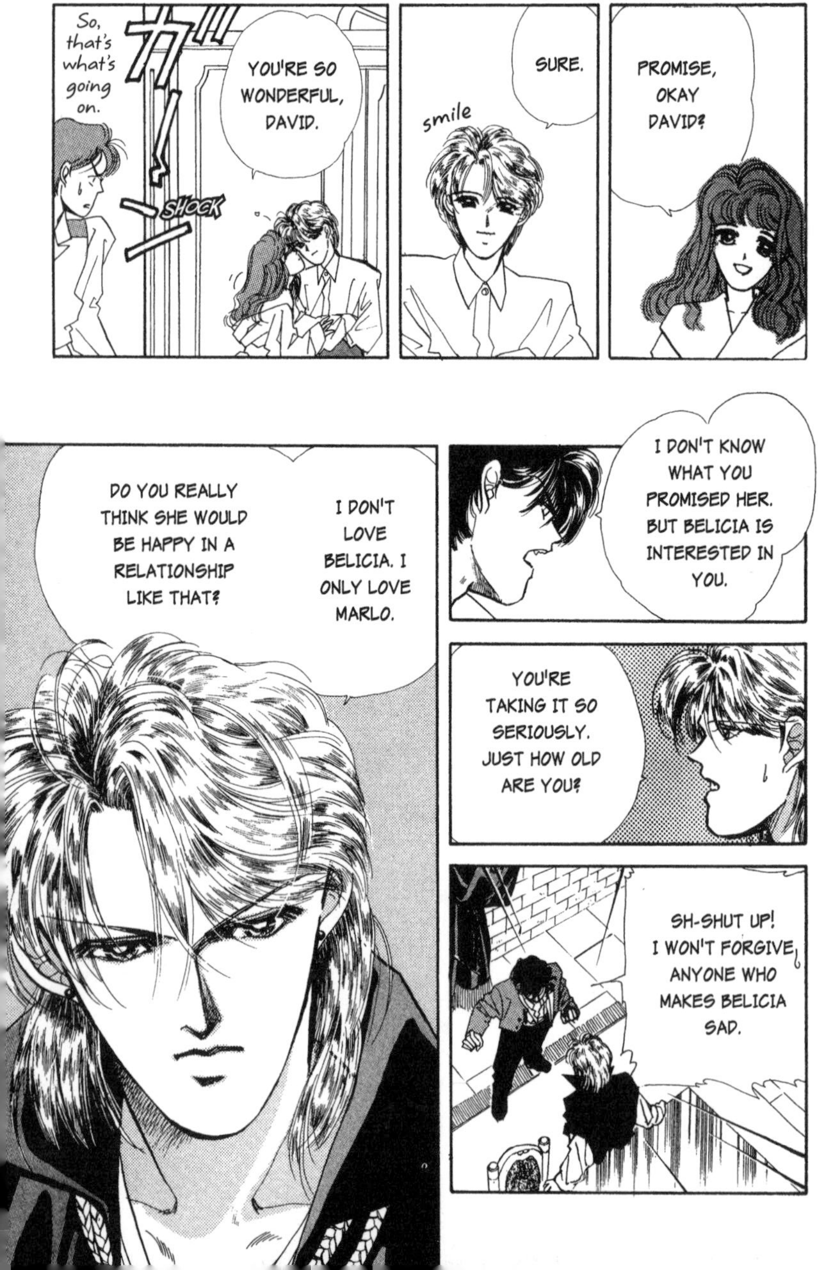
PROMISE, OKAY DAVID?
SURE.
smile
YOU'RE SO WONDERFUL, DAVID.
So, that's what's going on.
SHOCK
I DON'T KNOW WHAT YOU PROMISED HER. BUT BELICIA IS INTERESTED IN YOU.
YOU'RE TAKING IT SO SERIOUSLY. JUST HOW OLD ARE YOU?
SH-SHUT UP! I WON'T FORGIVE ANYONE WHO MAKES BELICIA SAD.
I DON'T LOVE BELICIA. I ONLY LOVE MARLO.
DO YOU REALLY THINK SHE WOULD BE HAPPY IN A RELATIONSHIP LIKE THAT?

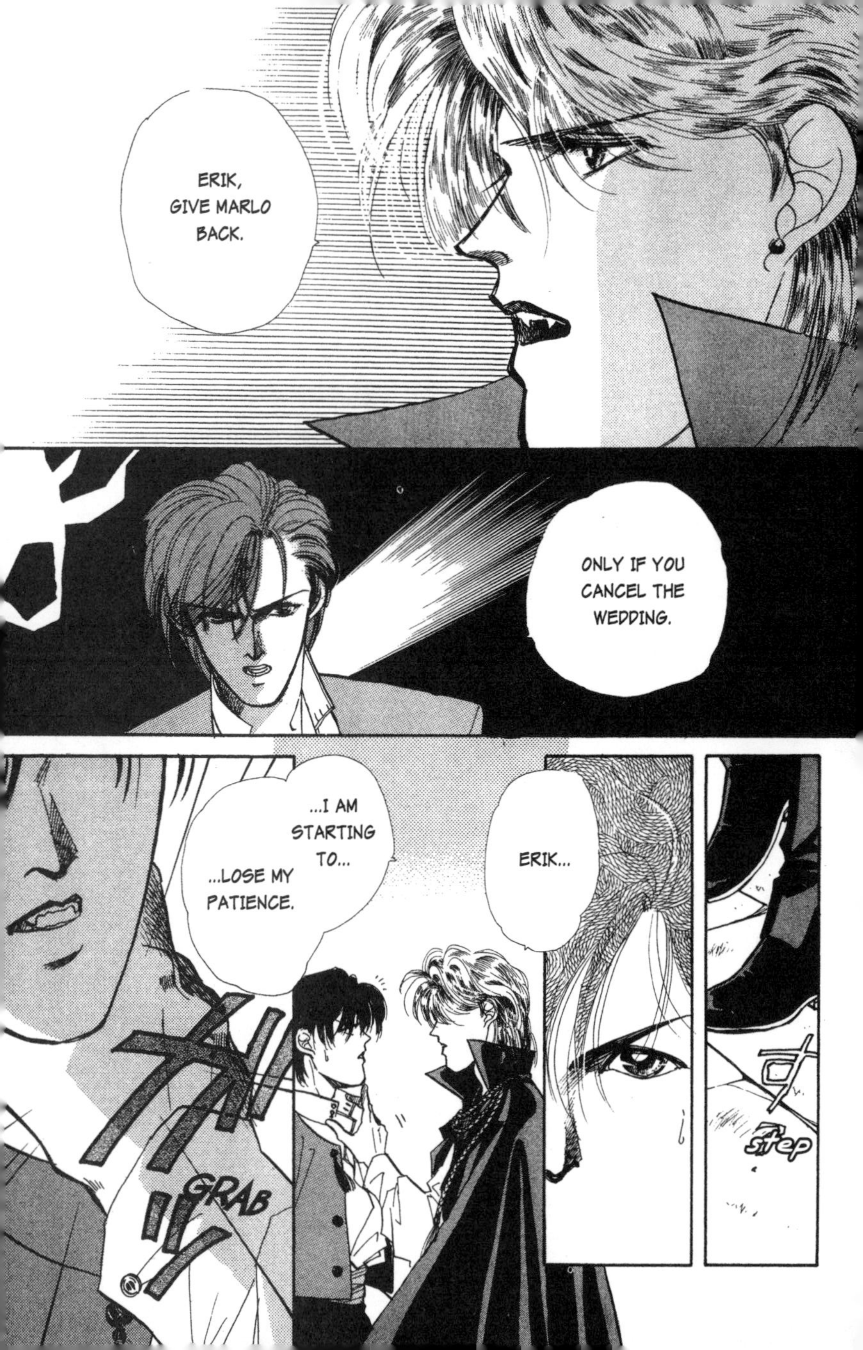
ERIK, GIVE MARLO BACK.
ONLY IF YOU CANCEL THE WEDDING.
step
ERIK...
...I AM STARTING TO...
...LOSE MY PATIENCE.
GRAB

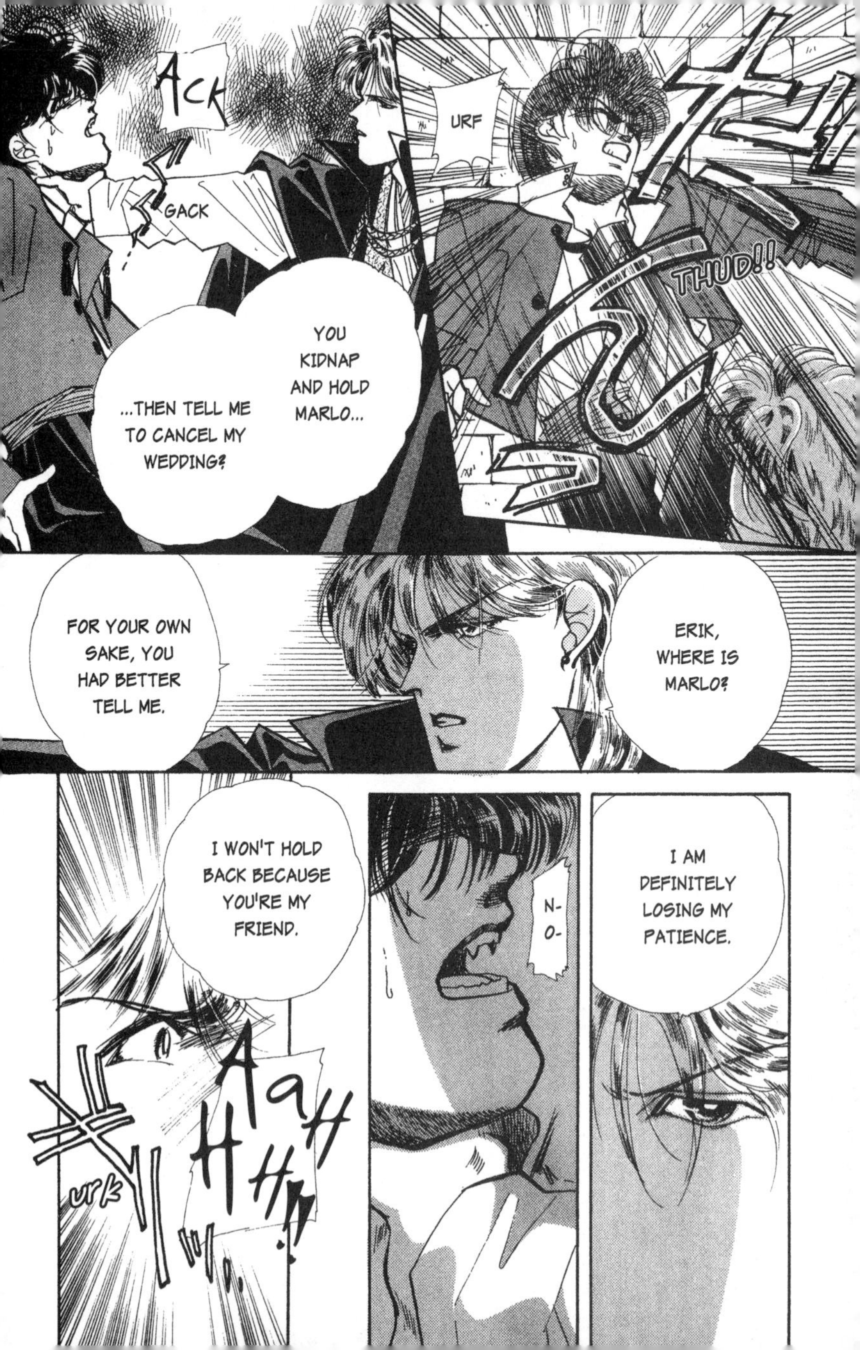
URF
THUD!!
ACK
GACK
YOU KIDNAP AND HOLD MARLO...
...THEN TELL ME TO CANCEL MY WEDDING?
ERIK, WHERE IS MARLO?
FOR YOUR OWN SAKE, YOU HAD BETTER TELL ME.
I AM DEFINITELY LOSING MY PATIENCE.
N-O-
I WON'T HOLD BACK BECAUSE YOU'RE MY FRIEND.
AaHHH!!
urk

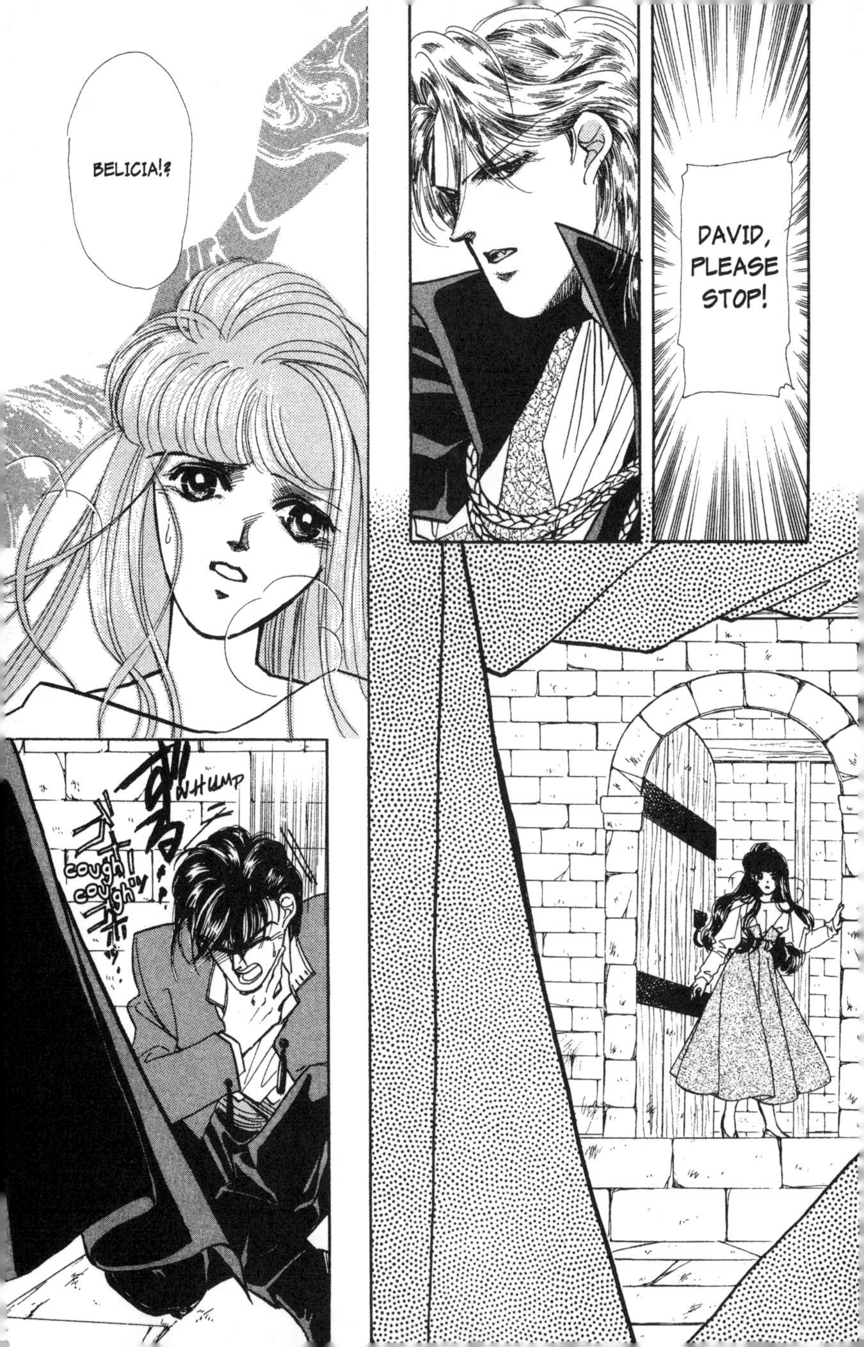
DAVID, PLEASE STOP!
BELICIA!?
WHUMP
cough! cough!

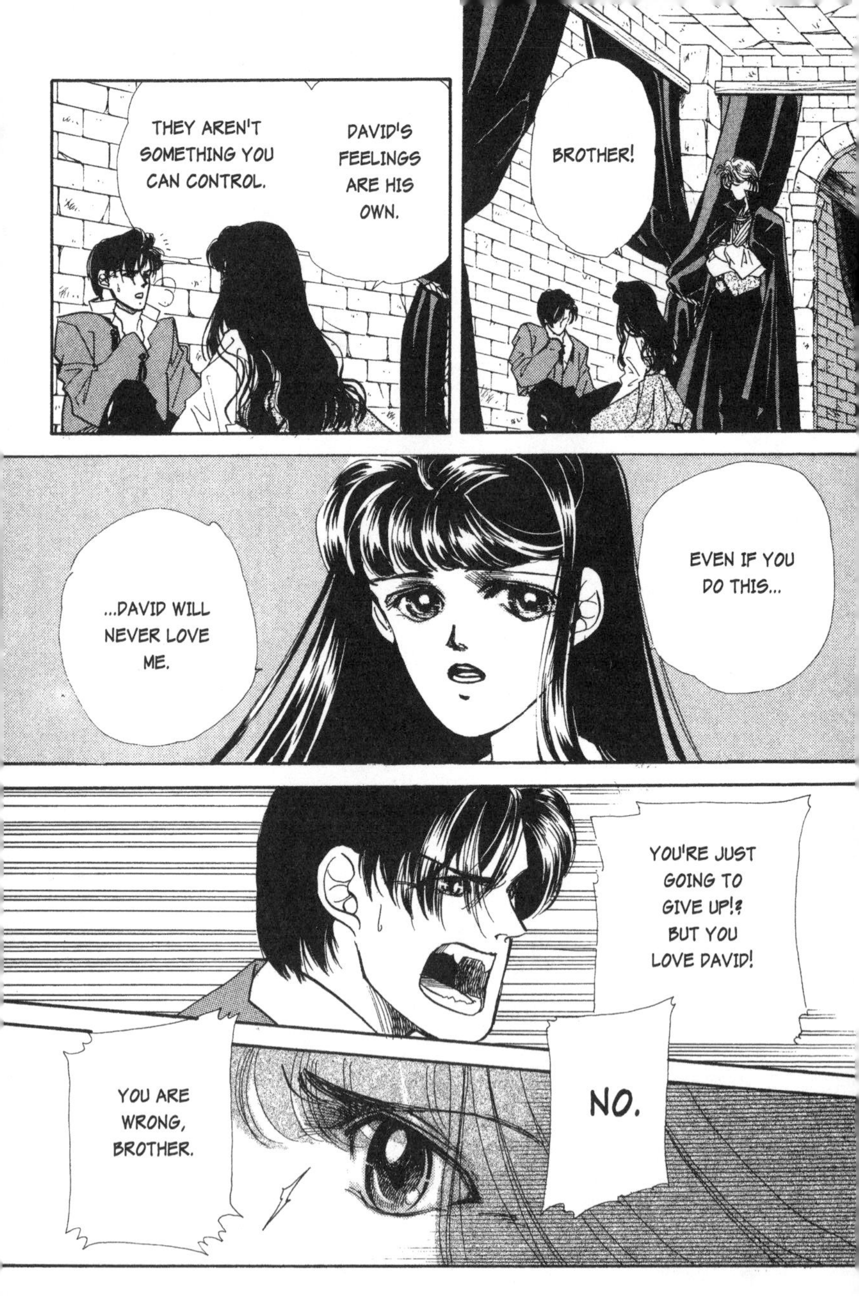
BROTHER!
DAVID'S FEELINGS ARE HIS OWN.
THEY AREN'T SOMETHING YOU CAN CONTROL.
EVEN IF YOU DO THIS...
...DAVID WILL NEVER LOVE ME.
YOU'RE JUST GOING TO GIVE UP!? BUT YOU LOVE DAVID!
NO.
YOU ARE WRONG, BROTHER.

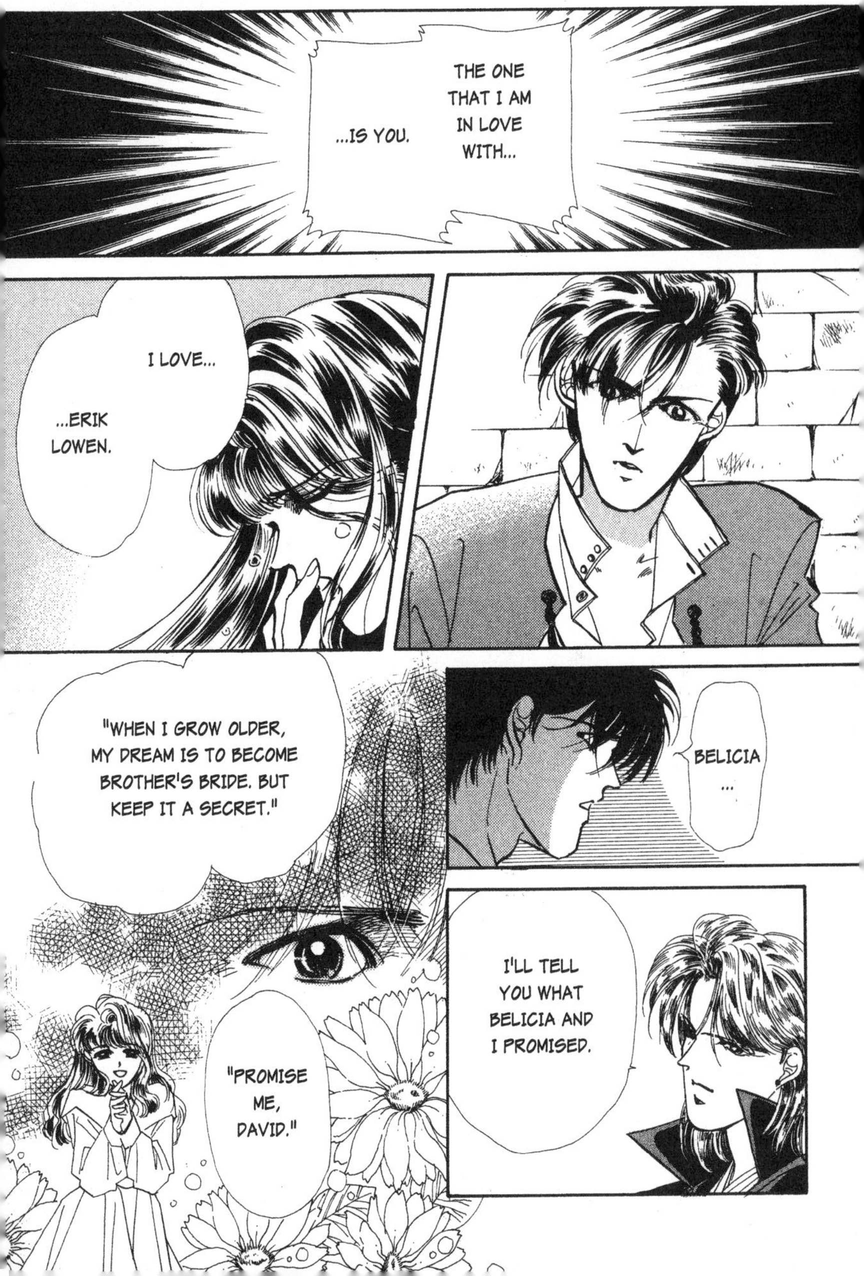
THE ONE THAT I AM IN LOVE WITH...
...IS YOU.
I LOVE...
...ERIK LOWEN.
BELICIA ...
I'LL TELL YOU WHAT BELICIA AND I PROMISED.
"WHEN I GROW OLDER, MY DREAM IS TO BECOME BROTHER'S BRIDE. BUT KEEP IT A SECRET."
"PROMISE ME, DAVID."

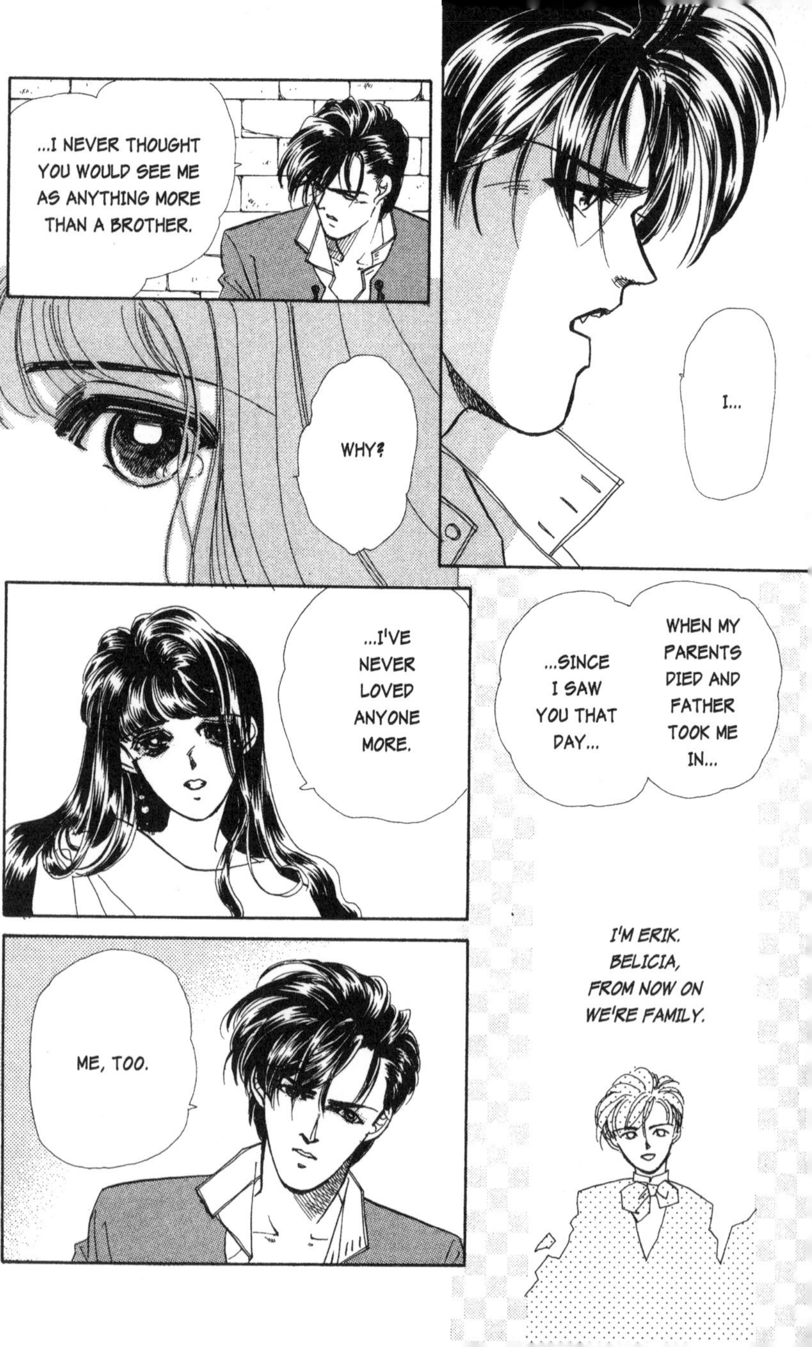
I...
...I NEVER THOUGHT YOU WOULD SEE ME AS ANYTHING MORE THAN A BROTHER.
WHY?
WHEN MY PARENTS DIED AND FATHER TOOK ME IN...
...SINCE I SAW YOU THAT DAY...
...I'VE NEVER LOVED ANYONE MORE.
I'M ERIK. BELICIA, FROM NOW ON WE'RE FAMILY.
ME, TOO.

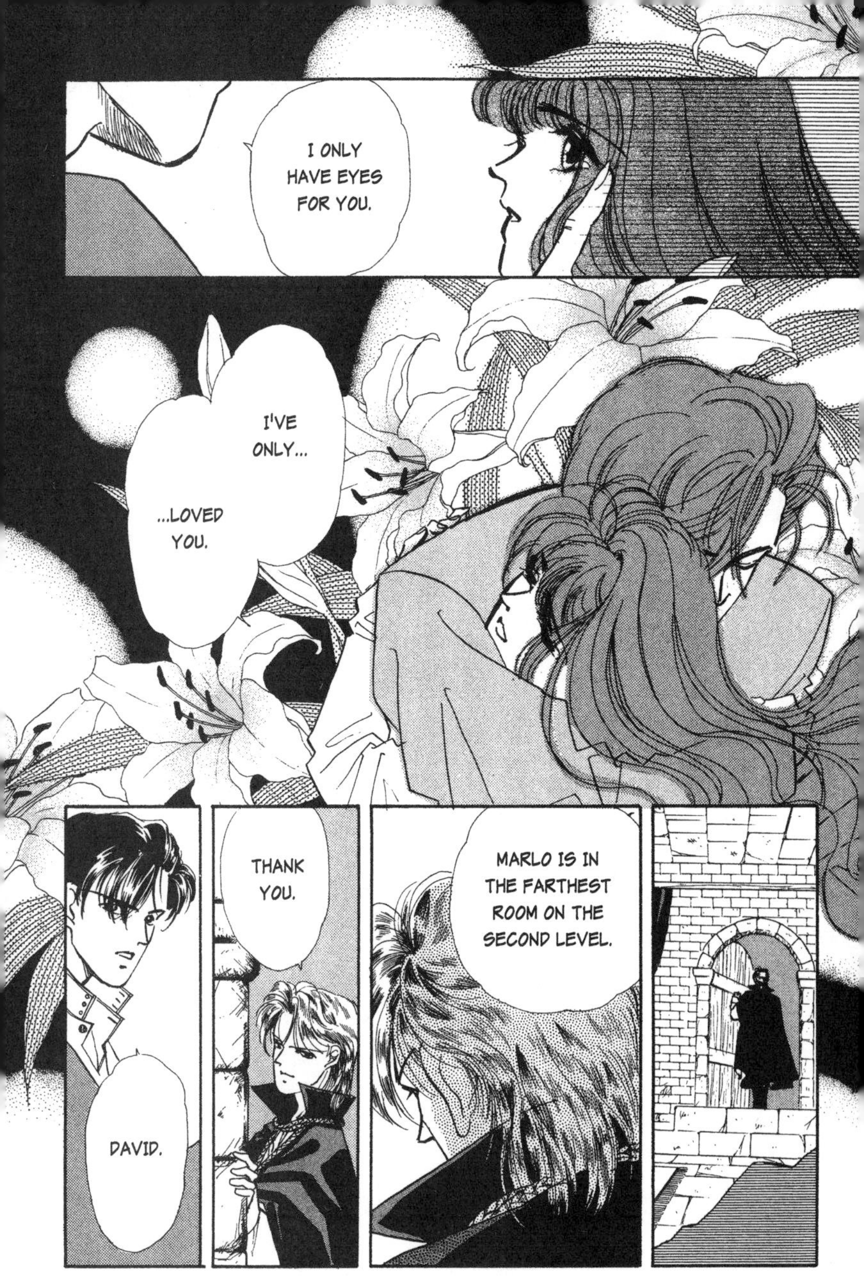
I ONLY HAVE EYES FOR YOU.
I'VE ONLY...
...LOVED YOU.
MARLO IS IN THE FARTHEST ROOM ON THE SECOND LEVEL.
THANK YOU.
DAVID.

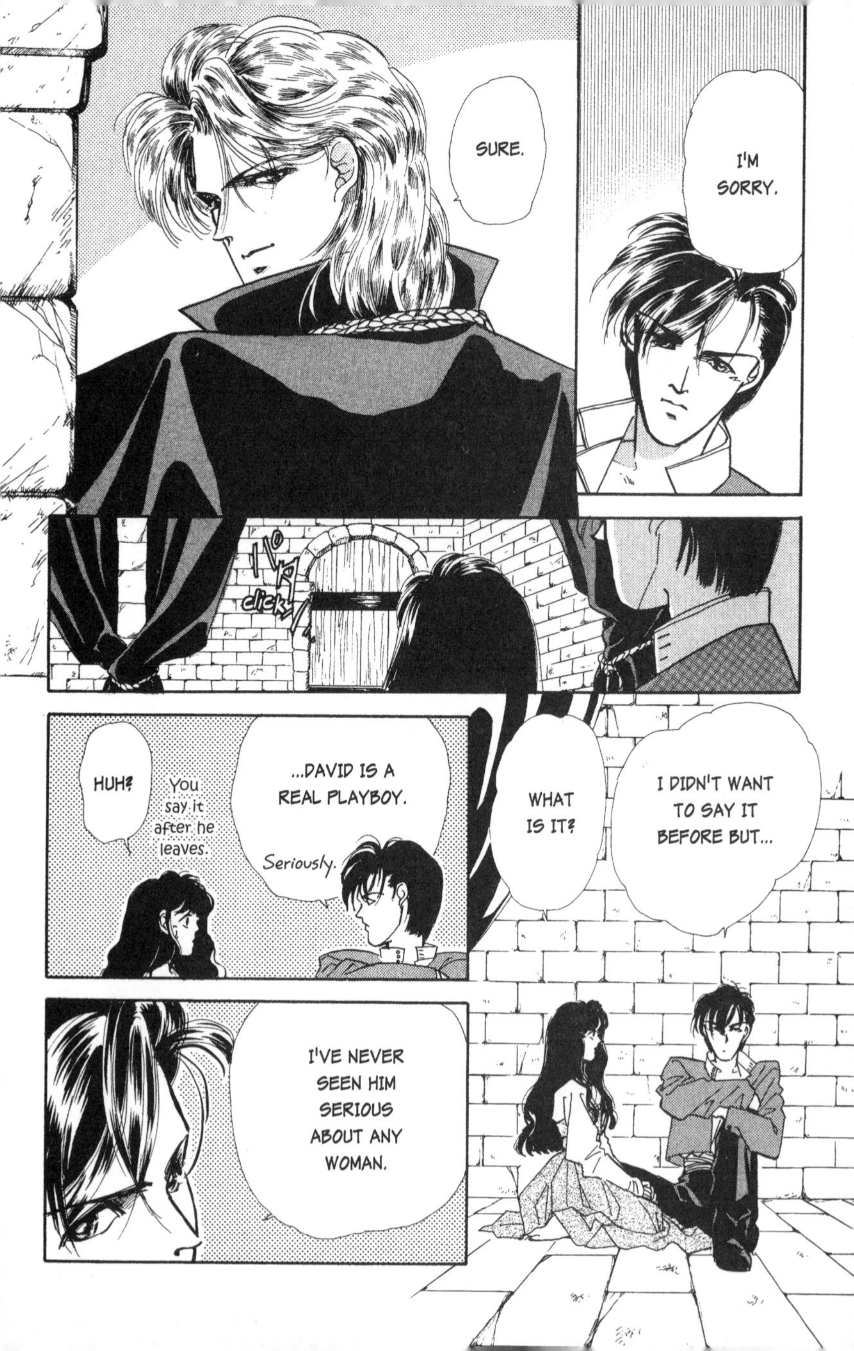
I'M SORRY.
SURE.
click
I DIDN'T WANT TO SAY IT BEFORE BUT...
WHAT IS IT?
...DAVID IS A REAL PLAYBOY.
HUH?
You say it after he leaves.
Seriously.
I'VE NEVER SEEN HIM SERIOUS ABOUT ANY WOMAN.

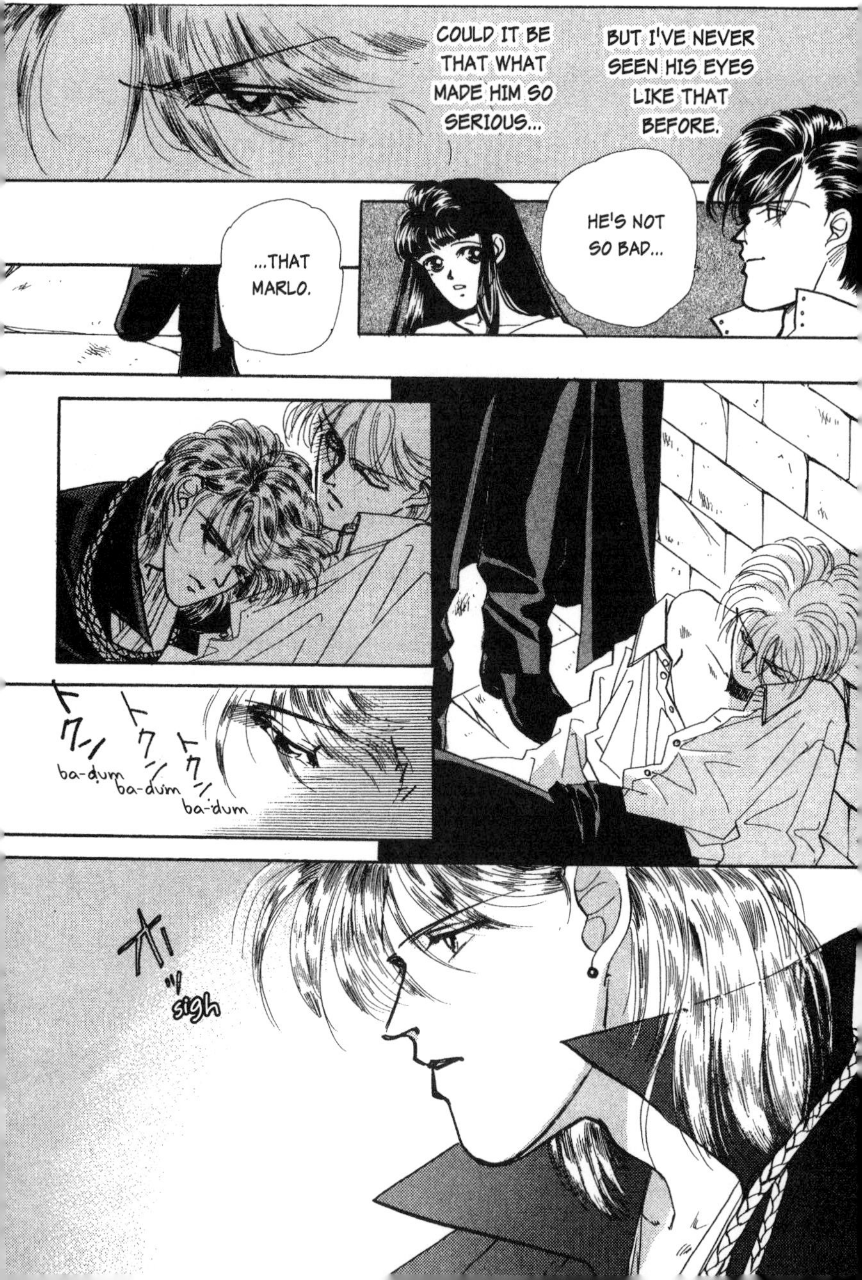
BUT I'VE NEVER SEEN HIS EYES LIKE THAT BEFORE.
COULD IT BE THAT WHAT MADE HIM SO SERIOUS...
HE'S NOT SO BAD...
...THAT MARLO.
ba-dum ba-dum ba-dum
sigh

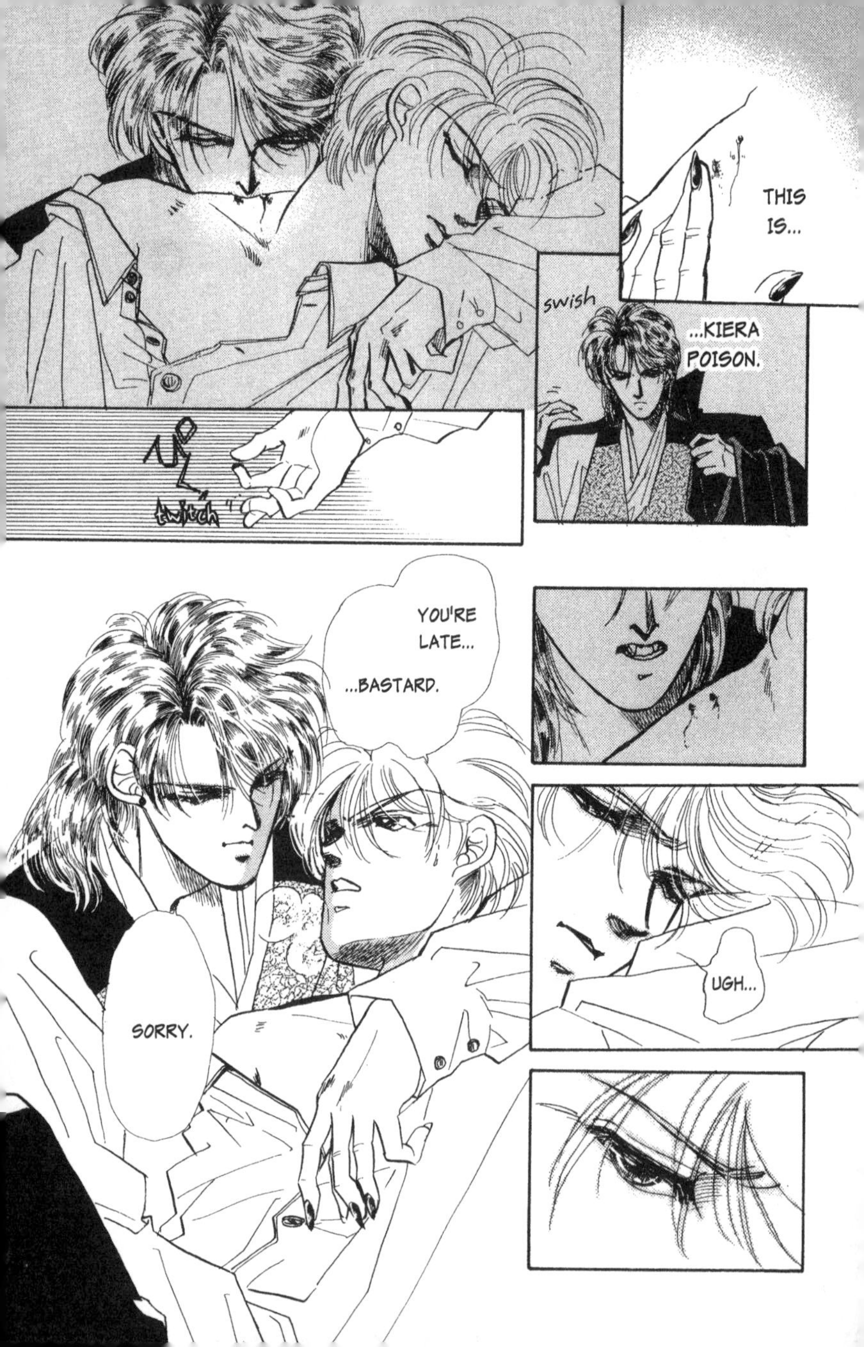
THIS IS...
swish
...KIERA POISON.
twitch
UGH...
YOU'RE LATE...
...BASTARD.
SORRY.

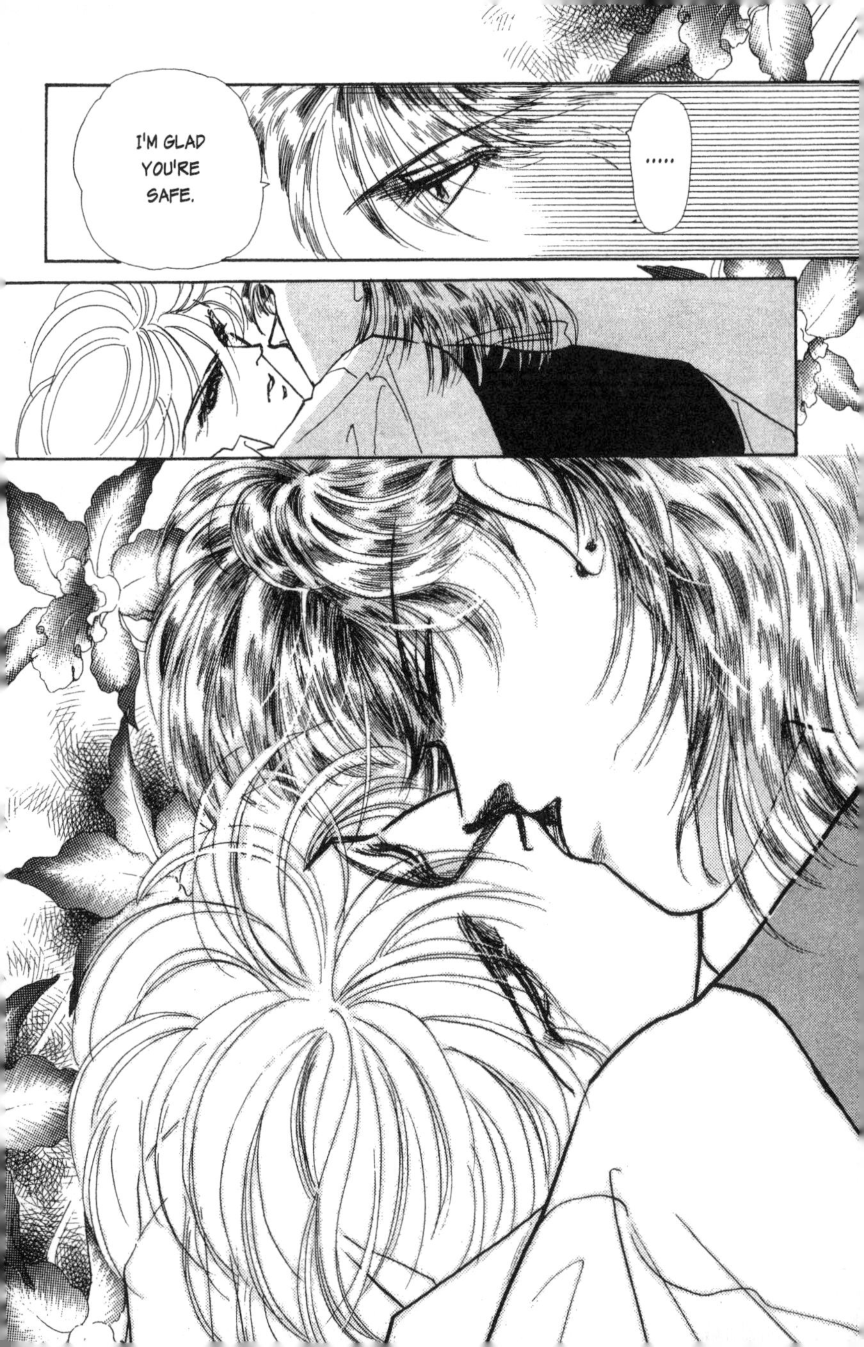
......
I'M GLAD YOU'RE SAFE.

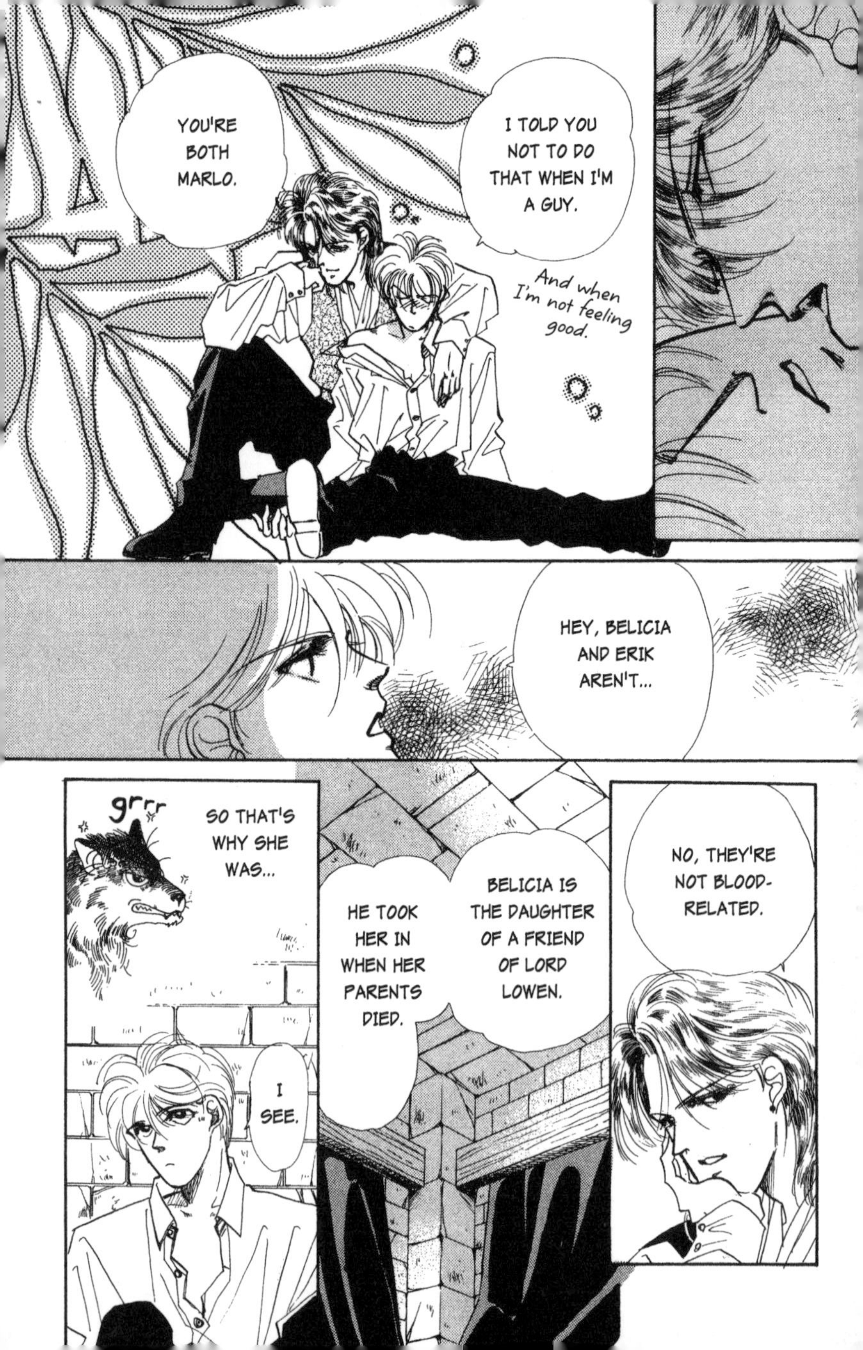
I TOLD YOU NOT TO DO THAT WHEN I'M A GUY.
And when I'm not feeling good.
YOU'RE BOTH MARLO.
HEY, BELICIA AND ERIK AREN'T...
NO, THEY'RE NOT BLOOD-RELATED.
BELICIA IS THE DAUGHTER OF A FRIEND OF LORD LOWEN.
HE TOOK HER IN WHEN HER PARENTS DIED.
grrr
SO THAT'S WHY SHE WAS...
I SEE.

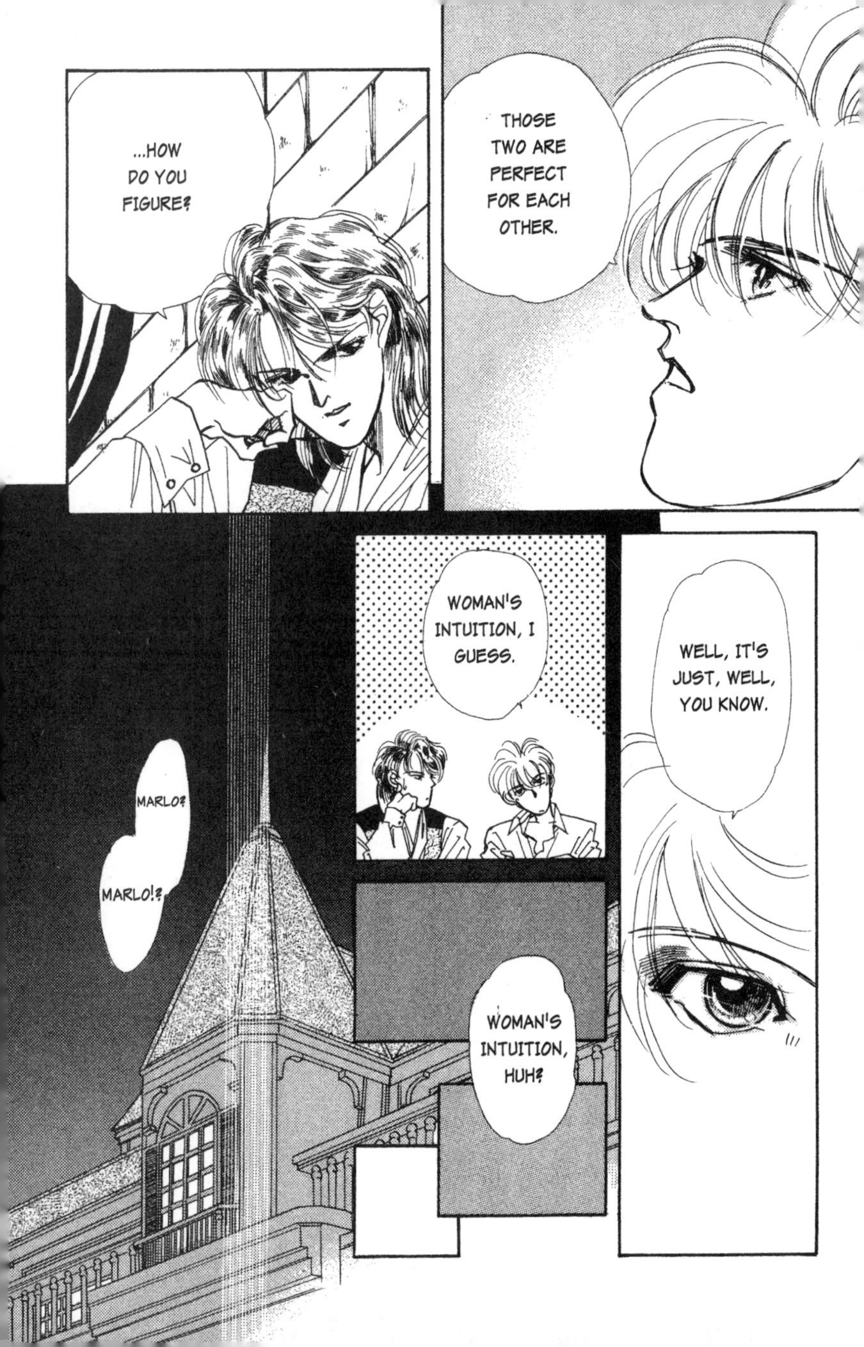
THOSE TWO ARE PERFECT FOR EACH OTHER.
...HOW DO YOU FIGURE?
WELL, IT'S JUST, WELL, YOU KNOW.
WOMAN'S INTUITION, I GUESS.
WOMAN'S INTUITION, HUH?
MARLO?
MARLO!?

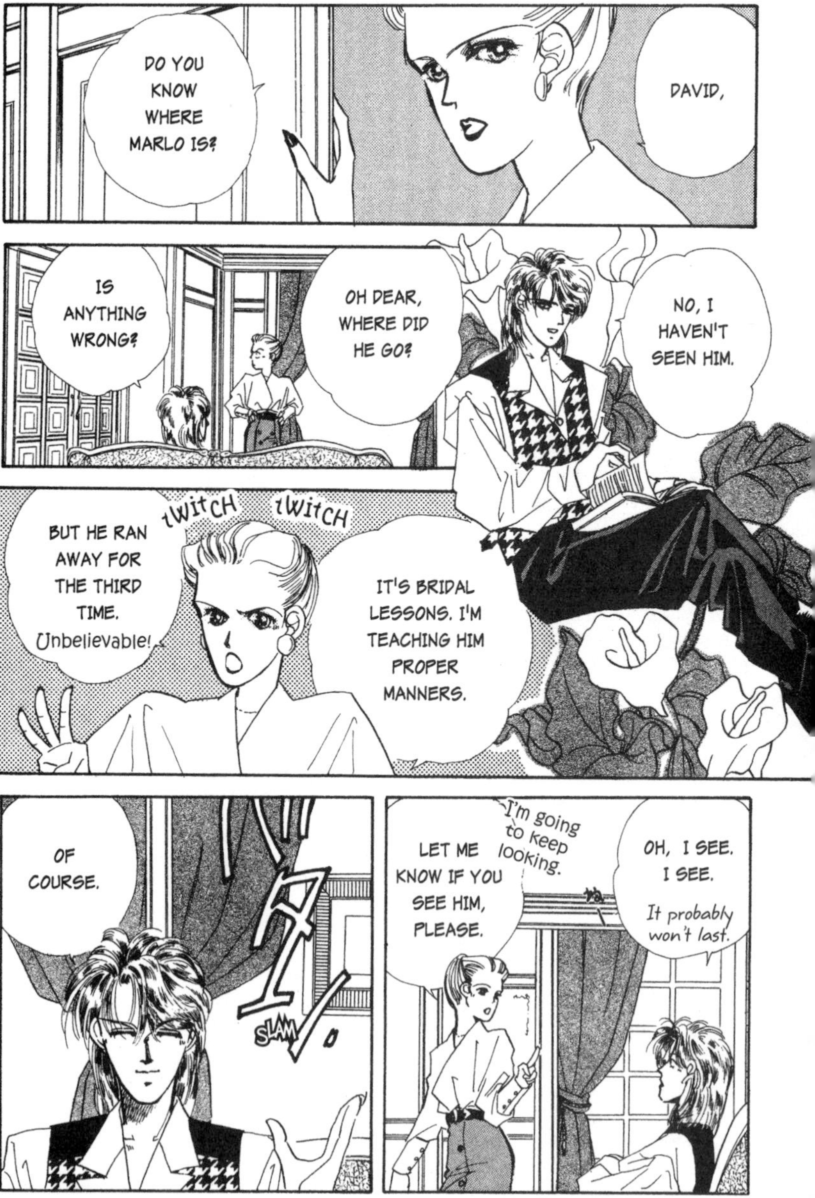
DAVID,
DO YOU KNOW WHERE MARLO IS?
NO, I HAVEN'T SEEN HIM.
OH DEAR, WHERE DID HE GO?
IS ANYTHING WRONG?
TWITCH TWITCH
IT'S BRIDAL LESSONS. I'M TEACHING HIM PROPER MANNERS.
BUT HE RAN AWAY FOR THE THIRD TIME. Unbelievable!
OH, I SEE. I SEE. It probably won't last.
I'm going to keep looking.
LET ME KNOW IF YOU SEE HIM, PLEASE.
OF COURSE.
SLAM

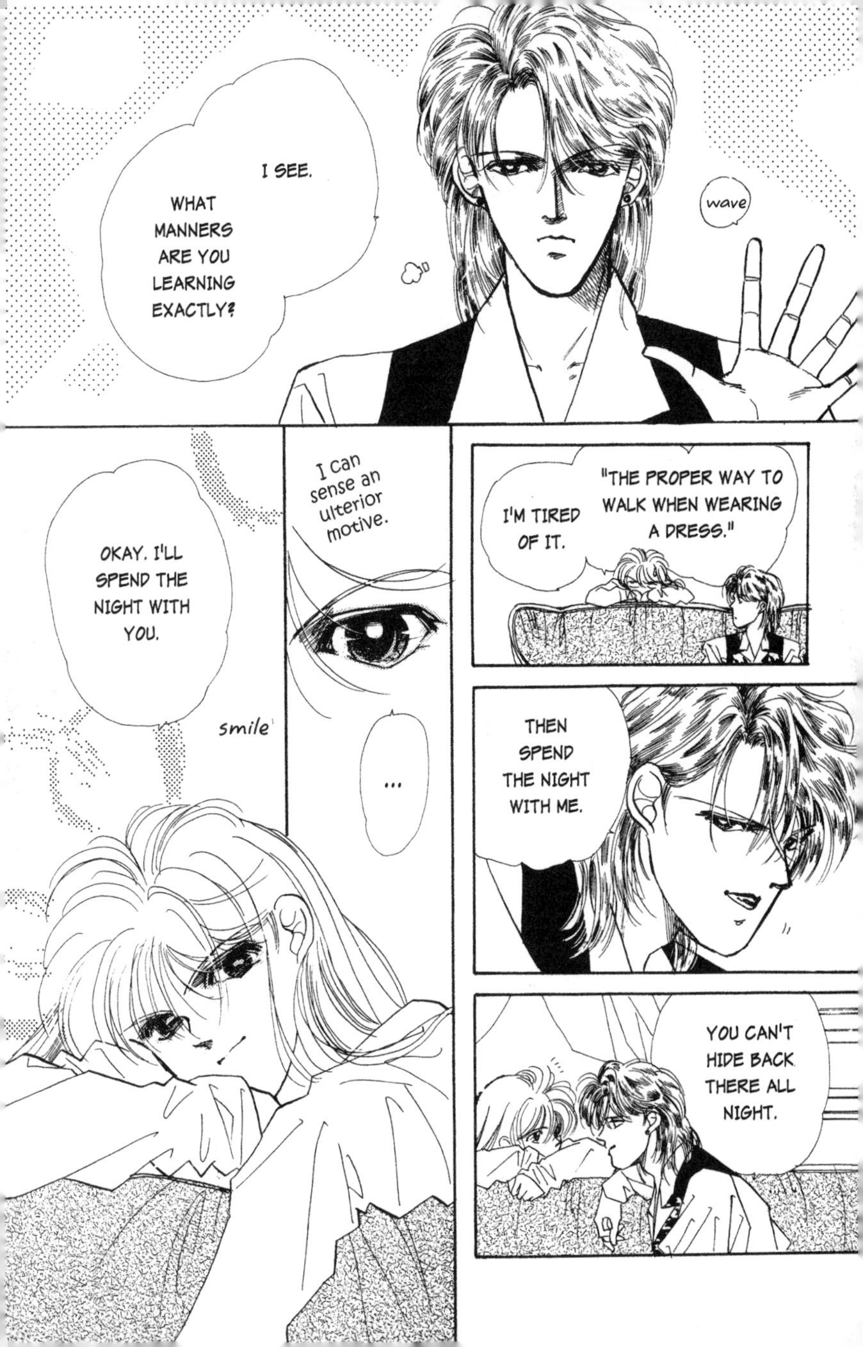
wave
I SEE.
WHAT MANNERS ARE YOU LEARNING EXACTLY?
"THE PROPER WAY TO WALK WHEN WEARING A DRESS."
I'M TIRED OF IT.
THEN SPEND THE NIGHT WITH ME.
YOU CAN'T HIDE BACK THERE ALL NIGHT.
I can sense an ulterior motive.
...
OKAY. I'LL SPEND THE NIGHT WITH YOU.
smile

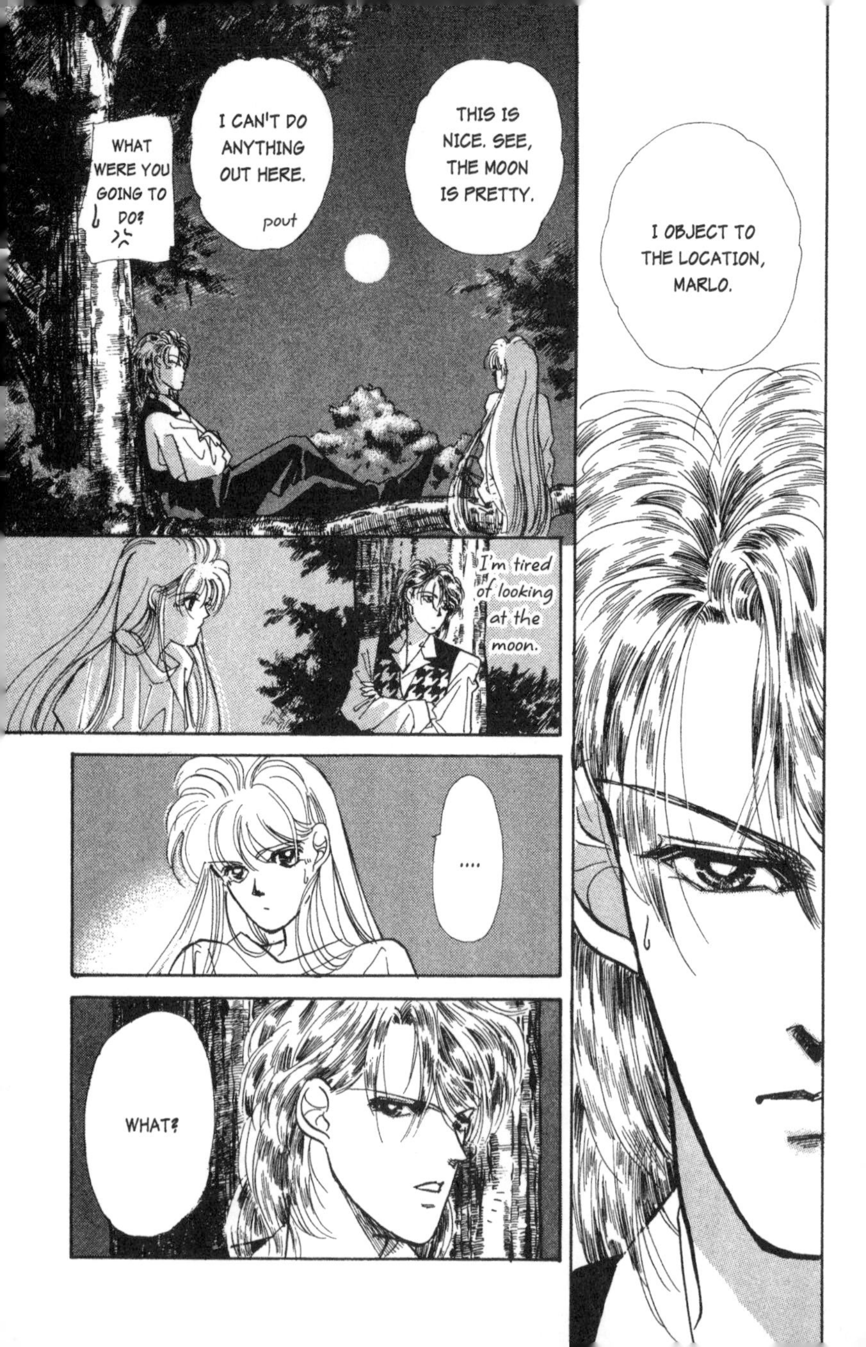
I OBJECT TO THE LOCATION, MARLO.
THIS IS NICE. SEE, THE MOON IS PRETTY.
I CAN'T DO ANYTHING OUT HERE.
pout
WHAT WERE YOU GOING TO DO?
I'm tired of looking at the moon.
....
WHAT?

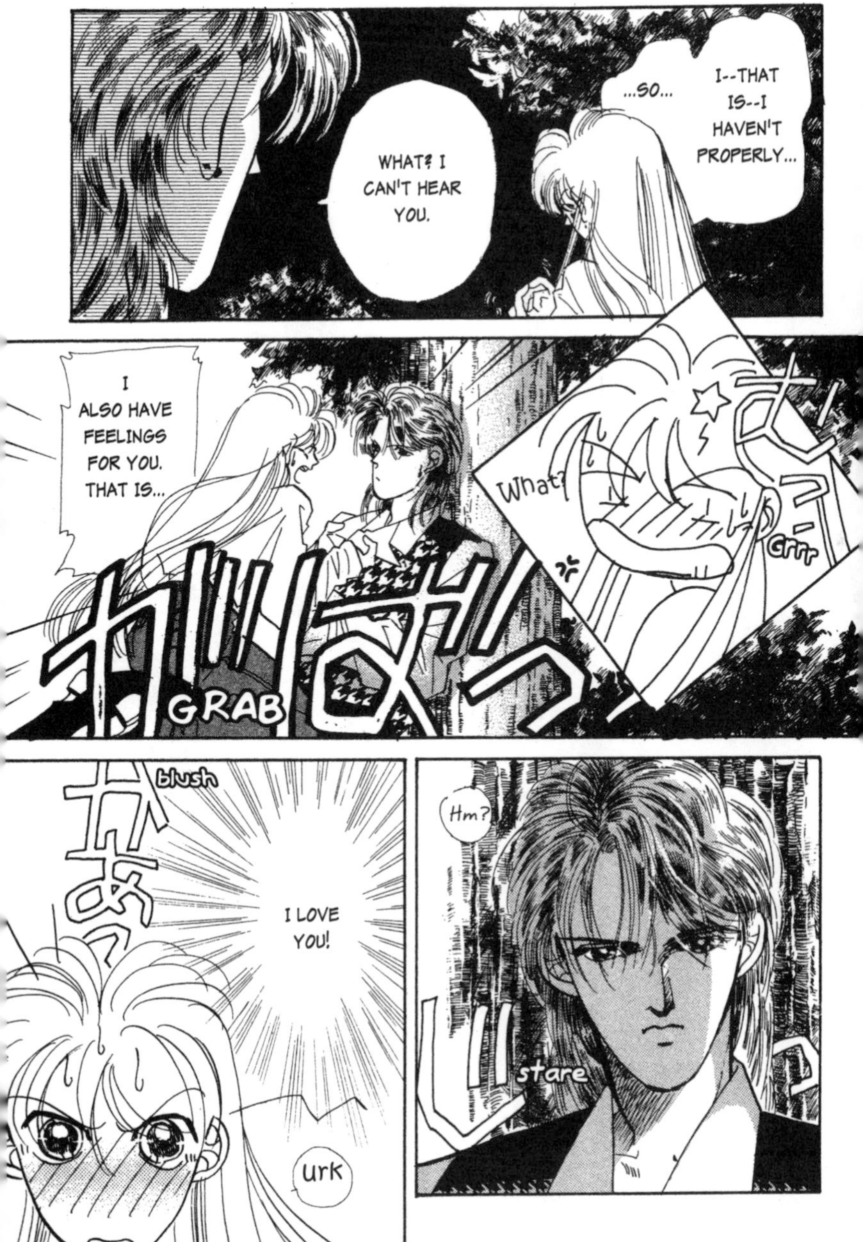
I--THAT IS--I HAVEN'T PROPERLY...
...SO...
WHAT? I CAN'T HEAR YOU.
What?
Grrr
I ALSO HAVE FEELINGS FOR YOU. THAT IS...
GRAB
Hm?
stare
blush
I LOVE YOU!
urk

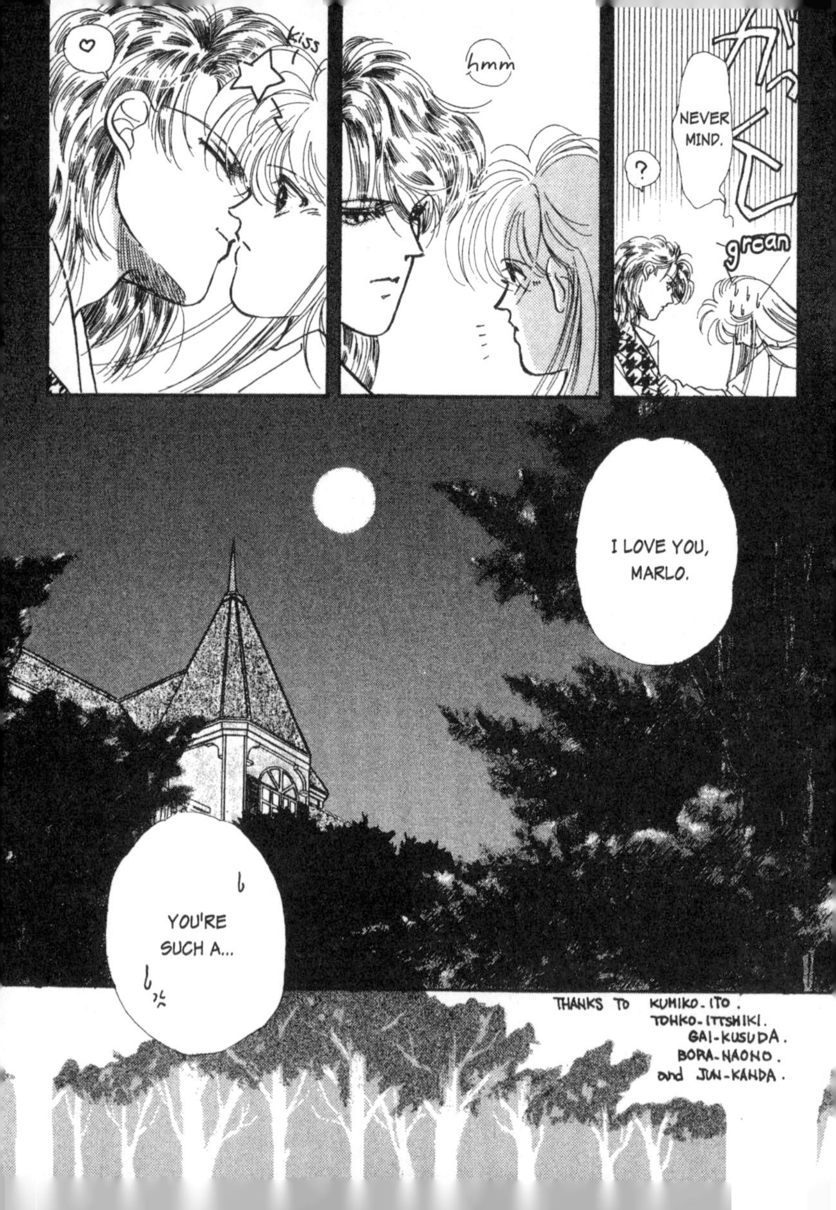
NEVER MIND.
?
groan
hmm
kiss
I LOVE YOU, MARLO.
YOU'RE SUCH A...
THANKS TO KUMIKO-ITO. TOHKO-ITTSHIKI. GAI-KUSUDA. BORA-NAONO. and JUN-KANDA.

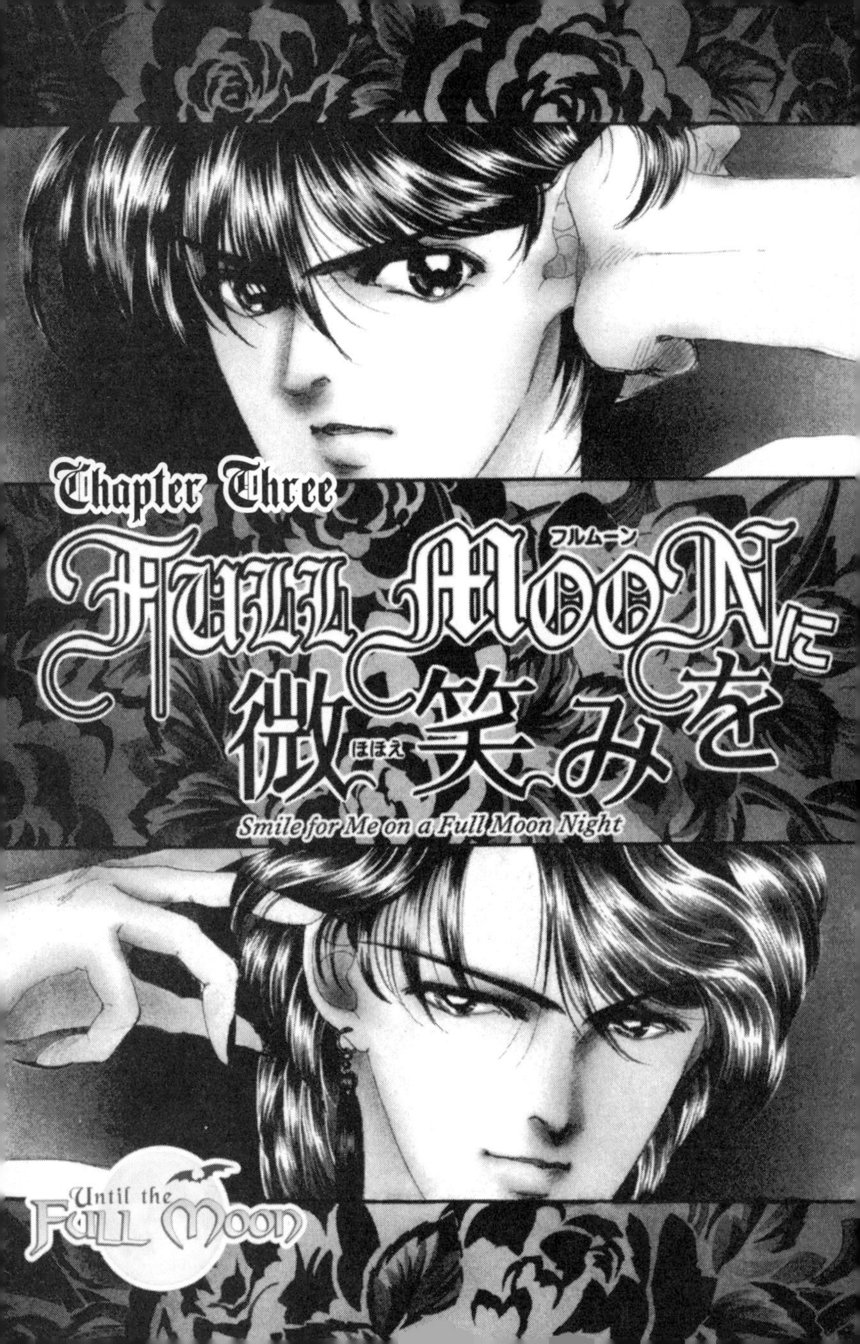
Chapter Three
FULL MOON に
フルムーン
微笑みを
ほほえ
Smile for Me on a Full Moon Night
Until the FULL MOON

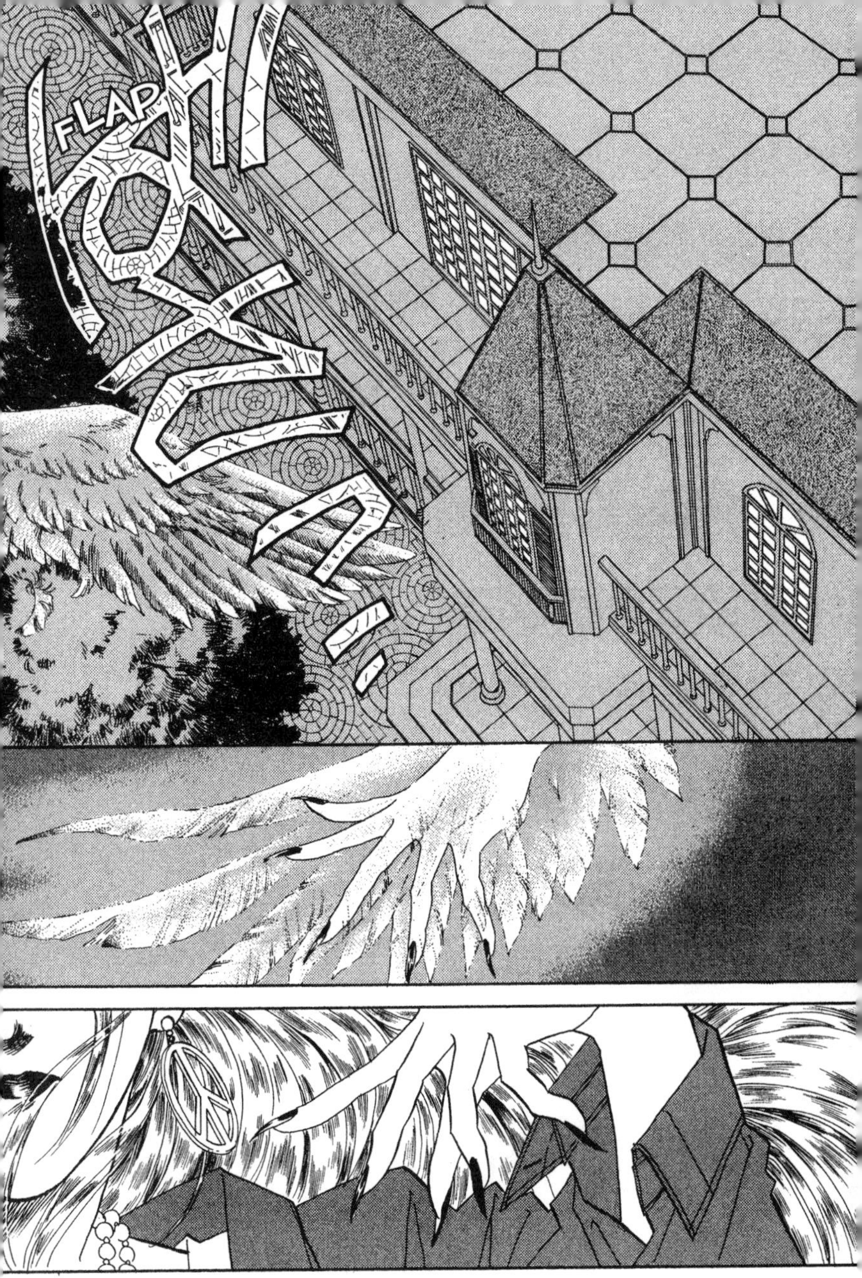
FLAP

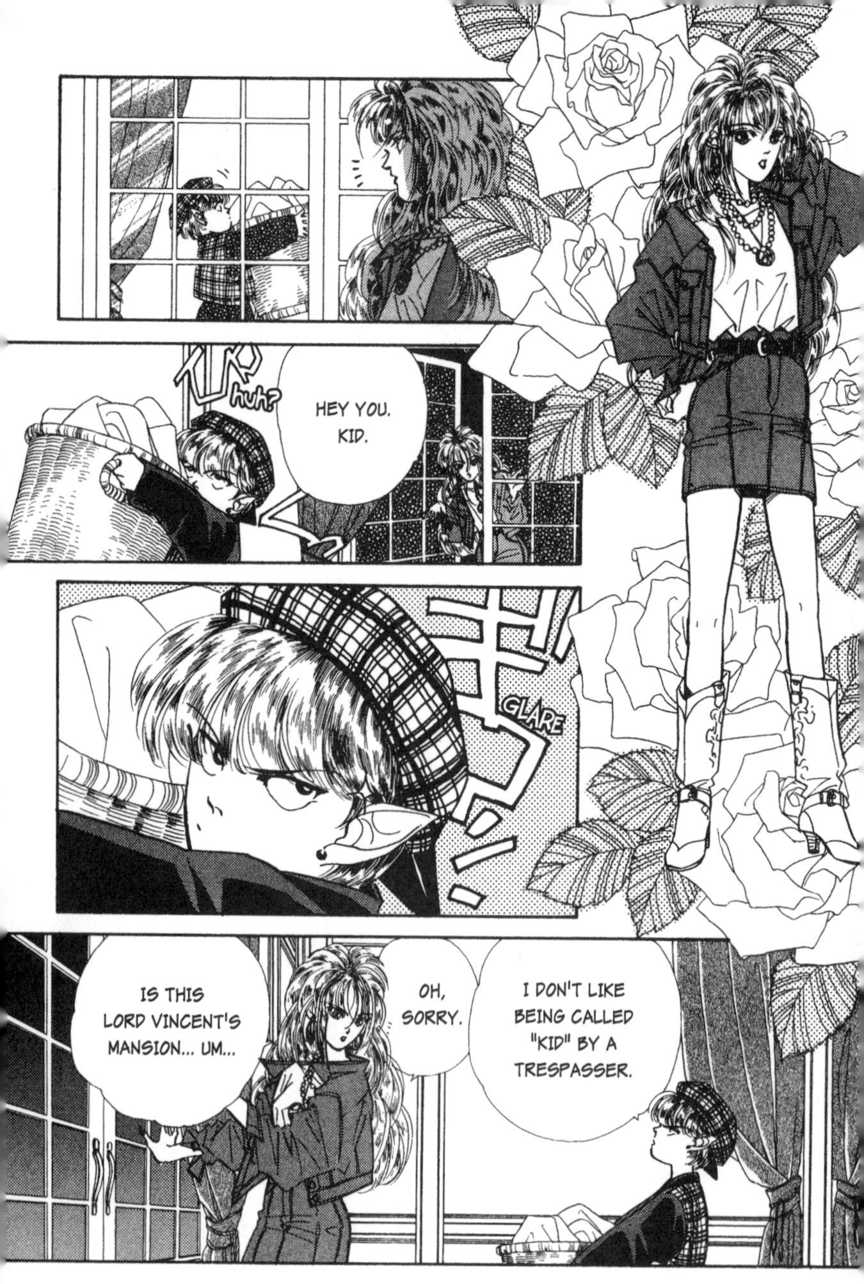
HEY YOU. KID.
huh?
GLARE
I DON'T LIKE BEING CALLED "KID" BY A TRESPASSER.
OH, SORRY.
IS THIS LORD VINCENT'S MANSION... UM...

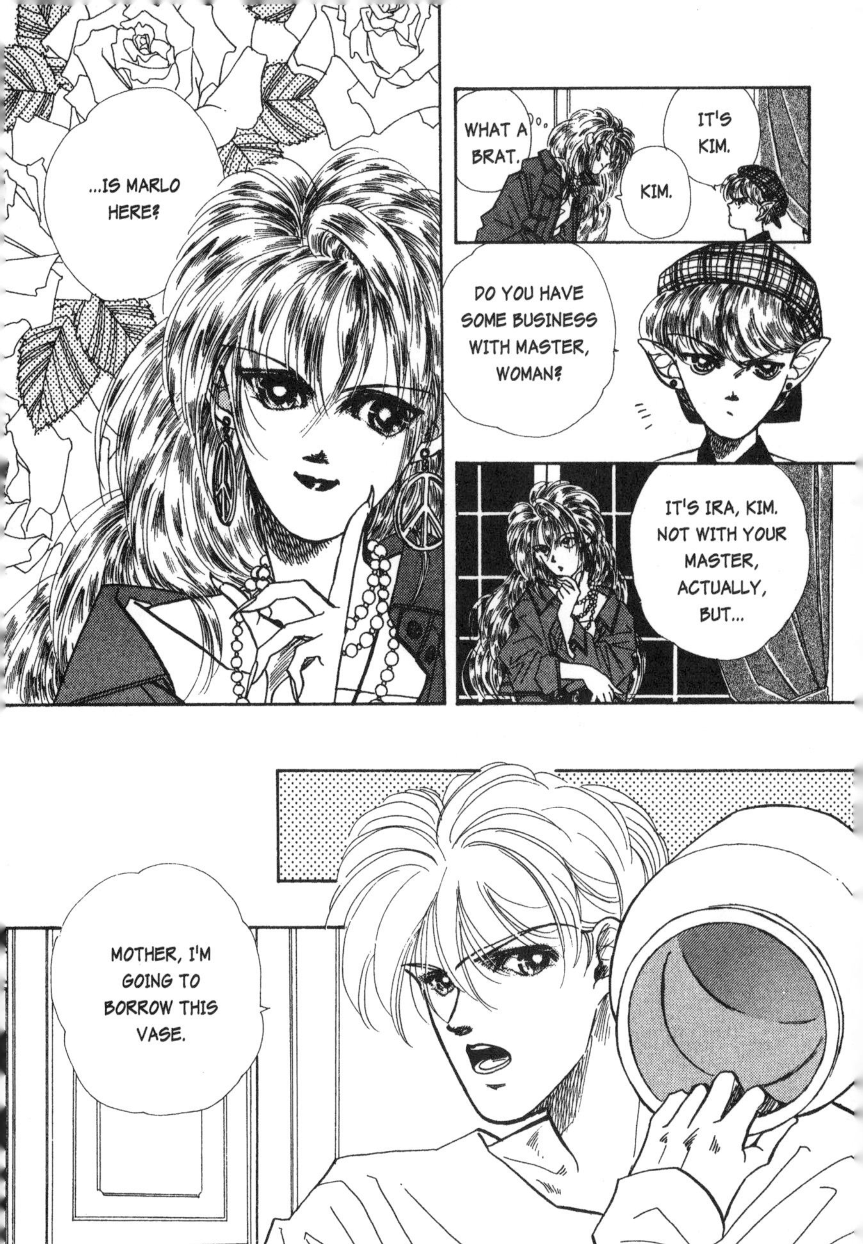
IT'S KIM.
WHAT A BRAT.
KIM.
DO YOU HAVE SOME BUSINESS WITH MASTER, WOMAN?
IT'S IRA, KIM. NOT WITH YOUR MASTER, ACTUALLY, BUT...
...IS MARLO HERE?
MOTHER, I'M GOING TO BORROW THIS VASE.

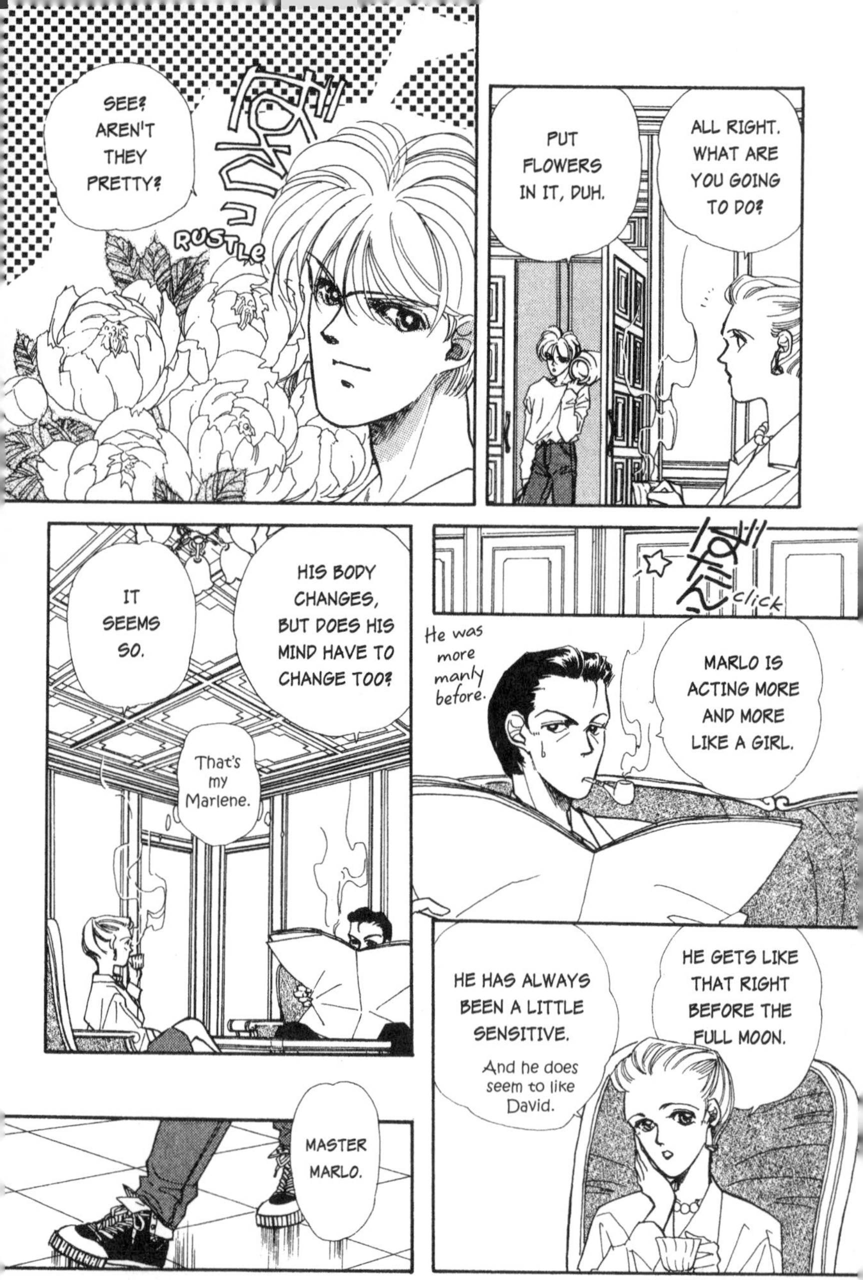
ALL RIGHT. WHAT ARE YOU GOING TO DO?
PUT FLOWERS IN IT, DUH.
SEE? AREN'T THEY PRETTY?
RUSTLE
click
MARLO IS ACTING MORE AND MORE LIKE A GIRL.
He was more manly before.
HE GETS LIKE THAT RIGHT BEFORE THE FULL MOON.
HE HAS ALWAYS BEEN A LITTLE SENSITIVE.
And he does seem to like David.
HIS BODY CHANGES, BUT DOES HIS MIND HAVE TO CHANGE TOO?
IT SEEMS SO.
That's my Marlene.
MASTER MARLO.

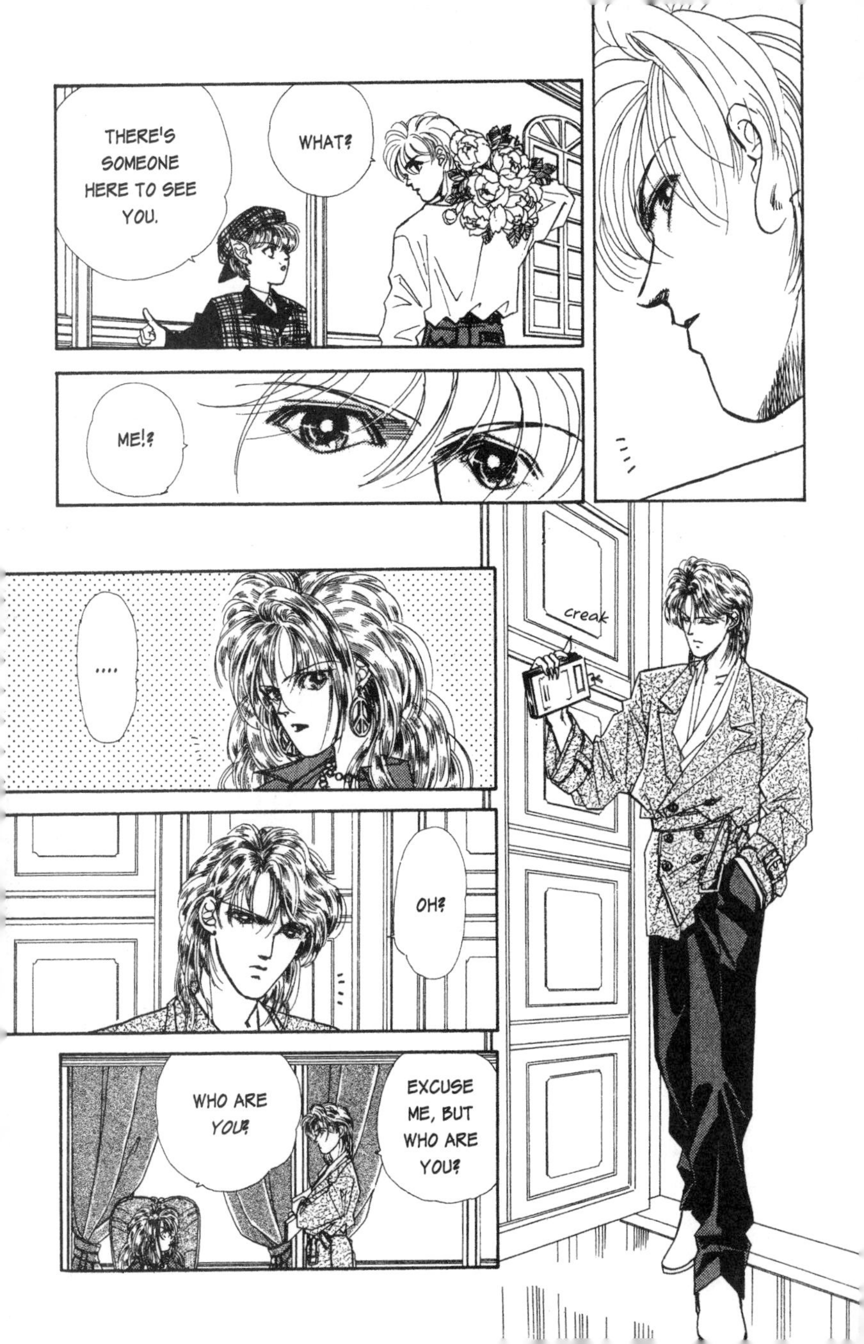
WHAT?
THERE'S SOMEONE HERE TO SEE YOU.
ME!?
creak
....
OH?
EXCUSE ME, BUT WHO ARE YOU?
WHO ARE YOU?

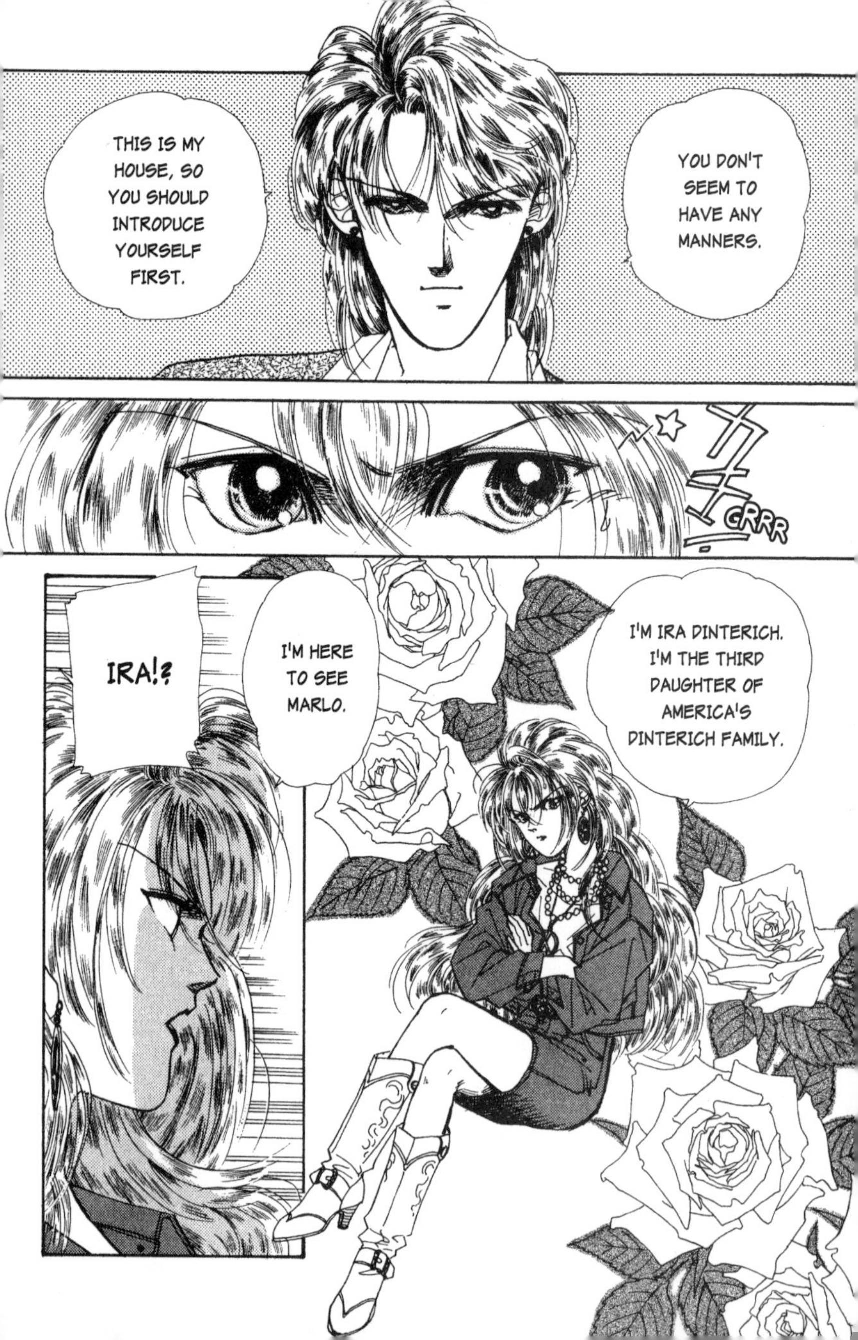
YOU DON'T SEEM TO HAVE ANY MANNERS.
THIS IS MY HOUSE, SO YOU SHOULD INTRODUCE YOURSELF FIRST.
GRRR
I'M IRA DINTERICH. I'M THE THIRD DAUGHTER OF AMERICA'S DINTERICH FAMILY.
I'M HERE TO SEE MARLO.
IRA!?

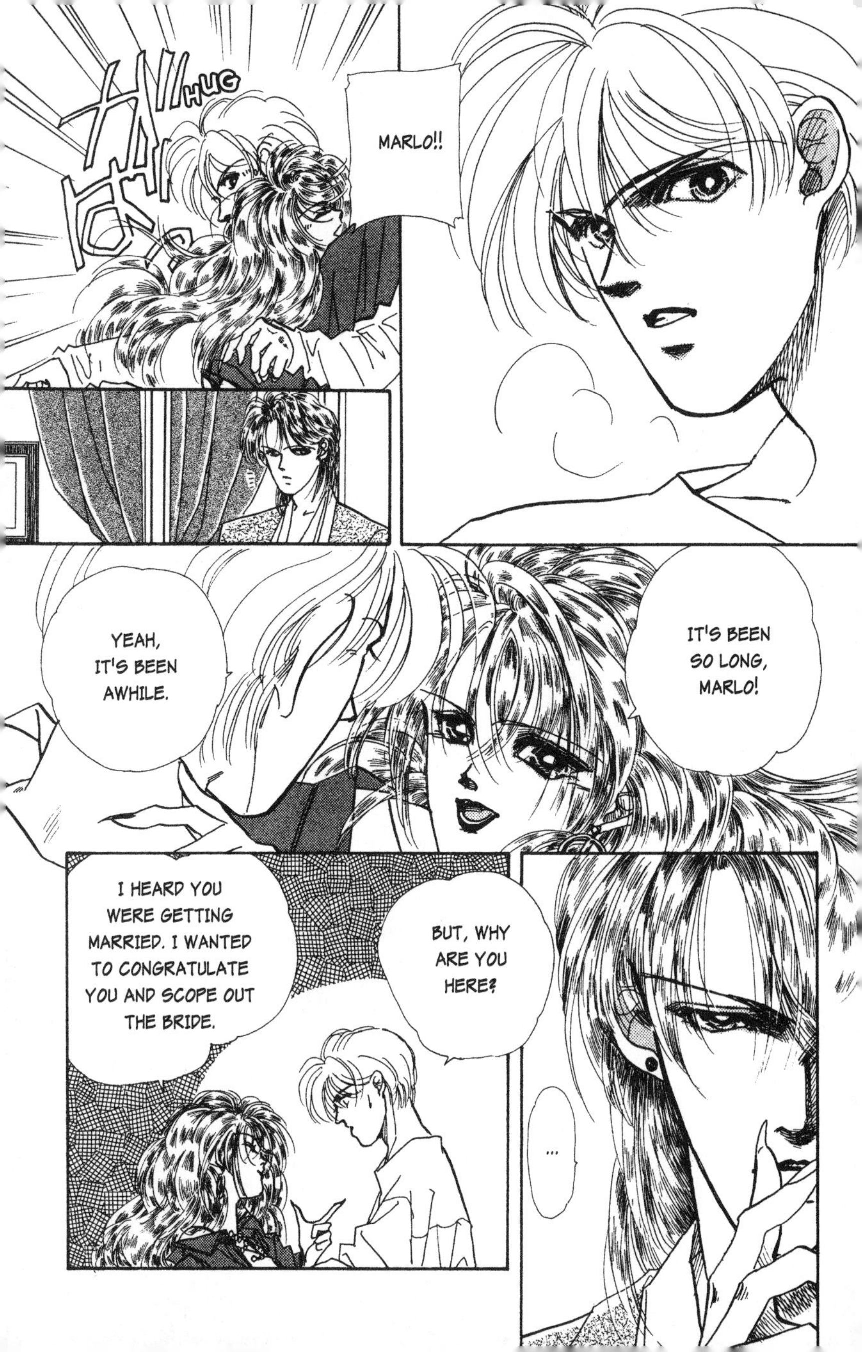
MARLO!!
HUG
IT'S BEEN SO LONG, MARLO!
YEAH, IT'S BEEN AWHILE.
...
BUT, WHY ARE YOU HERE?
I HEARD YOU WERE GETTING MARRIED. I WANTED TO CONGRATULATE YOU AND SCOPE OUT THE BRIDE.

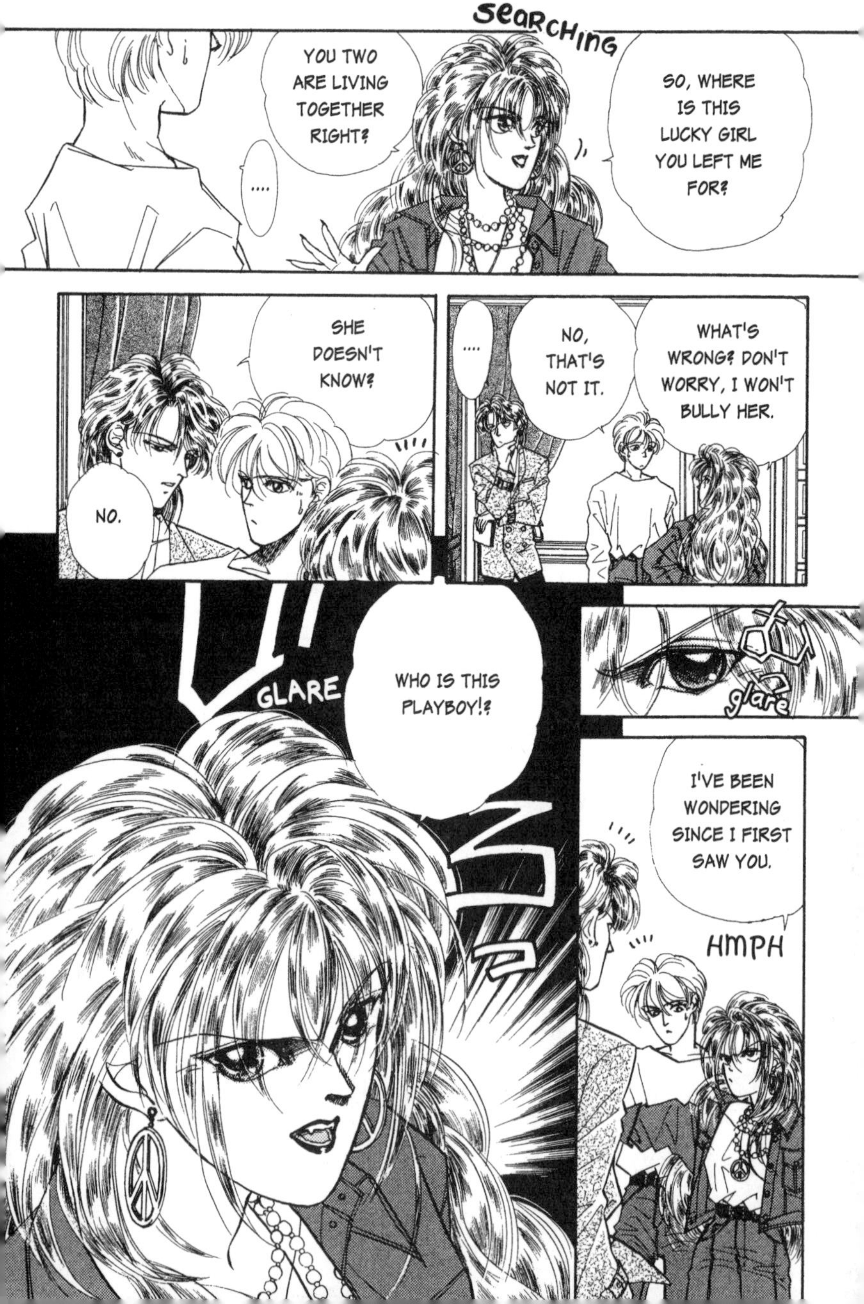
SEARCHING
SO, WHERE IS THIS LUCKY GIRL YOU LEFT ME FOR?
YOU TWO ARE LIVING TOGETHER RIGHT?
....
WHAT'S WRONG? DON'T WORRY, I WON'T BULLY HER.
NO, THAT'S NOT IT.
....
SHE DOESN'T KNOW?
NO.
glare
I'VE BEEN WONDERING SINCE I FIRST SAW YOU.
HMPH
WHO IS THIS PLAYBOY!?
GLARE

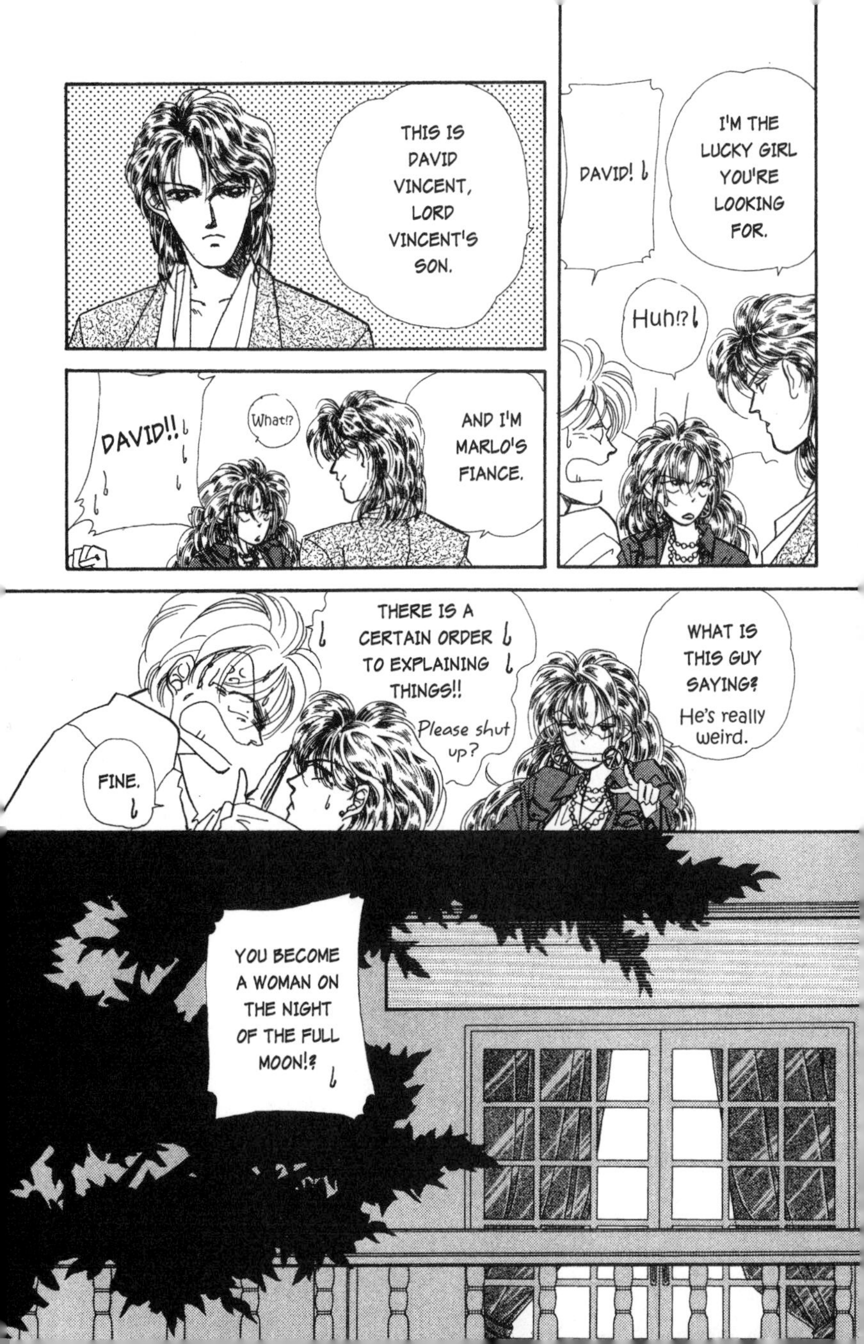
I'M THE LUCKY GIRL YOU'RE LOOKING FOR.
DAVID!
Huh!?
THIS IS DAVID VINCENT, LORD VINCENT'S SON.
AND I'M MARLO'S FIANCE.
What!?
DAVID!!
WHAT IS THIS GUY SAYING?
He's really weird.
THERE IS A CERTAIN ORDER TO EXPLAINING THINGS!!
Please shut up?
FINE.
YOU BECOME A WOMAN ON THE NIGHT OF THE FULL MOON!?

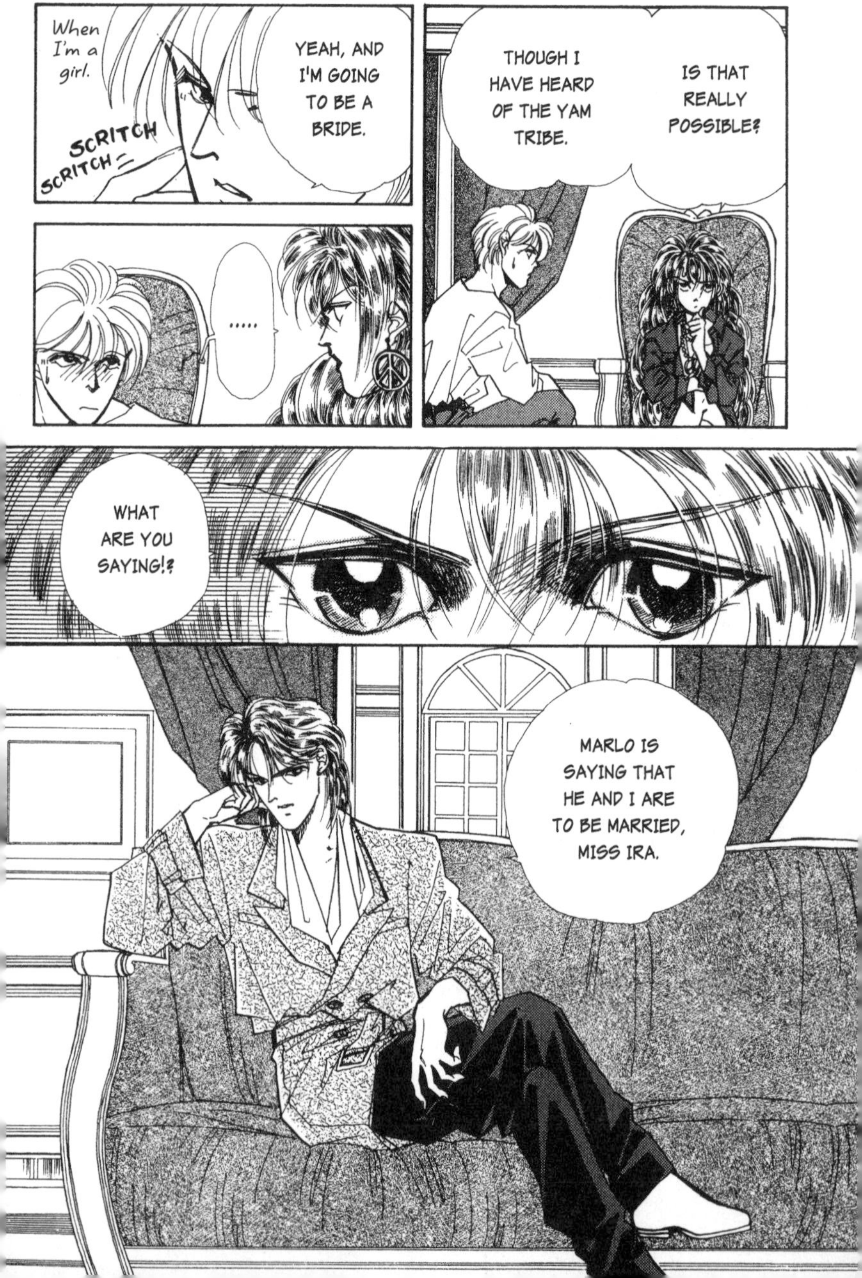
IS THAT REALLY POSSIBLE?
THOUGH I HAVE HEARD OF THE YAM TRIBE.
YEAH, AND I'M GOING TO BE A BRIDE.
When I'm a girl.
SCRITCH SCRITCH
.....
WHAT ARE YOU SAYING!?
MARLO IS SAYING THAT HE AND I ARE TO BE MARRIED, MISS IRA.

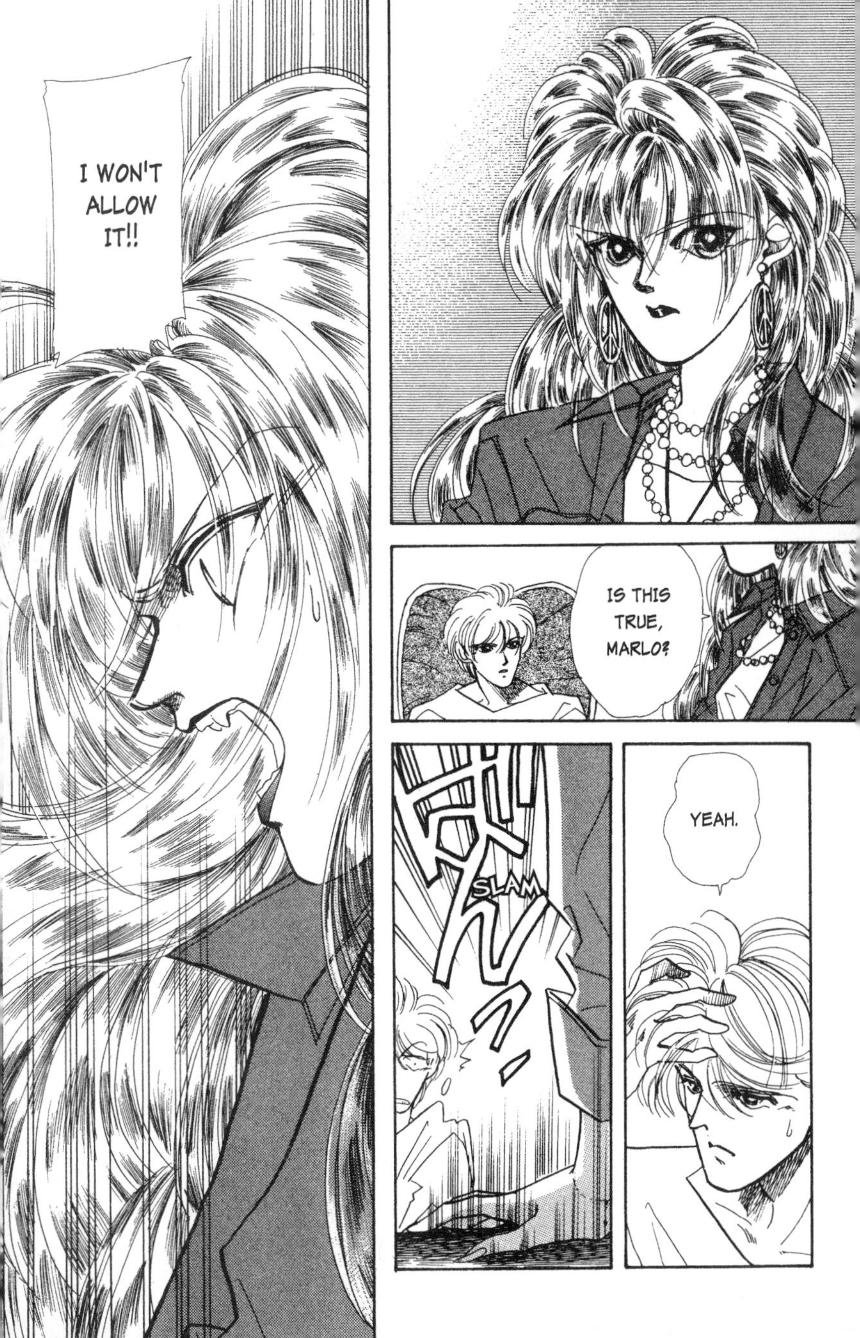
IS THIS TRUE, MARLO?
YEAH.
SLAM
I WON'T ALLOW IT!!

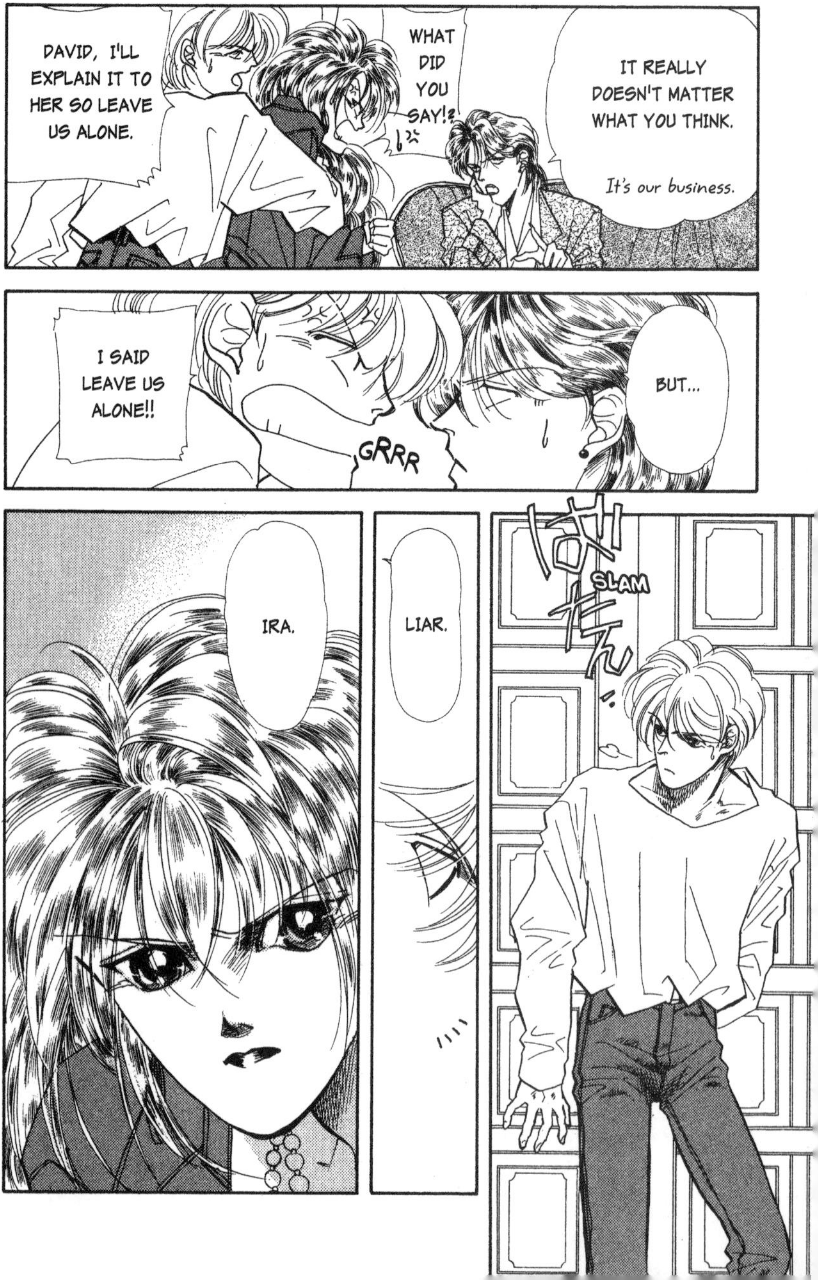
IT REALLY DOESN'T MATTER WHAT YOU THINK.
It's our business.
WHAT DID YOU SAY!?
DAVID, I'LL EXPLAIN IT TO HER SO LEAVE US ALONE.
BUT...
GRRR
I SAID LEAVE US ALONE!!
ばたん
SLAM
LIAR.
IRA.

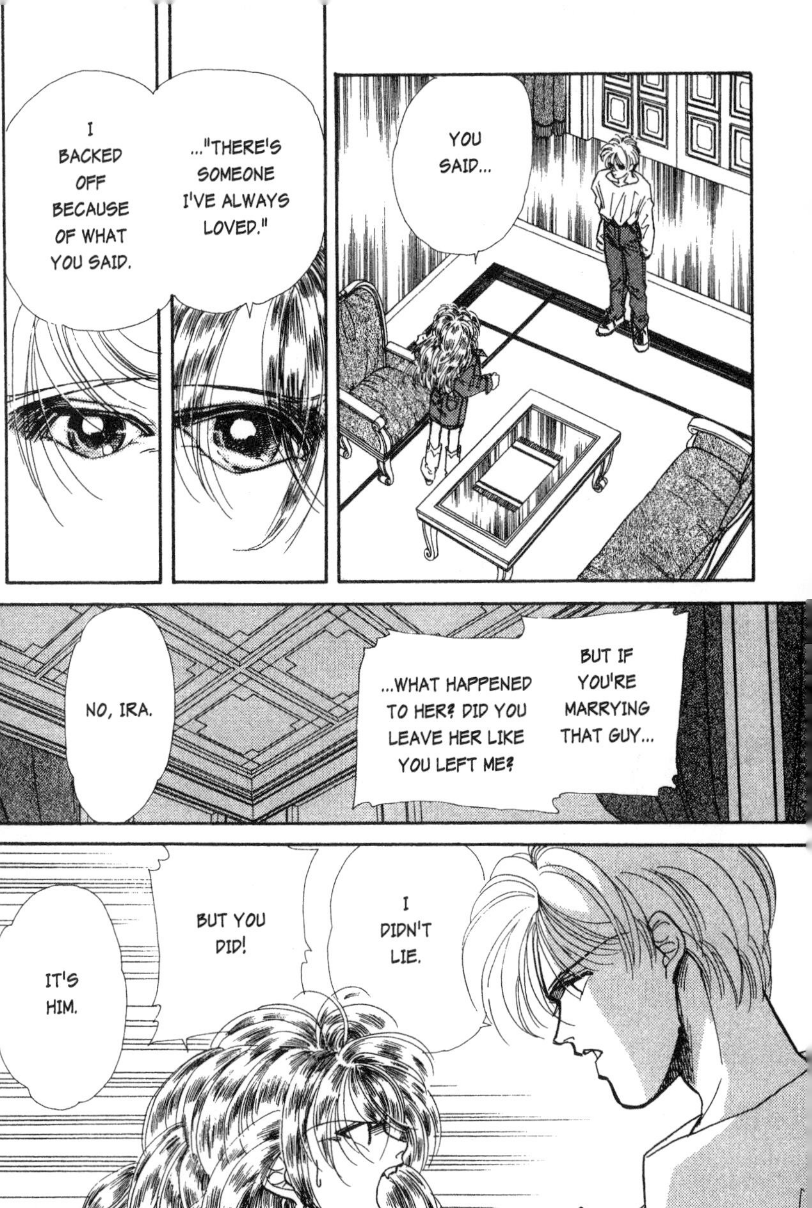
YOU SAID...
..."THERE'S SOMEONE I'VE ALWAYS LOVED."
I BACKED OFF BECAUSE OF WHAT YOU SAID.
BUT IF YOU'RE MARRYING THAT GUY...
...WHAT HAPPENED TO HER? DID YOU LEAVE HER LIKE YOU LEFT ME?
NO, IRA.
I DIDN'T LIE.
BUT YOU DID!
IT'S HIM.

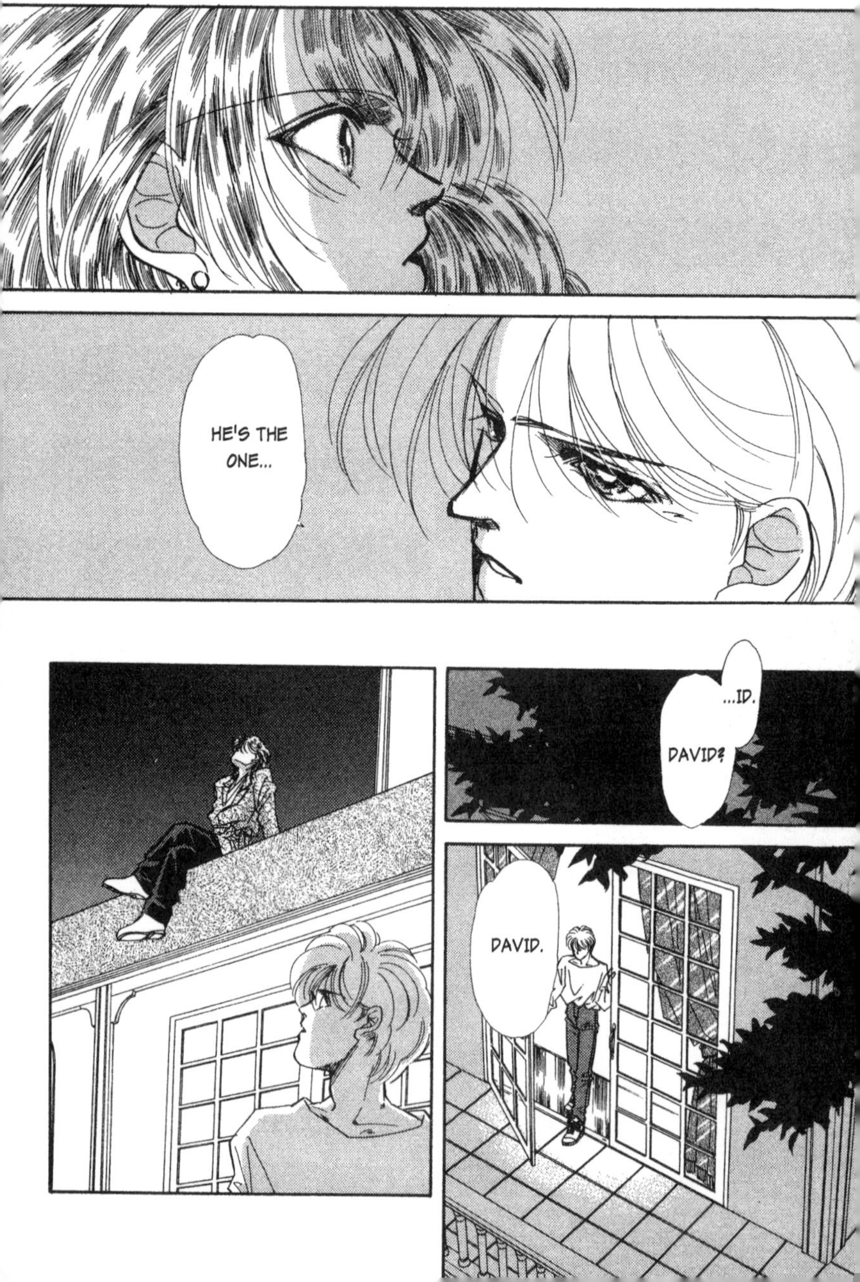
HE'S THE ONE...
...ID.
DAVID?
DAVID.

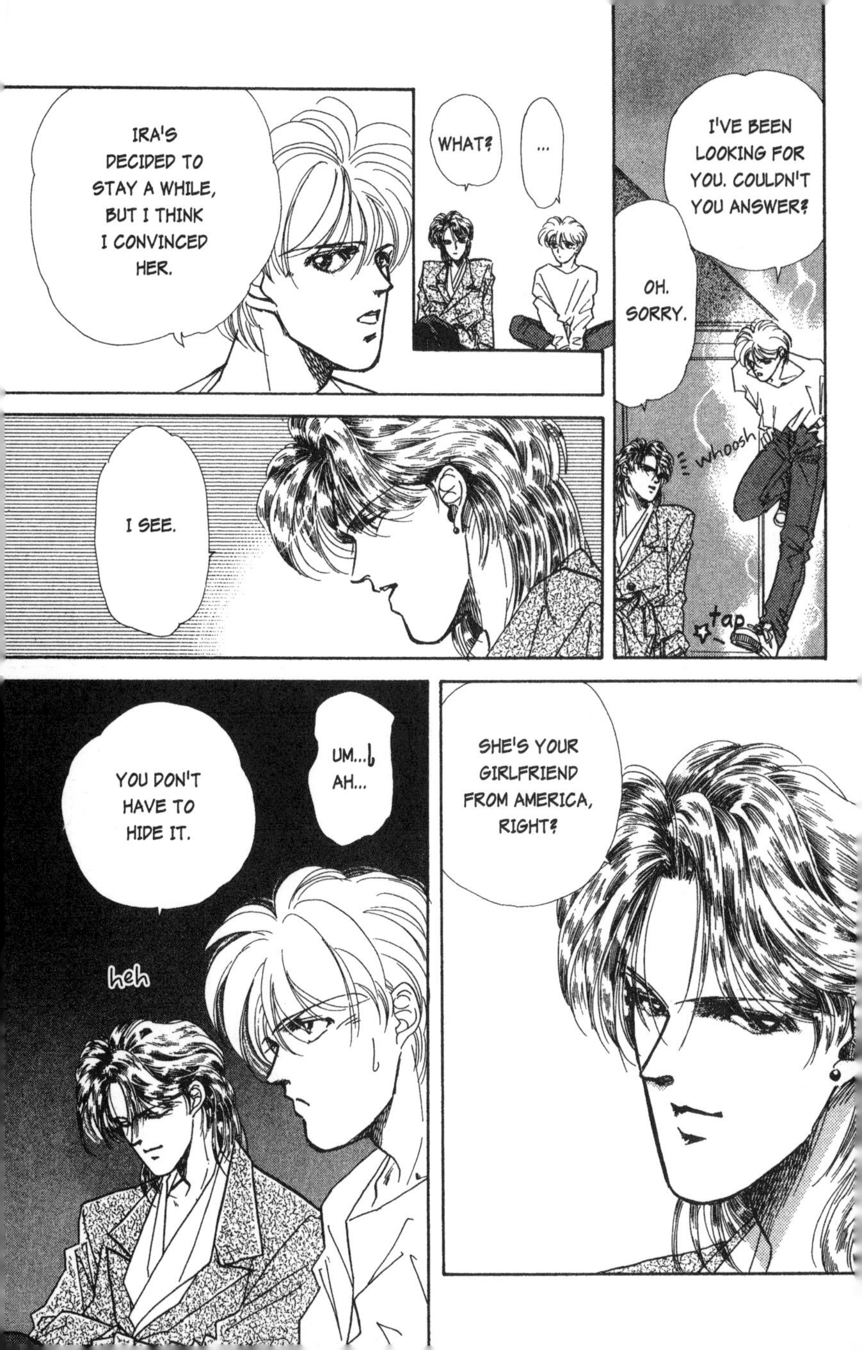
I'VE BEEN LOOKING FOR YOU. COULDN'T YOU ANSWER?
OH. SORRY.
whoosh
tap
WHAT?
...
IRA'S DECIDED TO STAY A WHILE, BUT I THINK I CONVINCED HER.
I SEE.
SHE'S YOUR GIRLFRIEND FROM AMERICA, RIGHT?
UM... AH...
YOU DON'T HAVE TO HIDE IT.
heh

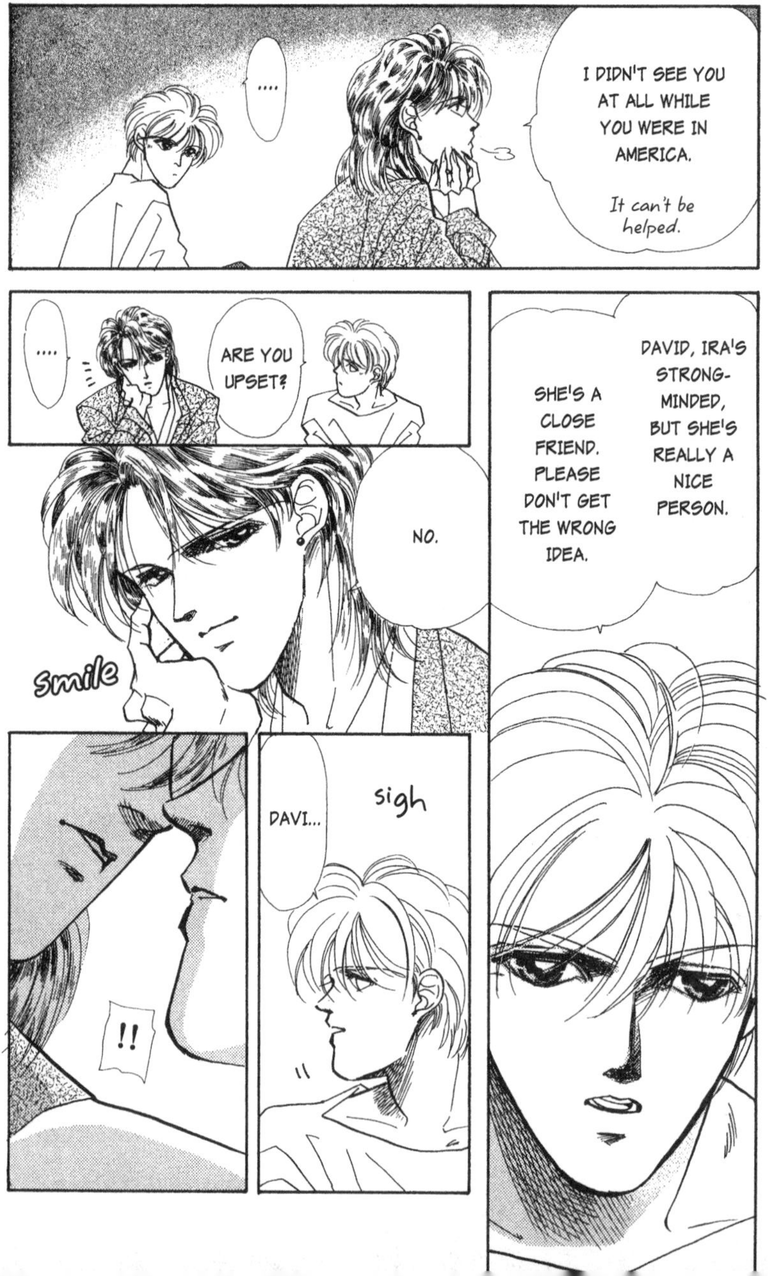
I DIDN'T SEE YOU AT ALL WHILE YOU WERE IN AMERICA.
It can't be helped.
....
DAVID, IRA'S STRONG-MINDED, BUT SHE'S REALLY A NICE PERSON.
SHE'S A CLOSE FRIEND. PLEASE DON'T GET THE WRONG IDEA.
ARE YOU UPSET?
....
NO.
Smile
DAVI...
sigh
!!

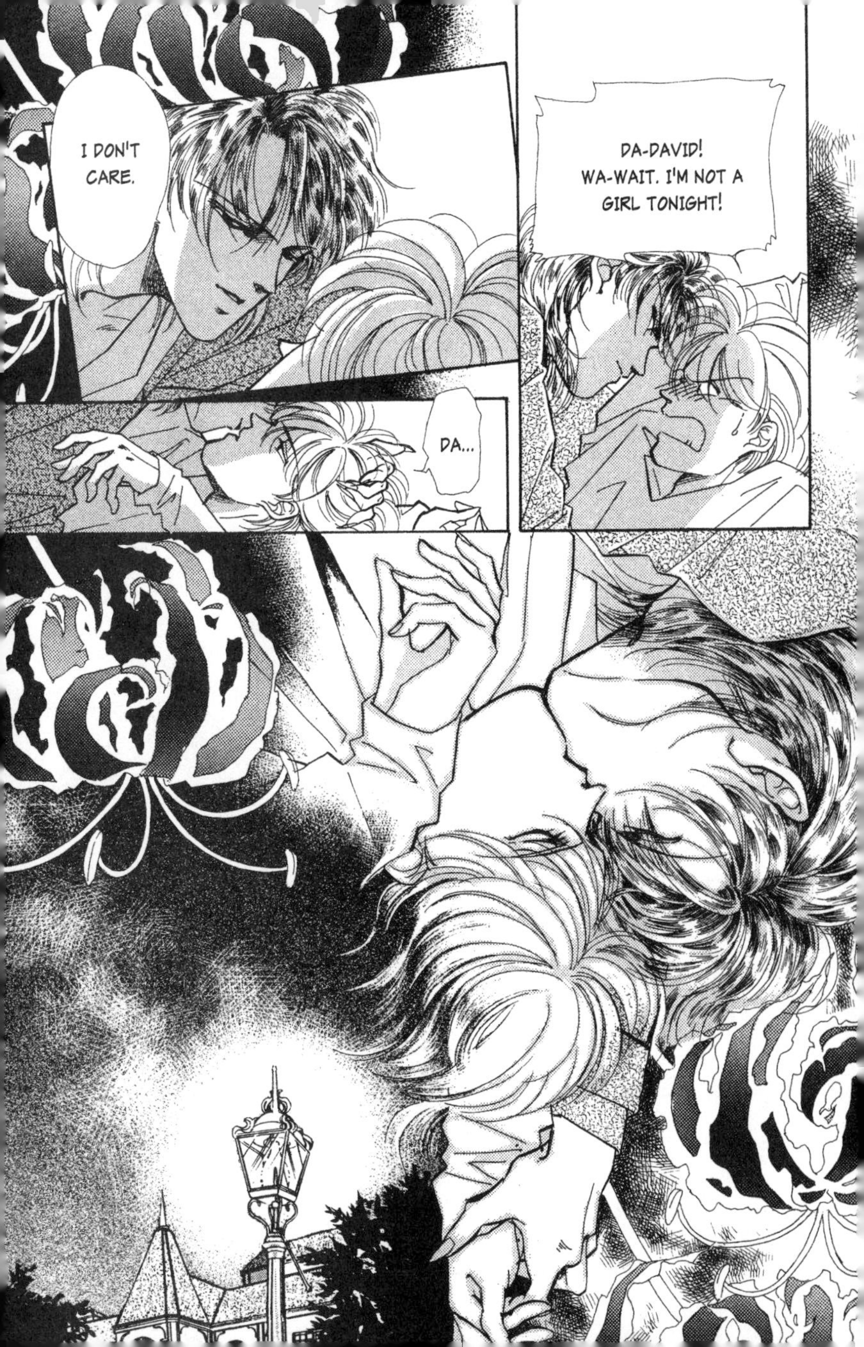
DA-DAVID! WA-WAIT. I'M NOT A GIRL TONIGHT!
I DON'T CARE.
DA...

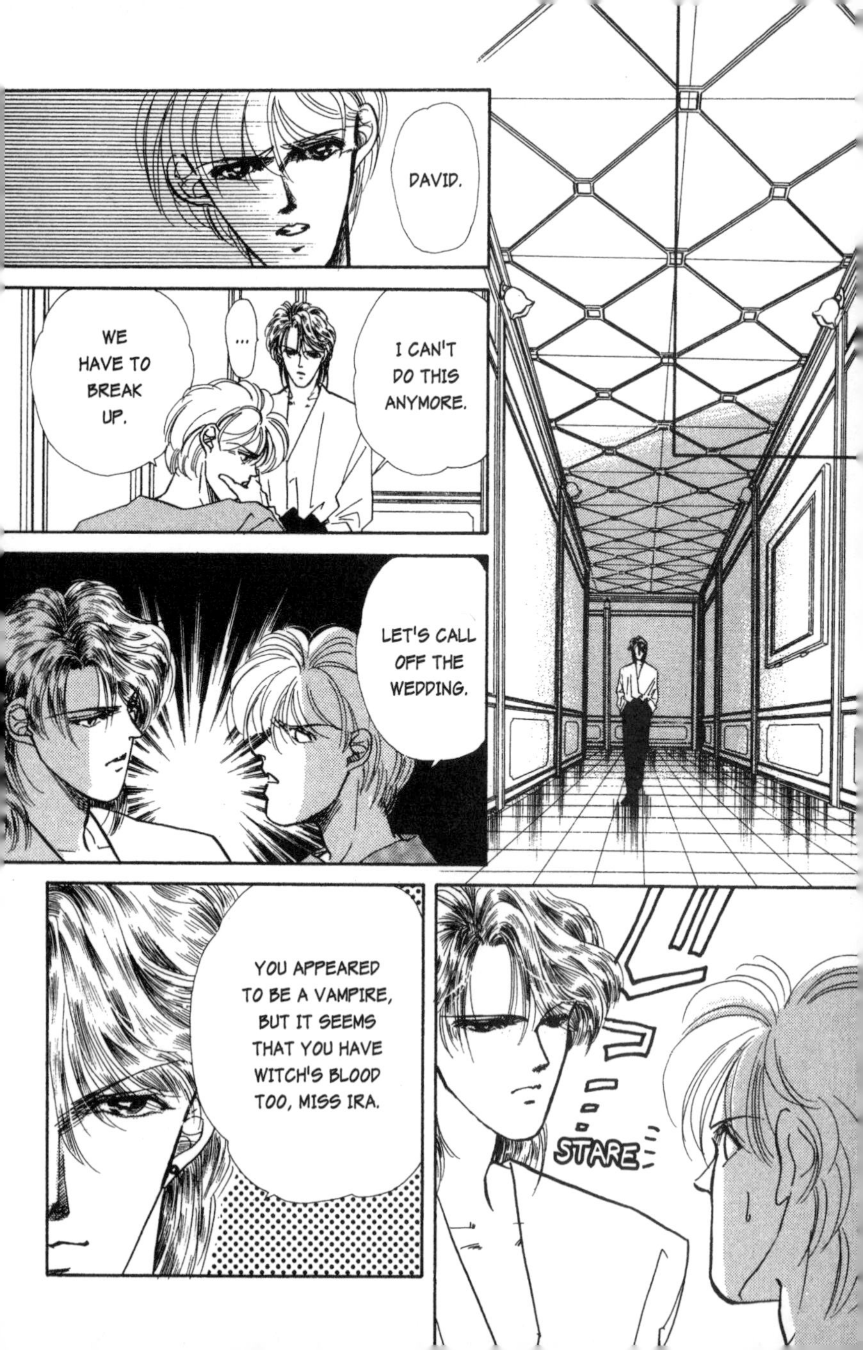
DAVID.
I CAN'T DO THIS ANYMORE.
...
WE HAVE TO BREAK UP.
LET'S CALL OFF THE WEDDING.
STARE
YOU APPEARED TO BE A VAMPIRE, BUT IT SEEMS THAT YOU HAVE WITCH'S BLOOD TOO, MISS IRA.

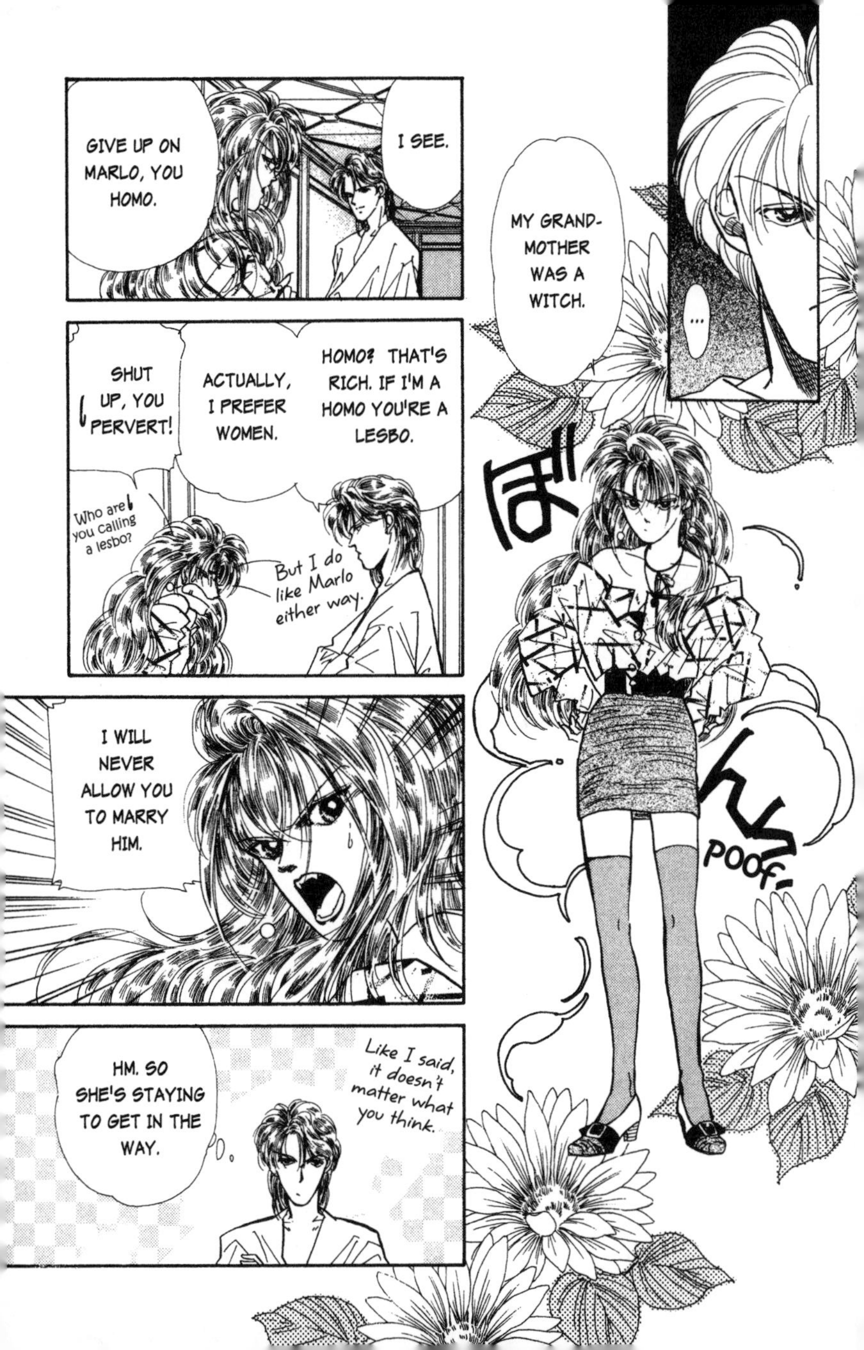
...
MY GRANDMOTHER WAS A WITCH.
ぽん
POOF
I SEE.
GIVE UP ON MARLO, YOU HOMO.
HOMO? THAT'S RICH. IF I'M A HOMO YOU'RE A LESBO.
ACTUALLY, I PREFER WOMEN.
SHUT UP, YOU PERVERT!
But I do like Marlo either way.
Who are you calling a lesbo?
I WILL NEVER ALLOW YOU TO MARRY HIM.
Like I said, it doesn't matter what you think.
HM. SO SHE'S STAYING TO GET IN THE WAY.

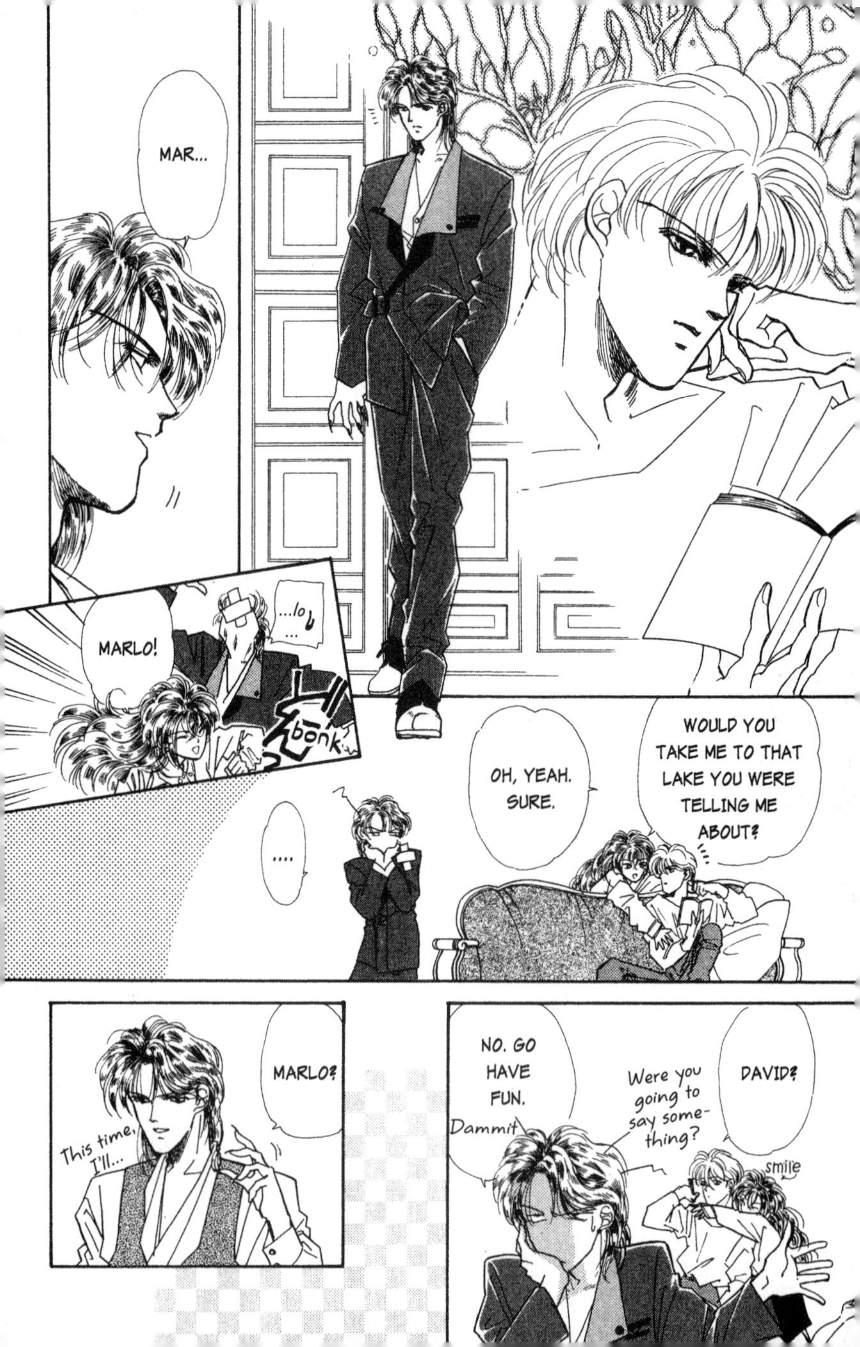
MAR...
...lo
...
MARLO!
bonk
WOULD YOU TAKE ME TO THAT LAKE YOU WERE TELLING ME ABOUT?
OH, YEAH. SURE.
....
DAVID?
Were you going to say some-thing?
NO. GO HAVE FUN.
Dammit
smile
MARLO?
This time, I'll...

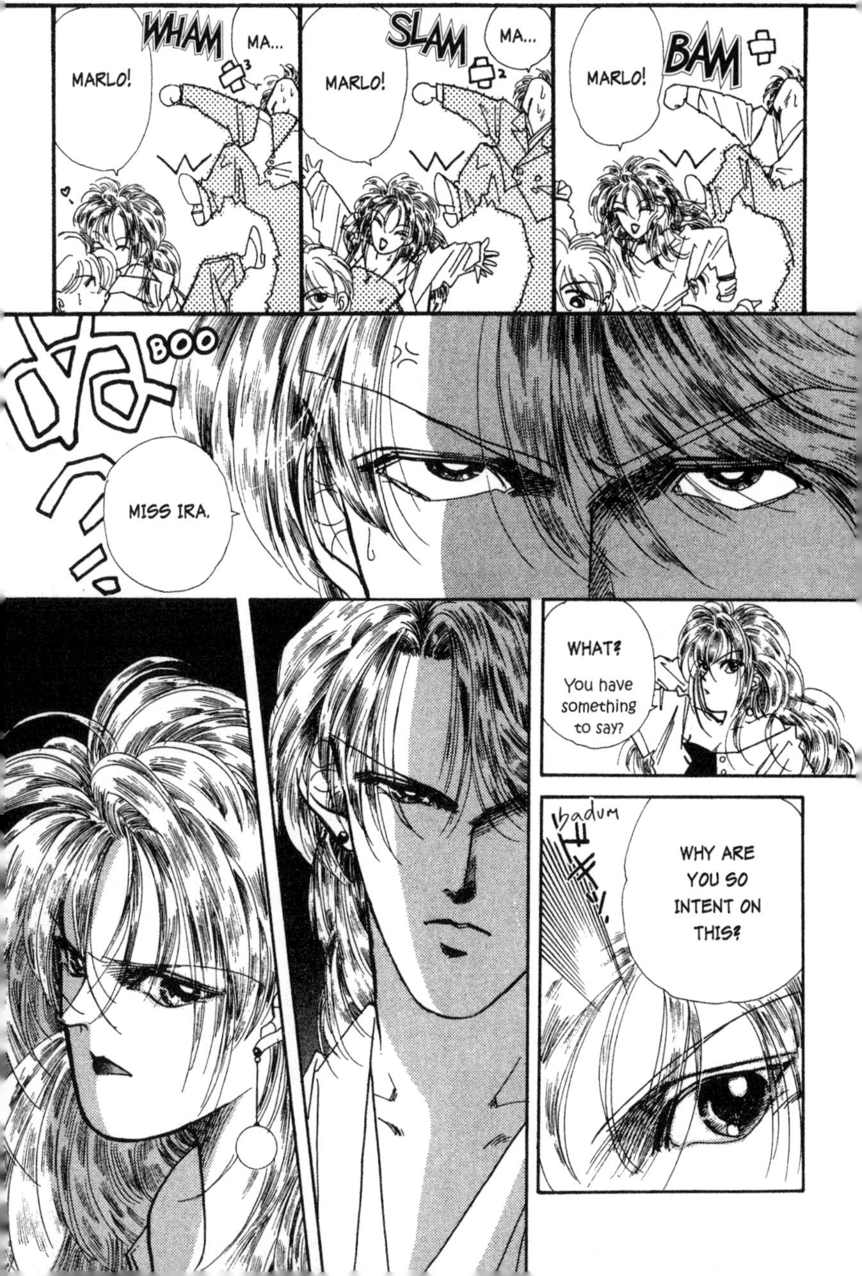
BAM
MARLO!
MA...
SLAM
MARLO!
MA...
WHAM
MARLO!
BOO
MISS IRA.
WHAT? You have something to say?
badum
WHY ARE YOU SO INTENT ON THIS?

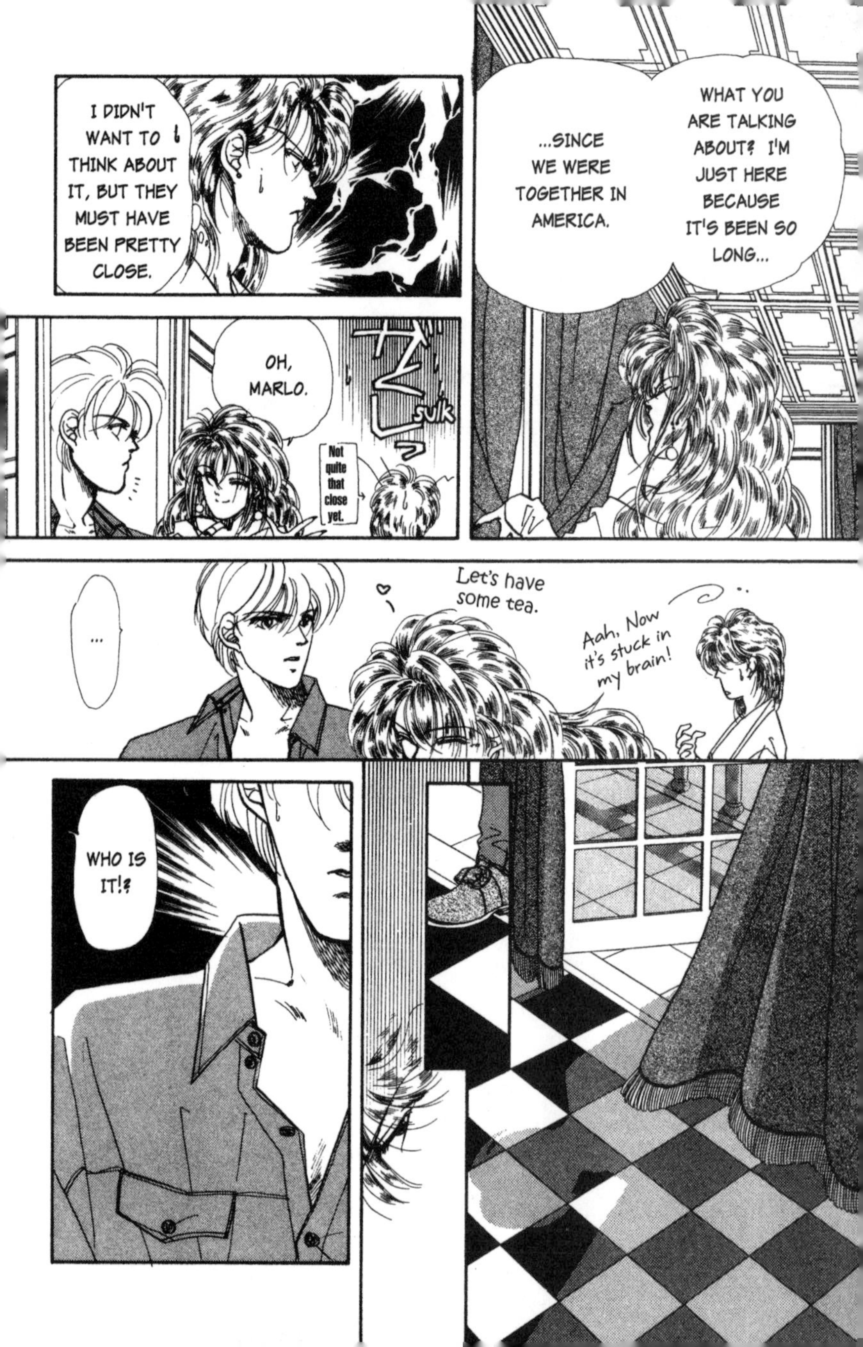
WHAT YOU ARE TALKING ABOUT? I'M JUST HERE BECAUSE IT'S BEEN SO LONG...
...SINCE WE WERE TOGETHER IN AMERICA.
I DIDN'T WANT TO THINK ABOUT IT, BUT THEY MUST HAVE BEEN PRETTY CLOSE.
OH, MARLO.
sulk
Not quite that close yet.
Aah, Now it's stuck in my brain!
Let's have some tea.
...
WHO IS IT!?

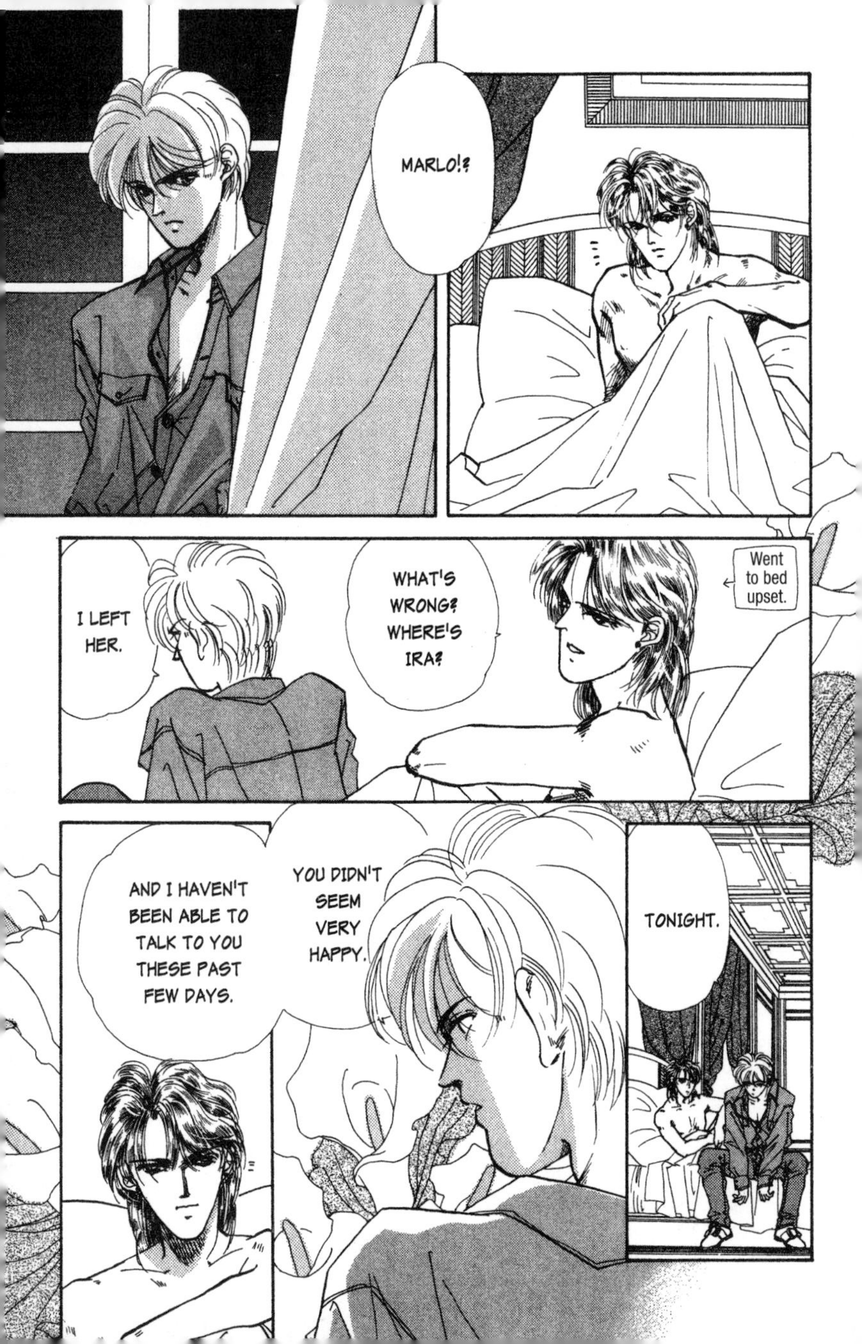
MARLO!?
Went to bed upset.
WHAT'S WRONG? WHERE'S IRA?
I LEFT HER.
TONIGHT.
YOU DIDN'T SEEM VERY HAPPY.
AND I HAVEN'T BEEN ABLE TO TALK TO YOU THESE PAST FEW DAYS.

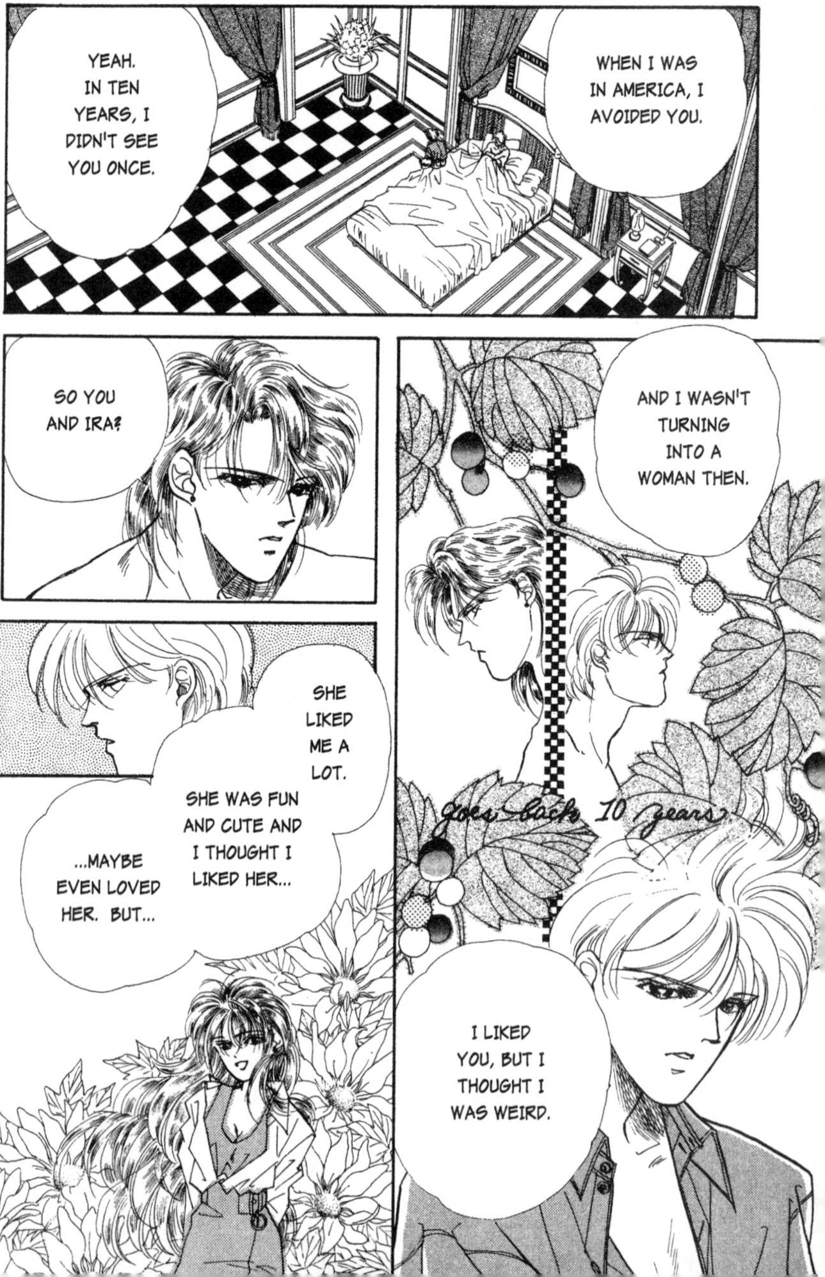
WHEN I WAS IN AMERICA, I AVOIDED YOU.
YEAH. IN TEN YEARS, I DIDN'T SEE YOU ONCE.
AND I WASN'T TURNING INTO A WOMAN THEN.
goes back 10 years
I LIKED YOU, BUT I THOUGHT I WAS WEIRD.
SO YOU AND IRA?
SHE LIKED ME A LOT.
SHE WAS FUN AND CUTE AND I THOUGHT I LIKED HER...
...MAYBE EVEN LOVED HER. BUT...

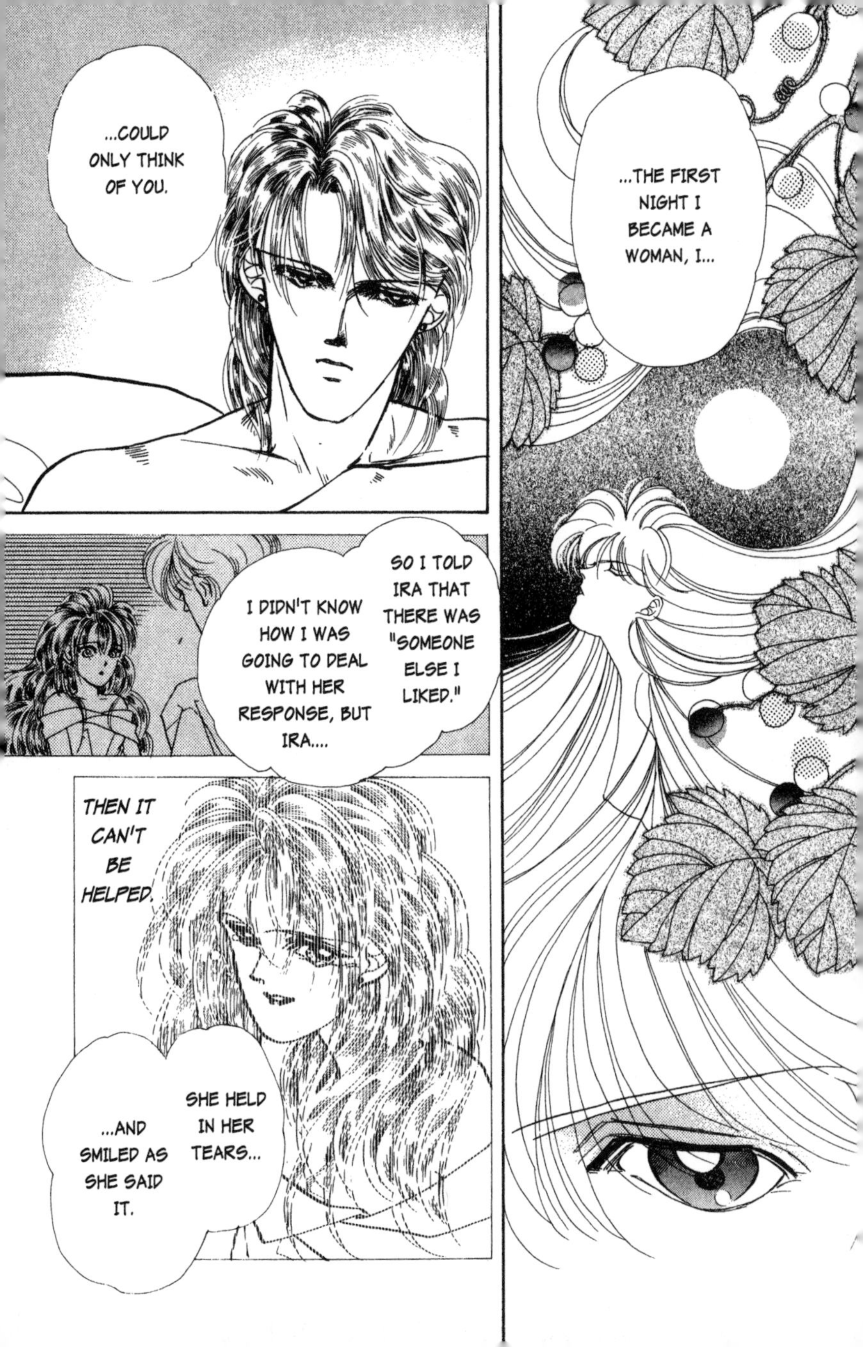
...THE FIRST NIGHT I BECAME A WOMAN, I...
...COULD ONLY THINK OF YOU.
SO I TOLD IRA THAT THERE WAS "SOMEONE ELSE I LIKED."
I DIDN'T KNOW HOW I WAS GOING TO DEAL WITH HER RESPONSE, BUT IRA....
THEN IT CAN'T BE HELPED.
SHE HELD IN HER TEARS...
...AND SMILED AS SHE SAID IT.

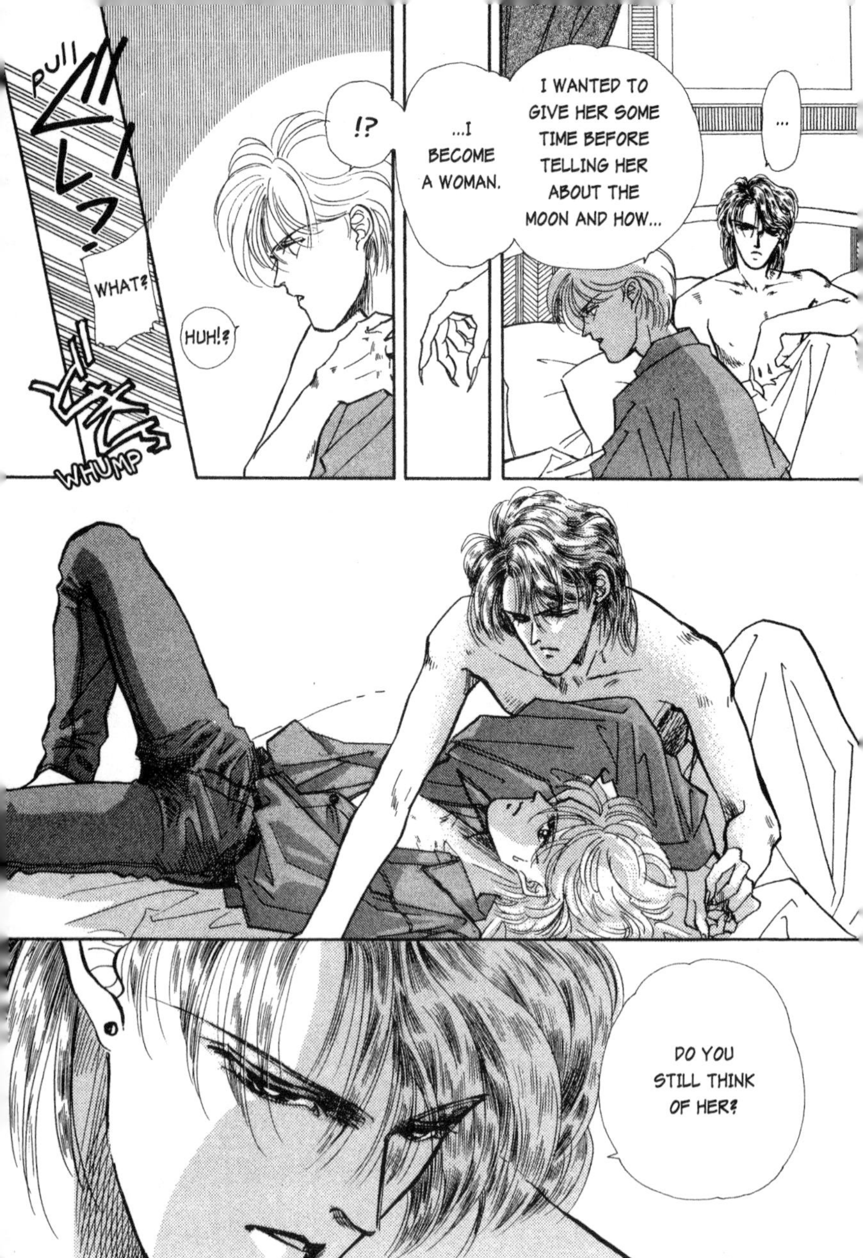
...
I WANTED TO GIVE HER SOME TIME BEFORE TELLING HER ABOUT THE MOON AND HOW...
...I BECOME A WOMAN.
!?
pull
WHAT?
HUH!?
WHUMP
DO YOU STILL THINK OF HER?

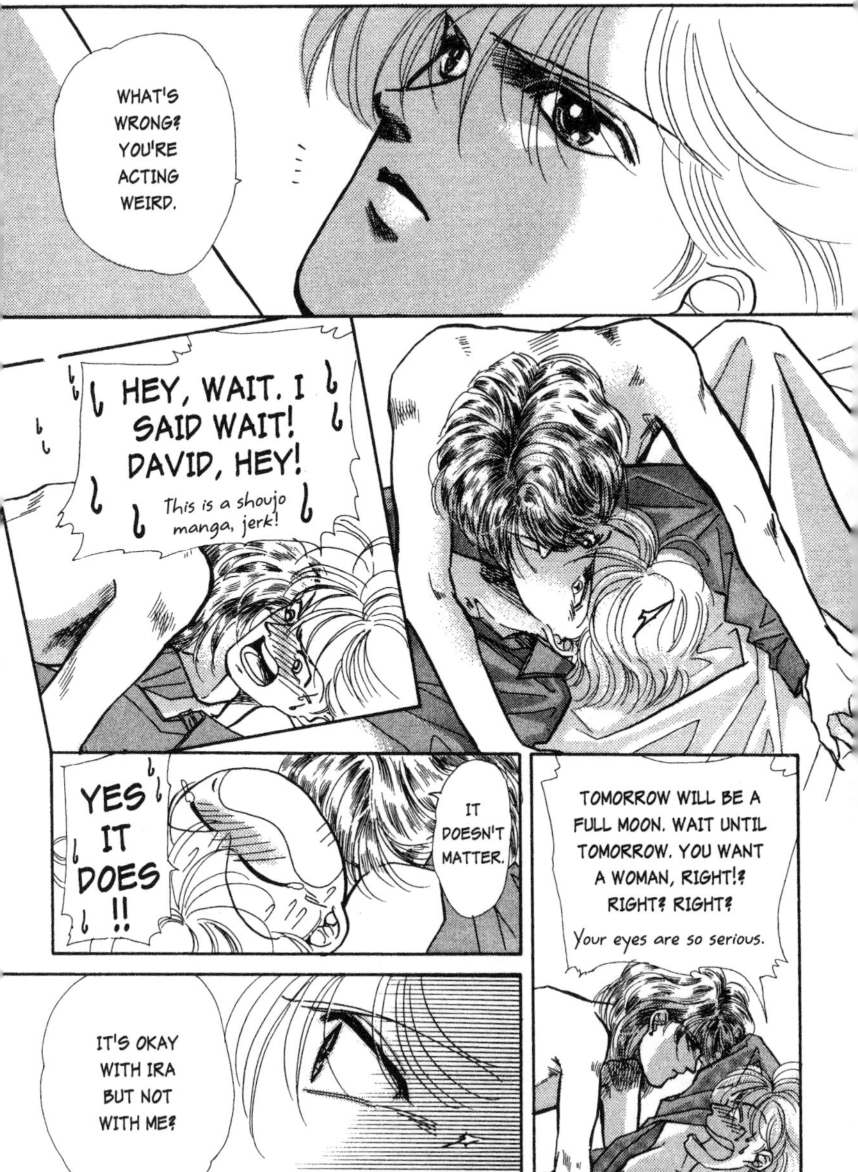
WHAT'S WRONG? YOU'RE ACTING WEIRD.
HEY, WAIT. I SAID WAIT! DAVID, HEY!
This is a shoujo manga, jerk!
TOMORROW WILL BE A FULL MOON. WAIT UNTIL TOMORROW. YOU WANT A WOMAN, RIGHT!? RIGHT? RIGHT?
Your eyes are so serious.
IT DOESN'T MATTER.
YES IT DOES!!
IT'S OKAY WITH IRA BUT NOT WITH ME?

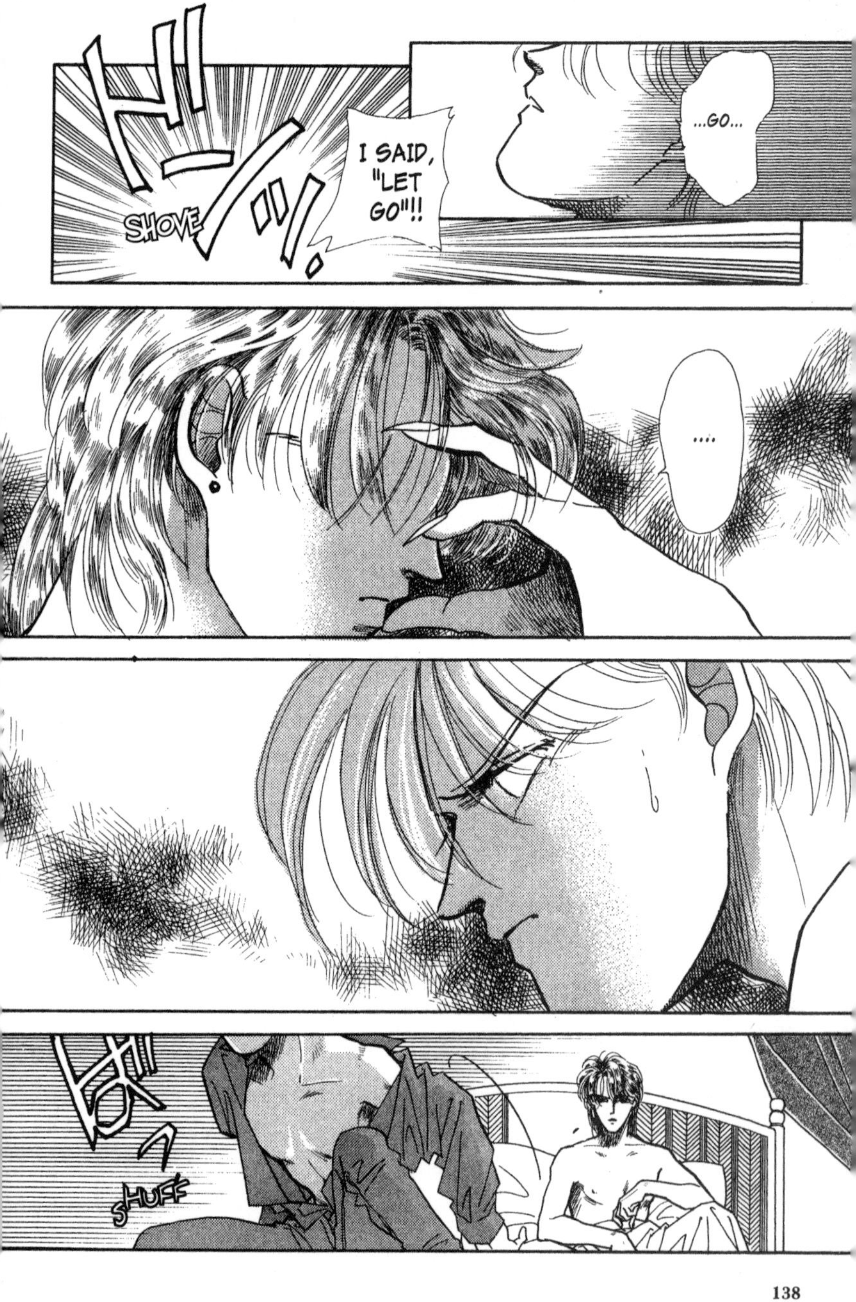
...GO...
I SAID, "LET GO"!!
SHOVE
....
SHUFF

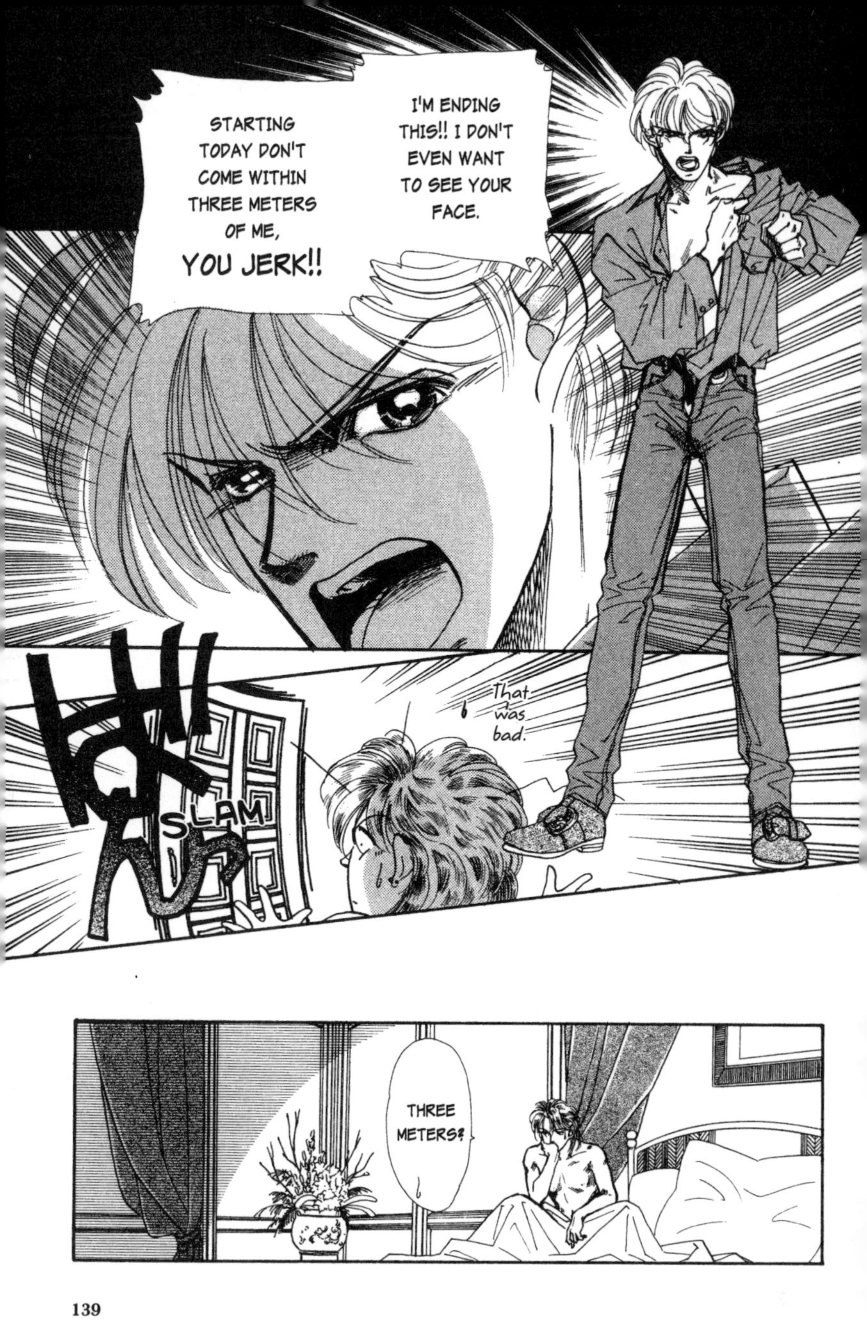
I'M ENDING THIS!! I DON'T EVEN WANT TO SEE YOUR FACE.
STARTING TODAY DON'T COME WITHIN THREE METERS OF ME, YOU JERK!!
That was bad.
SLAM
THREE METERS?

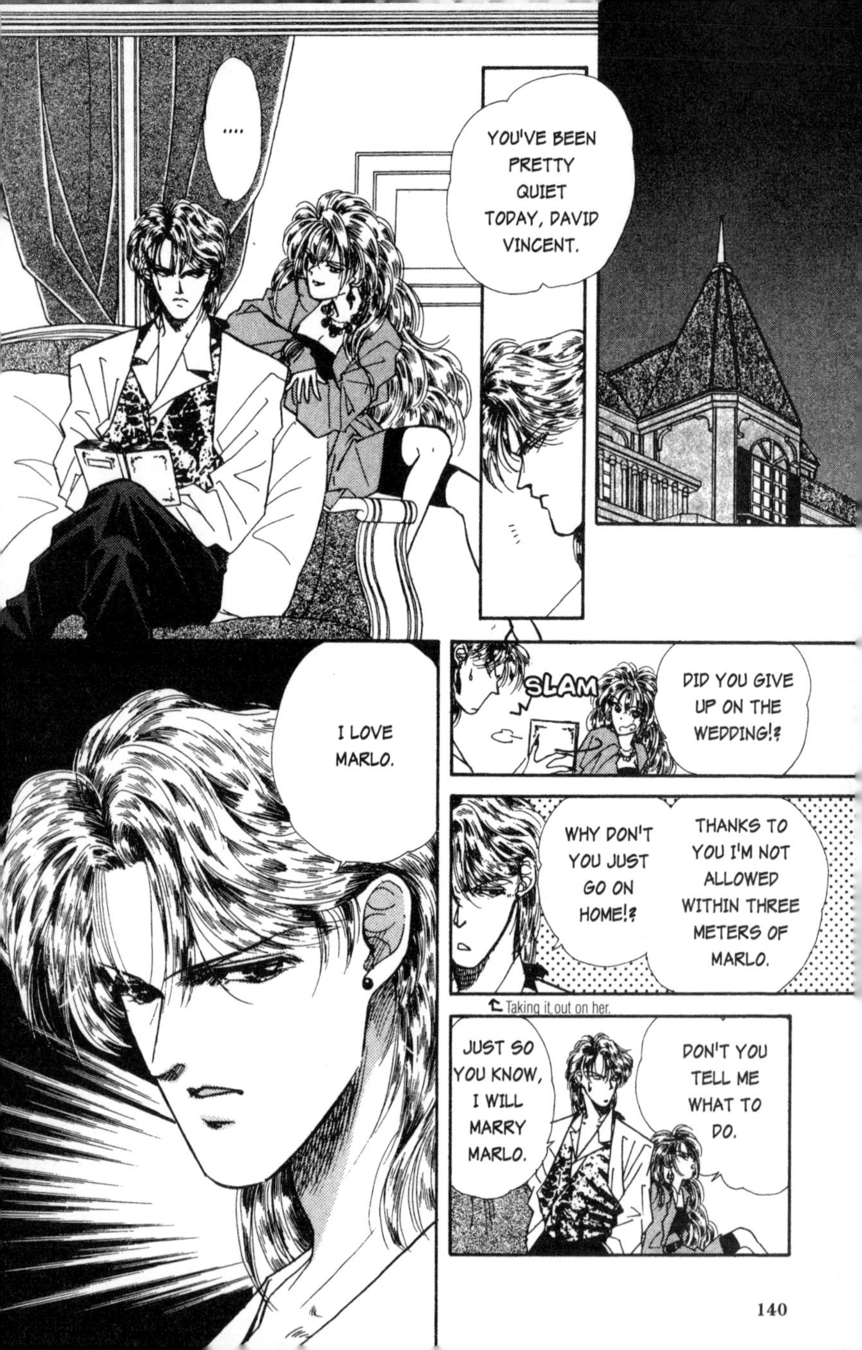
YOU'VE BEEN PRETTY QUIET TODAY, DAVID VINCENT.
....
DID YOU GIVE UP ON THE WEDDING!?
SLAM
THANKS TO YOU I'M NOT ALLOWED WITHIN THREE METERS OF MARLO.
WHY DON'T YOU JUST GO ON HOME!?
Taking it out on her.
DON'T YOU TELL ME WHAT TO DO.
JUST SO YOU KNOW, I WILL MARRY MARLO.
I LOVE MARLO.

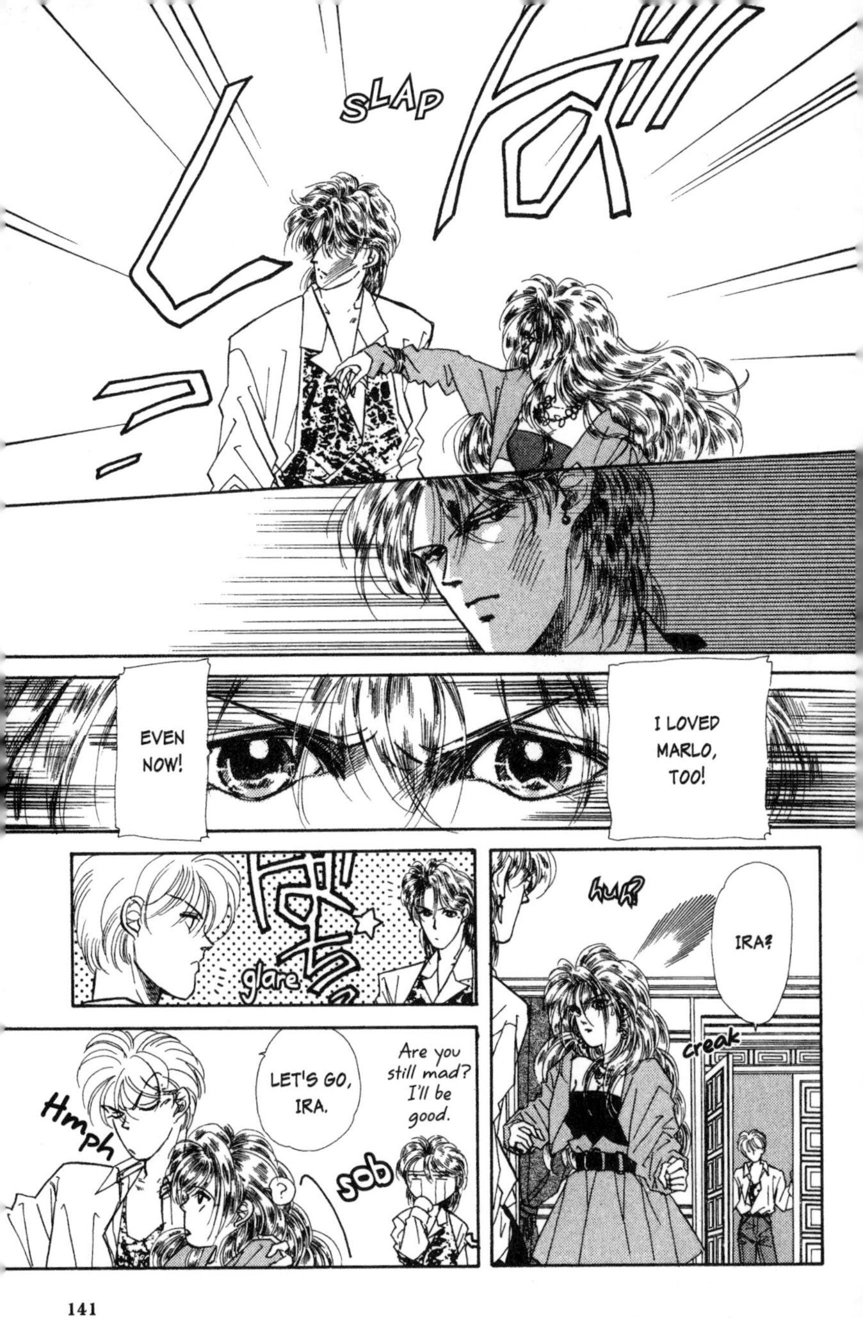
SLAP
I LOVED MARLO, TOO!
EVEN NOW!
huh?
IRA?
creak
glare
Are you still mad? I'll be good.
LET'S GO, IRA.
Hmph
sob

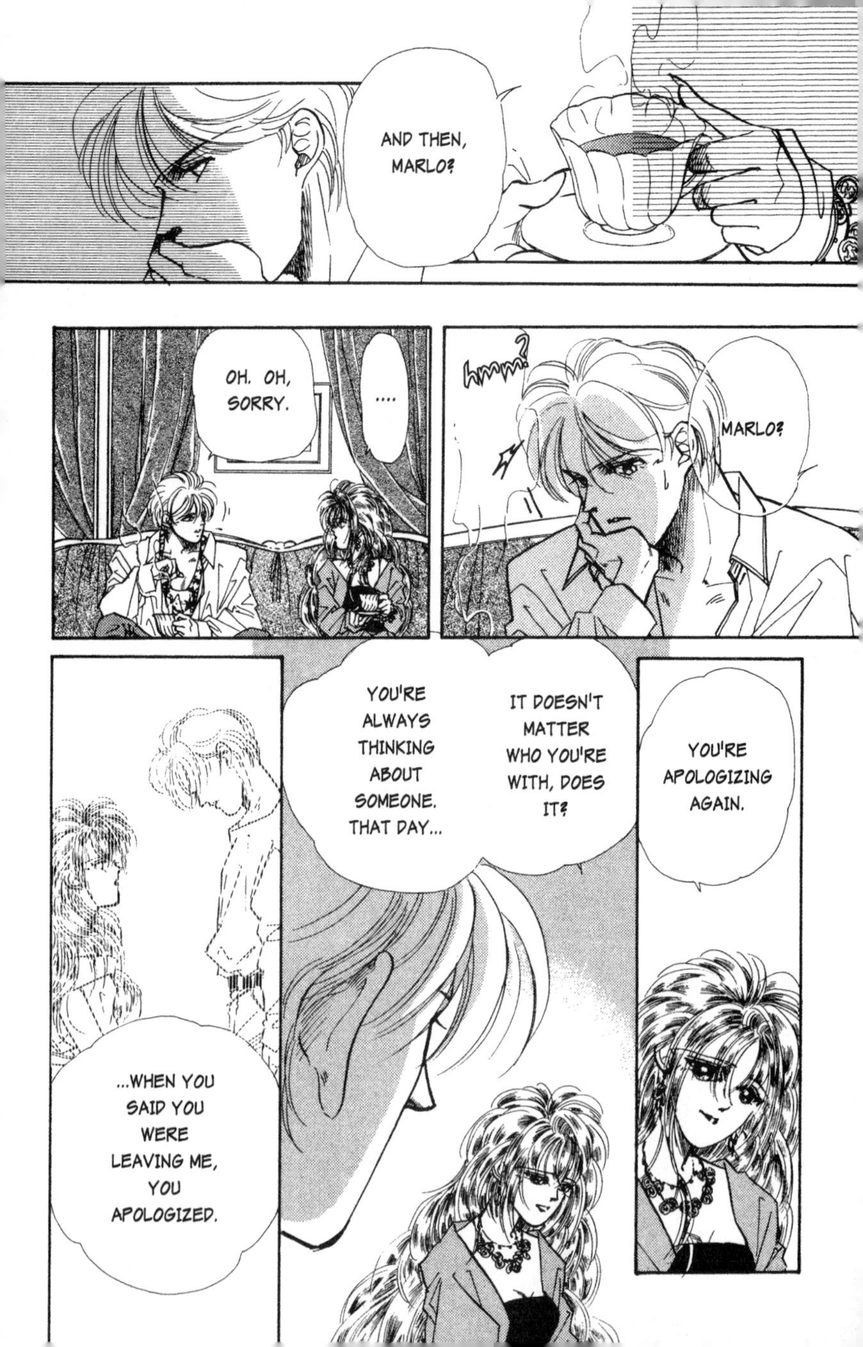
AND THEN, MARLO?
hmm?
MARLO?
....
OH. OH, SORRY.
YOU'RE APOLOGIZING AGAIN.
IT DOESN'T MATTER WHO YOU'RE WITH, DOES IT?
YOU'RE ALWAYS THINKING ABOUT SOMEONE. THAT DAY...
...WHEN YOU SAID YOU WERE LEAVING ME, YOU APOLOGIZED.

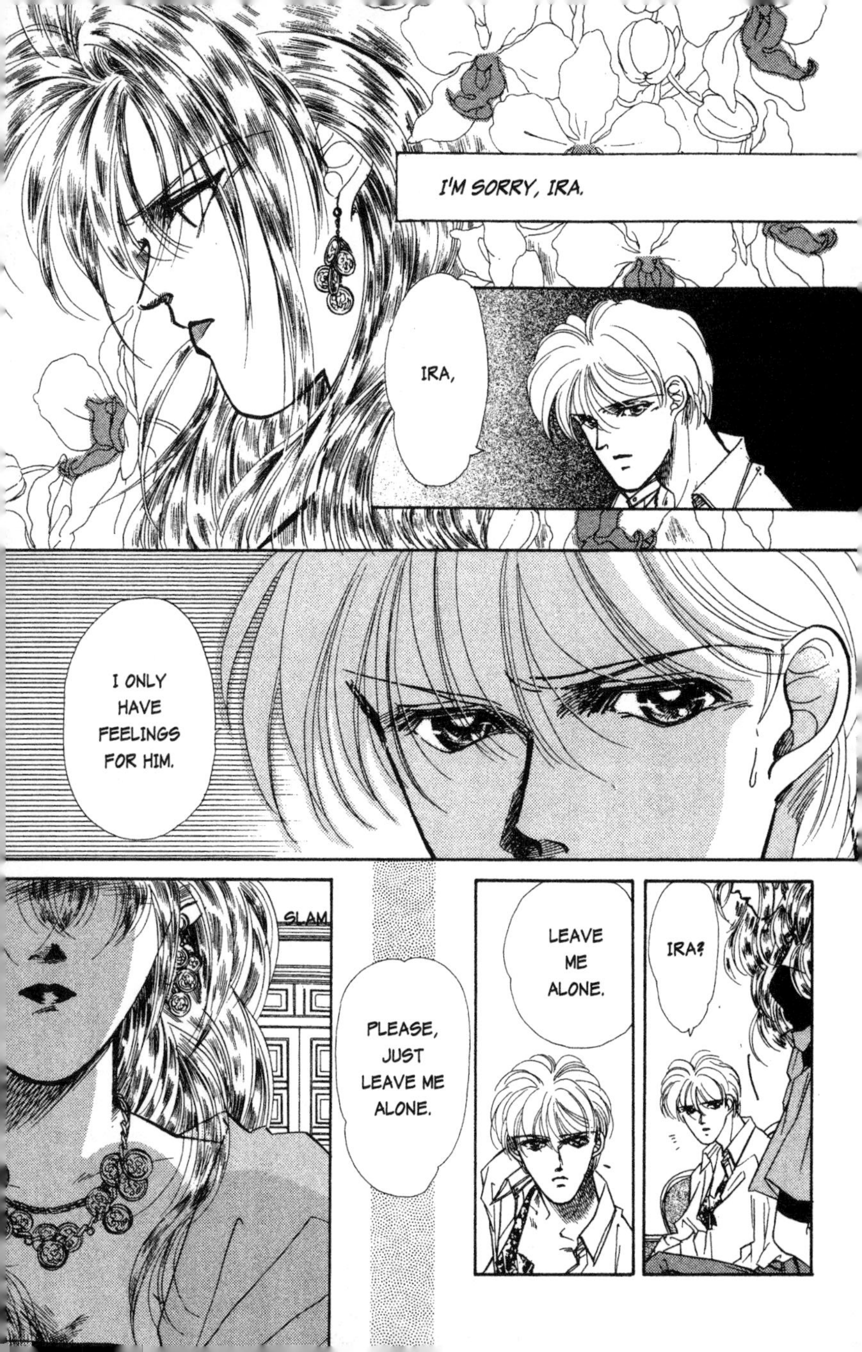
I'M SORRY, IRA.
IRA,
I ONLY HAVE FEELINGS FOR HIM.
IRA?
LEAVE ME ALONE.
PLEASE, JUST LEAVE ME ALONE.
SLAM

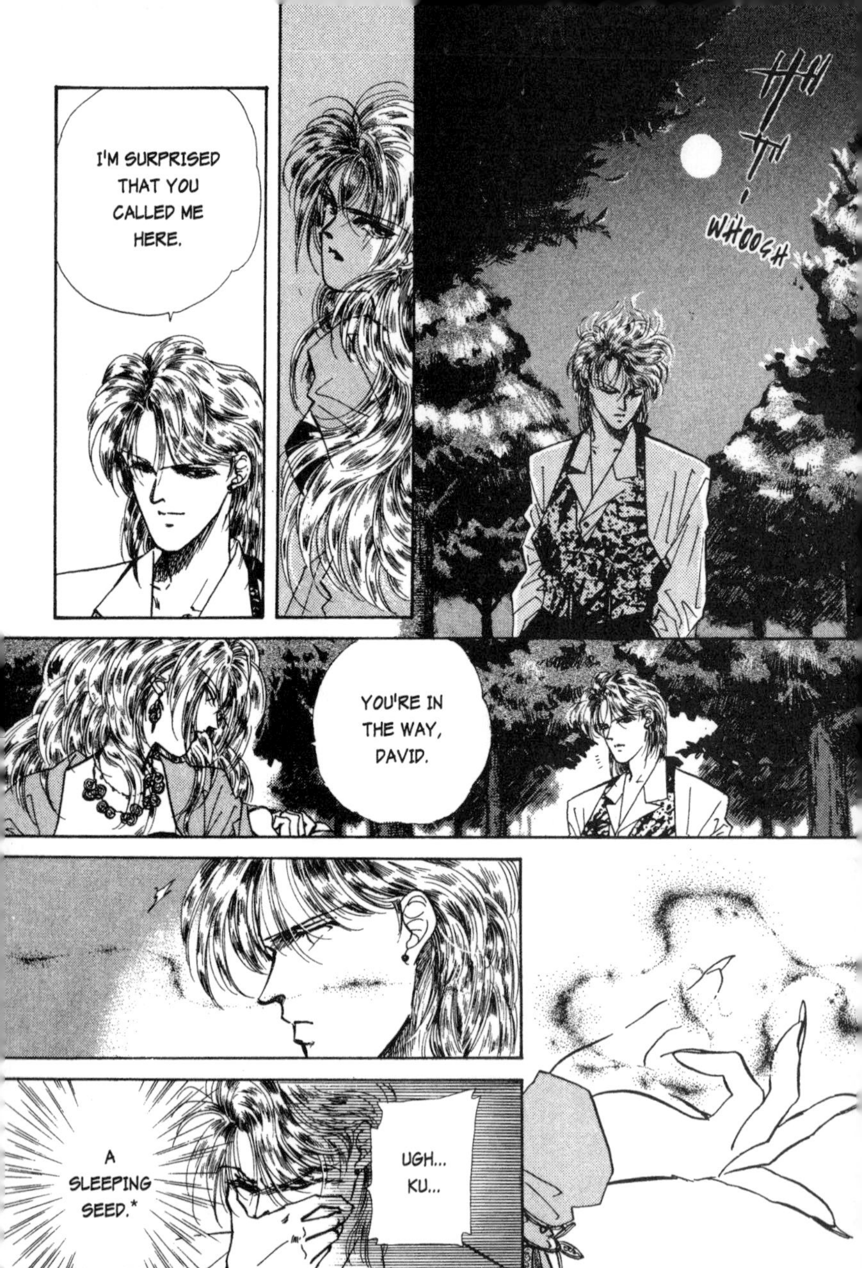
WHOOSH
I'M SURPRISED THAT YOU CALLED ME HERE.
YOU'RE IN THE WAY, DAVID.
UGH... KU...
A SLEEPING SEED.*

*Meaning sleeping potion

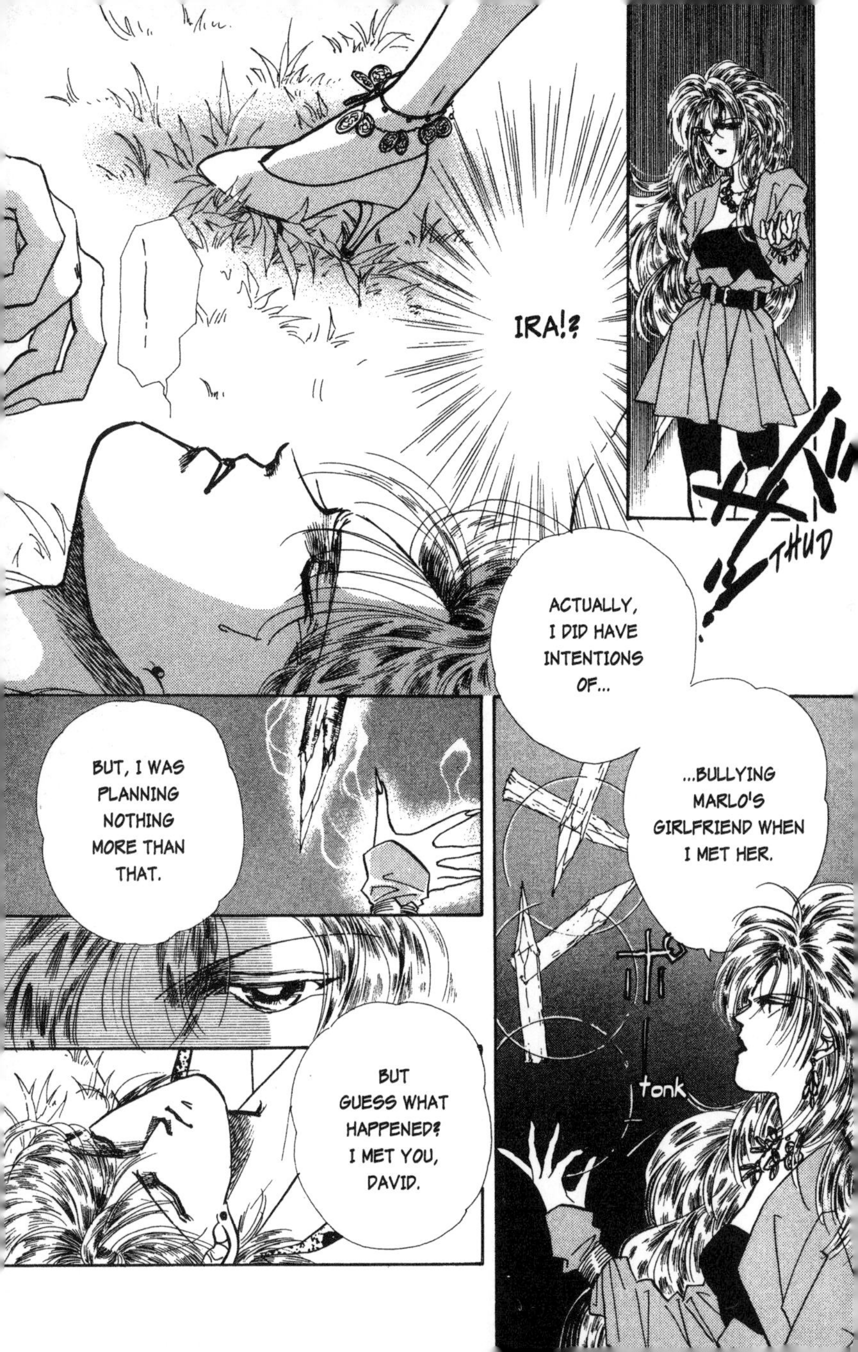
THUD
IRA!?
ACTUALLY, I DID HAVE INTENTIONS OF...
...BULLYING MARLO'S GIRLFRIEND WHEN I MET HER.
tonk
BUT, I WAS PLANNING NOTHING MORE THAN THAT.
BUT GUESS WHAT HAPPENED? I MET YOU, DAVID.

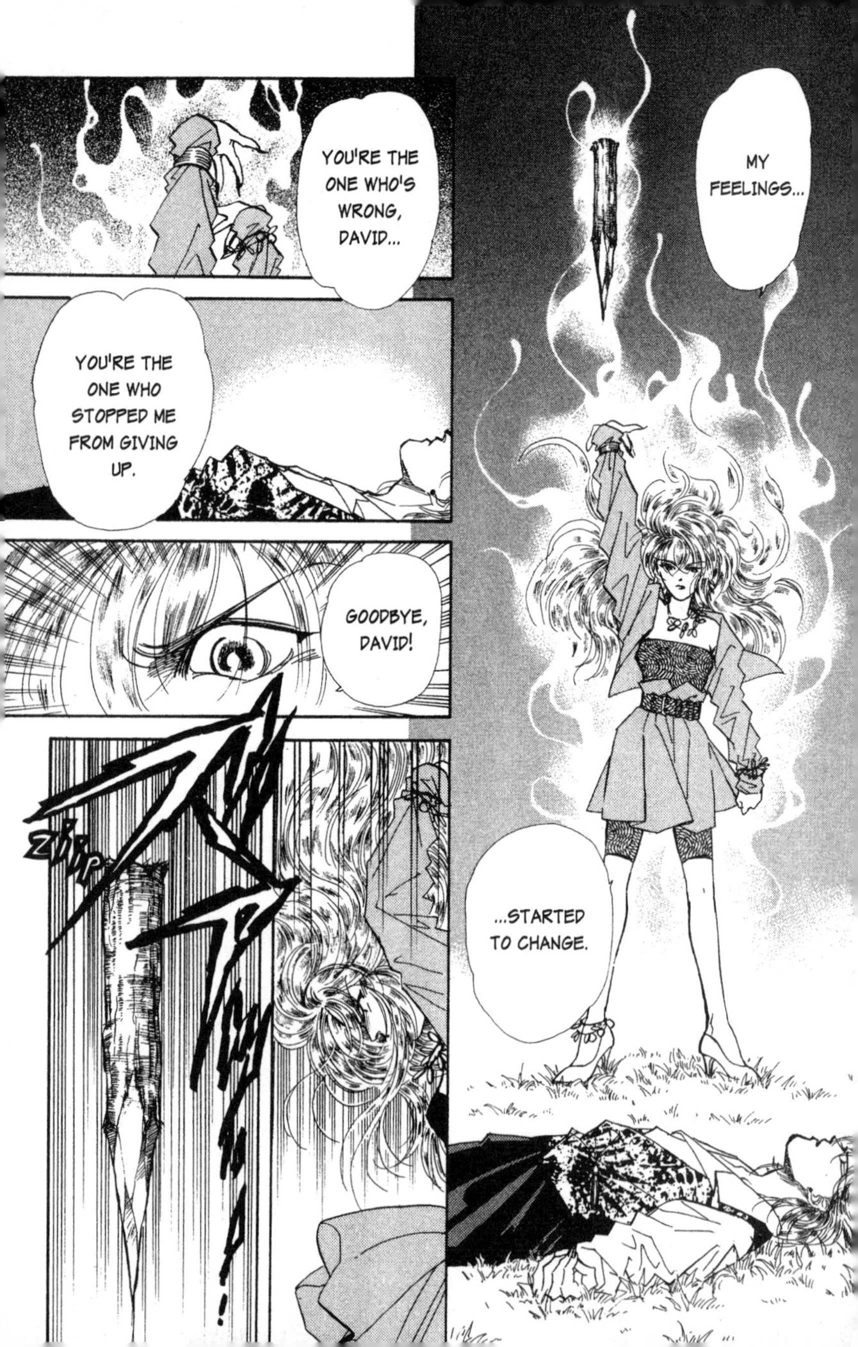
MY FEELINGS...
...STARTED TO CHANGE.
YOU'RE THE ONE WHO'S WRONG, DAVID...
YOU'RE THE ONE WHO STOPPED ME FROM GIVING UP.
GOODBYE, DAVID!

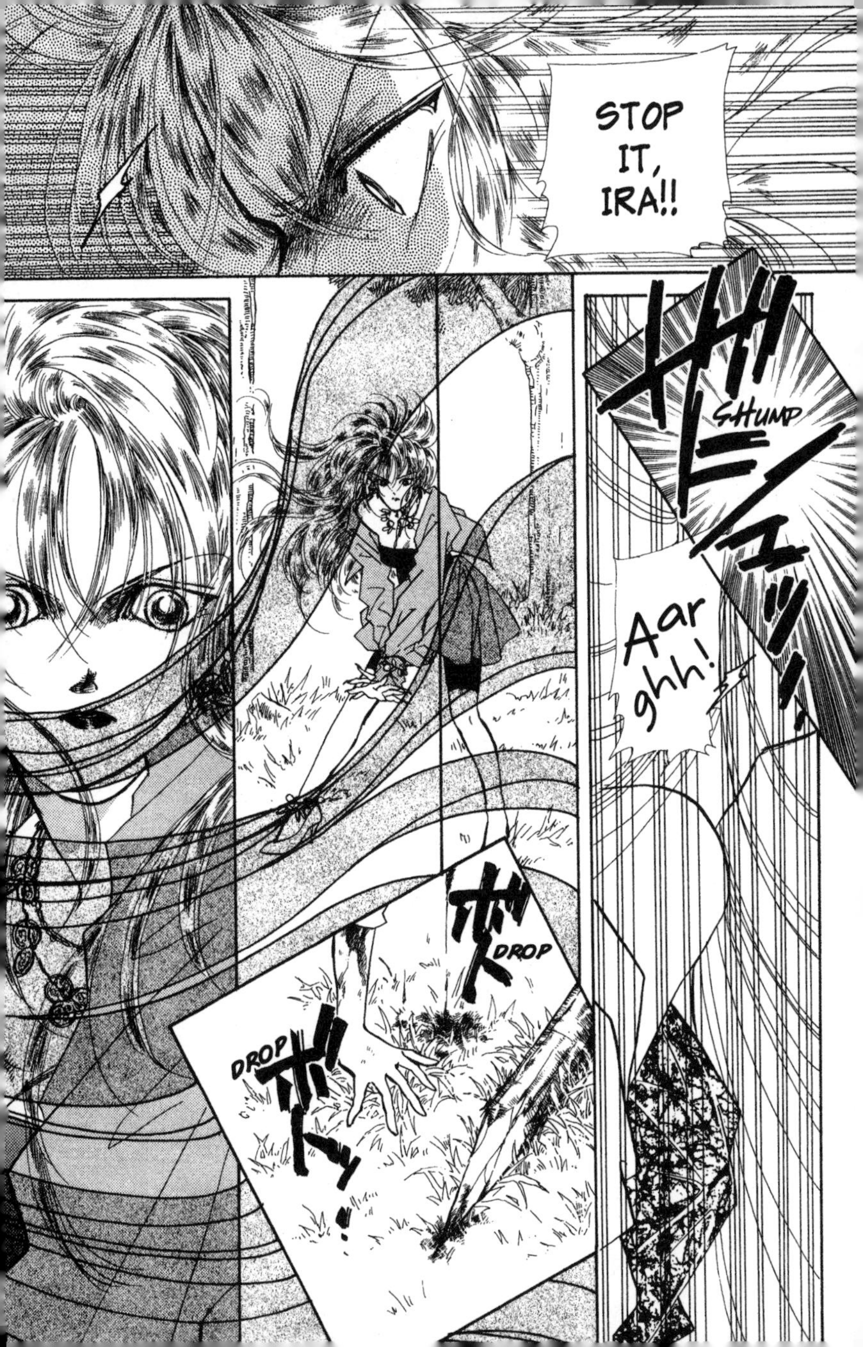
STOP IT, IRA!!
SHUMP
Aarghh!
DROP
DROP

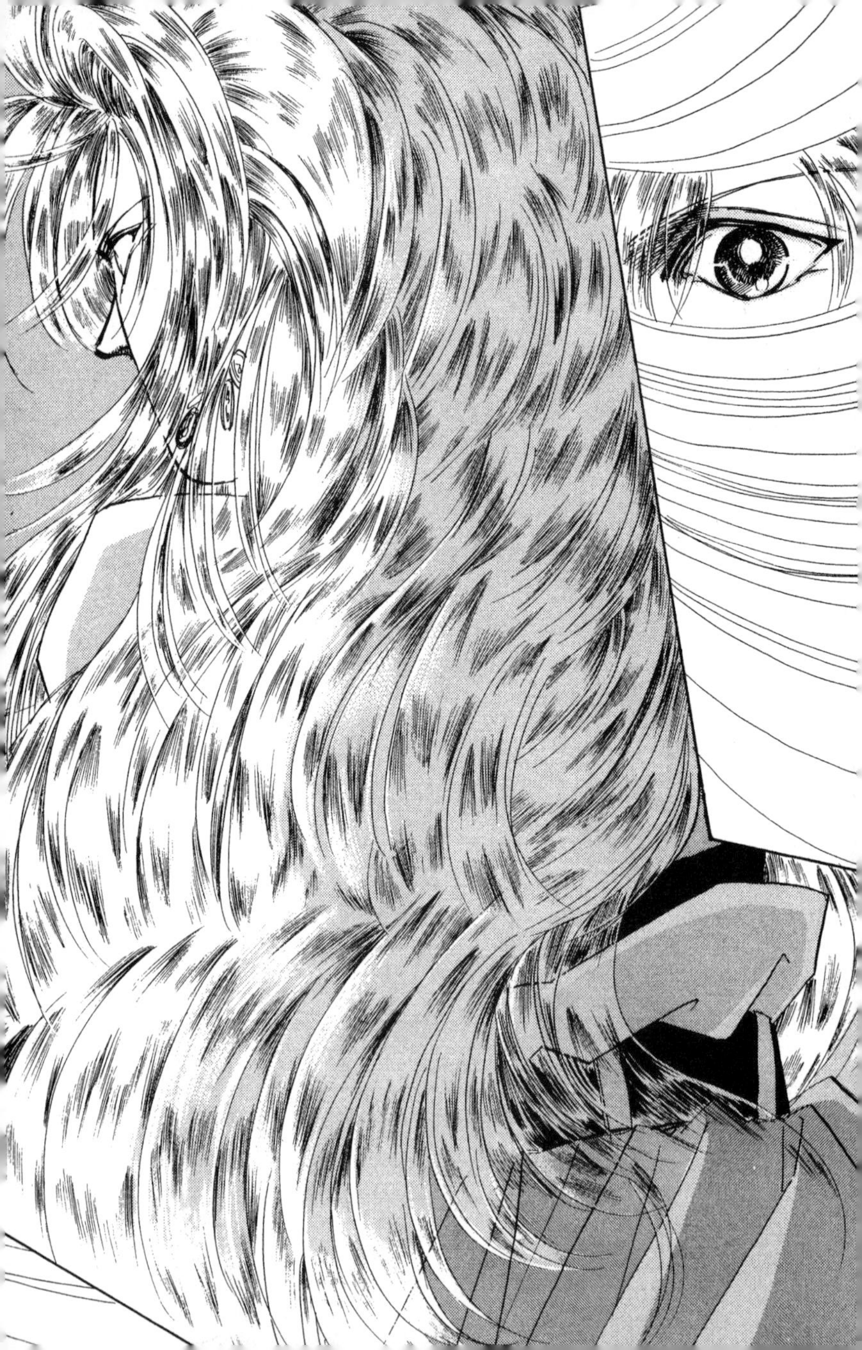

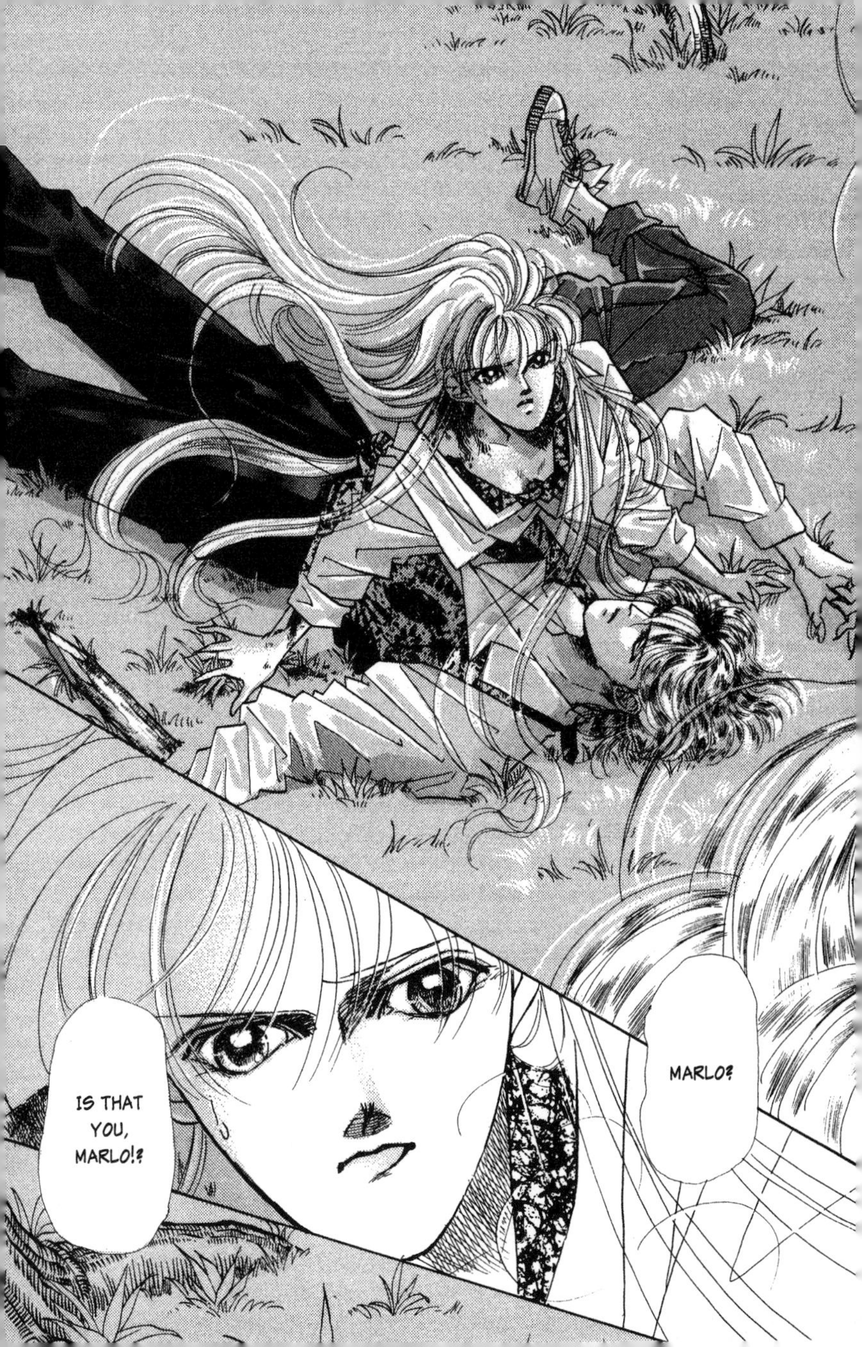
MARLO?
IS THAT YOU, MARLO!?

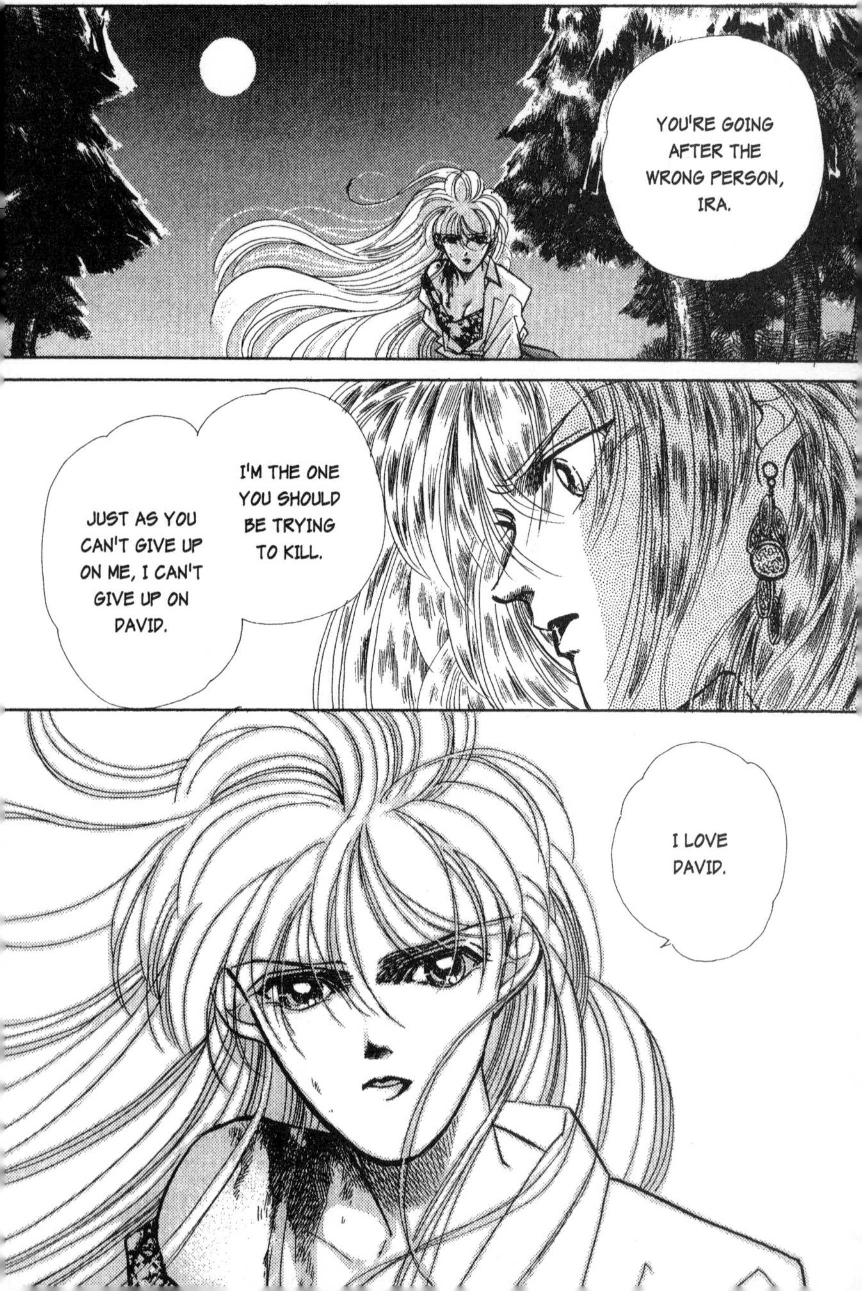
YOU'RE GOING AFTER THE WRONG PERSON, IRA.
I'M THE ONE YOU SHOULD BE TRYING TO KILL.
JUST AS YOU CAN'T GIVE UP ON ME, I CAN'T GIVE UP ON DAVID.
I LOVE DAVID.

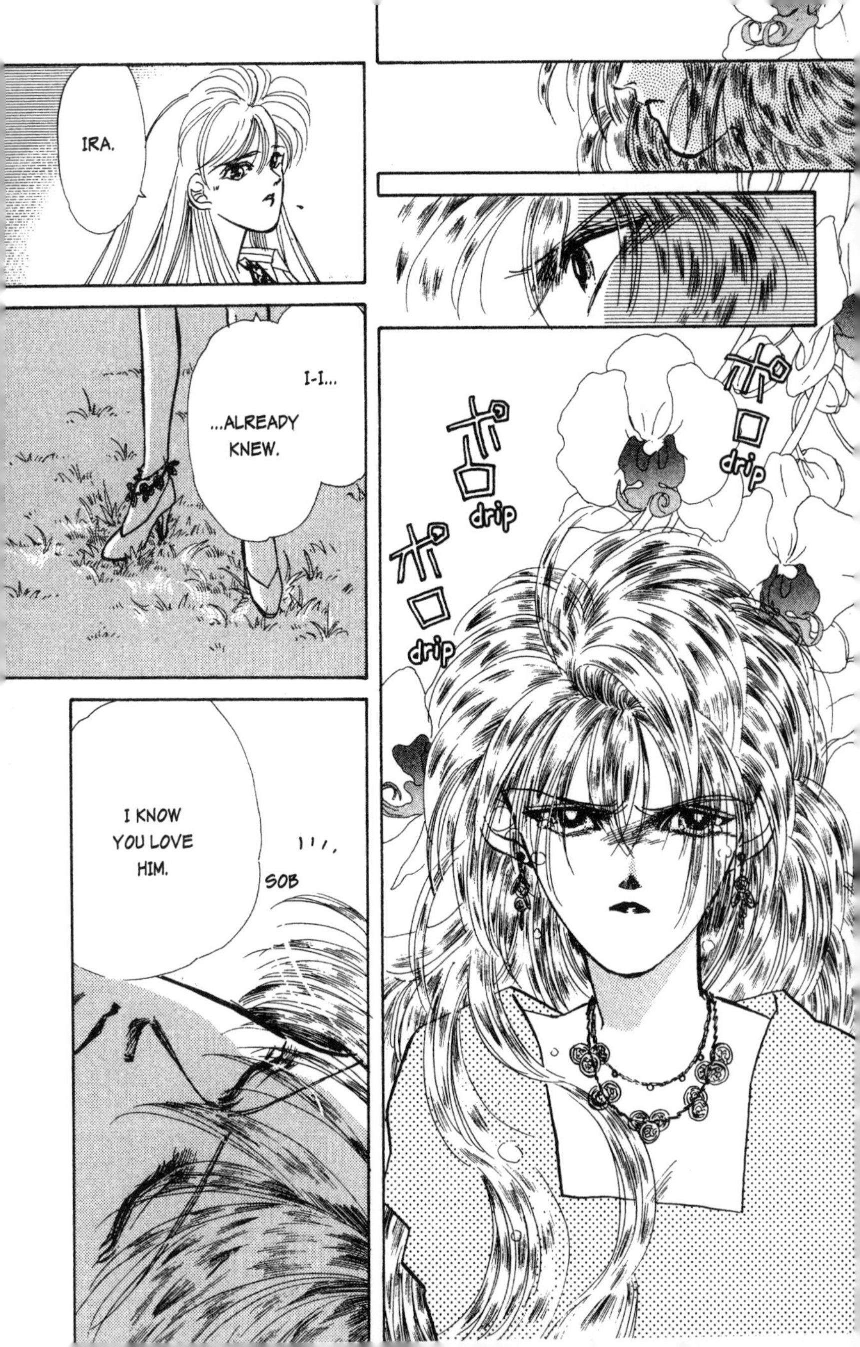
ポロ
drip
ポロ
drip
ポロ
drip
IRA.
I-I...
...ALREADY KNEW.
I KNOW YOU LOVE HIM.
SOB

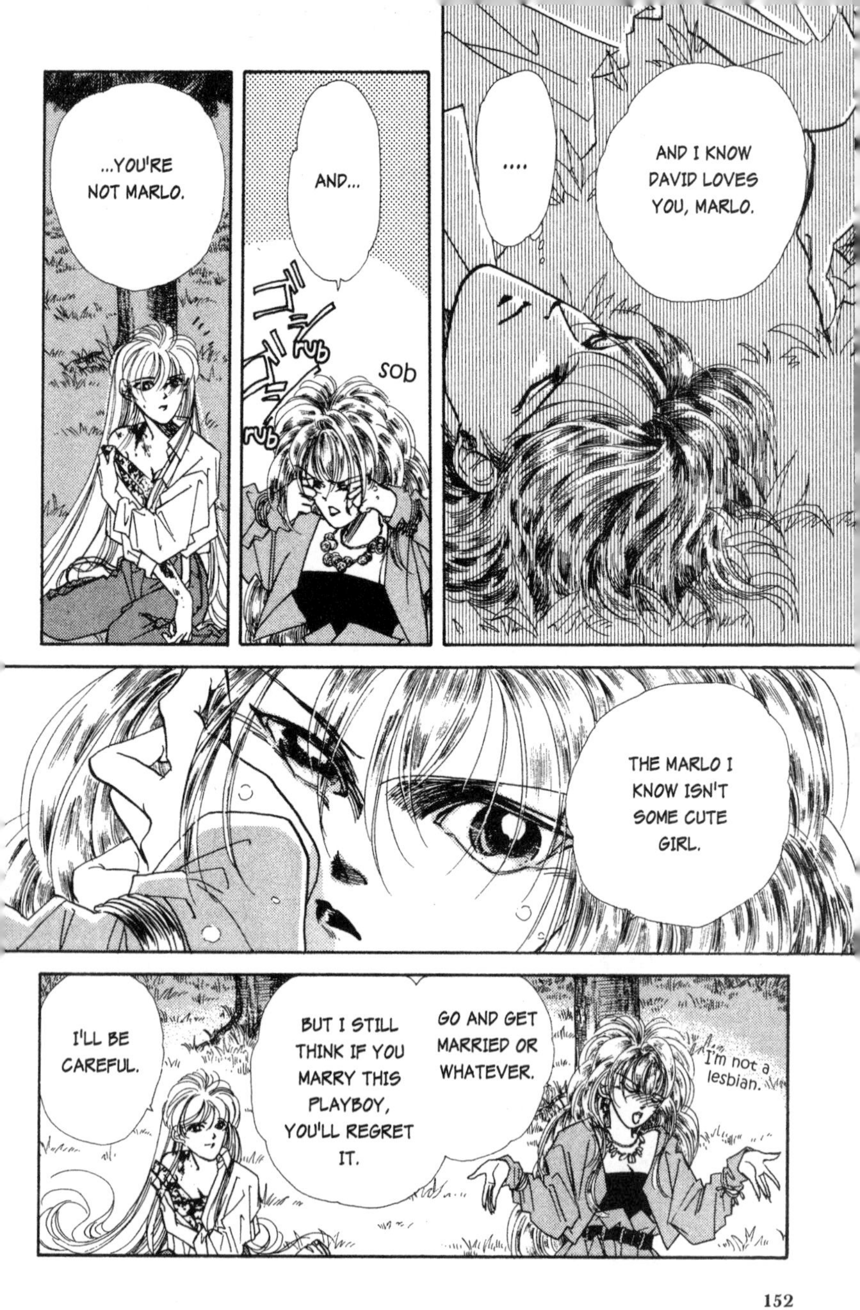

AND I KNOW DAVID LOVES YOU, MARLO.
....
AND...
rub
rub
sob
...YOU'RE NOT MARLO.
THE MARLO I KNOW ISN'T SOME CUTE GIRL.
I'm not a lesbian.
GO AND GET MARRIED OR WHATEVER.
BUT I STILL THINK IF YOU MARRY THIS PLAYBOY, YOU'LL REGRET IT.
I'LL BE CAREFUL.

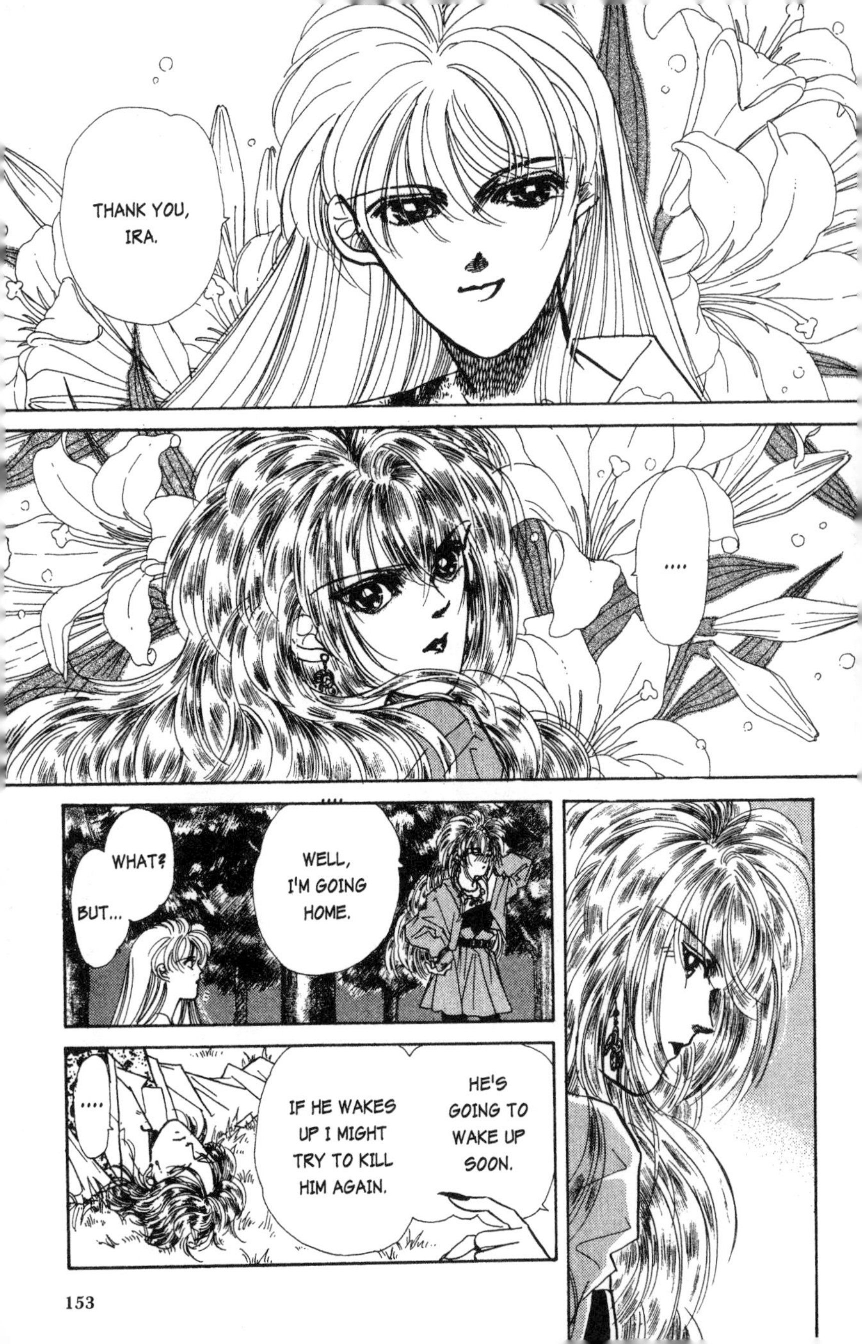
THANK YOU, IRA.
....
WELL, I'M GOING HOME.
WHAT? BUT...
HE'S GOING TO WAKE UP SOON.
IF HE WAKES UP I MIGHT TRY TO KILL HIM AGAIN.
....

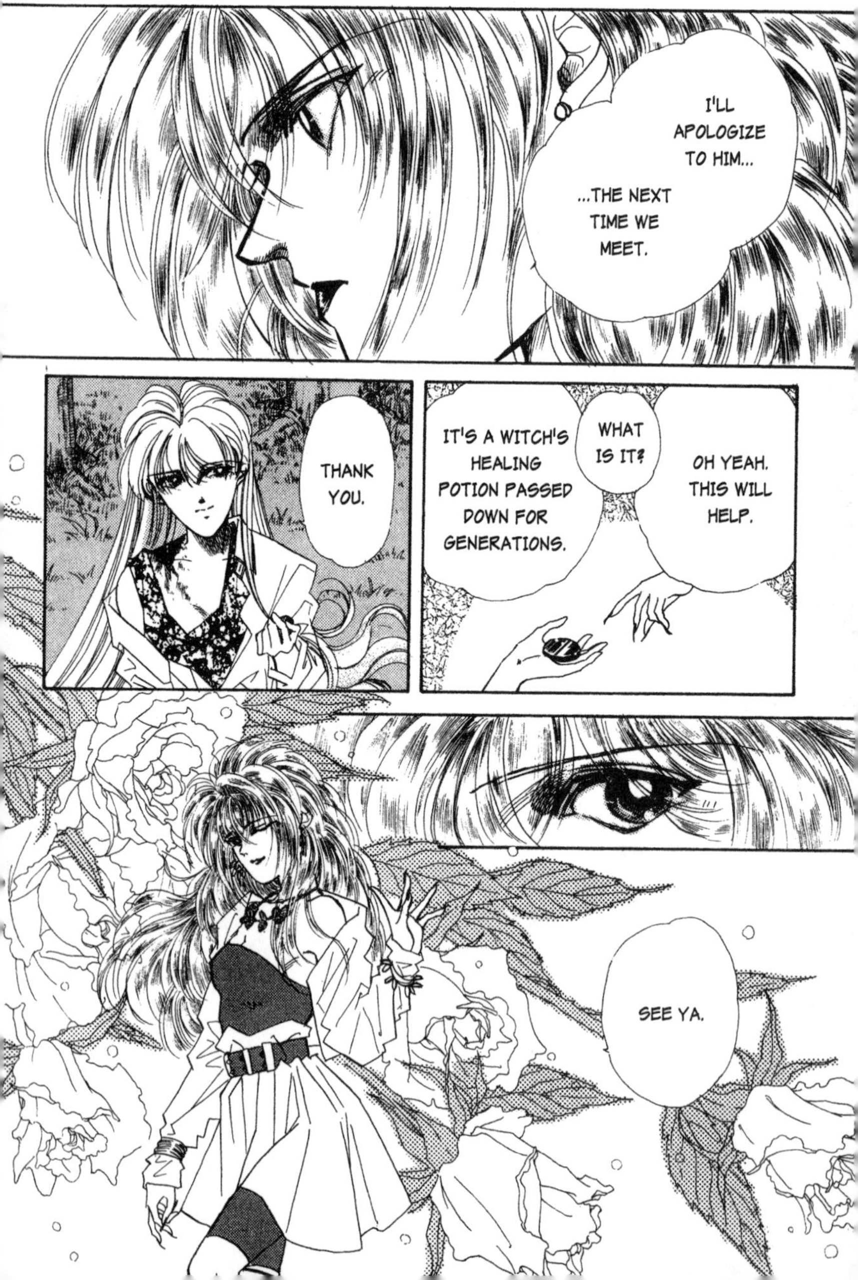
I'LL APOLOGIZE TO HIM...
...THE NEXT TIME WE MEET.
OH YEAH. THIS WILL HELP.
WHAT IS IT?
IT'S A WITCH'S HEALING POTION PASSED DOWN FOR GENERATIONS.
THANK YOU.
SEE YA.

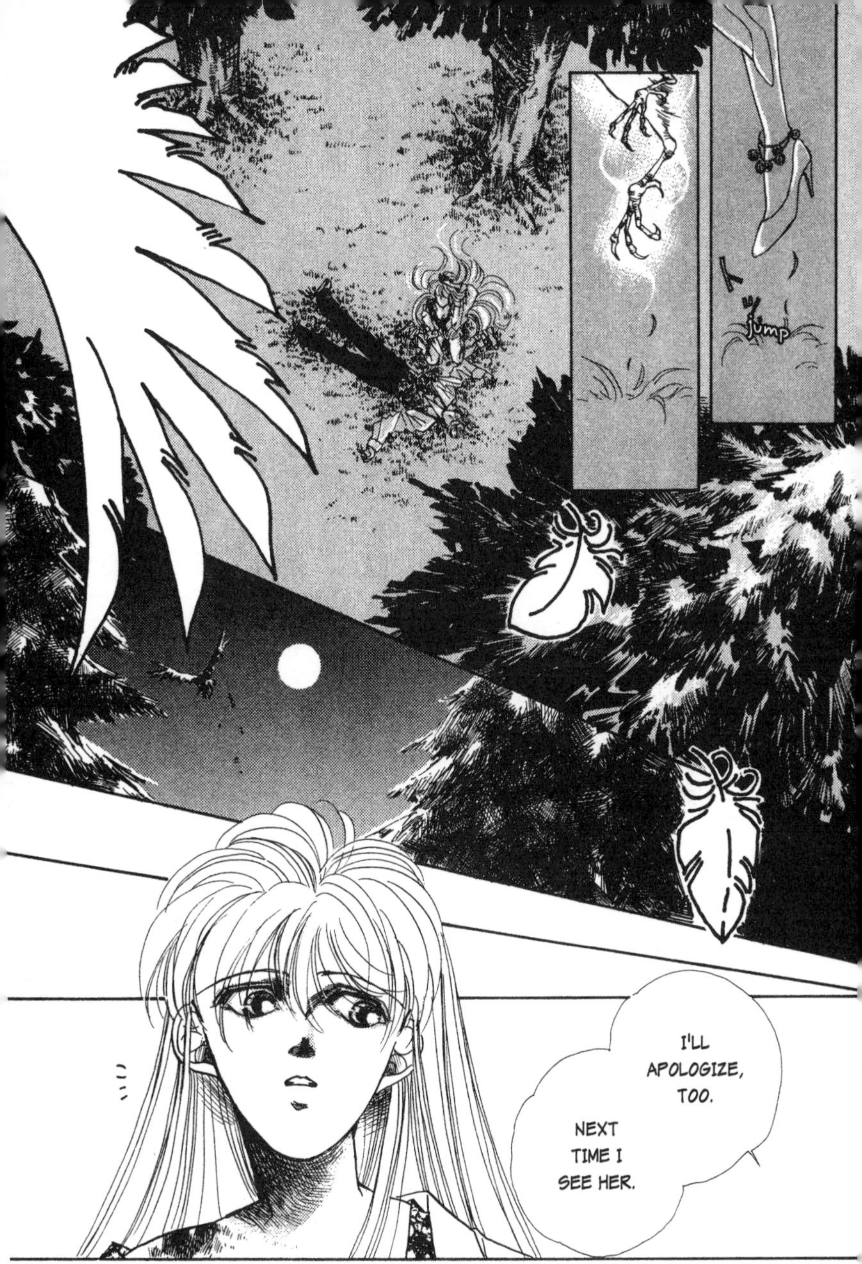
jump
I'LL APOLOGIZE, TOO.
NEXT TIME I SEE HER.

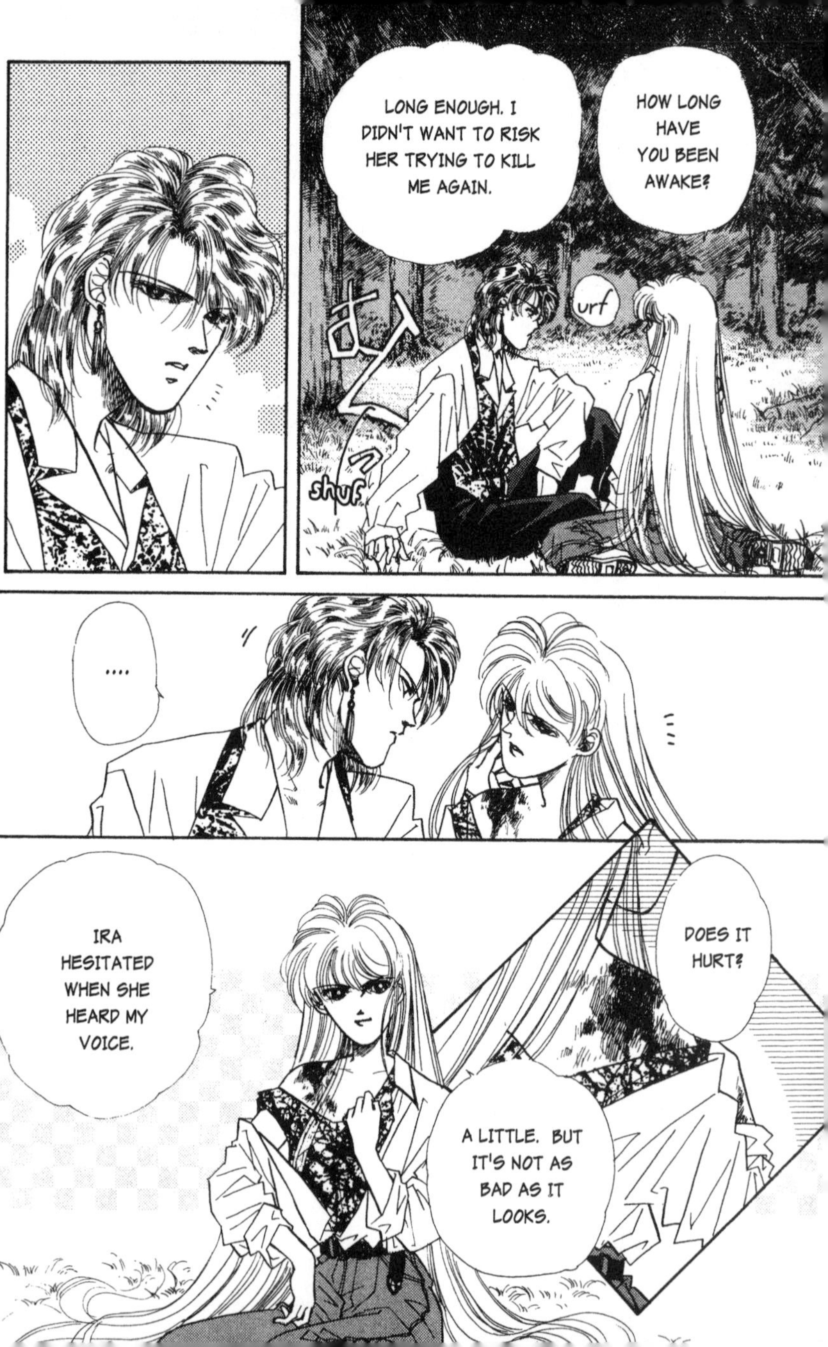
HOW LONG HAVE YOU BEEN AWAKE?
LONG ENOUGH. I DIDN'T WANT TO RISK HER TRYING TO KILL ME AGAIN.
urf
shuf
....
DOES IT HURT?
A LITTLE. BUT IT'S NOT AS BAD AS IT LOOKS.
IRA HESITATED WHEN SHE HEARD MY VOICE.

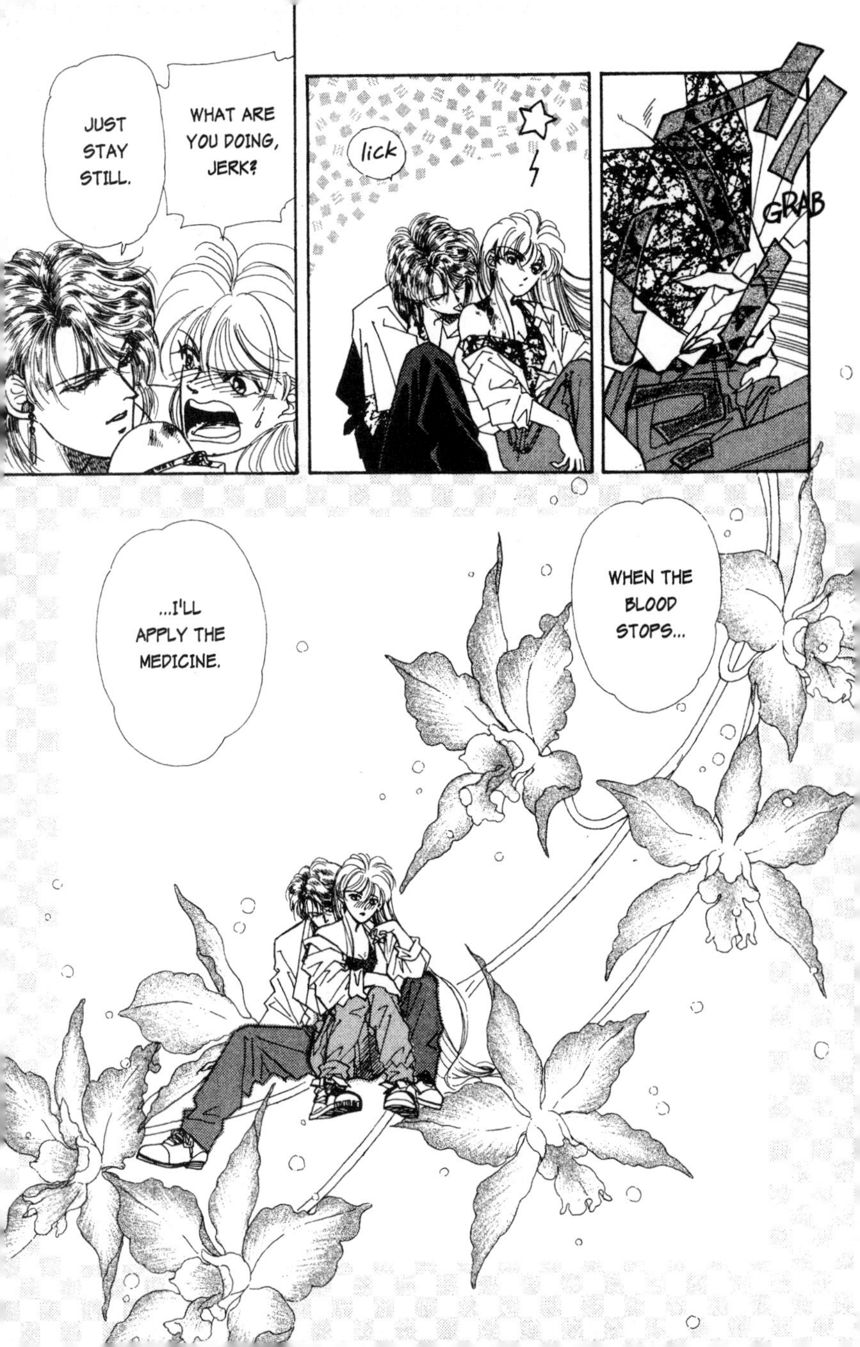
GRAB
lick
WHAT ARE YOU DOING, JERK?
JUST STAY STILL.
WHEN THE BLOOD STOPS...
...I'LL APPLY THE MEDICINE.

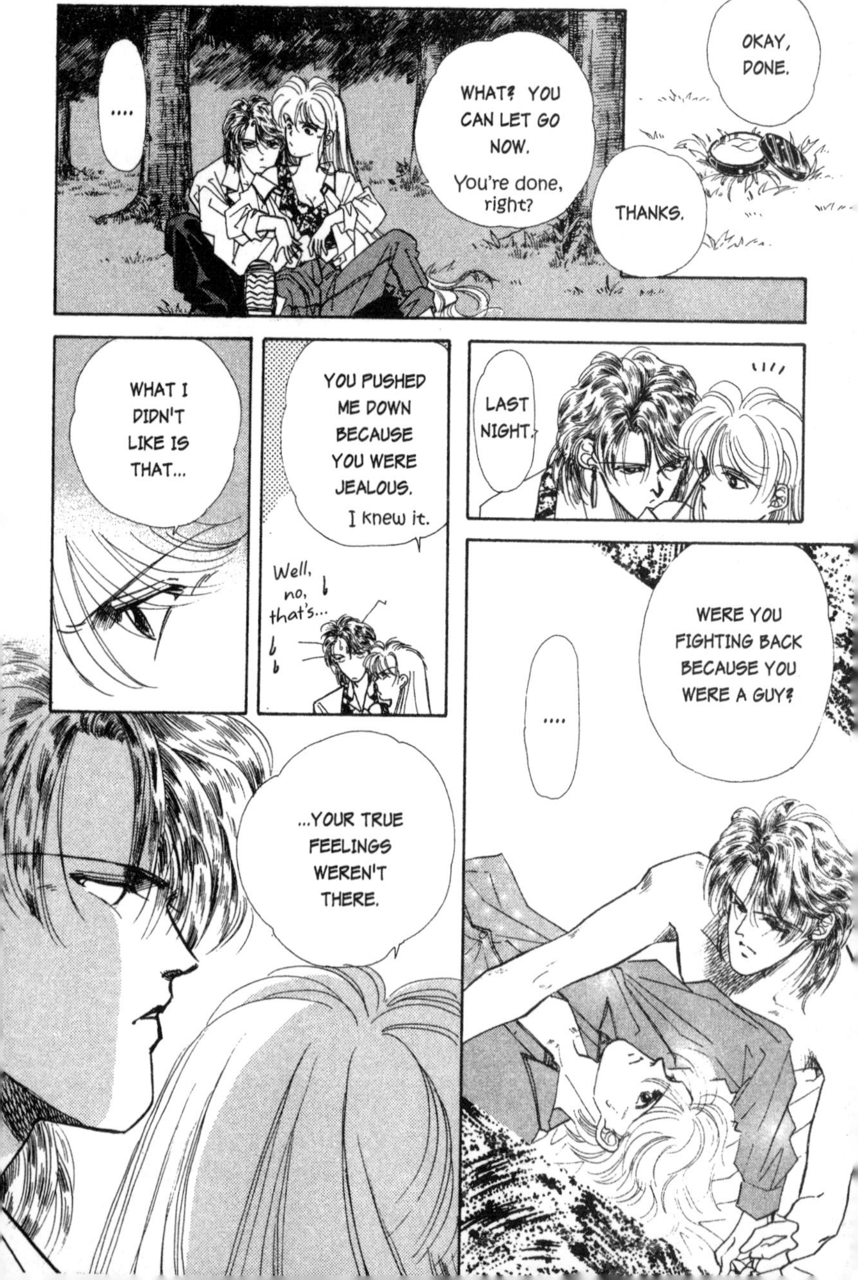
OKAY, DONE.
THANKS.
WHAT? YOU CAN LET GO NOW.
You're done, right?
....
LAST NIGHT,
YOU PUSHED ME DOWN BECAUSE YOU WERE JEALOUS.
I knew it.
Well, no, that's...
WHAT I DIDN'T LIKE IS THAT...
WERE YOU FIGHTING BACK BECAUSE YOU WERE A GUY?
....
...YOUR TRUE FEELINGS WEREN'T THERE.

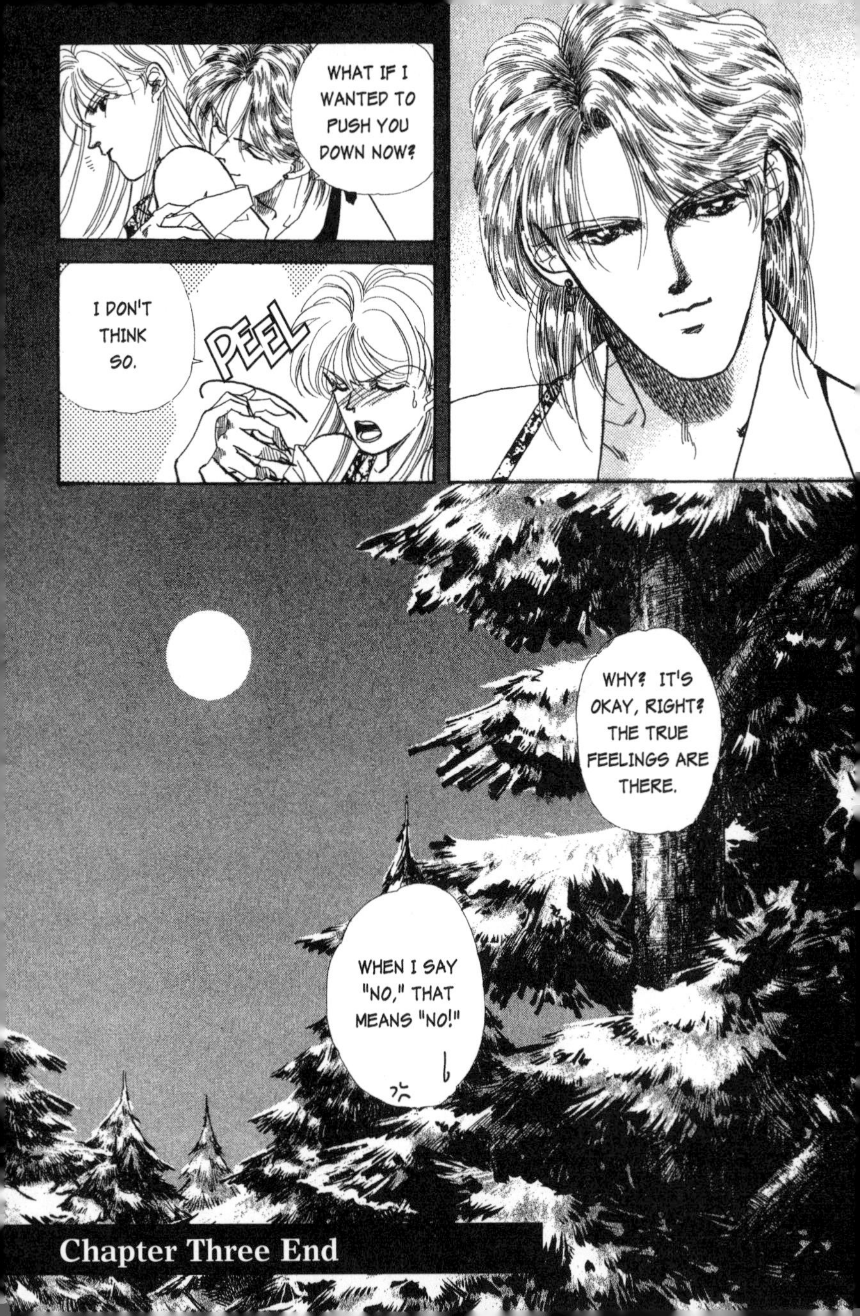
WHAT IF I WANTED TO PUSH YOU DOWN NOW?
I DON'T THINK SO.
PEEL
WHY? IT'S OKAY, RIGHT? THE TRUE FEELINGS ARE THERE.
WHEN I SAY "NO," THAT MEANS "NO!"

Chapter Three End

Chapter Four
FULL MOON にくちづけを
フルムーン
Kiss Me on a Full Moon Night
Until the FULL MOON

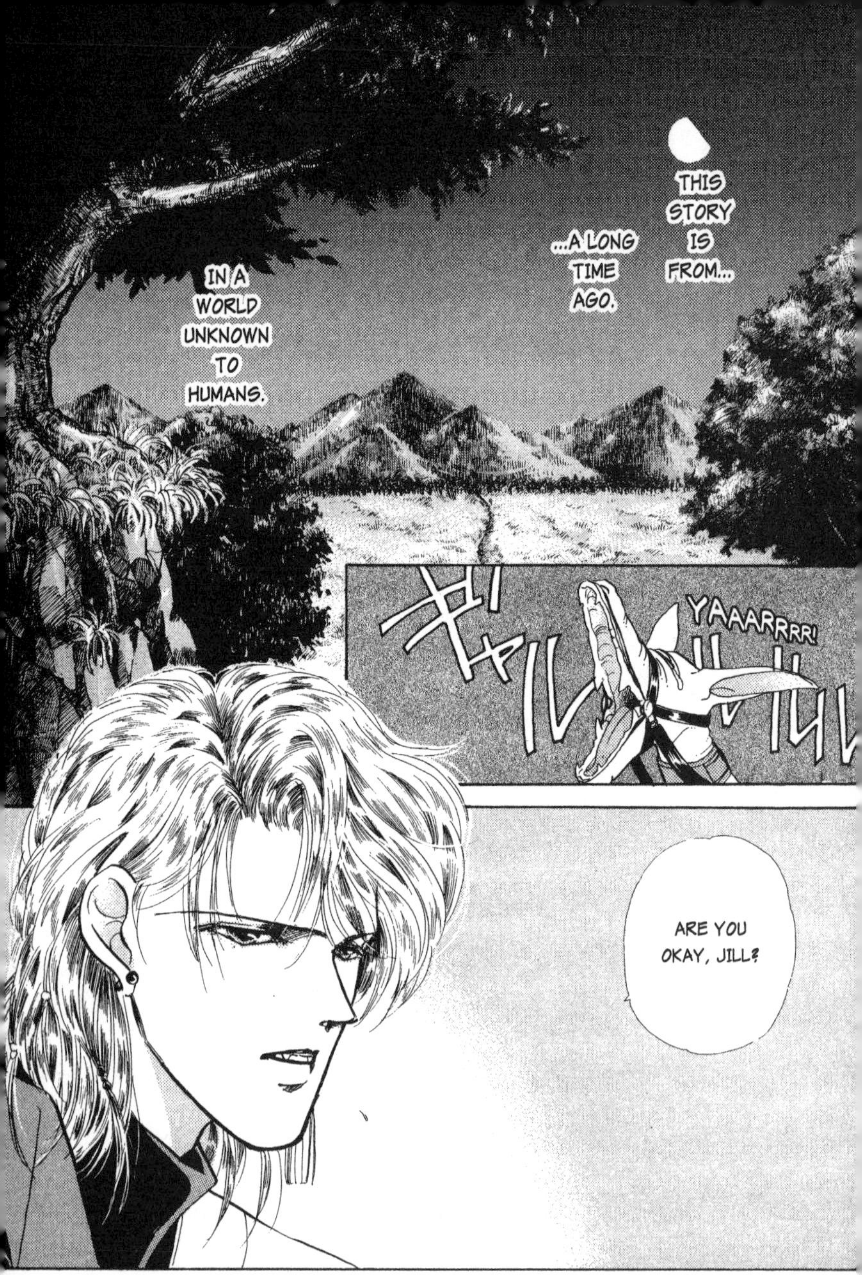
THIS STORY IS FROM...
...A LONG TIME AGO.
IN A WORLD UNKNOWN TO HUMANS.
YAAARRRR!
ARE YOU OKAY, JILL?

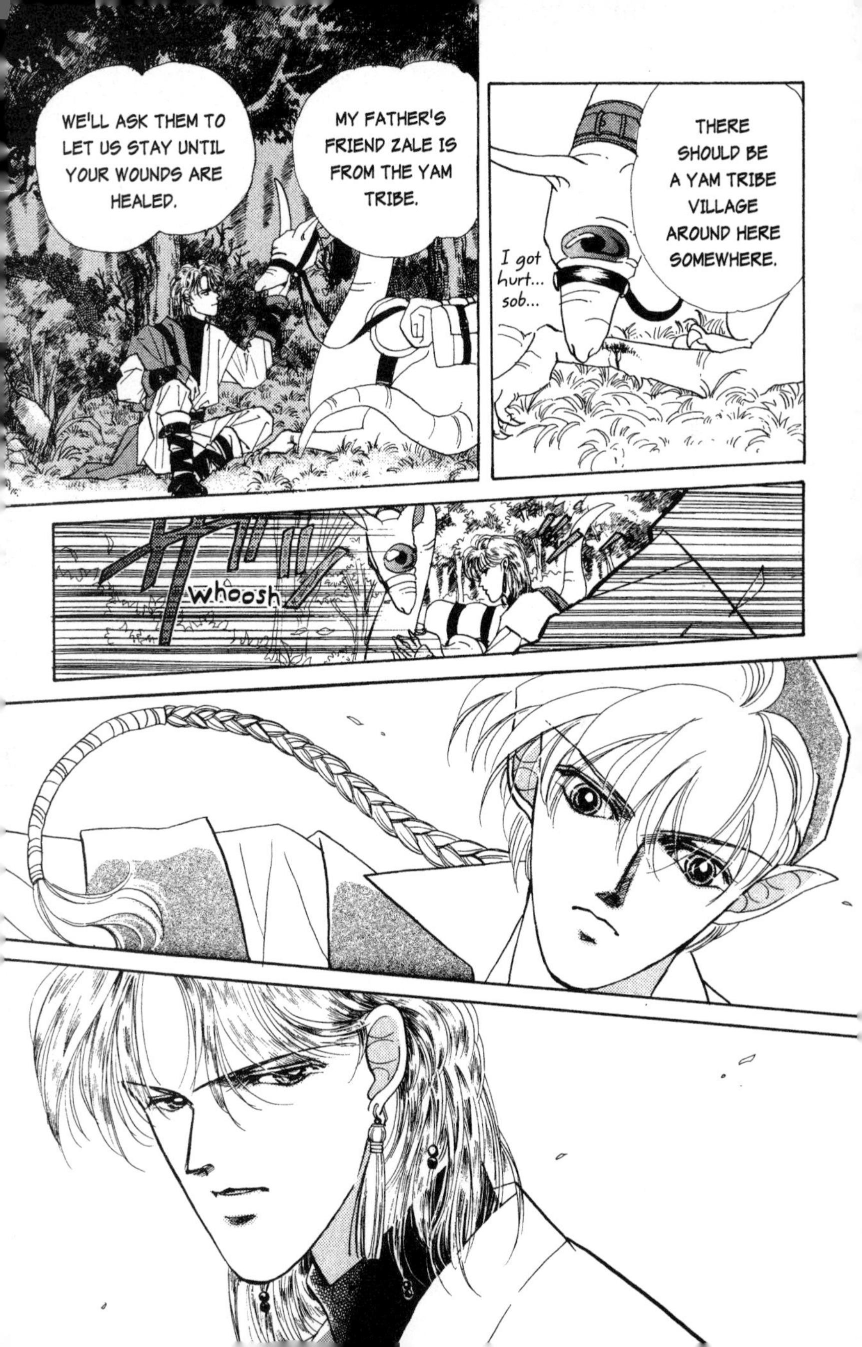
THERE SHOULD BE A YAM TRIBE VILLAGE AROUND HERE SOMEWHERE.
I got hurt... sob...
MY FATHER'S FRIEND ZALE IS FROM THE YAM TRIBE.
WE'LL ASK THEM TO LET US STAY UNTIL YOUR WOUNDS ARE HEALED.
whoosh

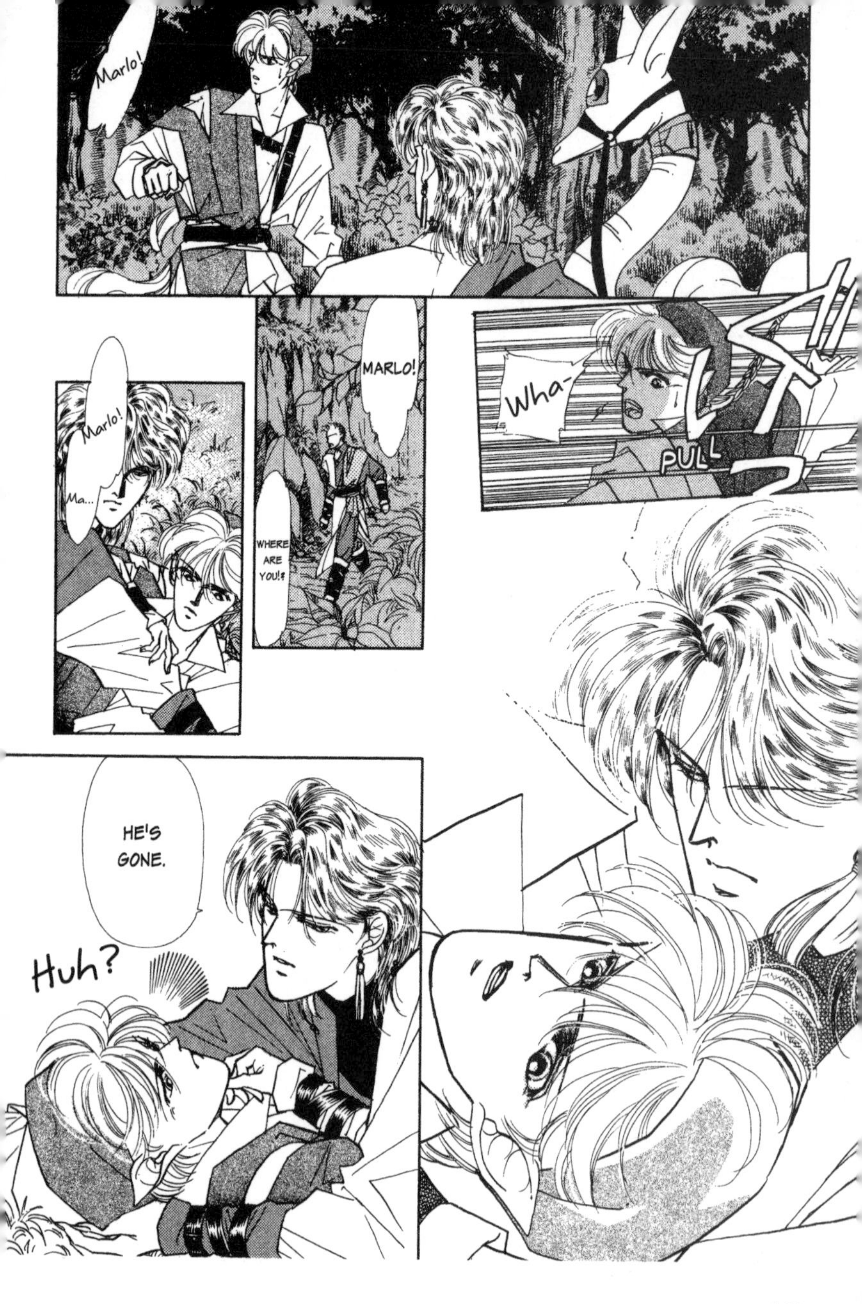
Marlo!
Wha-
PULL
MARLO!
WHERE ARE YOU!?
Marlo!
Ma...
HE'S GONE.
Huh?

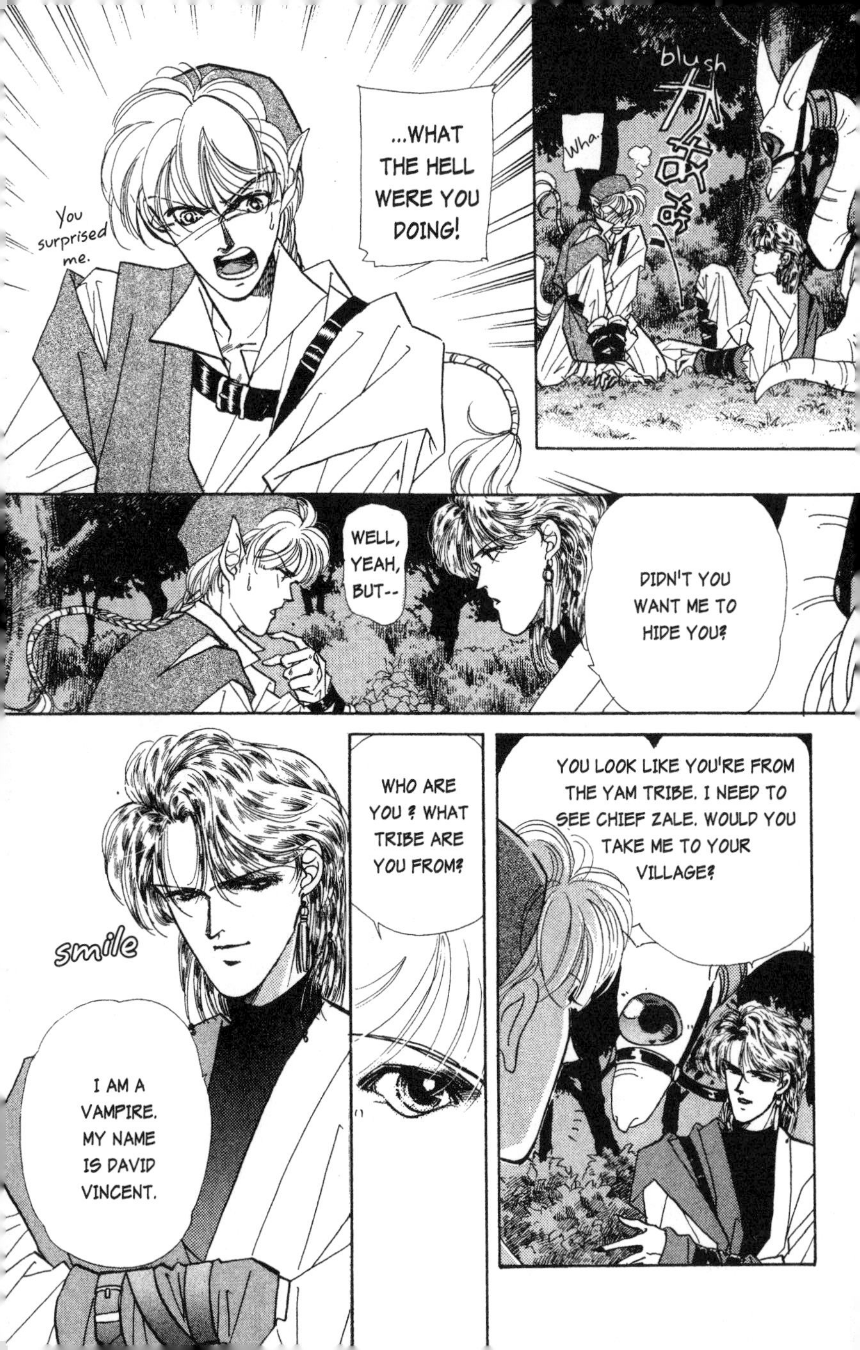
blush
Wha.
...WHAT THE HELL WERE YOU DOING!
You surprised me.
DIDN'T YOU WANT ME TO HIDE YOU?
WELL, YEAH, BUT--
YOU LOOK LIKE YOU'RE FROM THE YAM TRIBE. I NEED TO SEE CHIEF ZALE. WOULD YOU TAKE ME TO YOUR VILLAGE?
WHO ARE YOU? WHAT TRIBE ARE YOU FROM?
smile
I AM A VAMPIRE. MY NAME IS DAVID VINCENT.

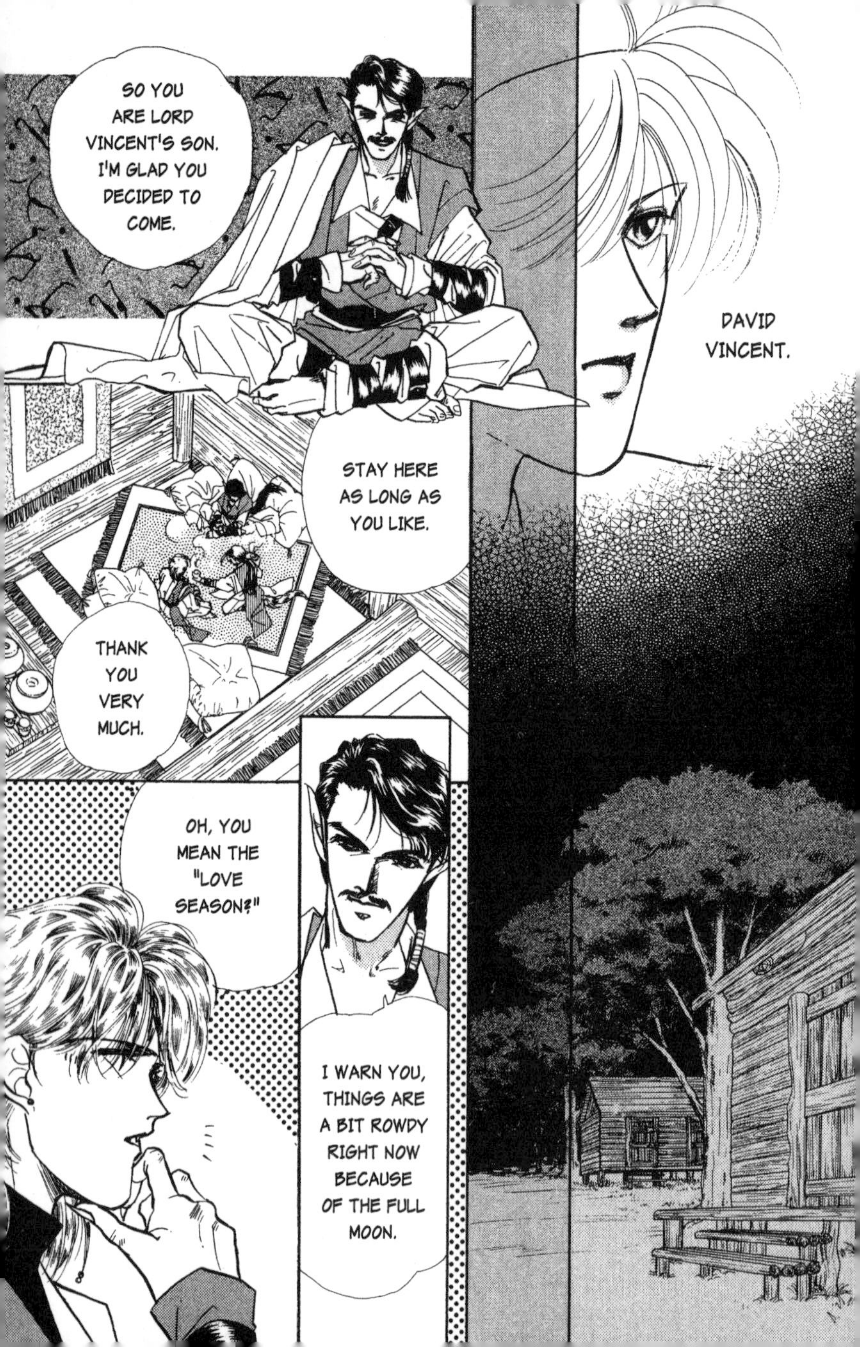
DAVID VINCENT.
SO YOU ARE LORD VINCENT'S SON. I'M GLAD YOU DECIDED TO COME.
STAY HERE AS LONG AS YOU LIKE.
THANK YOU VERY MUCH.
I WARN YOU, THINGS ARE A BIT ROWDY RIGHT NOW BECAUSE OF THE FULL MOON.
OH, YOU MEAN THE "LOVE SEASON?"

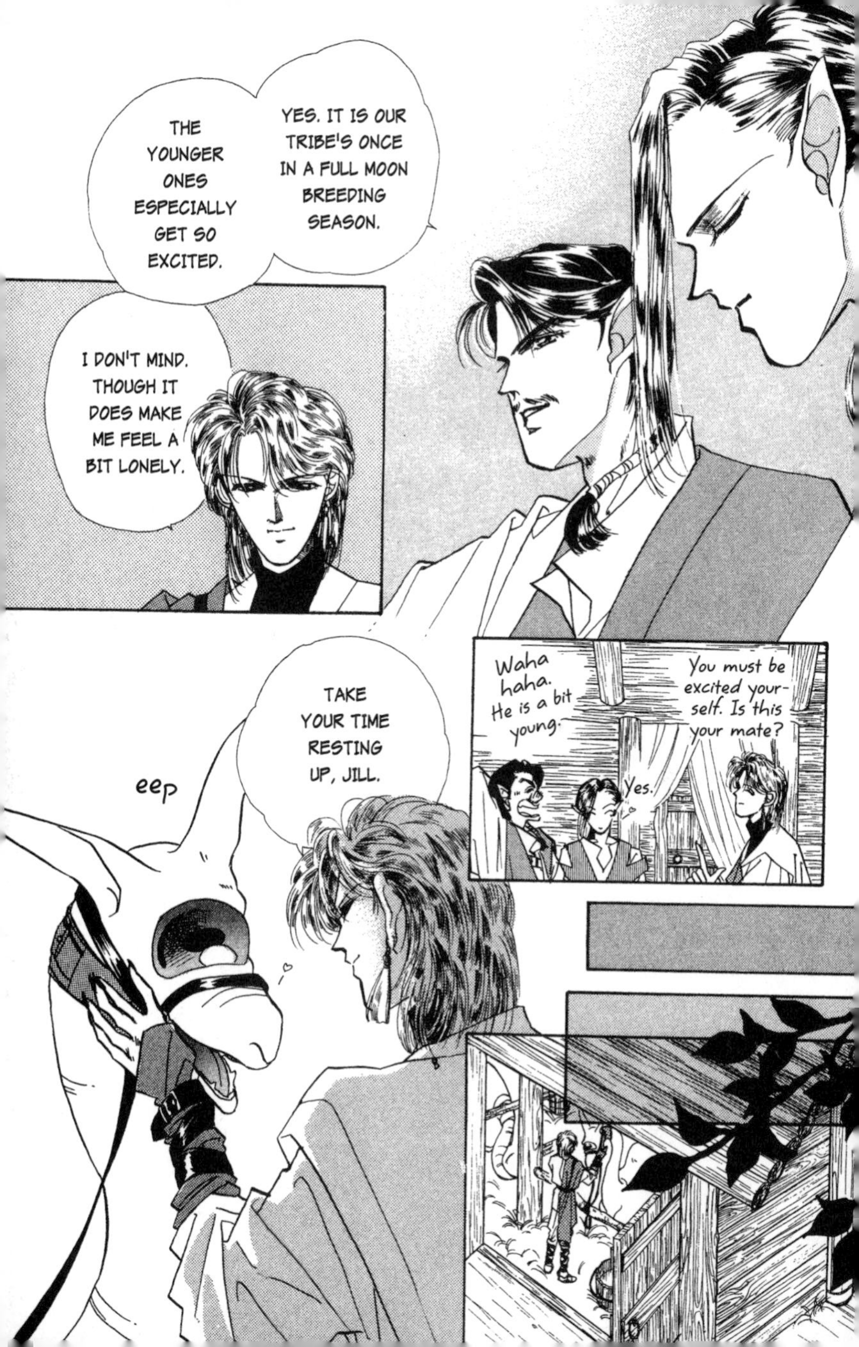
YES. IT IS OUR TRIBE'S ONCE IN A FULL MOON BREEDING SEASON.
THE YOUNGER ONES ESPECIALLY GET SO EXCITED.
I DON'T MIND. THOUGH IT DOES MAKE ME FEEL A BIT LONELY.
You must be excited your-self. Is this your mate?
Yes.
Waha haha. He is a bit young.
TAKE YOUR TIME RESTING UP, JILL.
eep

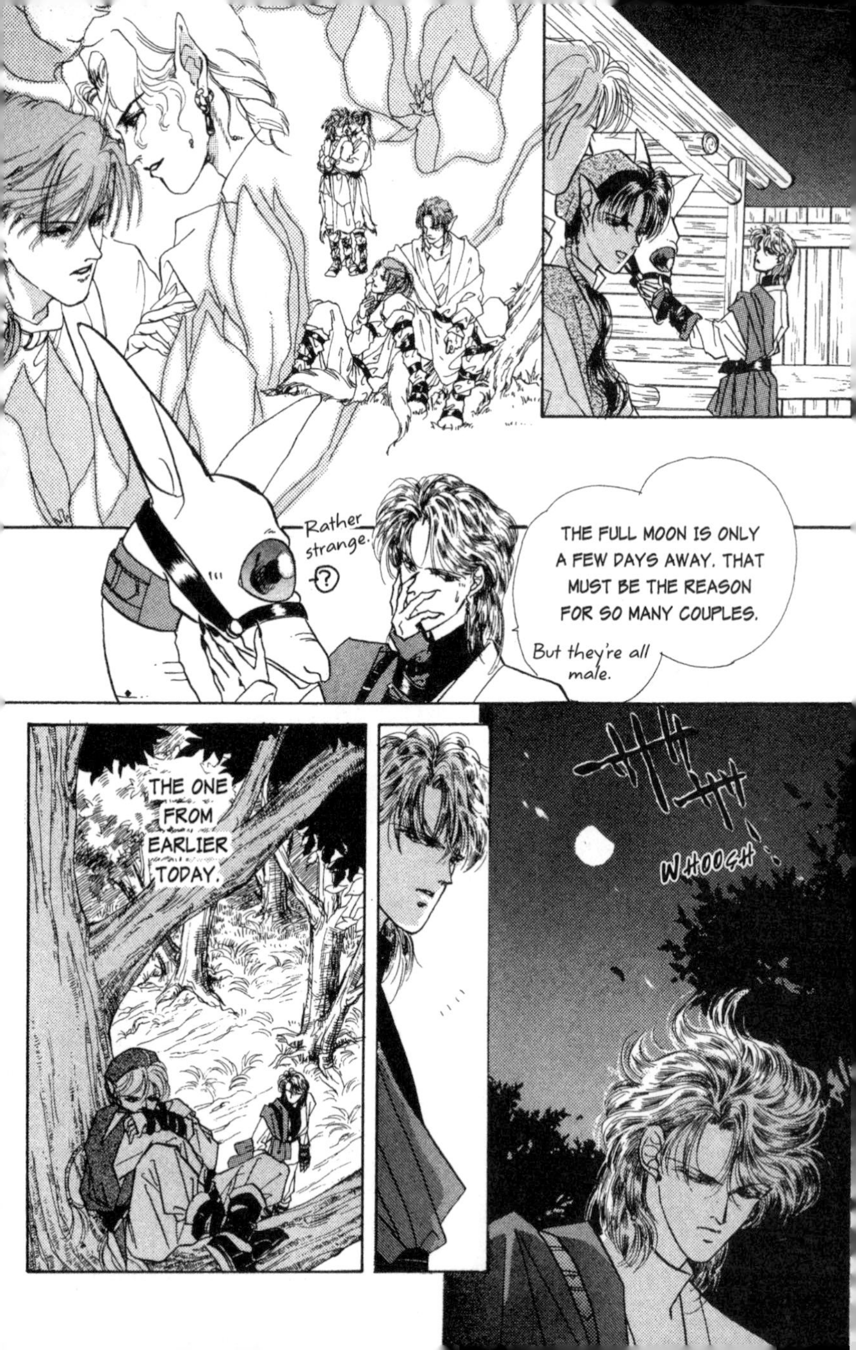
THE FULL MOON IS ONLY A FEW DAYS AWAY. THAT MUST BE THE REASON FOR SO MANY COUPLES.
But they're all male.
Rather strange.
?
WHOOSH
THE ONE FROM EARLIER TODAY.

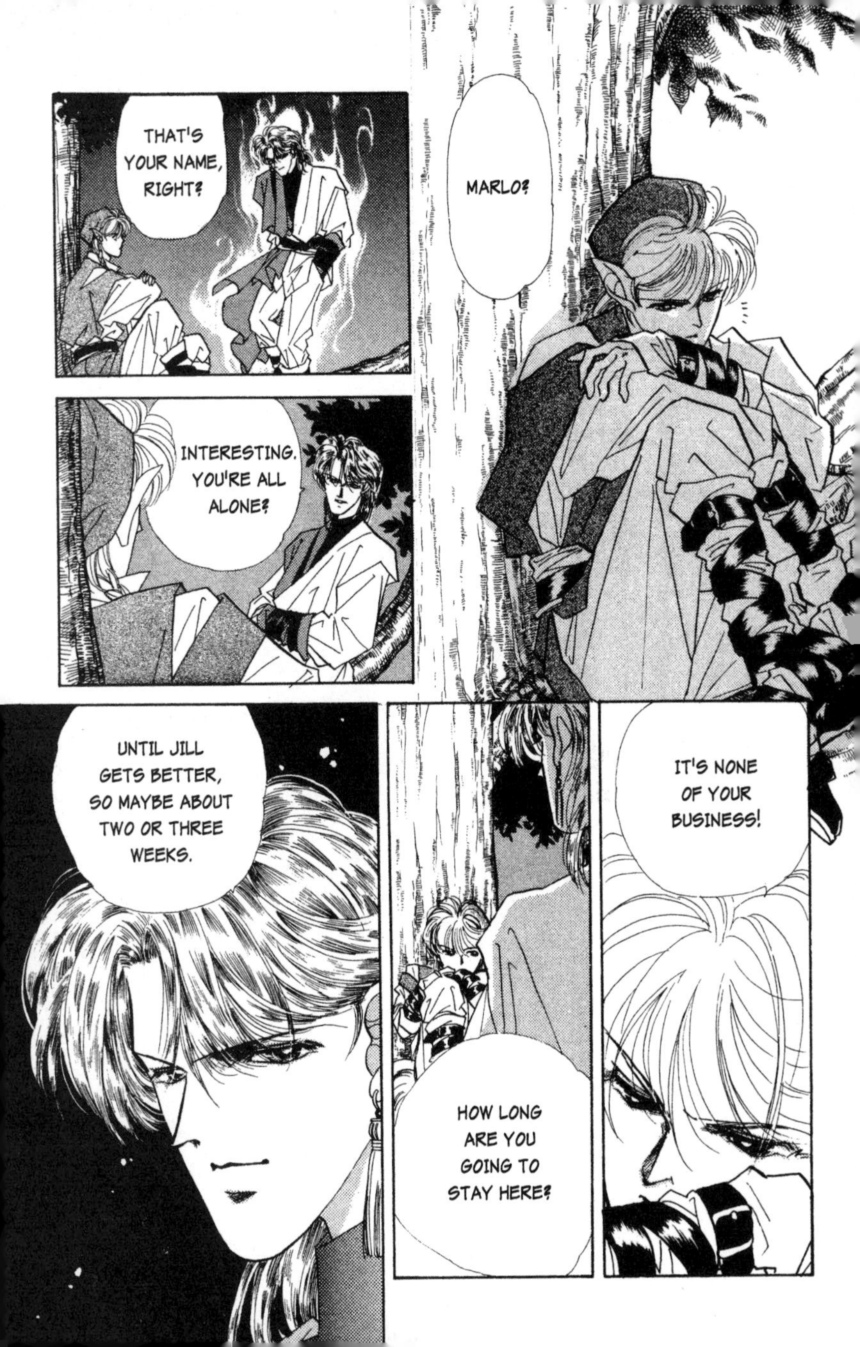
MARLO?
THAT'S YOUR NAME, RIGHT?
INTERESTING. YOU'RE ALL ALONE?
IT'S NONE OF YOUR BUSINESS!
HOW LONG ARE YOU GOING TO STAY HERE?
UNTIL JILL GETS BETTER, SO MAYBE ABOUT TWO OR THREE WEEKS.

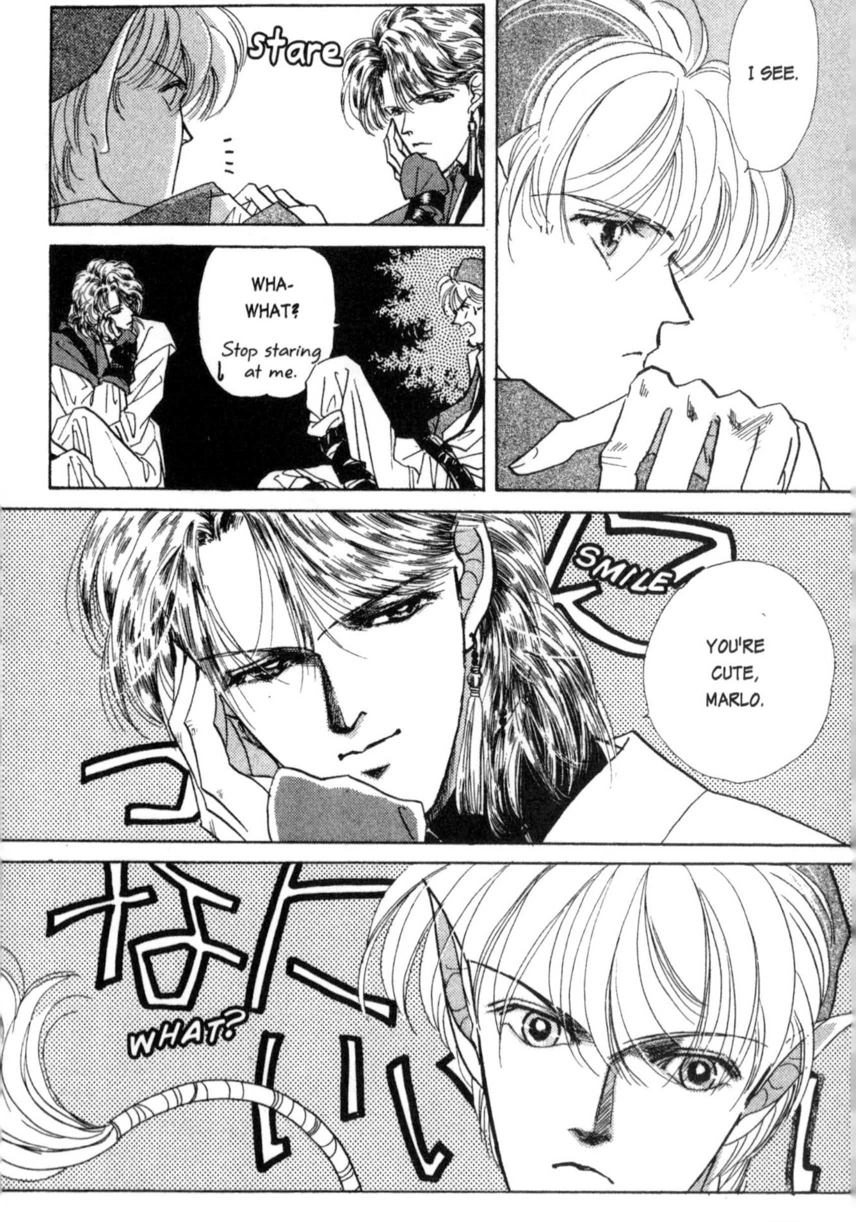
I SEE.
stare
WHA-WHAT?
Stop staring at me.
SMILE
YOU'RE CUTE, MARLO.
WHAT?

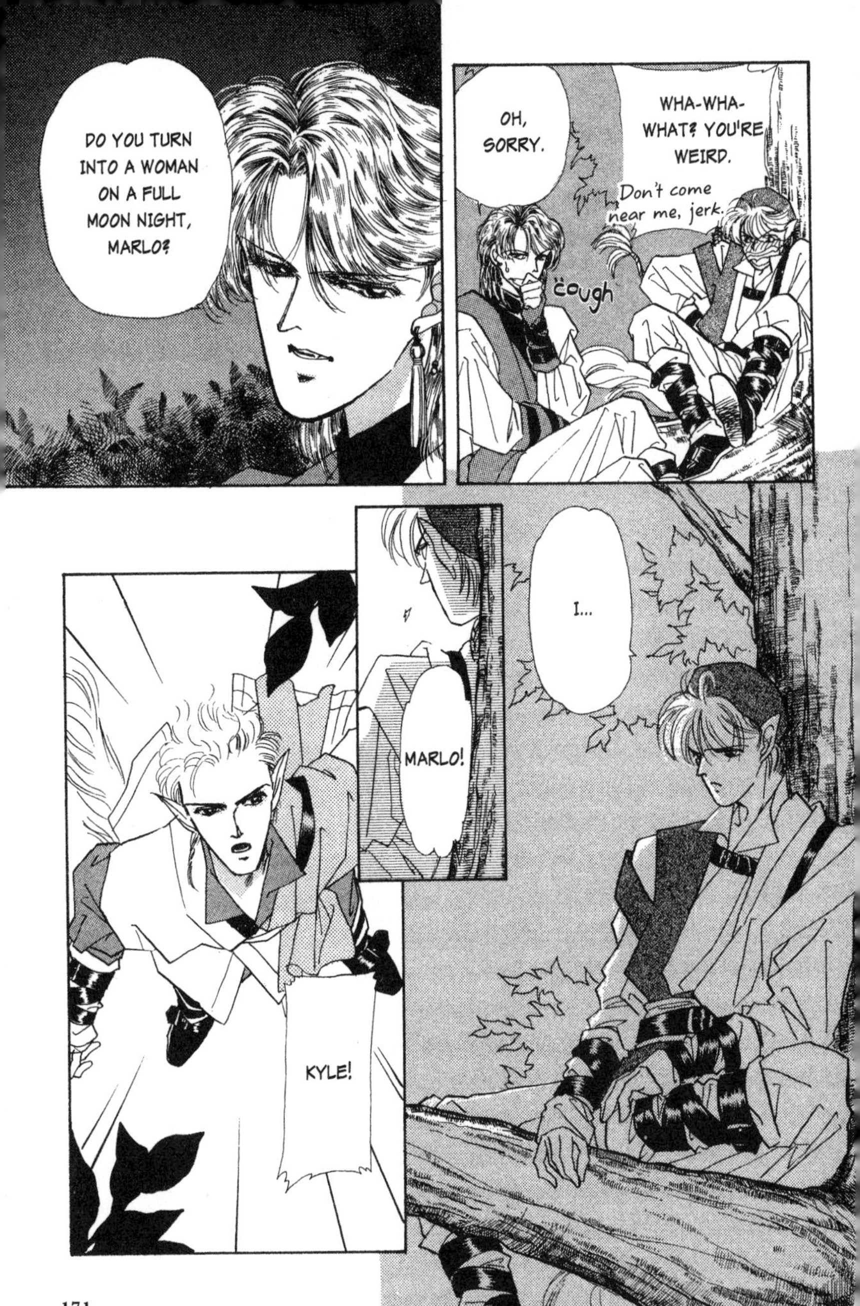
WHA-WHA-WHAT? YOU'RE WEIRD.
Don't come near me, jerk.
OH, SORRY.
cough
DO YOU TURN INTO A WOMAN ON A FULL MOON NIGHT, MARLO?
I...
MARLO!
KYLE!

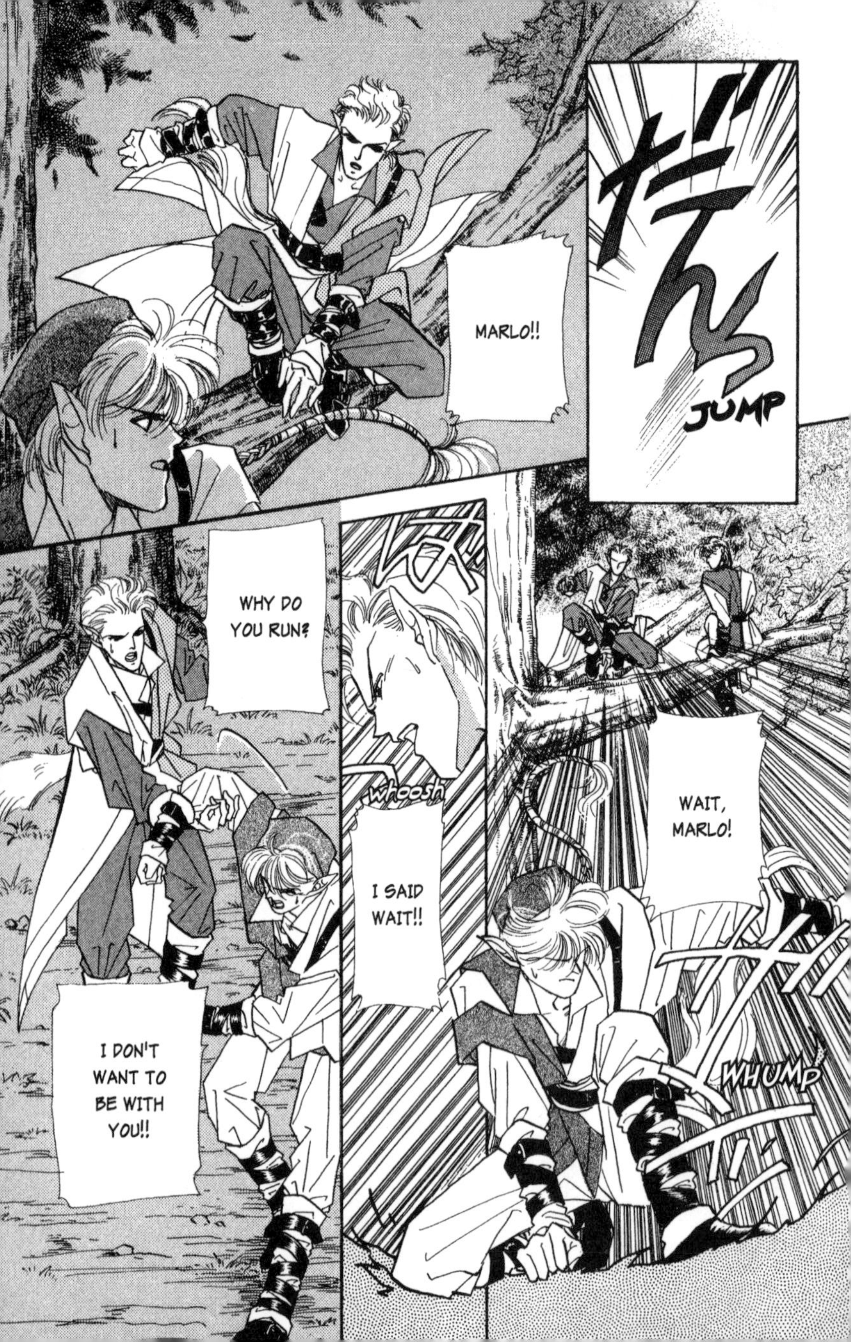
JUMP
MARLO!!
WAIT, MARLO!
WHUMP
whoosh
I SAID WAIT!!
WHY DO YOU RUN?
I DON'T WANT TO BE WITH YOU!!

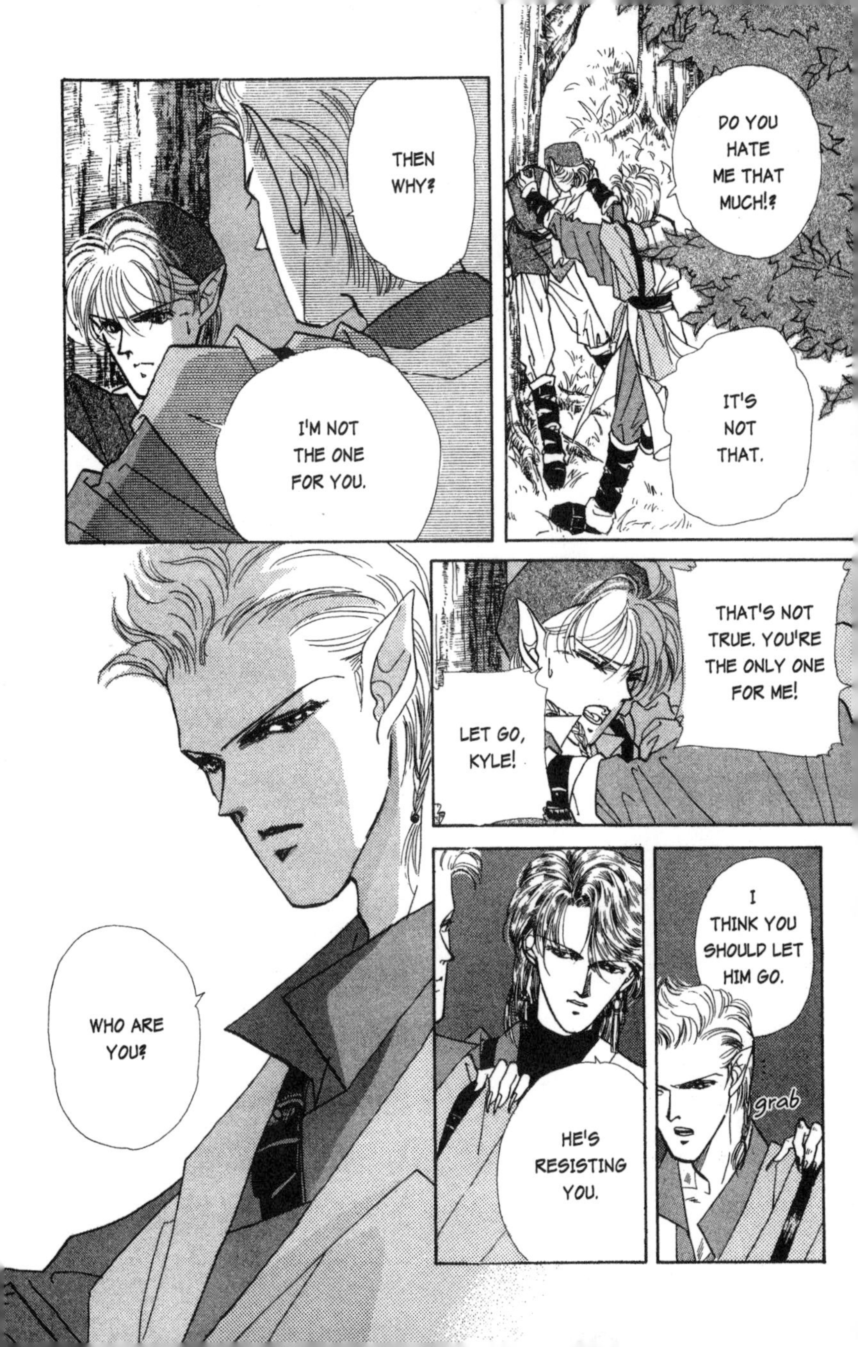
DO YOU HATE ME THAT MUCH!?
IT'S NOT THAT.
THEN WHY?
I'M NOT THE ONE FOR YOU.
THAT'S NOT TRUE. YOU'RE THE ONLY ONE FOR ME!
LET GO, KYLE!
I THINK YOU SHOULD LET HIM GO.
grab
HE'S RESISTING YOU.
WHO ARE YOU?

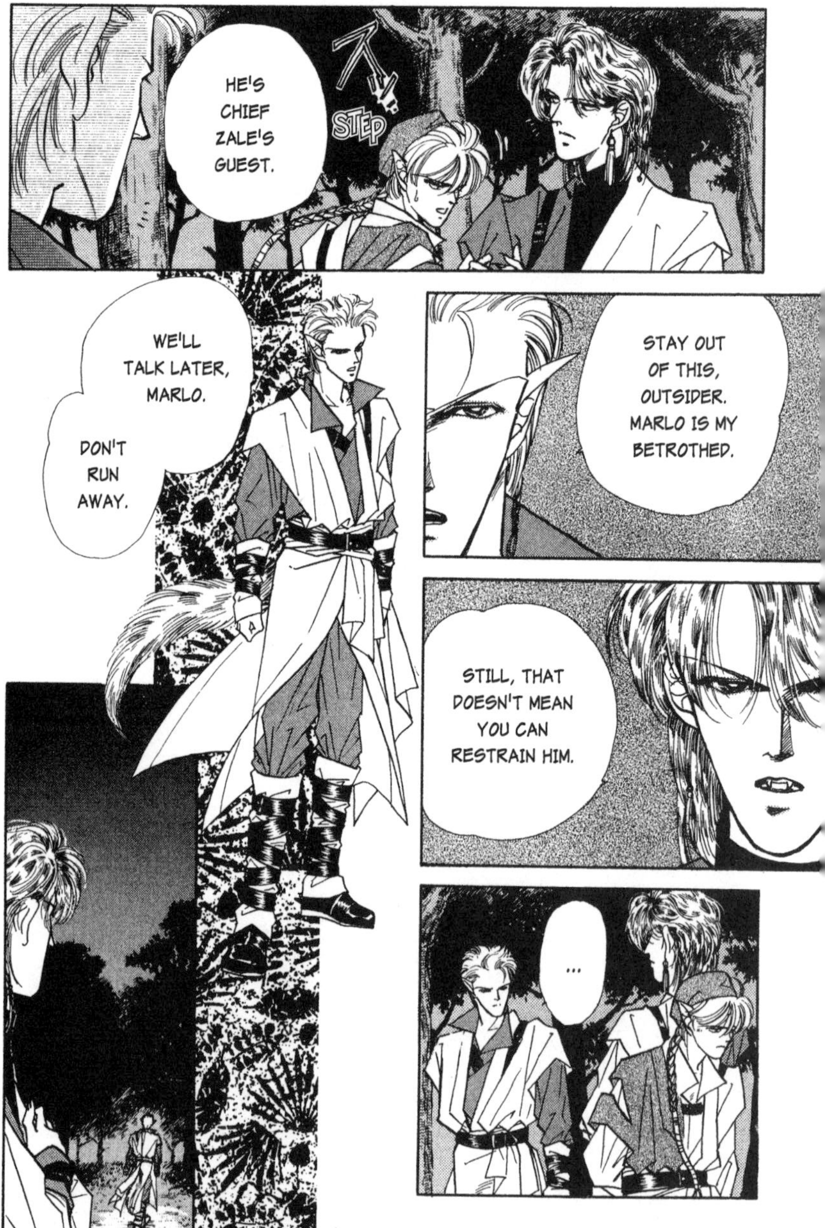
STEP
HE'S CHIEF ZALE'S GUEST.
STAY OUT OF THIS, OUTSIDER. MARLO IS MY BETROTHED.
STILL, THAT DOESN'T MEAN YOU CAN RESTRAIN HIM.
...
WE'LL TALK LATER, MARLO.
DON'T RUN AWAY.

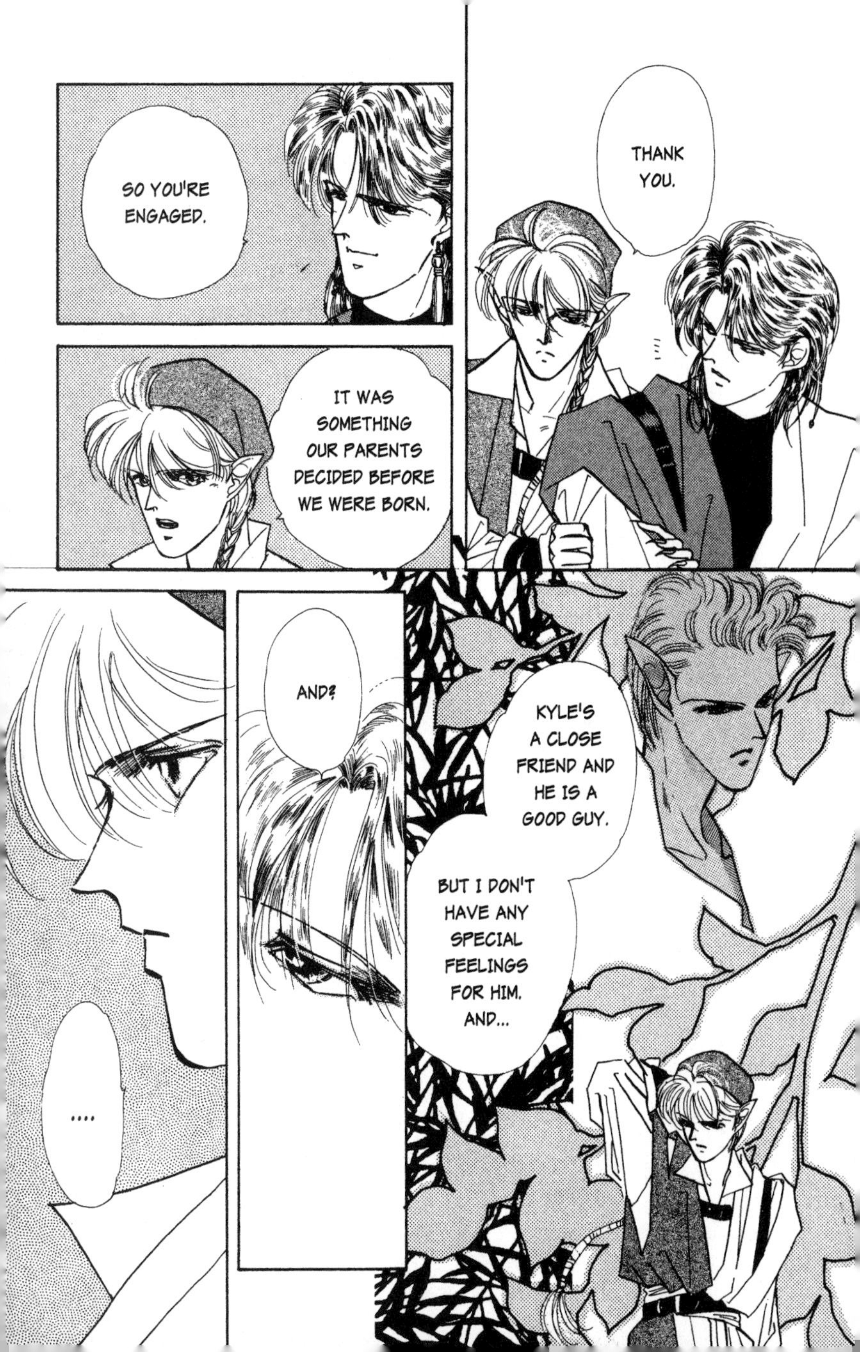
THANK YOU.
SO YOU'RE ENGAGED.
IT WAS SOMETHING OUR PARENTS DECIDED BEFORE WE WERE BORN.
KYLE'S A CLOSE FRIEND AND HE IS A GOOD GUY.
BUT I DON'T HAVE ANY SPECIAL FEELINGS FOR HIM. AND...
AND?
....

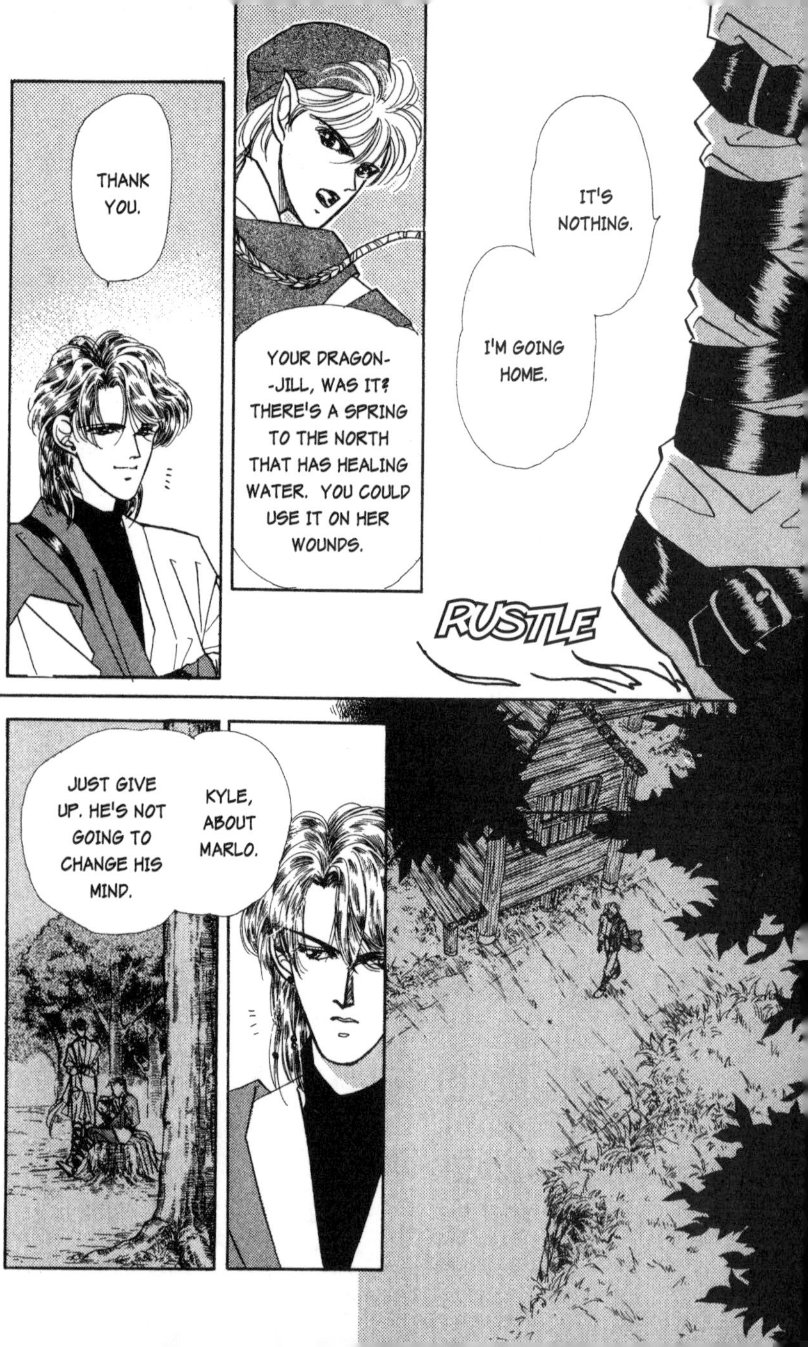
IT'S NOTHING.
I'M GOING HOME.
RUSTLE
YOUR DRAGON- -JILL, WAS IT? THERE'S A SPRING TO THE NORTH THAT HAS HEALING WATER. YOU COULD USE IT ON HER WOUNDS.
THANK YOU.
KYLE, ABOUT MARLO.
JUST GIVE UP. HE'S NOT GOING TO CHANGE HIS MIND.

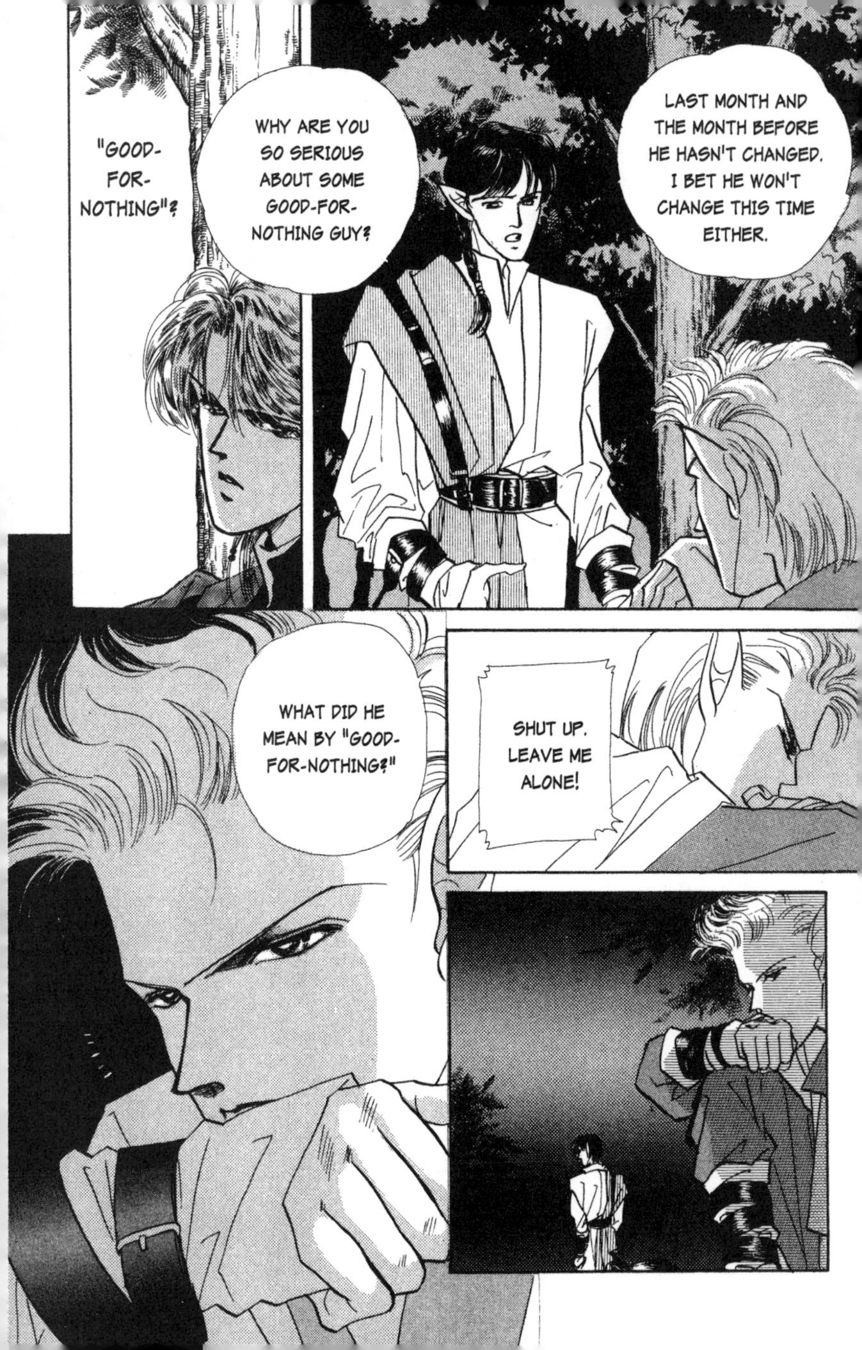
LAST MONTH AND THE MONTH BEFORE HE HASN'T CHANGED. I BET HE WON'T CHANGE THIS TIME EITHER.
WHY ARE YOU SO SERIOUS ABOUT SOME GOOD-FOR-NOTHING GUY?
"GOOD-FOR-NOTHING"?
SHUT UP. LEAVE ME ALONE!
WHAT DID HE MEAN BY "GOOD-FOR-NOTHING?"

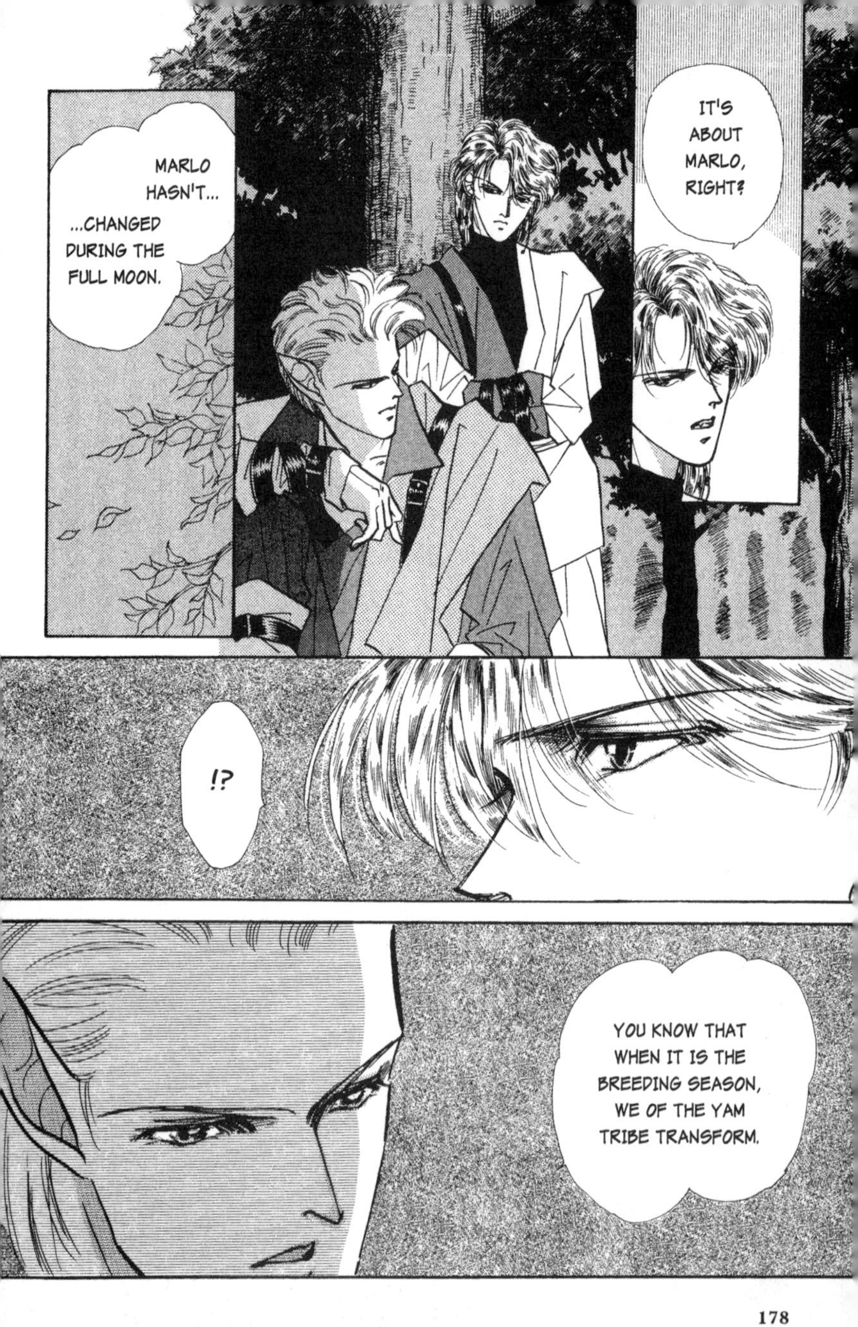
IT'S ABOUT MARLO, RIGHT?
MARLO HASN'T... ...CHANGED DURING THE FULL MOON.
!?
YOU KNOW THAT WHEN IT IS THE BREEDING SEASON, WE OF THE YAM TRIBE TRANSFORM.

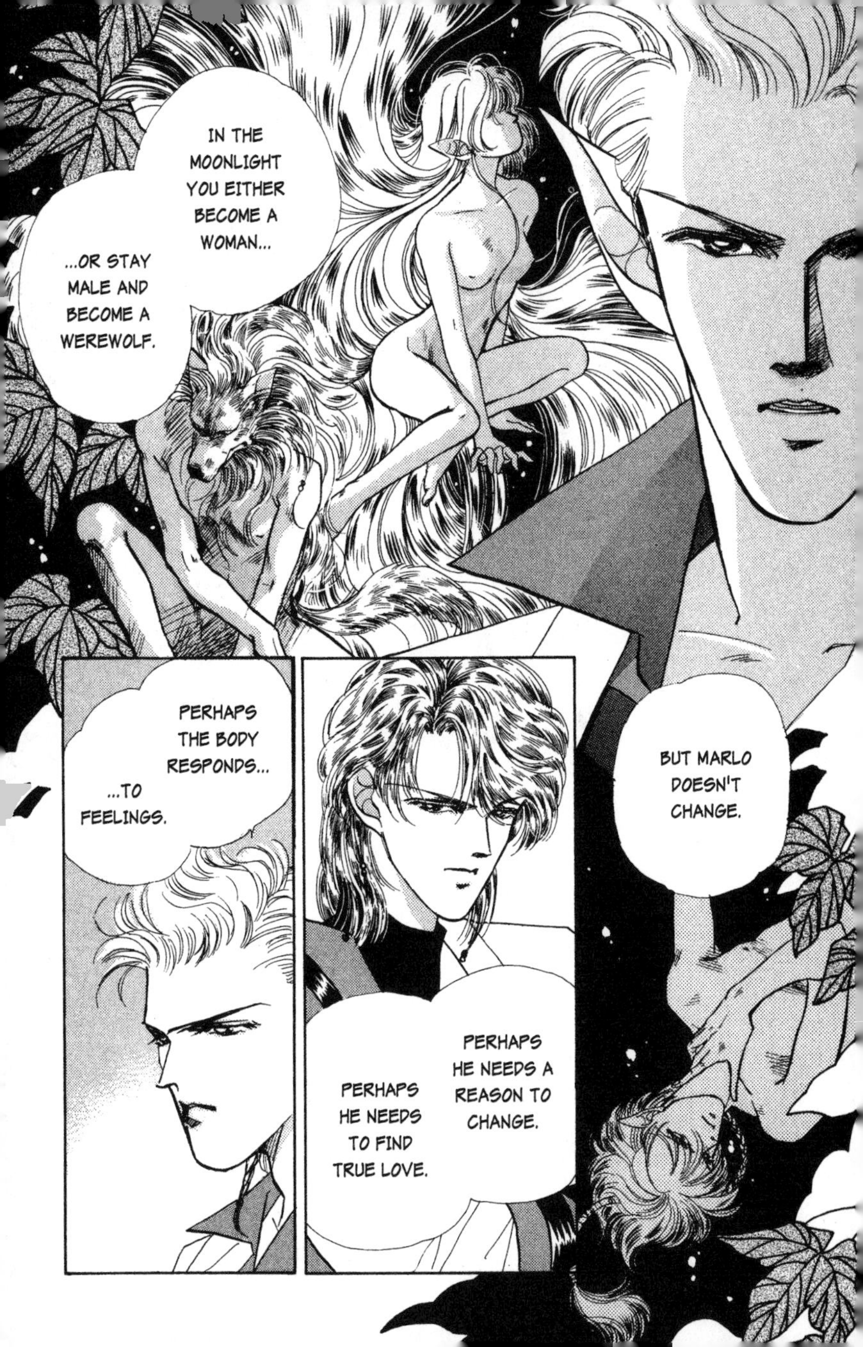
IN THE MOONLIGHT YOU EITHER BECOME A WOMAN...
...OR STAY MALE AND BECOME A WEREWOLF.
BUT MARLO DOESN'T CHANGE.
PERHAPS HE NEEDS A REASON TO CHANGE.
PERHAPS HE NEEDS TO FIND TRUE LOVE.
PERHAPS THE BODY RESPONDS...
...TO FEELINGS.

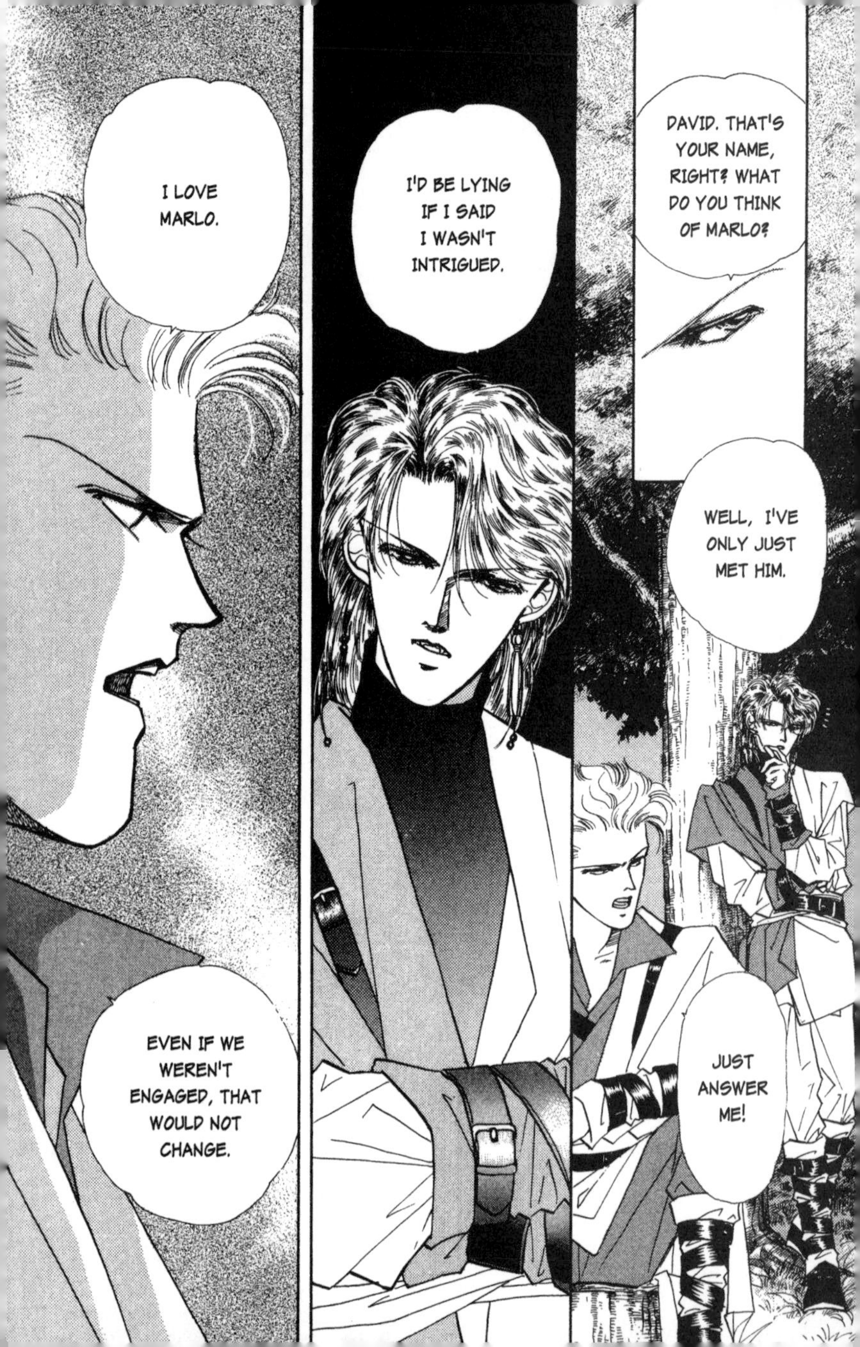
DAVID. THAT'S YOUR NAME, RIGHT? WHAT DO YOU THINK OF MARLO?
WELL, I'VE ONLY JUST MET HIM.
JUST ANSWER ME!
I'D BE LYING IF I SAID I WASN'T INTRIGUED.
I LOVE MARLO.
EVEN IF WE WEREN'T ENGAGED, THAT WOULD NOT CHANGE.

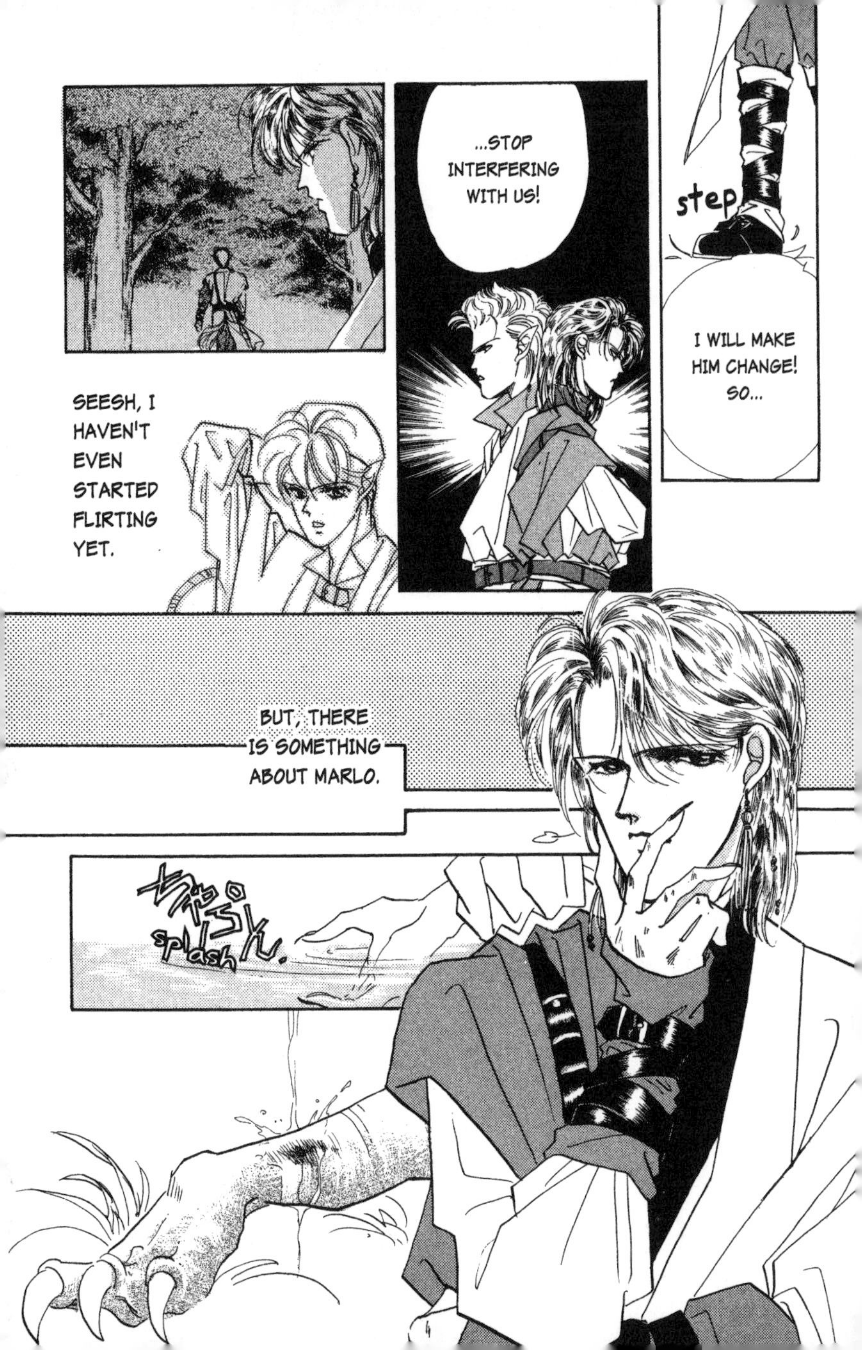
step
I WILL MAKE HIM CHANGE! SO...
...STOP INTERFERING WITH US!
SEESH, I HAVEN'T EVEN STARTED FLIRTING YET.
BUT, THERE IS SOMETHING ABOUT MARLO.
splash

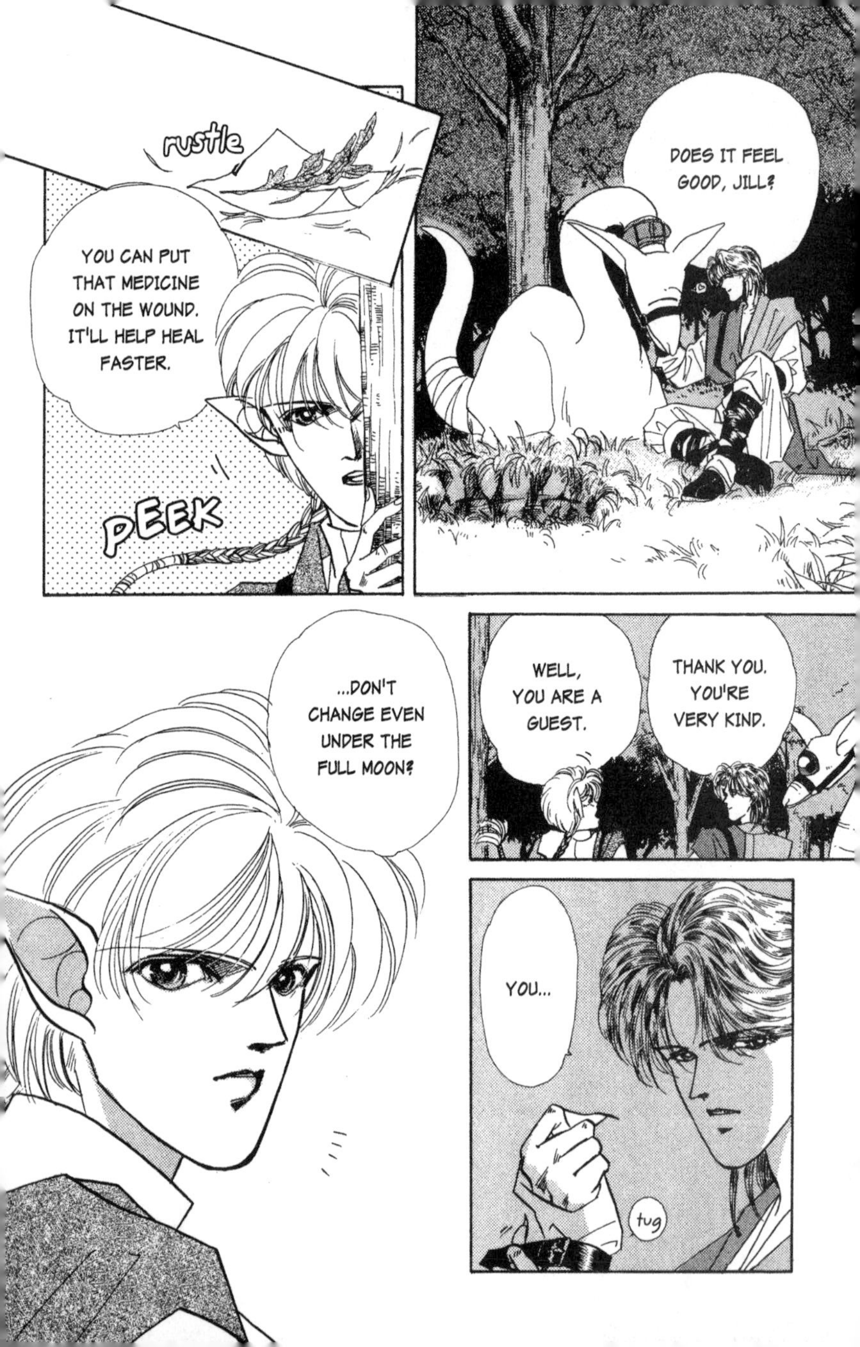
DOES IT FEEL GOOD, JILL?
rustle
YOU CAN PUT THAT MEDICINE ON THE WOUND. IT'LL HELP HEAL FASTER.
PEEK
THANK YOU. YOU'RE VERY KIND.
WELL, YOU ARE A GUEST.
YOU...
tug
...DON'T CHANGE EVEN UNDER THE FULL MOON?

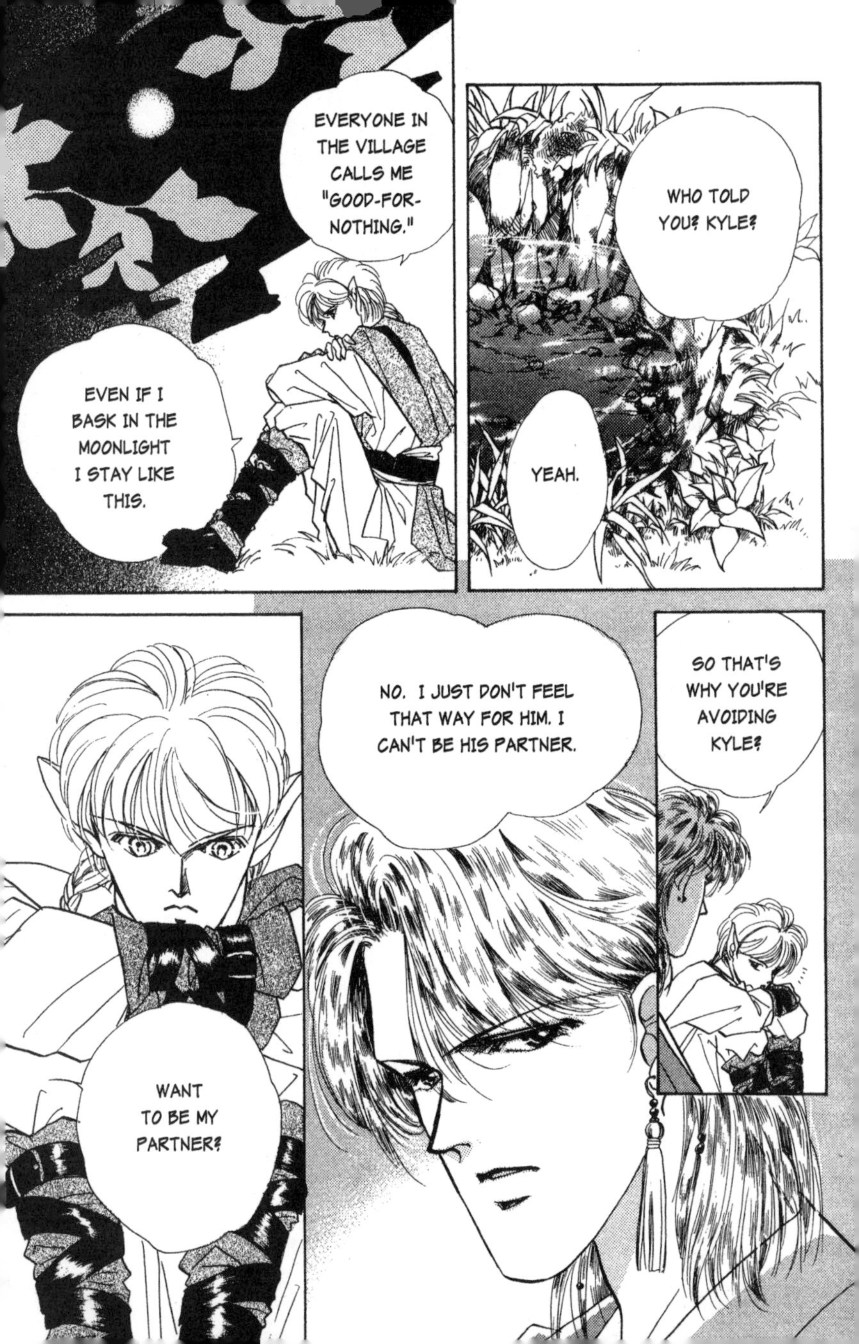
WHO TOLD YOU? KYLE?
YEAH.
EVERYONE IN THE VILLAGE CALLS ME "GOOD-FOR-NOTHING."
EVEN IF I BASK IN THE MOONLIGHT I STAY LIKE THIS.
SO THAT'S WHY YOU'RE AVOIDING KYLE?
NO. I JUST DON'T FEEL THAT WAY FOR HIM. I CAN'T BE HIS PARTNER.
WANT TO BE MY PARTNER?

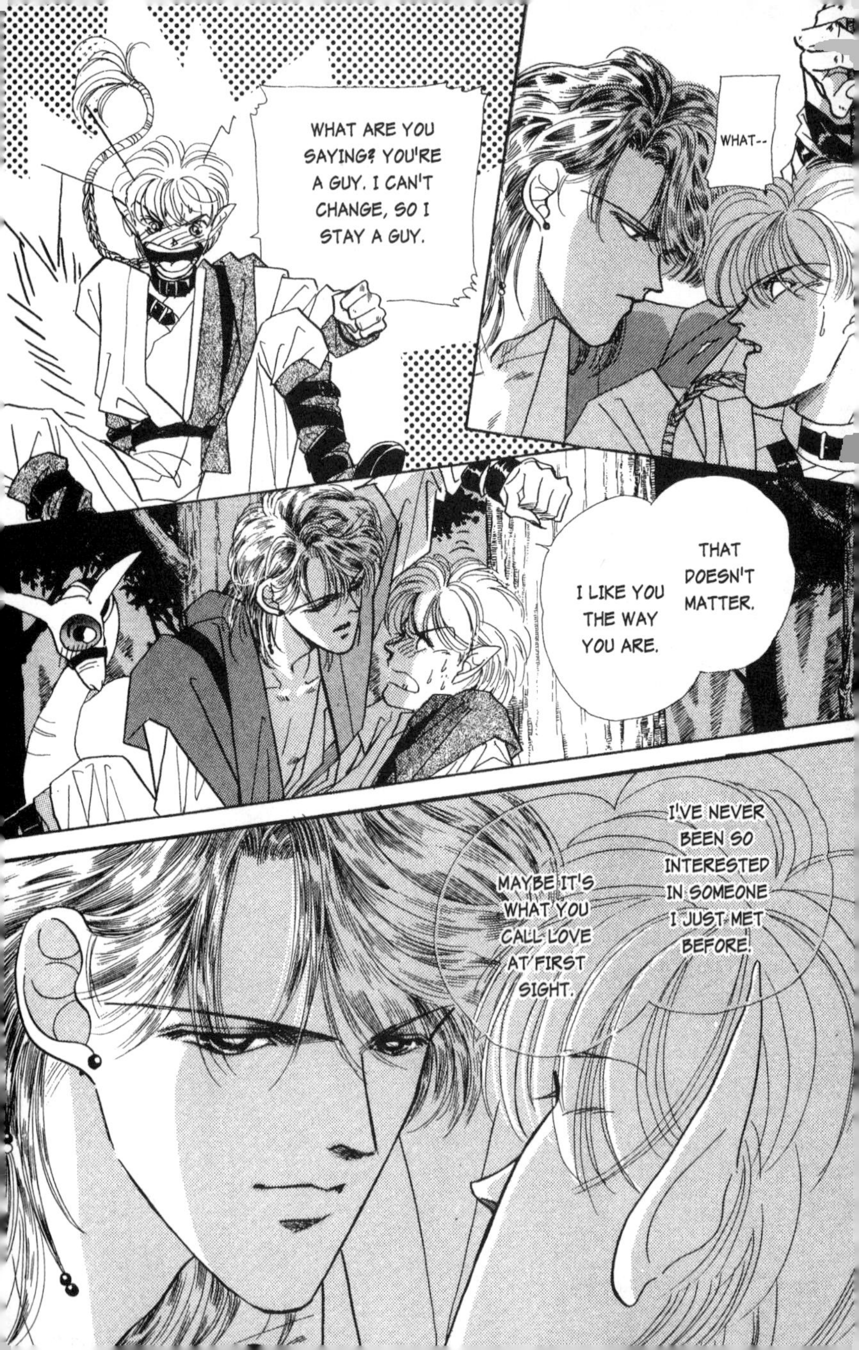
WHAT--
WHAT ARE YOU SAYING? YOU'RE A GUY. I CAN'T CHANGE, SO I STAY A GUY.
THAT DOESN'T MATTER.
I LIKE YOU THE WAY YOU ARE.
I'VE NEVER BEEN SO INTERESTED IN SOMEONE I JUST MET BEFORE.
MAYBE IT'S WHAT YOU CALL LOVE AT FIRST SIGHT.

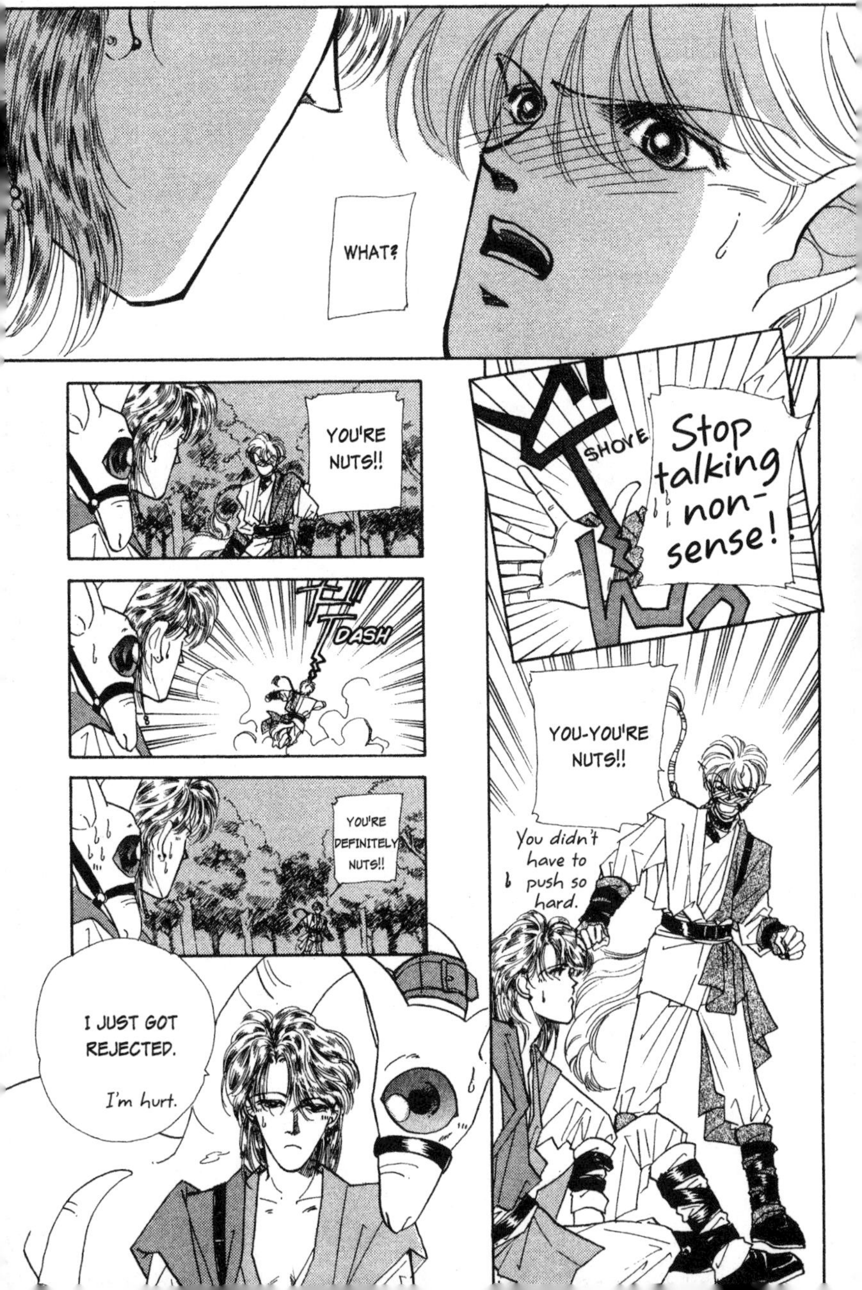
WHAT?
Stop talking nonsense!!
SHOVE
YOU-YOU'RE NUTS!!
You didn't have to push so hard.
YOU'RE NUTS!!
DASH
YOU'RE DEFINITELY NUTS!!
I JUST GOT REJECTED.
I'm hurt.

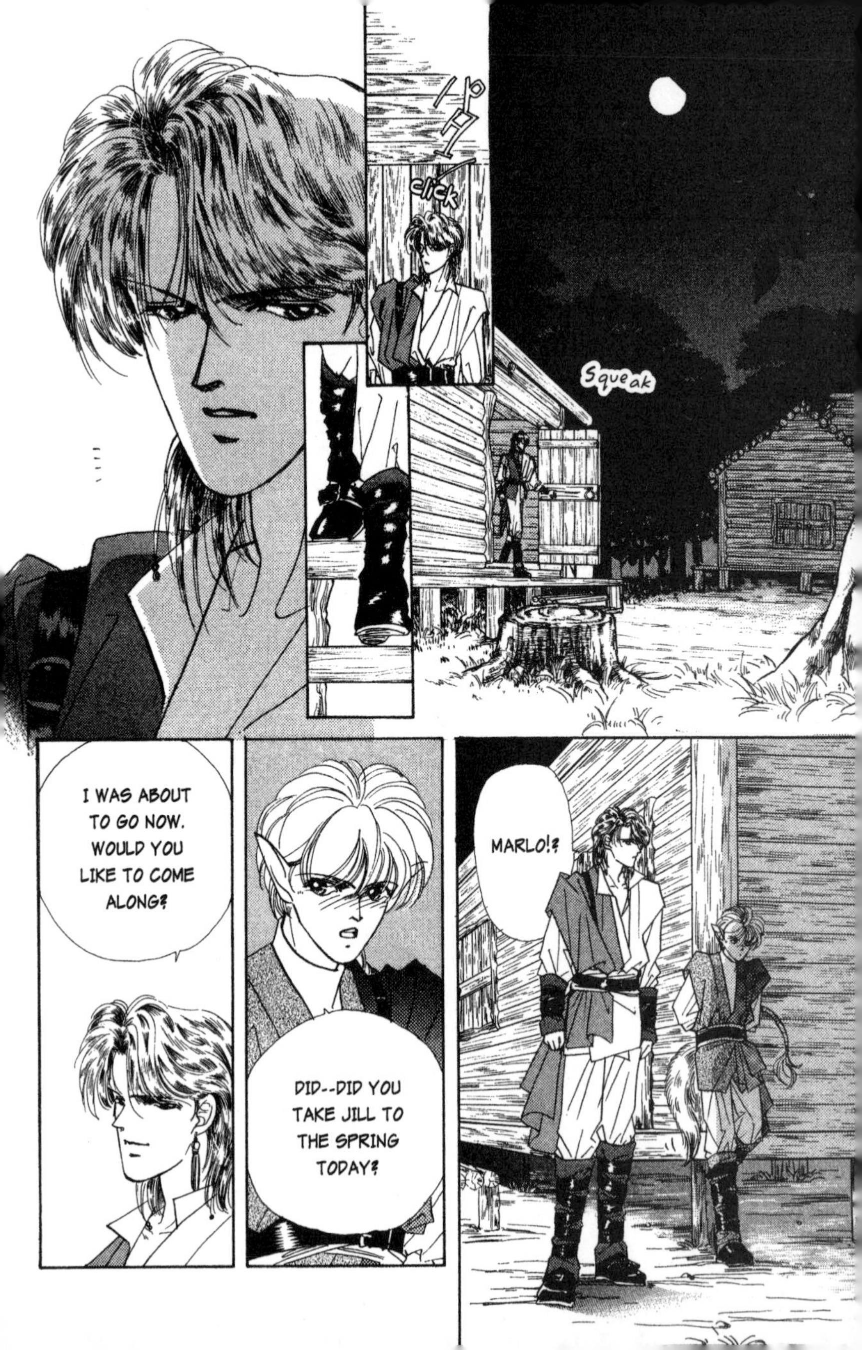
Squeak
click
MARLO!?
DID--DID YOU TAKE JILL TO THE SPRING TODAY?
I WAS ABOUT TO GO NOW. WOULD YOU LIKE TO COME ALONG?

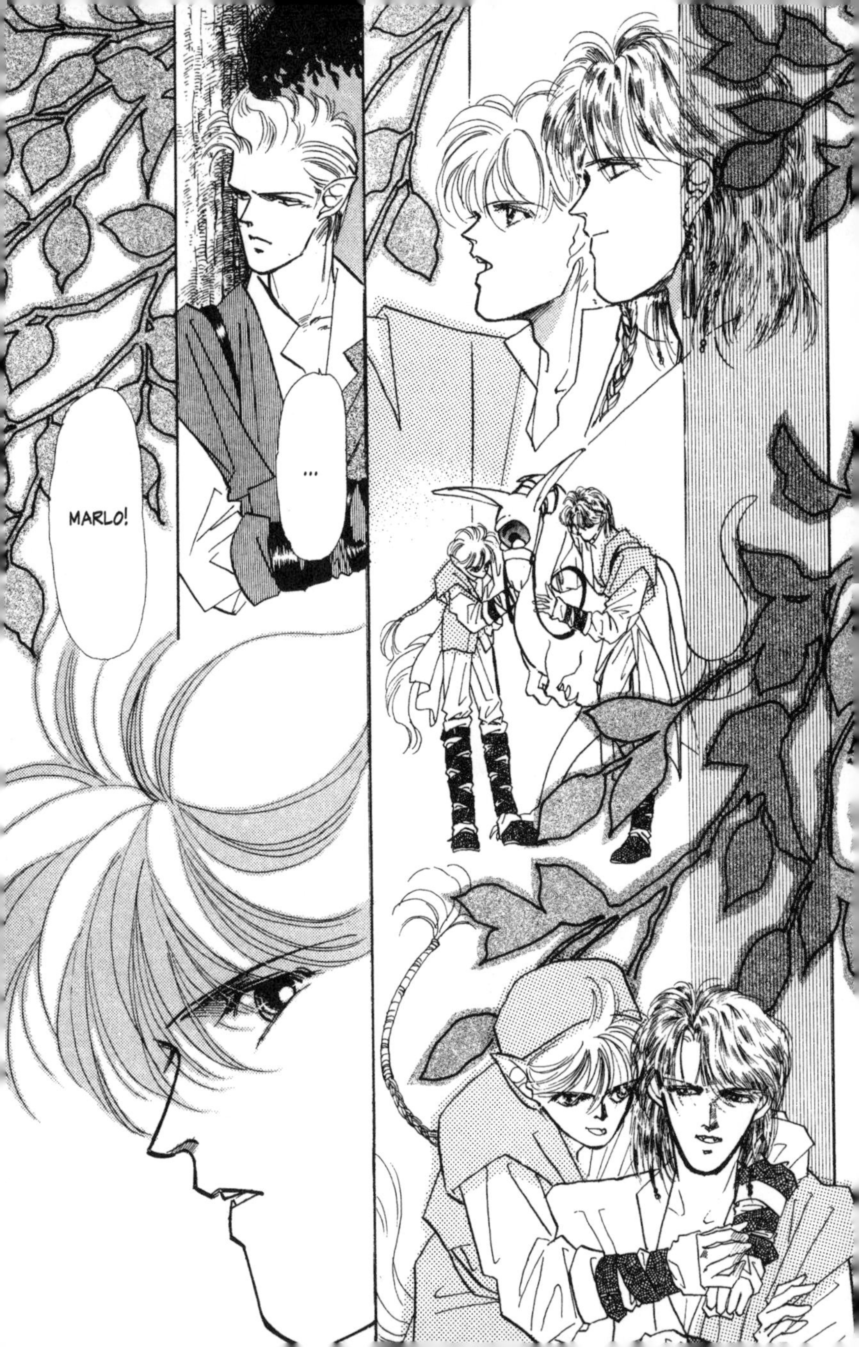
...
MARLO!

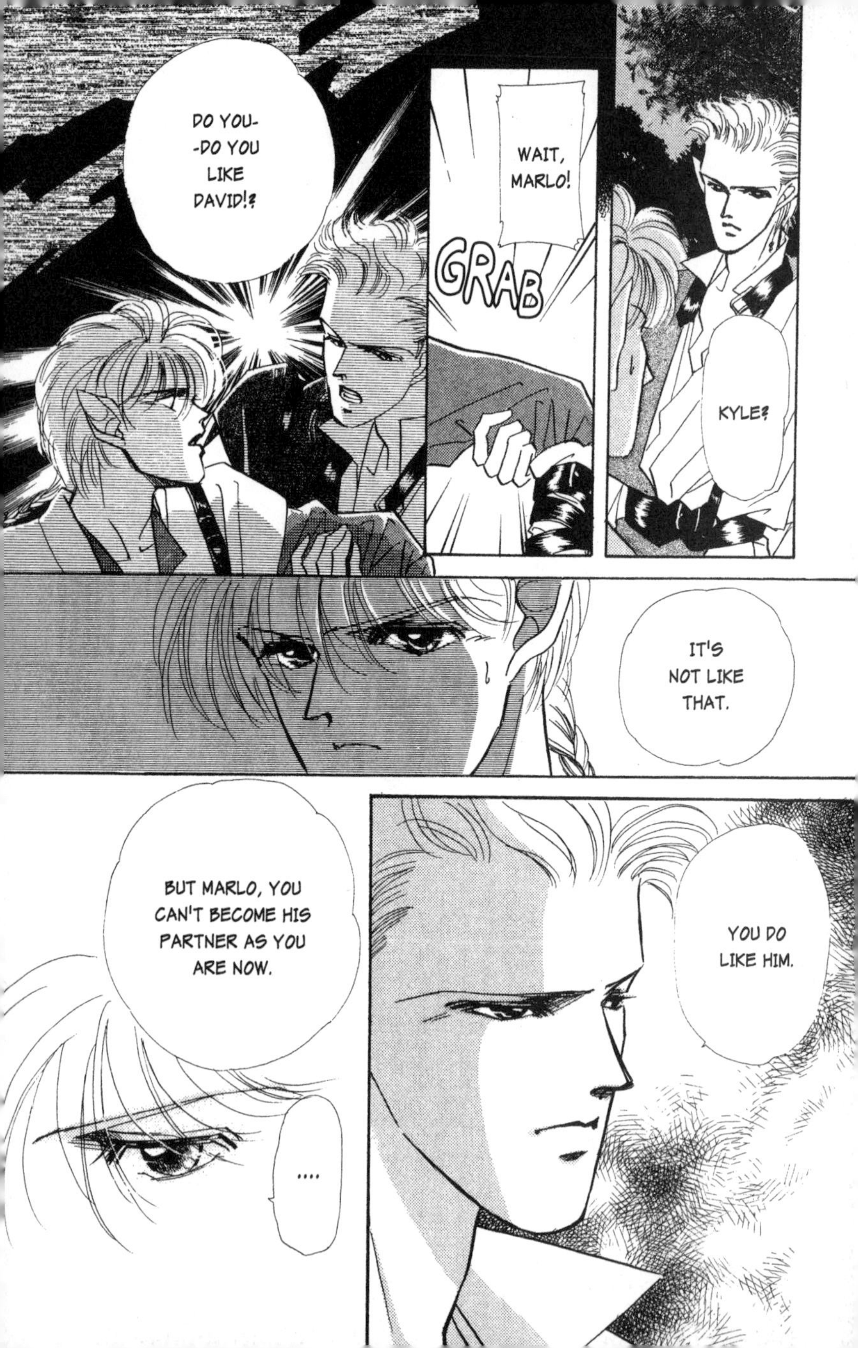
KYLE?
WAIT, MARLO!
GRAB
DO YOU-
-DO YOU LIKE DAVID!?
IT'S NOT LIKE THAT.
YOU DO LIKE HIM.
BUT MARLO, YOU CAN'T BECOME HIS PARTNER AS YOU ARE NOW.
....

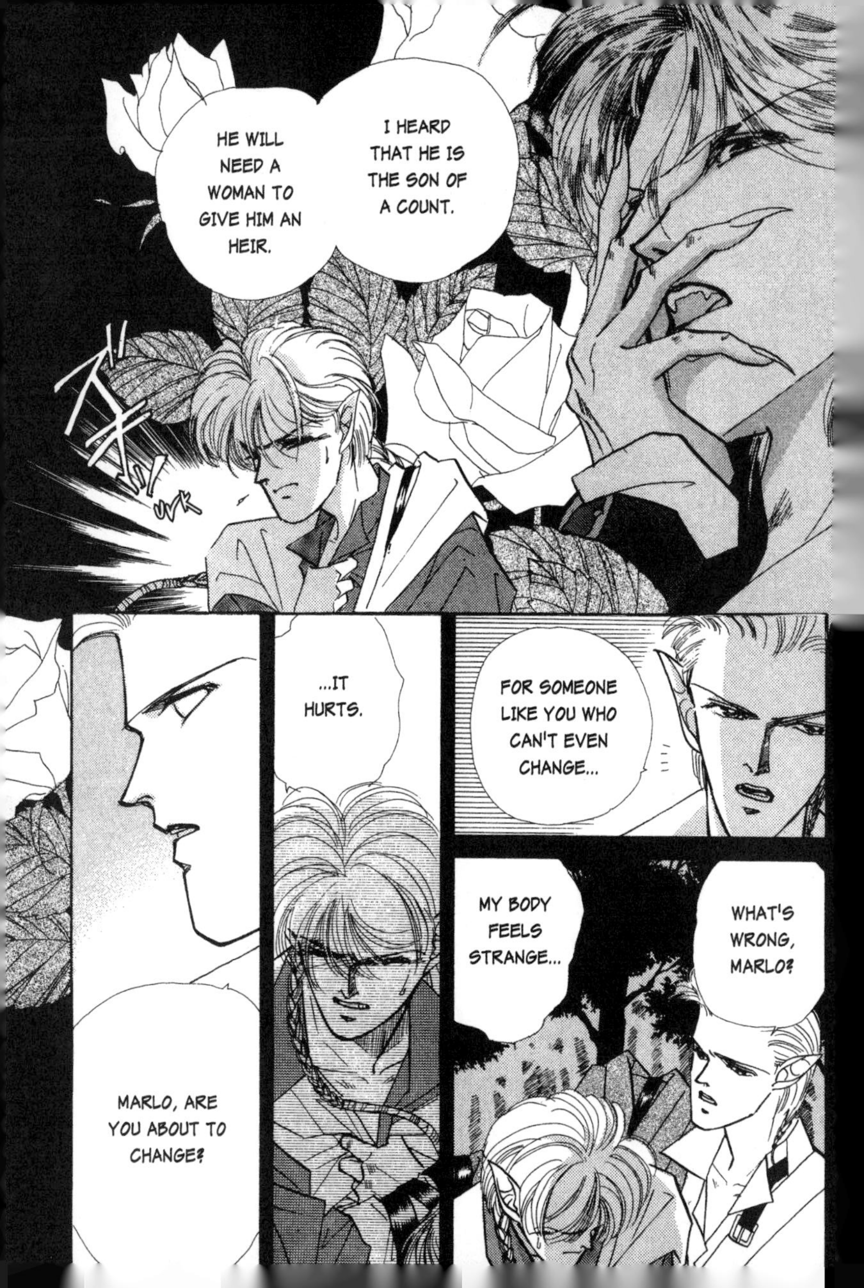
I HEARD THAT HE IS THE SON OF A COUNT.
HE WILL NEED A WOMAN TO GIVE HIM AN HEIR.
ズキッ
UVK
FOR SOMEONE LIKE YOU WHO CAN'T EVEN CHANGE...
WHAT'S WRONG, MARLO?
MY BODY FEELS STRANGE...
...IT HURTS.
MARLO, ARE YOU ABOUT TO CHANGE?

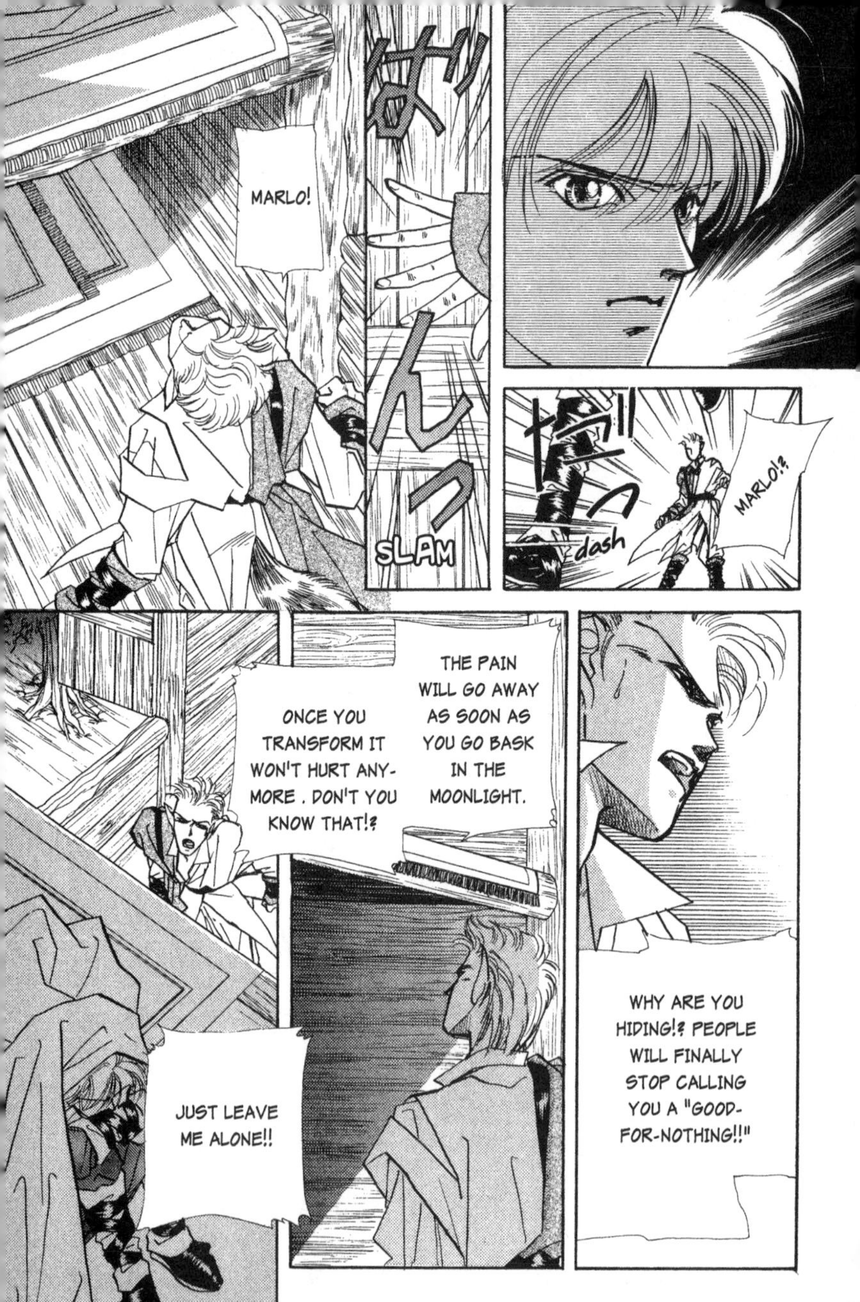
MARLO!?
dash
SLAM
MARLO!
WHY ARE YOU HIDING!? PEOPLE WILL FINALLY STOP CALLING YOU A "GOOD-FOR-NOTHING!!"
THE PAIN WILL GO AWAY AS SOON AS YOU GO BASK IN THE MOONLIGHT.
ONCE YOU TRANSFORM IT WON'T HURT ANY-MORE . DON'T YOU KNOW THAT!?
JUST LEAVE ME ALONE!!

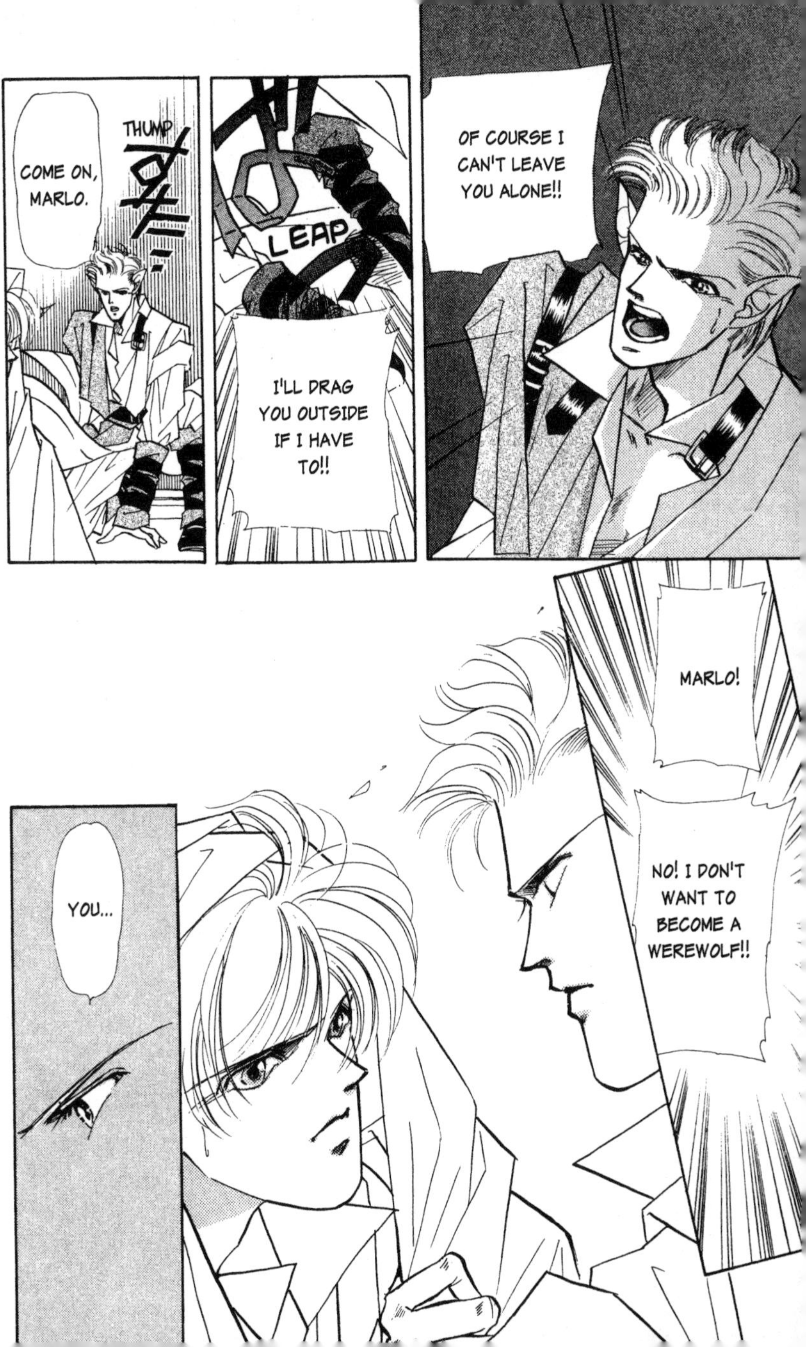
OF COURSE I CAN'T LEAVE YOU ALONE!!
LEAP
I'LL DRAG YOU OUTSIDE IF I HAVE TO!!
THUMP
COME ON, MARLO.
MARLO!
NO! I DON'T WANT TO BECOME A WEREWOLF!!
YOU...

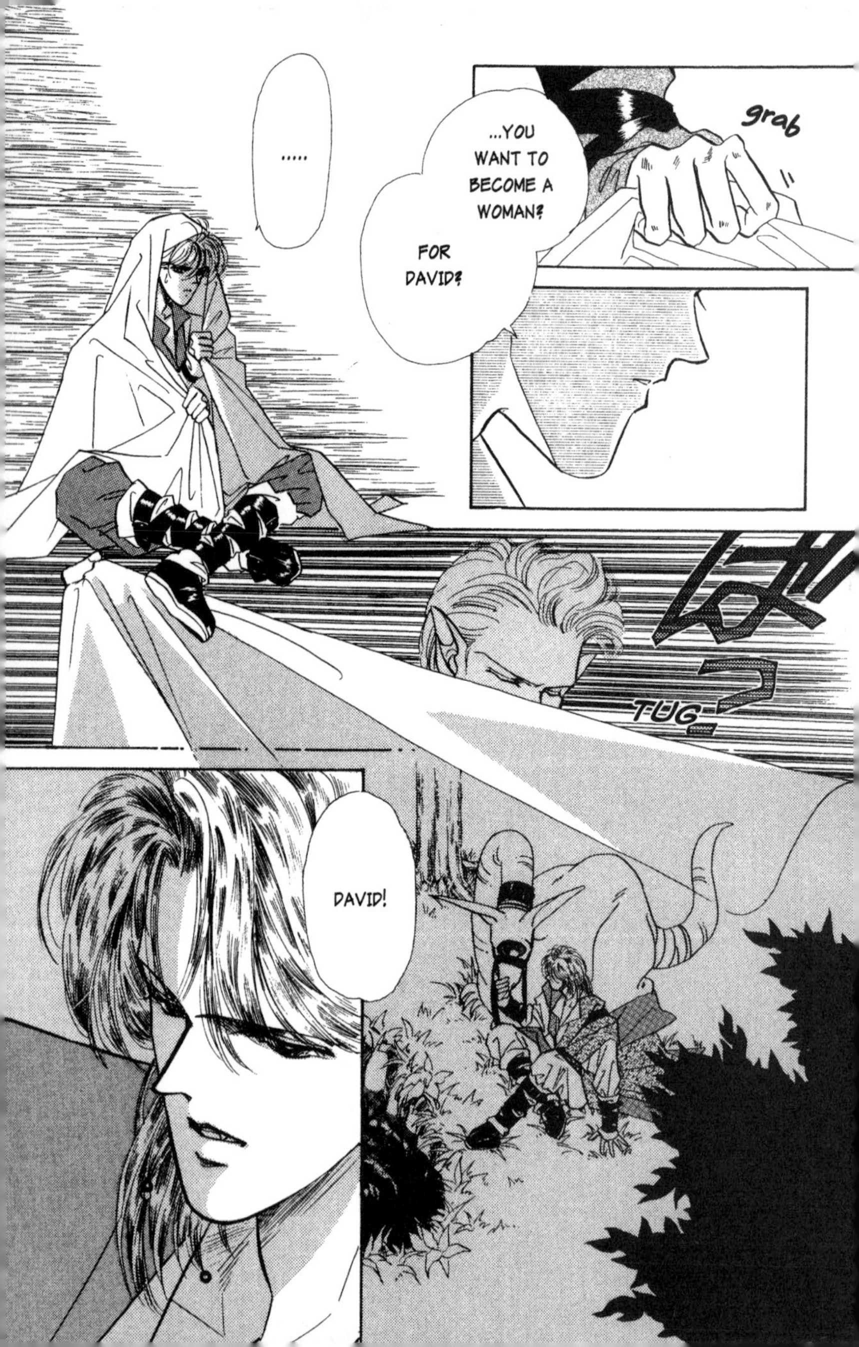
grab
...YOU WANT TO BECOME A WOMAN?
FOR DAVID?
.....
TUG
DAVID!

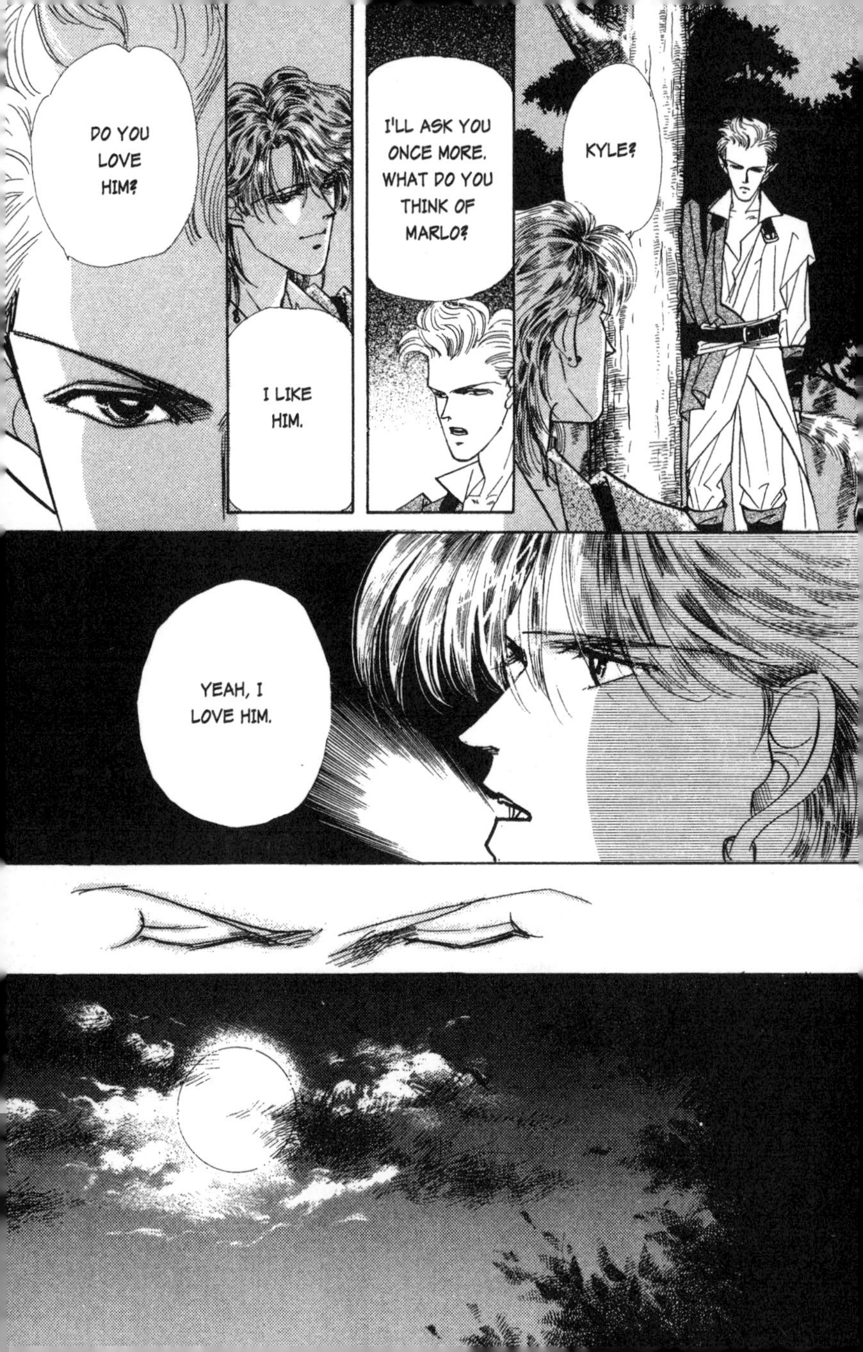
KYLE?
I'LL ASK YOU ONCE MORE. WHAT DO YOU THINK OF MARLO?
I LIKE HIM.
DO YOU LOVE HIM?
YEAH, I LOVE HIM.

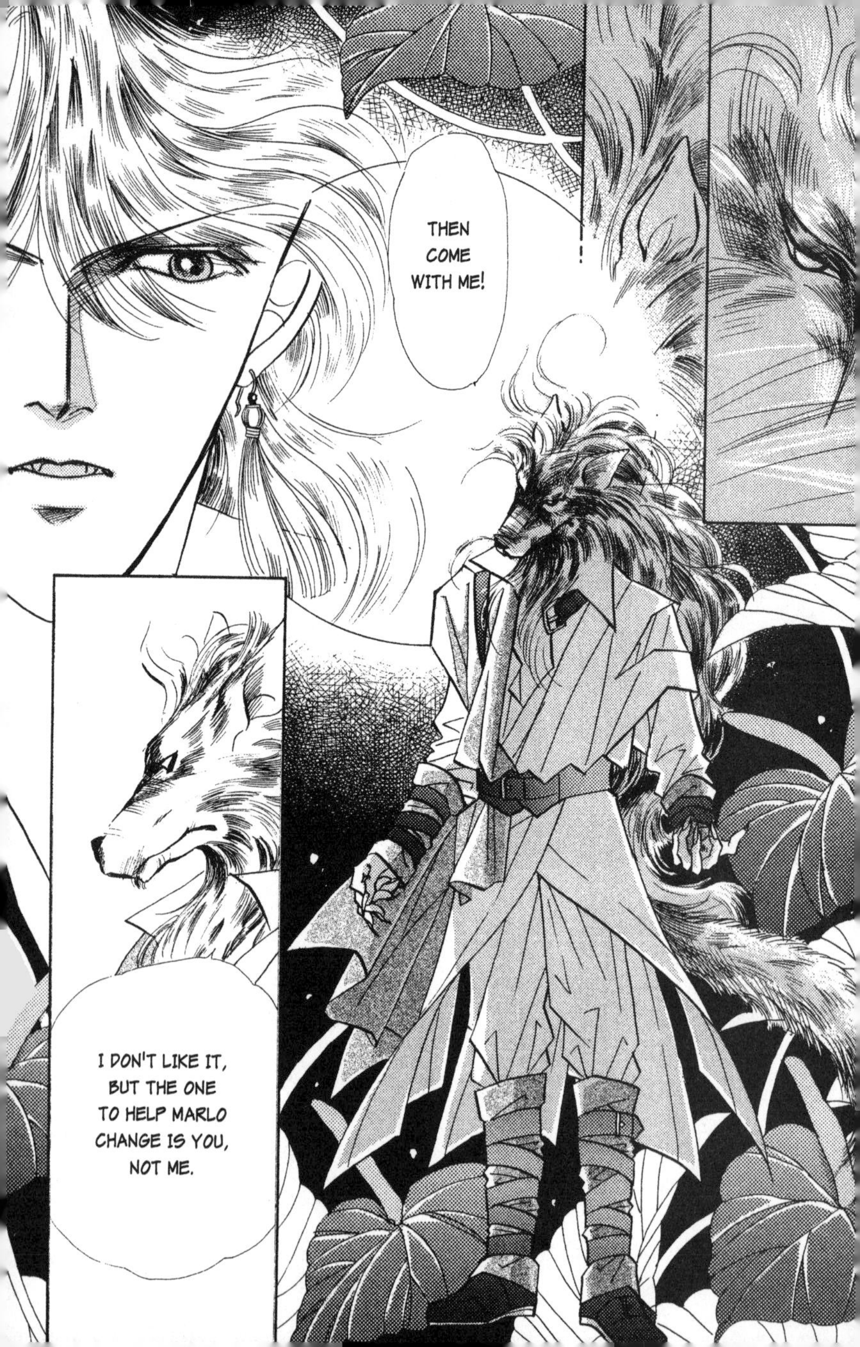
THEN COME WITH ME!
I DON'T LIKE IT, BUT THE ONE TO HELP MARLO CHANGE IS YOU, NOT ME.

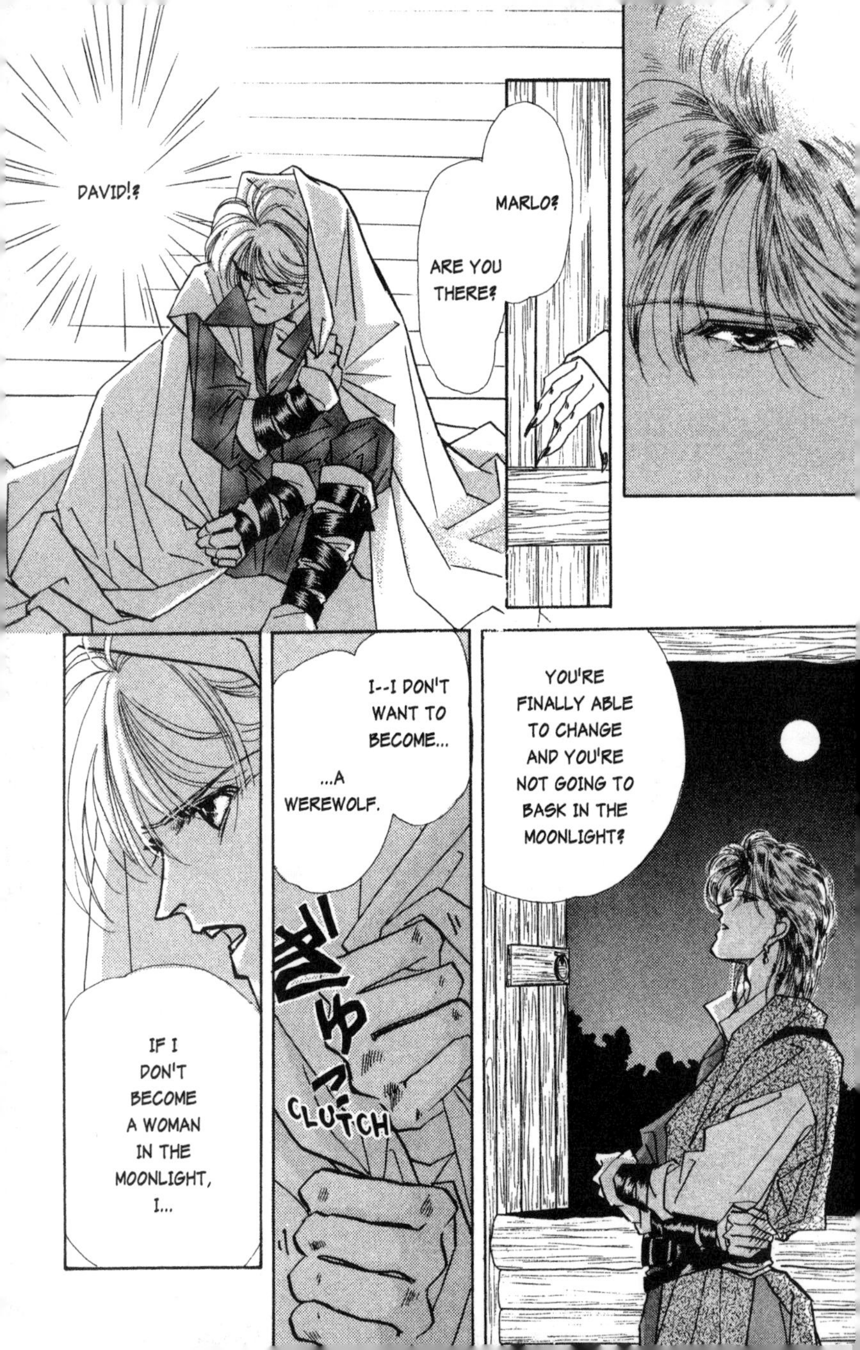
MARLO? ARE YOU THERE?
DAVID!?
YOU'RE FINALLY ABLE TO CHANGE AND YOU'RE NOT GOING TO BASK IN THE MOONLIGHT?
I--I DON'T WANT TO BECOME...
...A WEREWOLF.
CLUTCH
IF I DON'T BECOME A WOMAN IN THE MOONLIGHT, I...

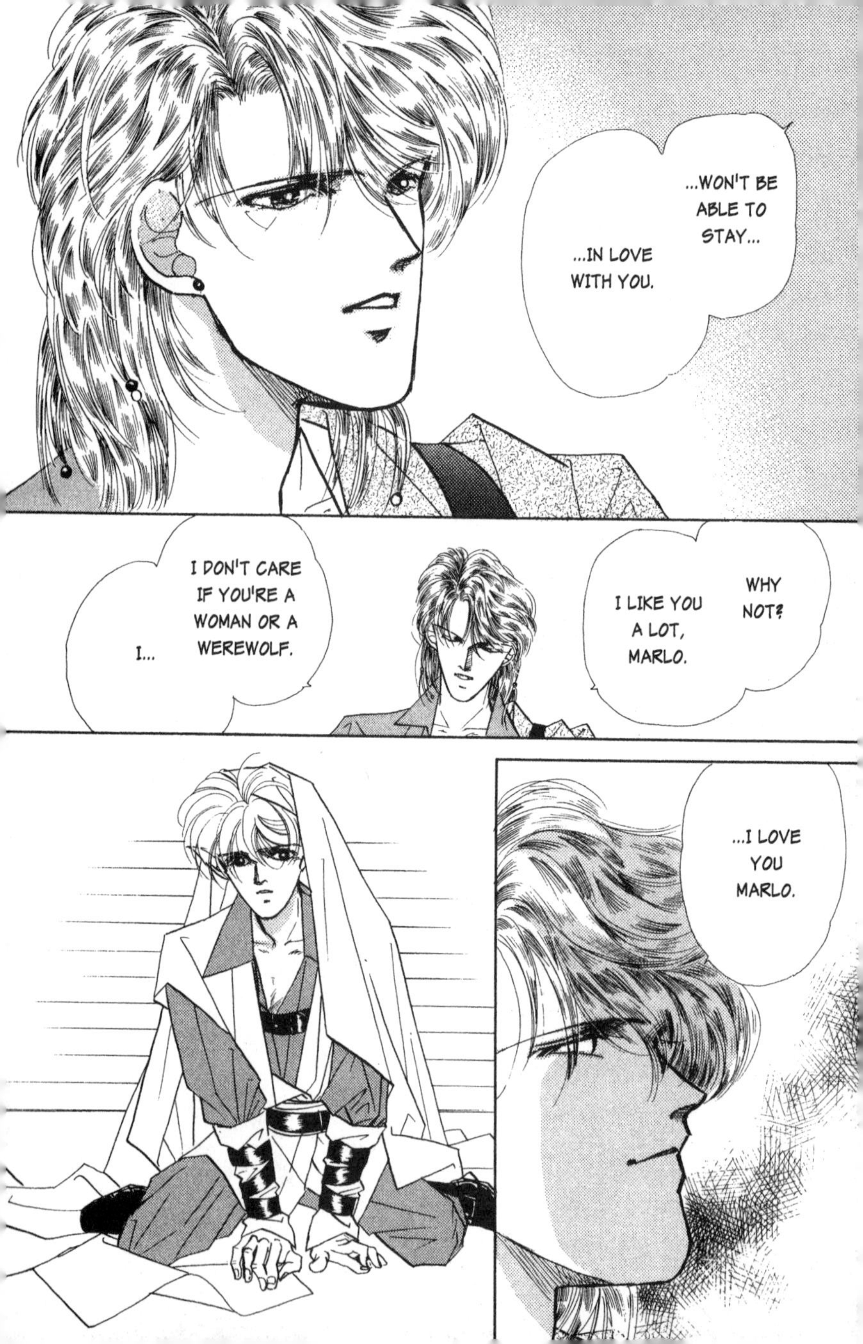
...WON'T BE ABLE TO STAY...
...IN LOVE WITH YOU.
WHY NOT?
I LIKE YOU A LOT, MARLO.
I DON'T CARE IF YOU'RE A WOMAN OR A WEREWOLF.
I...
...I LOVE YOU MARLO.

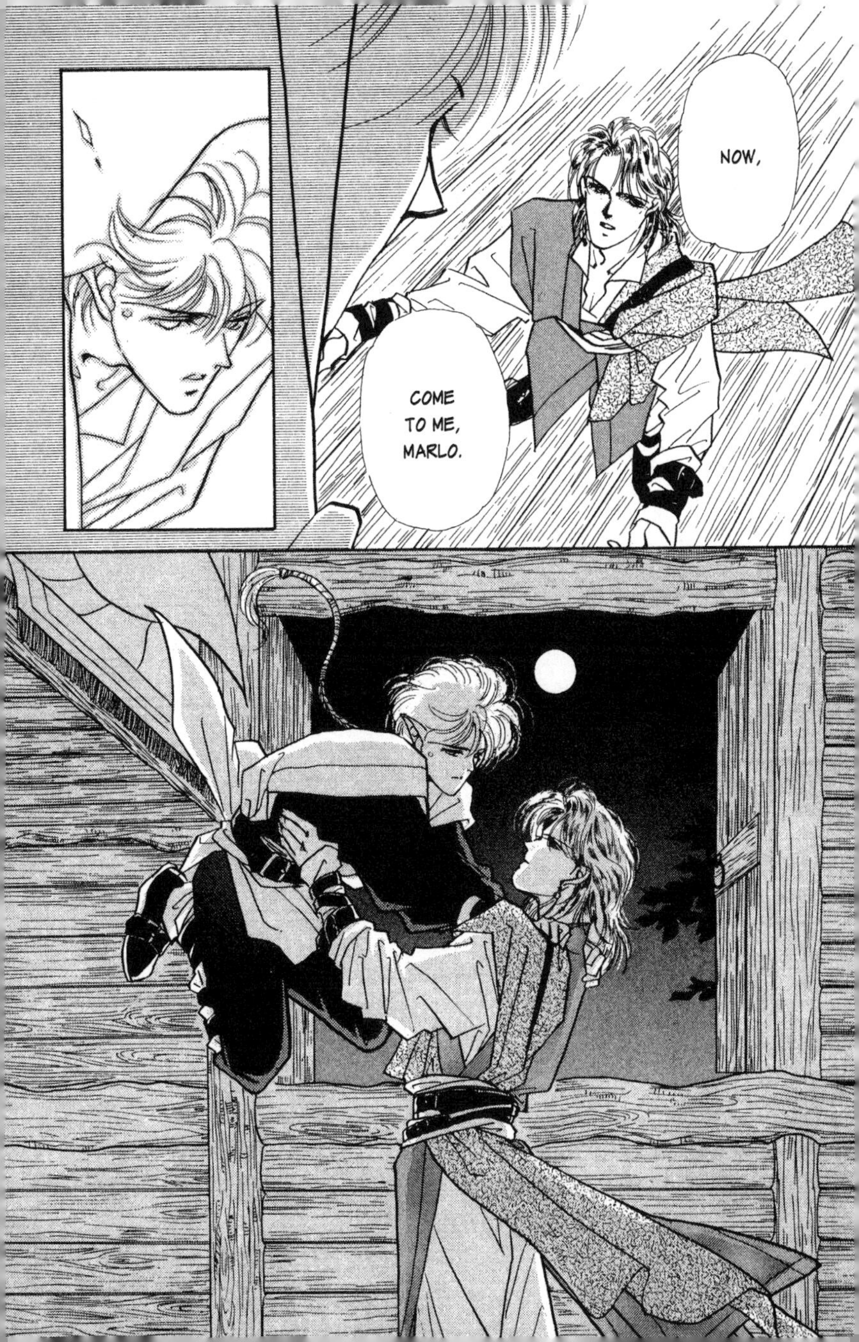
NOW,
COME TO ME, MARLO.

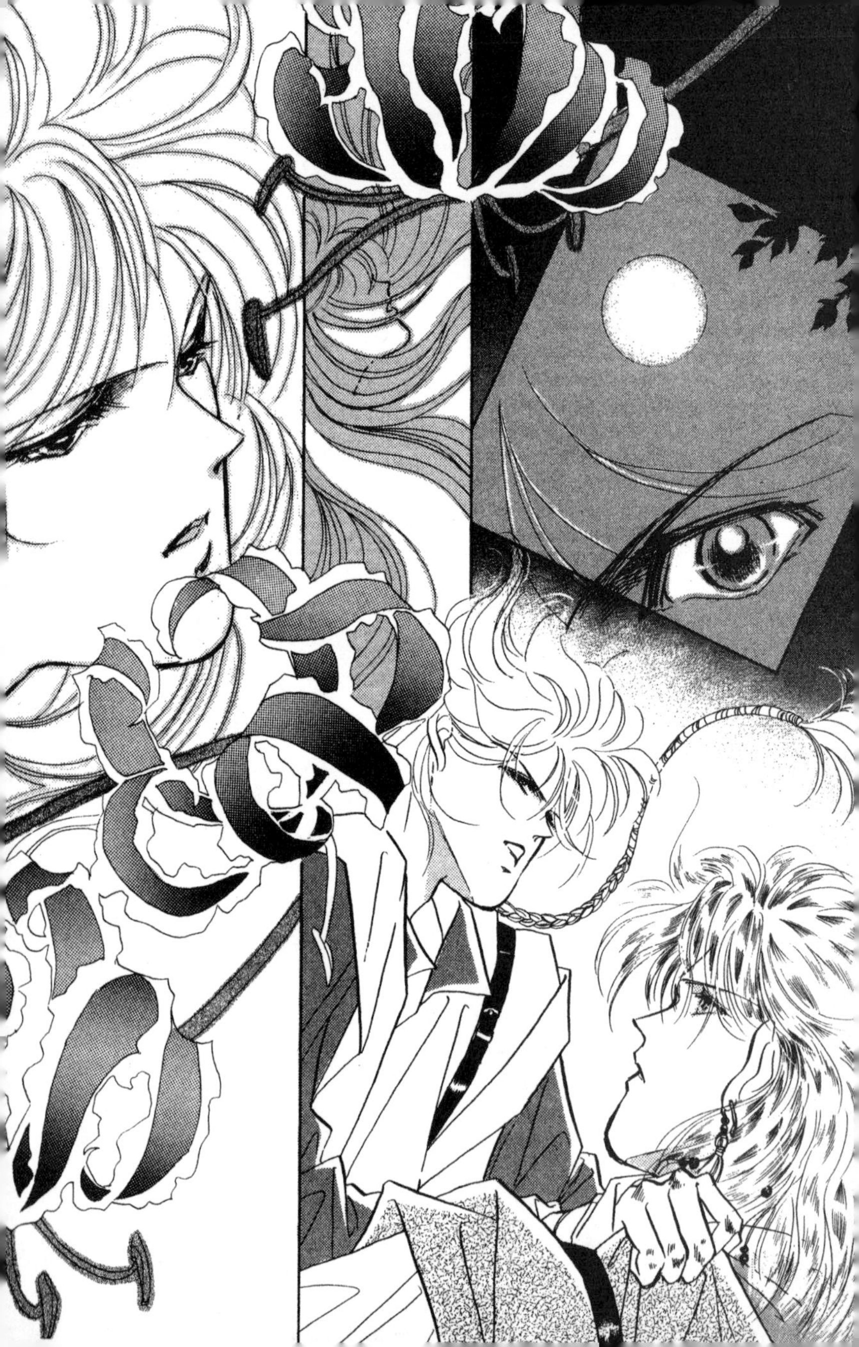

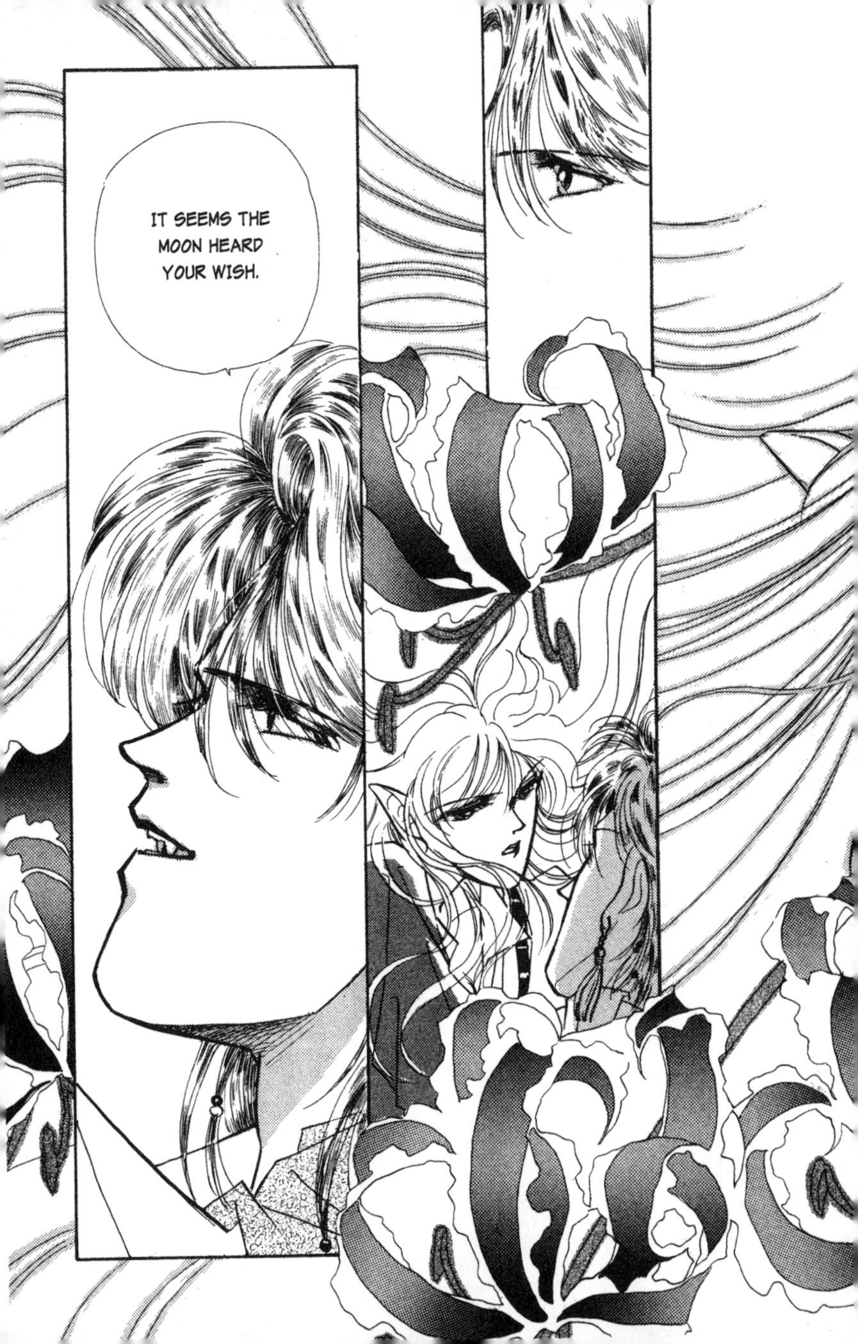
IT SEEMS THE MOON HEARD YOUR WISH.

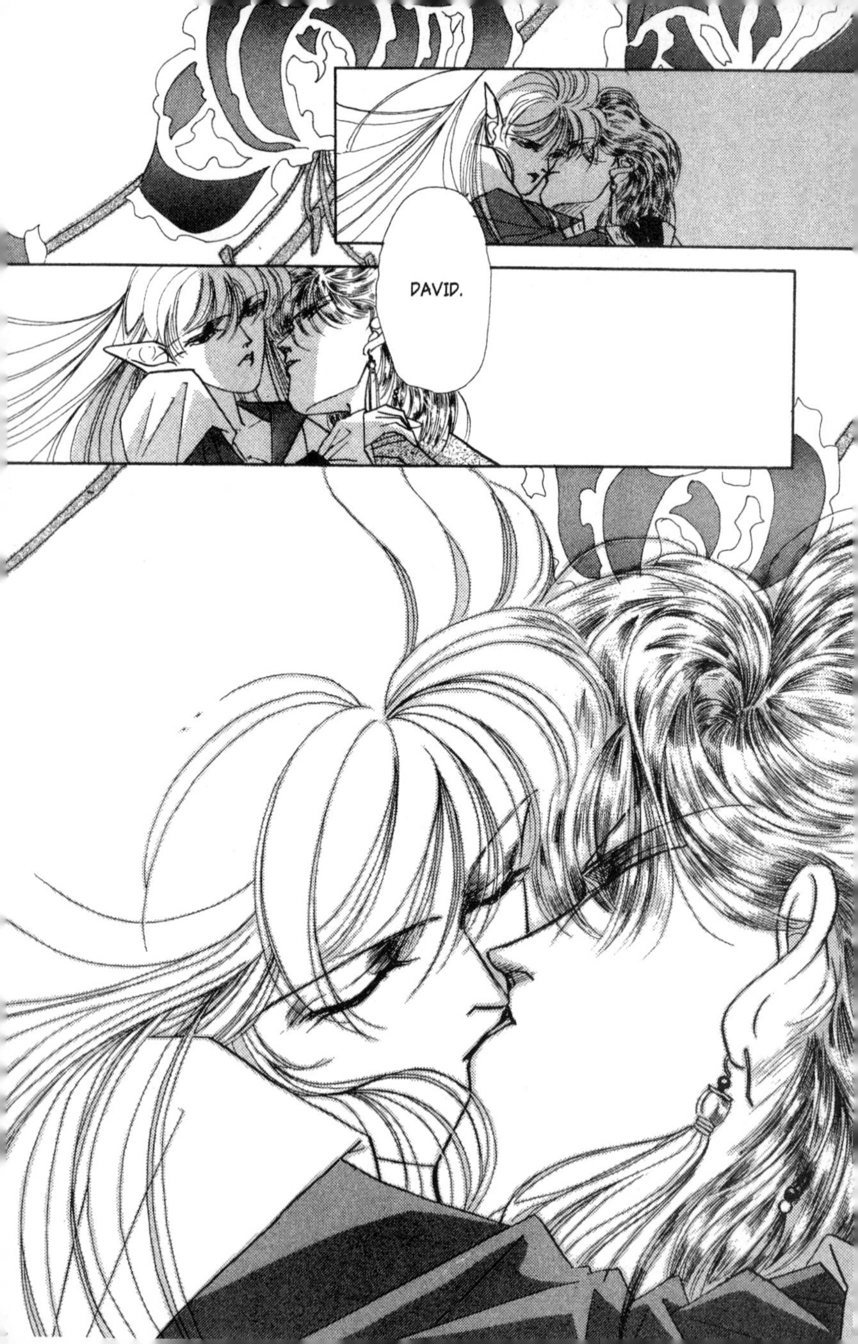
DAVID.

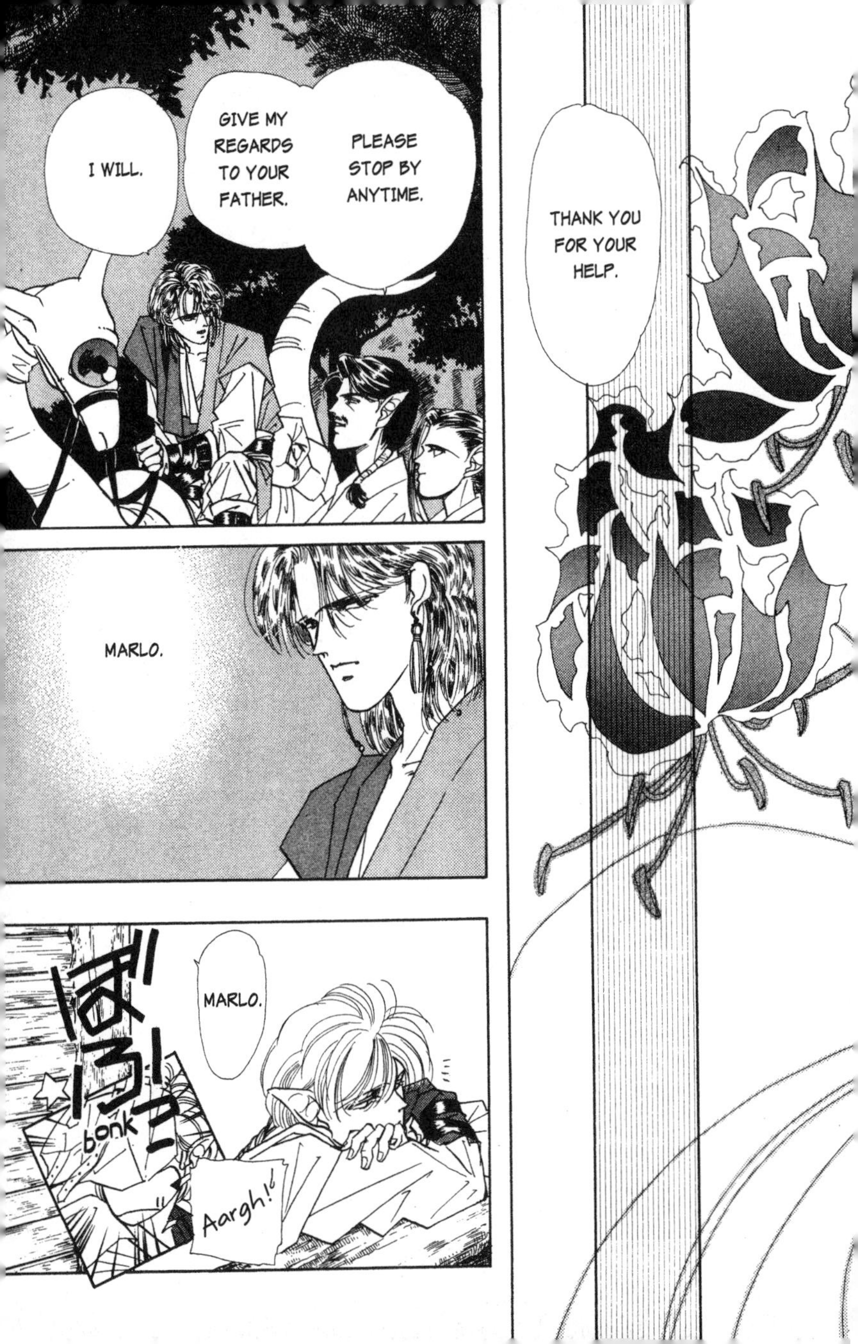
THANK YOU FOR YOUR HELP.
PLEASE STOP BY ANYTIME.
GIVE MY REGARDS TO YOUR FATHER.
I WILL.
MARLO.
MARLO.
bonk
Aargh!

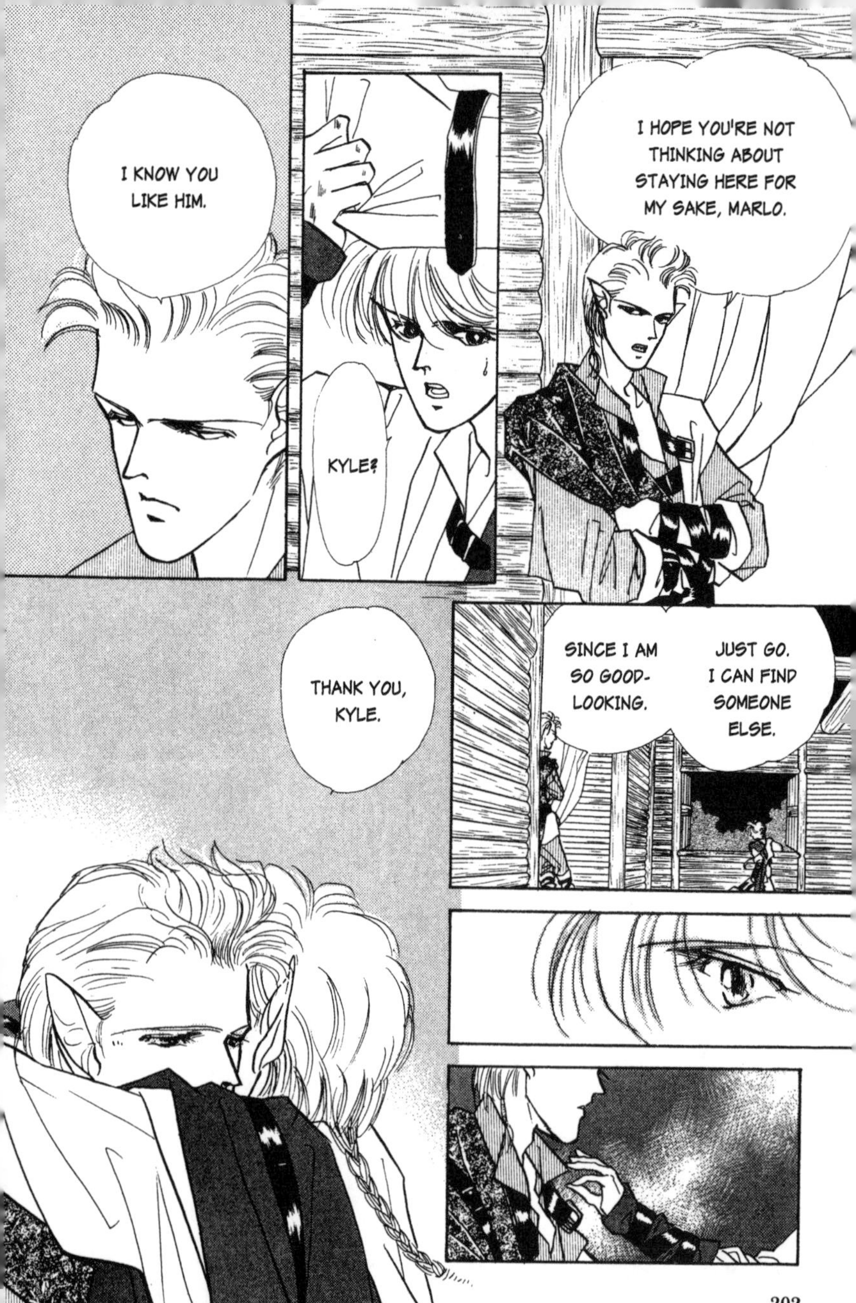
I HOPE YOU'RE NOT THINKING ABOUT STAYING HERE FOR MY SAKE, MARLO.
KYLE?
I KNOW YOU LIKE HIM.
JUST GO. I CAN FIND SOMEONE ELSE.
SINCE I AM SO GOOD-LOOKING.
THANK YOU, KYLE.

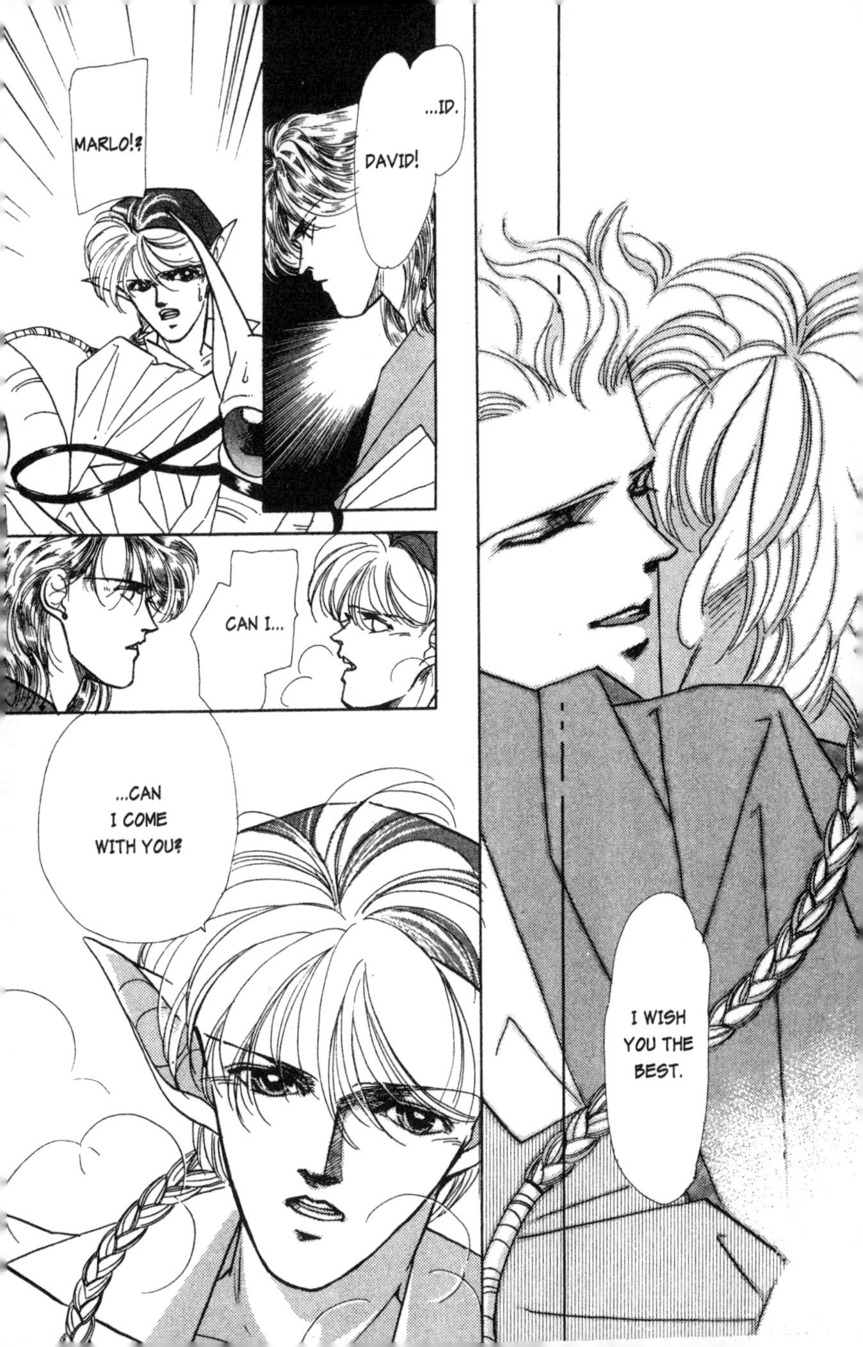
...ID.
DAVID!
MARLO!?
CAN I...
...CAN I COME WITH YOU?
I WISH YOU THE BEST.

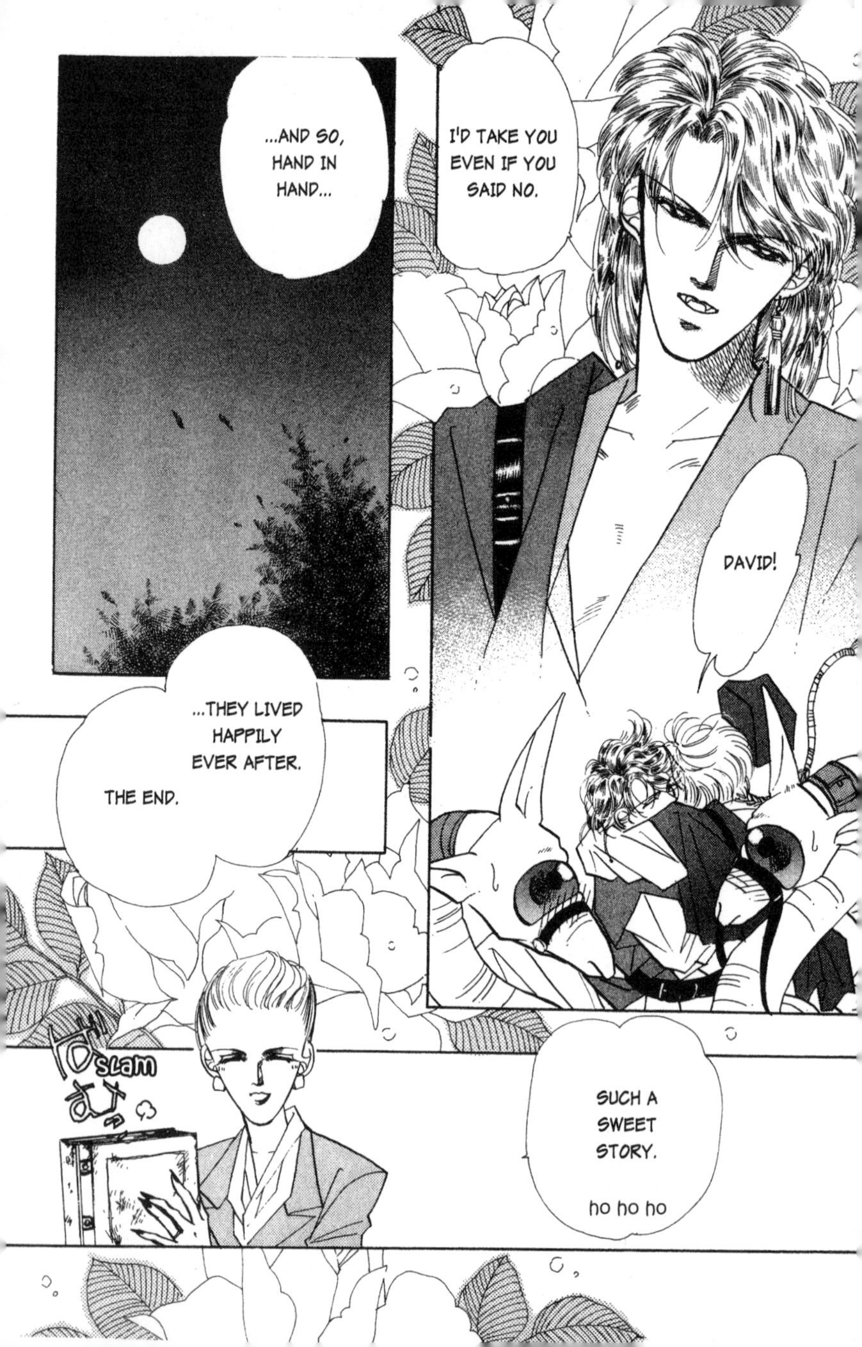
I'D TAKE YOU EVEN IF YOU SAID NO.
DAVID!
...AND SO, HAND IN HAND...
...THEY LIVED HAPPILY EVER AFTER.
THE END.
SUCH A SWEET STORY.
ho ho ho
slam

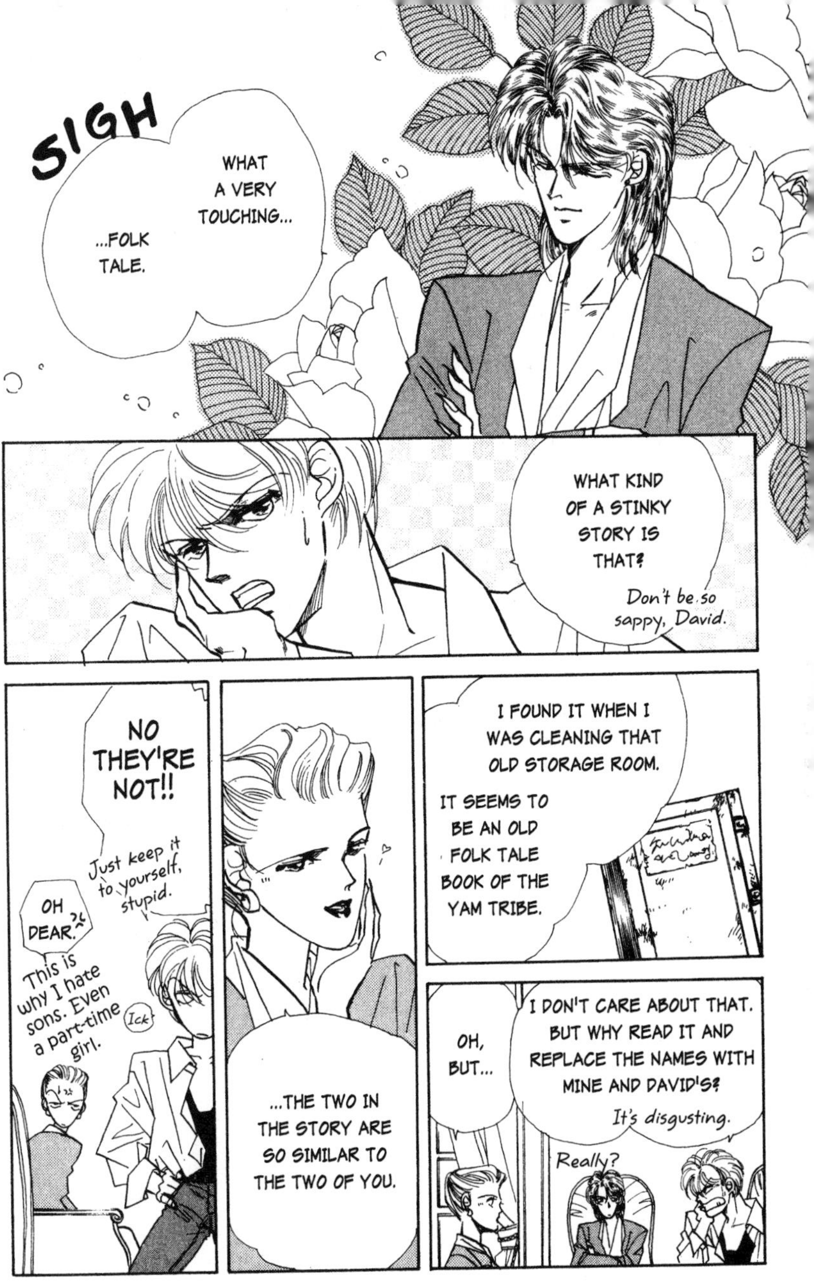
SIGH
WHAT A VERY TOUCHING...
...FOLK TALE.
WHAT KIND OF A STINKY STORY IS THAT?
Don't be so sappy, David.
I FOUND IT WHEN I WAS CLEANING THAT OLD STORAGE ROOM.
IT SEEMS TO BE AN OLD FOLK TALE BOOK OF THE YAM TRIBE.
I DON'T CARE ABOUT THAT. BUT WHY READ IT AND REPLACE THE NAMES WITH MINE AND DAVID'S?
It's disgusting.
OH, BUT...
Really?
...THE TWO IN THE STORY ARE SO SIMILAR TO THE TWO OF YOU.
NO THEY'RE NOT!!
Just keep it to yourself, stupid.
OH DEAR.
This is why I hate sons. Even a part-time girl.
Ick

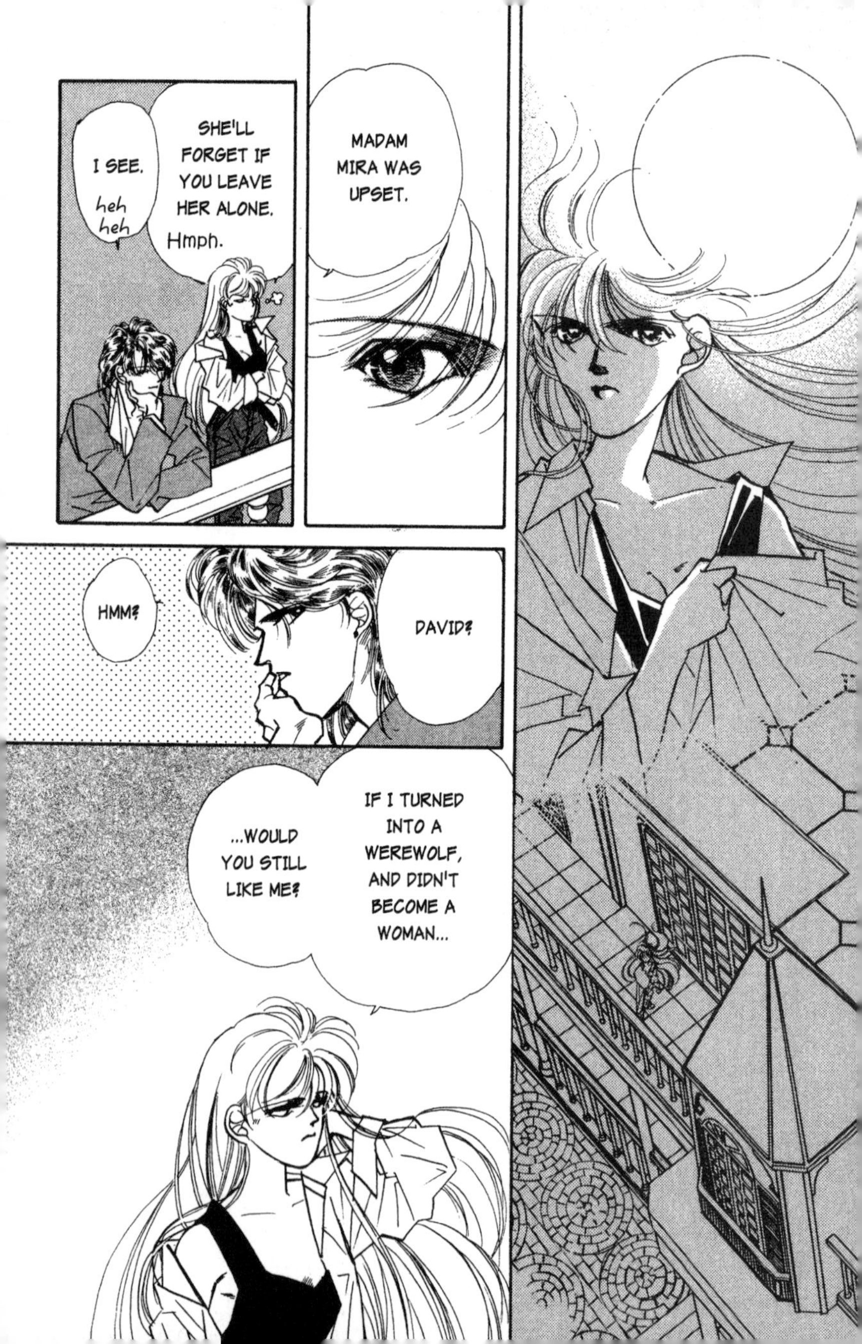
MADAM MIRA WAS UPSET.
SHE'LL FORGET IF YOU LEAVE HER ALONE.
Hmph.
I SEE.
heh heh
DAVID?
HMM?
IF I TURNED INTO A WEREWOLF, AND DIDN'T BECOME A WOMAN...
...WOULD YOU STILL LIKE ME?

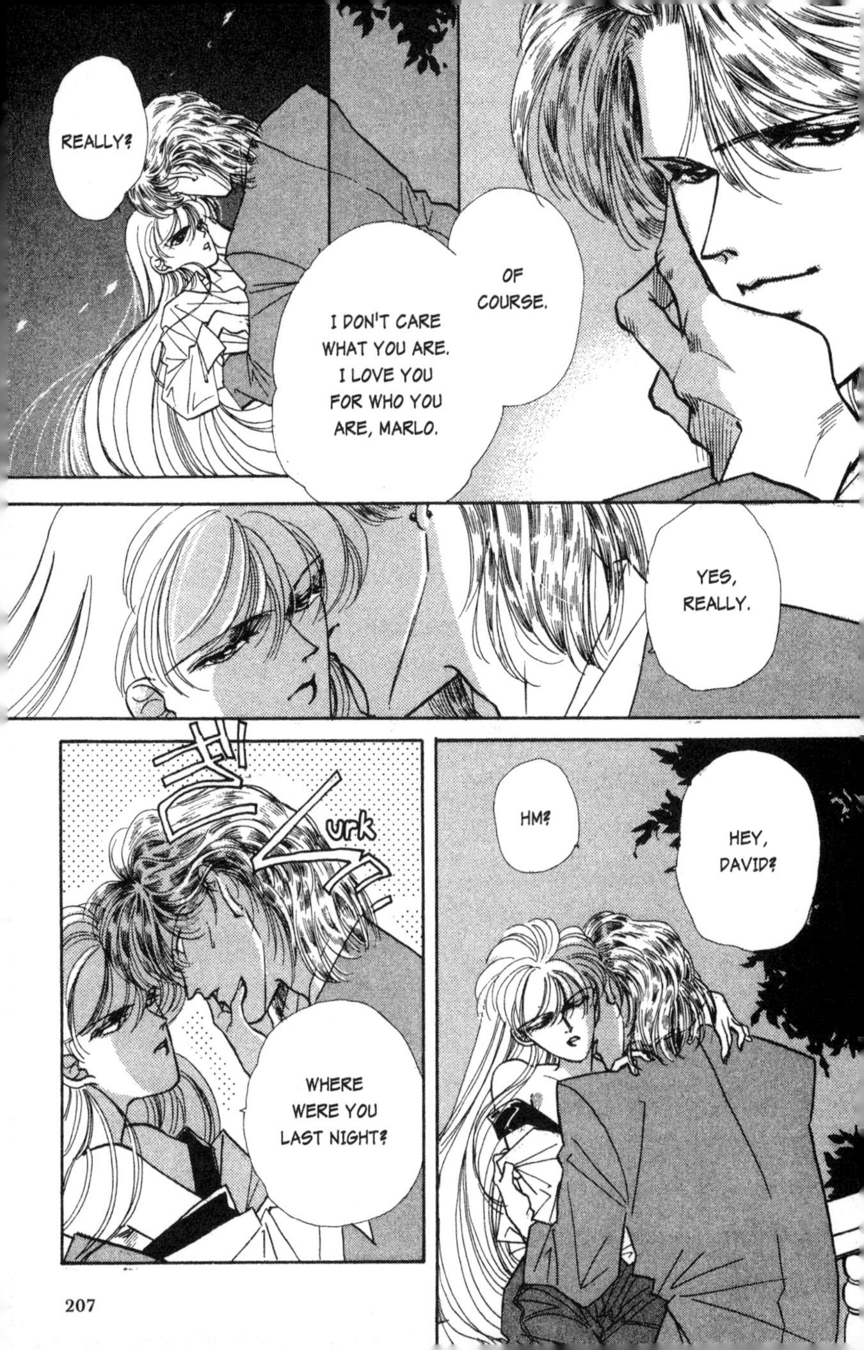
OF COURSE.
I DON'T CARE WHAT YOU ARE. I LOVE YOU FOR WHO YOU ARE, MARLO.
REALLY?
YES, REALLY.
HEY, DAVID?
HM?
urk
WHERE WERE YOU LAST NIGHT?

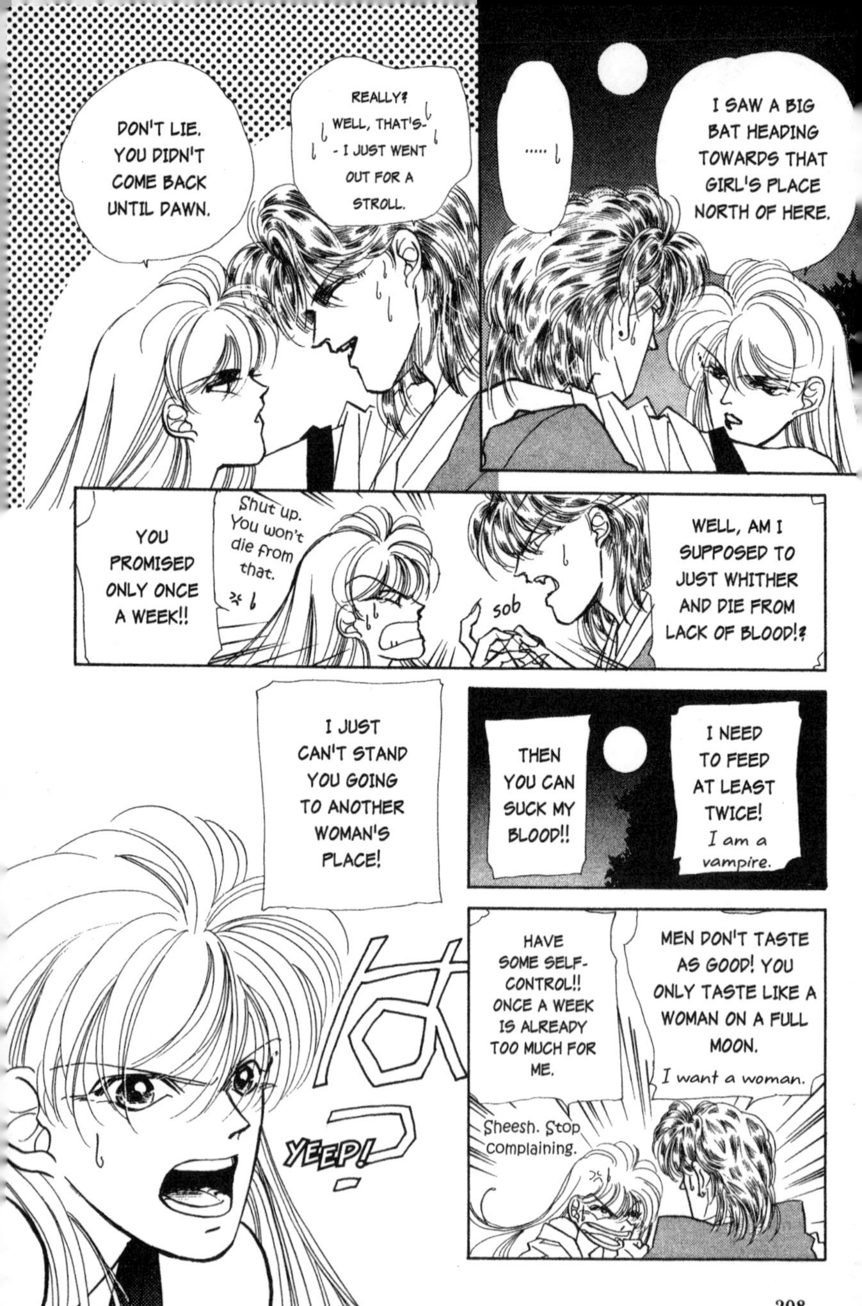
I SAW A BIG BAT HEADING TOWARDS THAT GIRL'S PLACE NORTH OF HERE.
.....
REALLY? WELL, THAT'S- - I JUST WENT OUT FOR A STROLL.
DON'T LIE. YOU DIDN'T COME BACK UNTIL DAWN.
WELL, AM I SUPPOSED TO JUST WHITHER AND DIE FROM LACK OF BLOOD!?
sob
Shut up. You won't die from that.
YOU PROMISED ONLY ONCE A WEEK!!
I NEED TO FEED AT LEAST TWICE!
I am a vampire.
THEN YOU CAN SUCK MY BLOOD!!
MEN DON'T TASTE AS GOOD! YOU ONLY TASTE LIKE A WOMAN ON A FULL MOON.
I want a woman.
HAVE SOME SELF-CONTROL!! ONCE A WEEK IS ALREADY TOO MUCH FOR ME.
Sheesh. Stop complaining.
I JUST CAN'T STAND YOU GOING TO ANOTHER WOMAN'S PLACE!
YEEP!

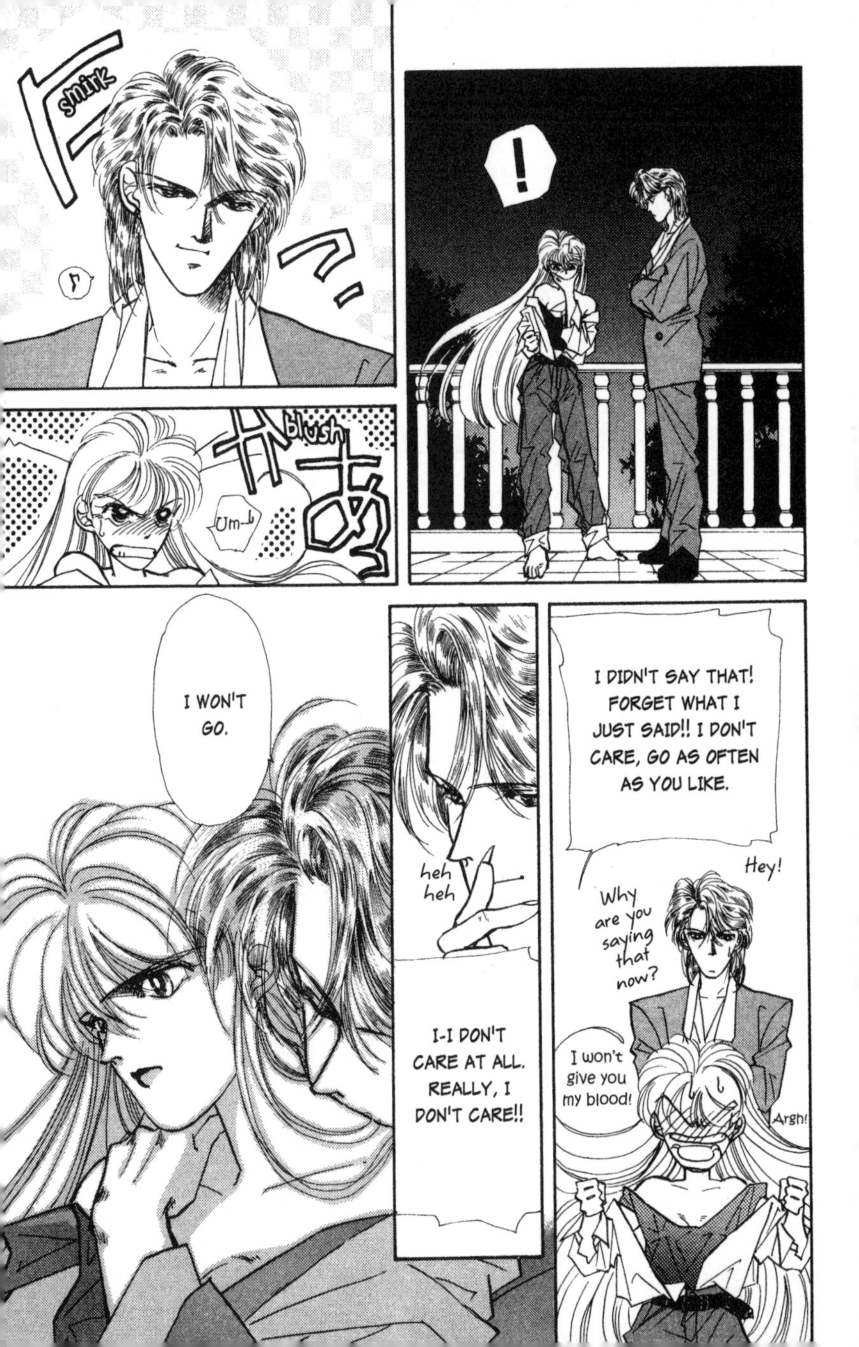
!
smirk
♪
blush
Um--
I DIDN'T SAY THAT! FORGET WHAT I JUST SAID!! I DON'T CARE, GO AS OFTEN AS YOU LIKE.
Hey!
Why are you saying that now?
I won't give you my blood!
Argh!
heh heh
I-I DON'T CARE AT ALL. REALLY, I DON'T CARE!!
I WON'T GO.

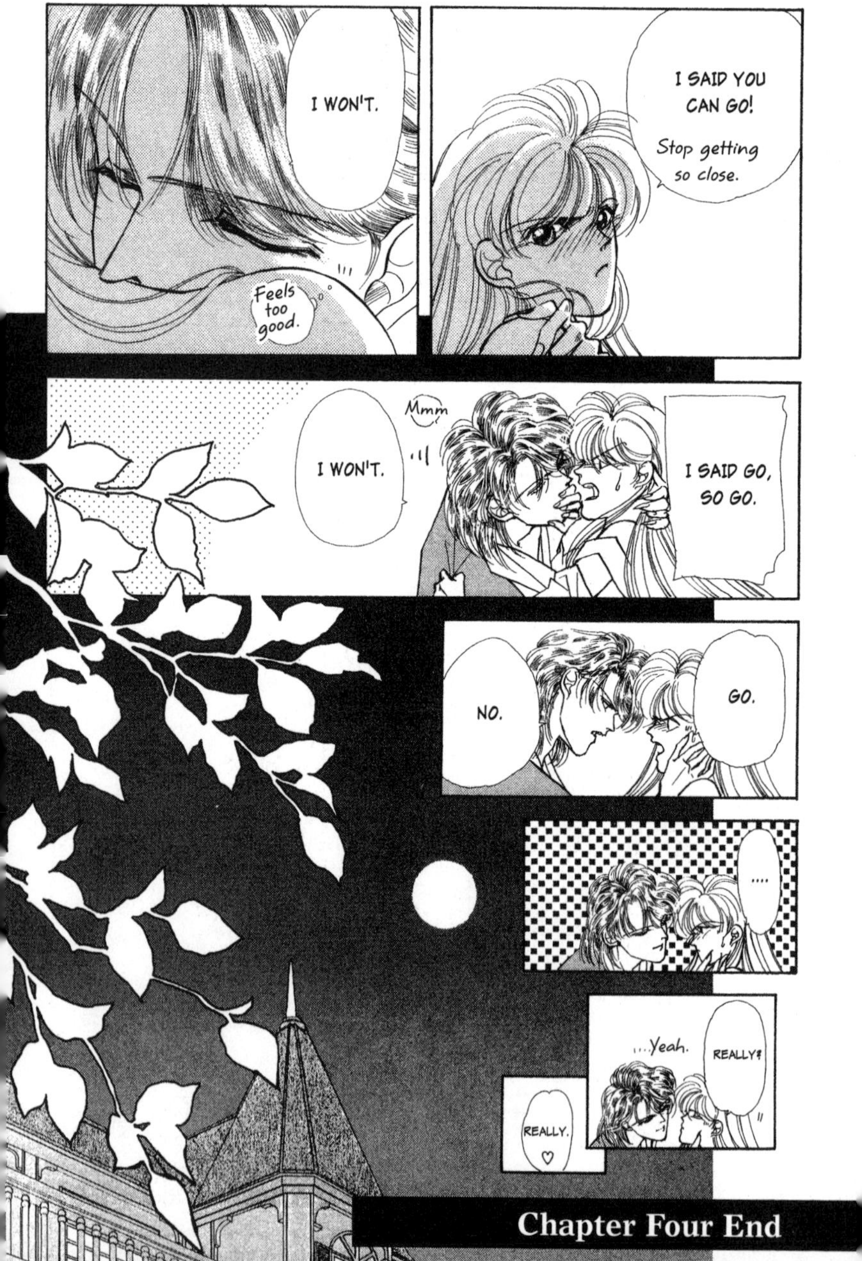
I SAID YOU CAN GO!
Stop getting so close.
I WON'T.
Feels too good.
I SAID GO, SO GO.
Mmm
I WON'T.
GO.
NO.
....
REALLY?
...Yeah.
REALLY. ♡
Chapter Four End

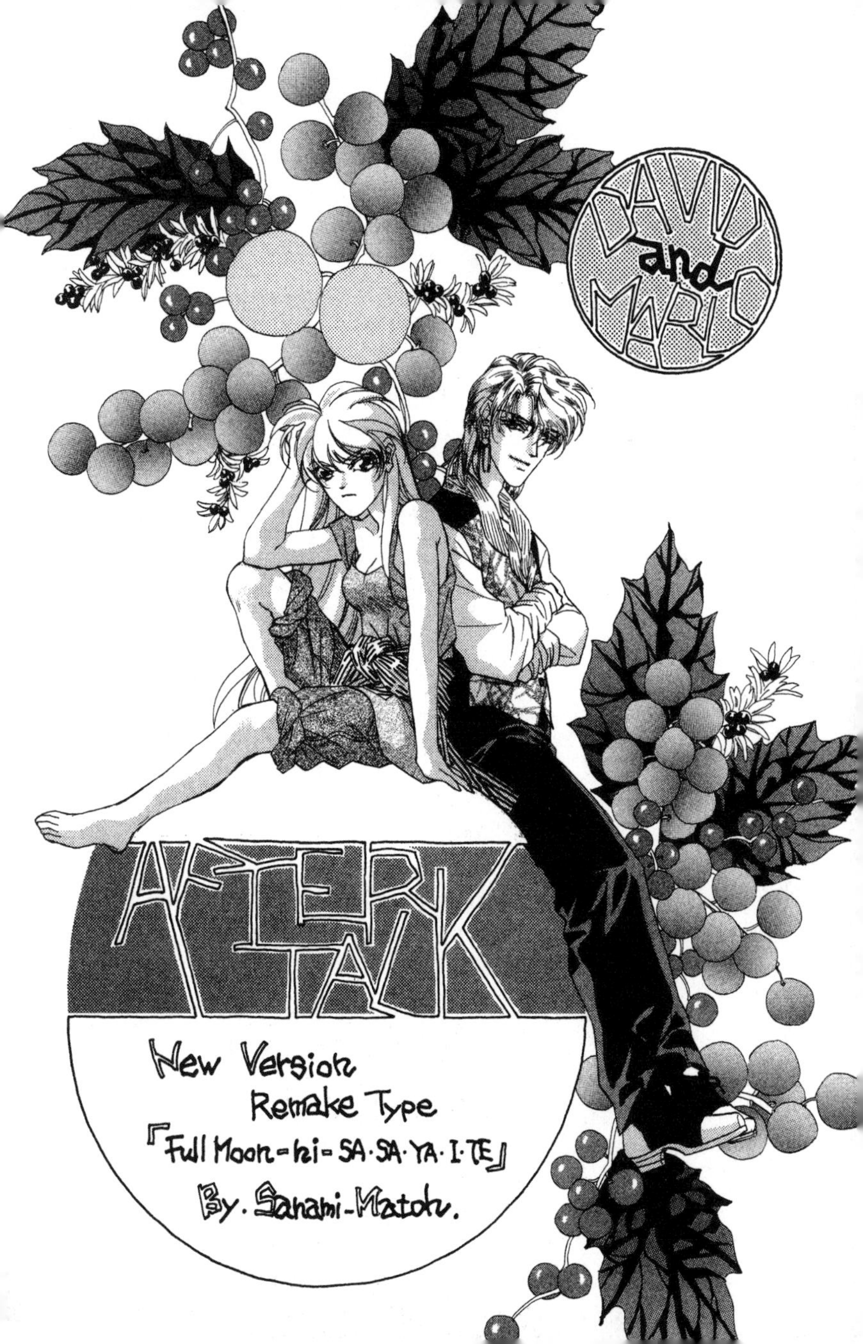
DAVID and MARLO
AFTER TALK
New Version
Remake Type
「Full Moon-ni-SA·SA·YA·I·TE」
By. Sanami-Matoh.

Kim.

THANK YOU FOR BUYING THIS BOOK. THE "FULL MOON" SERIES WAS ORIGINALLY DRAWN FOR A DIFFERENT PUBLISHER, BUT THE MAGAZINE WAS NO LONGER IN PUBLICATION, SO BIBLOS LET ME CONTINUE THE SERIES ON THEIR MAGAZINE. BIBLOS WAS ALSO KIND ENOUGH TO RE-RELEASE VOLUME 1. SINCE "FULL MOON" RECEIVED A LOT OF INQUIRIES FROM FANS, I'M GLAD THAT I WAS ABLE TO COMPLETE THE SERIES.

I DREW NEW COLOR ART FOR THE COVERS. HOPE YOU LIKE THEM.

THIS SERIES IS SCHEDULED TO BE COMPLETED IN TWO VOLUMES, BUT I'D LIKE TO DO MORE WITH THE CHARACTERS AND WRITE A SIDE STORY ONE OF THESE DAYS. I WOULD LIKE TO FIT IT INTO MY SCHEDULE, BUT I CAN'T MAKE ANY PROMISES OF WHEN THAT WILL BE, SINCE MY OTHER SERIES NEED MY ATTENTION FIRST. (AND I WRITE SO SLOWLY.) BUT I WILL TRY MY BEST. A LONG TIME AGO, I TOLD ANOTHER ARTIST FRIEND "IF THERE WERE TEN MORE OF ME, I COULD GET WORK DONE TEN TIMES AS FAST." SHE RESPONDED, "TEN PEOPLE MADE UP OF TEN PARTS OF ONE BODY WOULD ACTUALLY MAKE THE WORK GO MORE SLOWLY, I BET." THAT MADE SENSE...

I'm always making promises like this.

Claudia & Louis.

MOVIE

I'M NOT SURE IF YOU WOULD GO SO FAR AS TO CALL IT A HOBBY, BUT I LOVE MOVIES REGARDLESS OF THE GENRE, ESPECIALLY IF THEY'RE FUNNY. MOST OFTEN I WATCH FOR THE ACTOR. THE ACTRESSES I LIKE ARE KIM BASINGER, RENE RUSSO, GEENA DAVIS, JULIETTE LEWIS, GOLDIE HAWN, JODIE FOSTER, ISABELLE ADJANI, MICHELLE PFIEFFER, AND SHARON STONE. THERE ARE LOTS MORE BUT LATELY I HAVE REALLY GOTTEN INTERESTED IN KATE WINSLET. ACTORS I LIKE ARE SEAN CONNERY, DUSTIN HOFFMAN, NICHOLAS CAGE, ED HARRIS, AL PACINO, RUTGER HAUER, BRUCE WILLIS, GARY OLDMAN, WILLEM DAFOE, CHRISTOPHER WALKEN, MICHEAL BIEHN, AND STEVE MARTIN. I LIKE THE OLDER MOVIES JUST AS MUCH AS I LIKE THE NEW ONES. IF THERE IS AN ACTOR OR ACTRESS I LIKE IN A MOVIE, I WILL WATCH IT. AND I LIKE LOW BUDGET MOVIES THAT LOOK DIFFERENT AND UNUSUAL. (HONG KONG MOVIES ARE COMMON.) I'D LIKE TO MAKE A LIST OF MY FAVORITE MOVIES SOMEDAY. FOR THOSE THAT LIKE LEONARDO DICAPRIO, I HIGHLY RECOMMEND "WHAT'S EATING GILBERT GRAPE?" HE'S NOT THE LEAD, BUT IT'S MY FAVORITE MOVIE THAT HE IS IN.

Marlo & David.

Full Moon's most popular character, female Marlo.

READ THE SECOND VOLUME, TOO.

THANK YOU VERY MUCH.

Aftertalk End

Until the Full Moon II

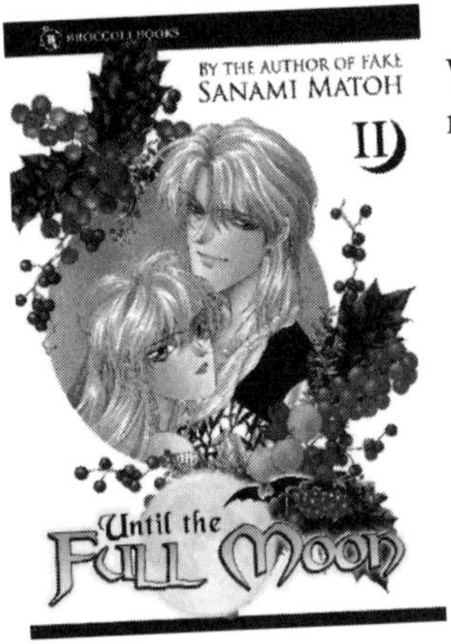
BY THE AUTHOR OF FAKE
SANAMI MATOH
II
Until the Full Moon

Who would have thought that there would be more trouble than changing into a woman on the evening of a full moon?

The love between Marlo and David is put to the test in the second and final volume.

Here's a sneak preview!

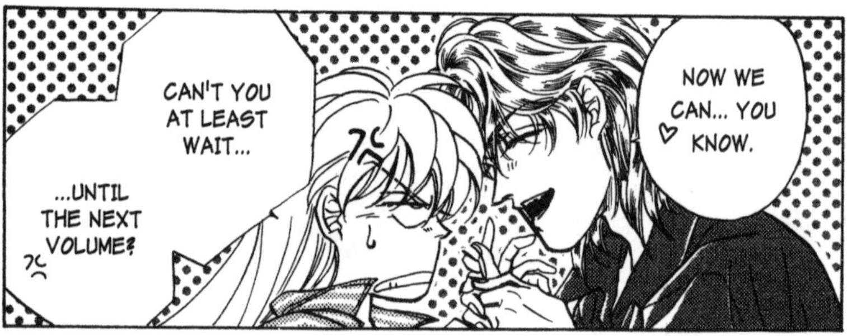
NOW WE CAN... YOU KNOW.
CAN'T YOU AT LEAST WAIT...
...UNTIL THE NEXT VOLUME?

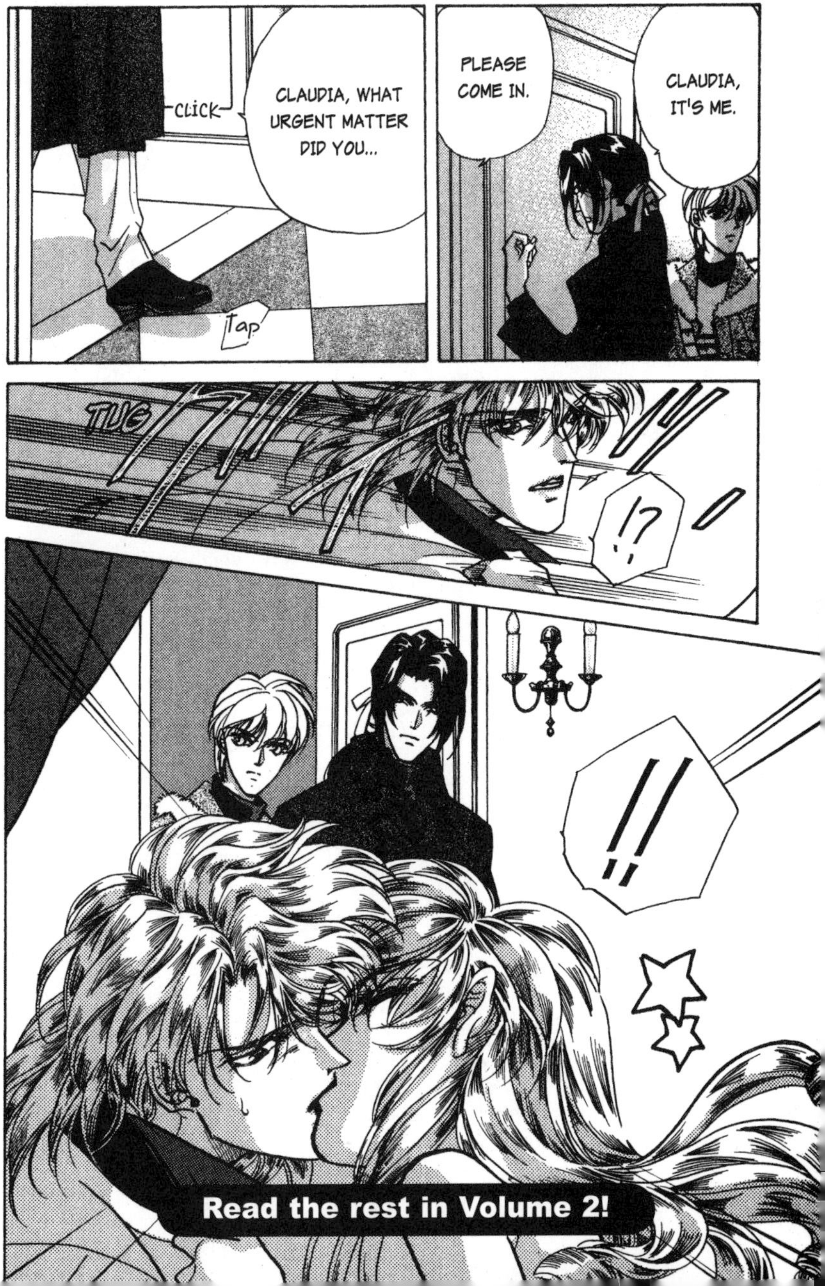
CLAUDIA, IT'S ME.
PLEASE COME IN.
CLICK
CLAUDIA, WHAT URGENT MATTER DID YOU...
Tap
TUG
!?
!!
Read the rest in Volume 2!

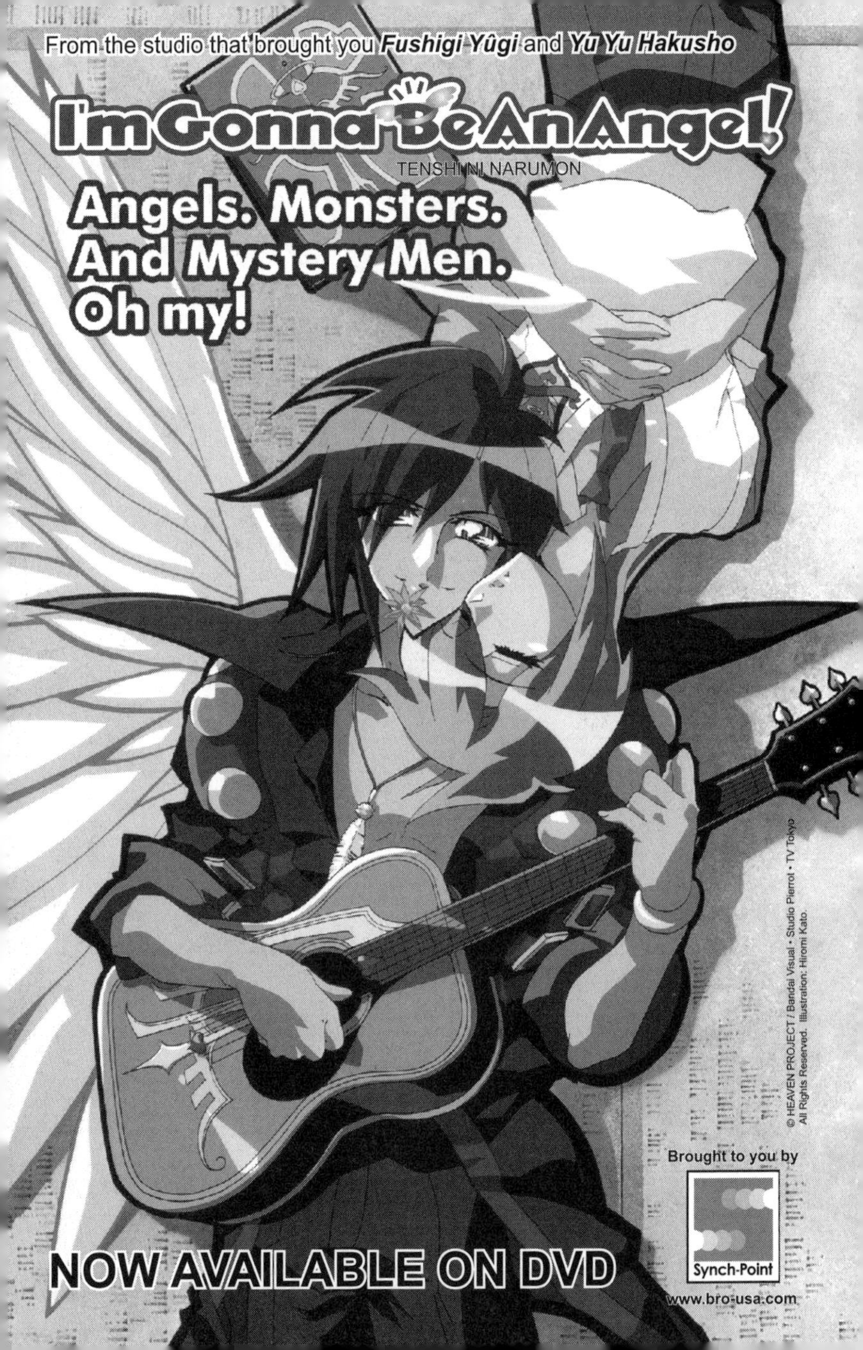
From the studio that brought you Fushigi Yûgi and Yu Yu Hakusho
I'm Gonna Be An Angel!
TENSHI NI NARUMON
Angels. Monsters.
And Mystery Men.
Oh my!
© HEAVEN PROJECT / Bandai Visual • Studio Pierrot • TV Tokyo
All Rights Reserved. Illustration: Hiromi Kato.
Brought to you by
Synch-Point
NOW AVAILABLE ON DVD
www.bro-usa.com

Join the celebration!
Di Gi Charat Theater - Leave it to Piyoko!, starring none other than Pyocola-sama, is coming out!

Support us, the Black Gema Gema Gang, and our mission to save Planet Analogue by buying the manga!!

Coming soon to your local bookstores!

brought to you by
BROCCOLI BOOKS
www.bro-usa.com

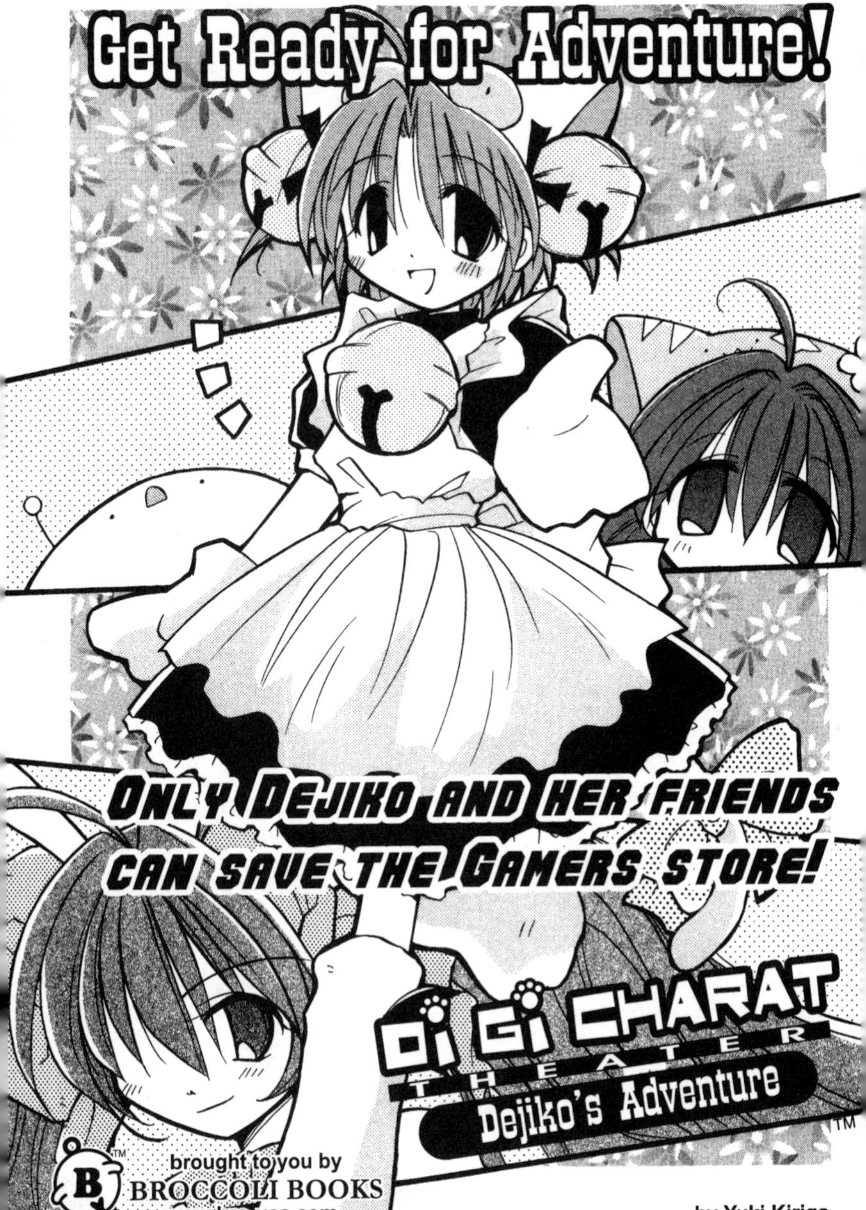
Get Ready for Adventure!
ONLY DEJIKO AND HER FRIENDS
CAN SAVE THE GAMERS STORE!
DI GI CHARAT THEATER
Dejiko's Adventure
by Yuki Kiriga
brought to you by
BROCCOLI BOOKS
www.bro-usa.com

YOU'RE READING THE WRONG WAY!

This is the end of the book! In Japan, manga is generally read from right to left. All reading starts on the upper right corner, and ends on the lower left. American comics are generally read from left to right, starting on the upper left of each page. In order to preserve the true nature of the work, we printed this book in a right to left fashion. Those who are unfamiliar with manga may find this confusing at first, but once you start getting into the story, you will wonder how you ever read manga any other way!

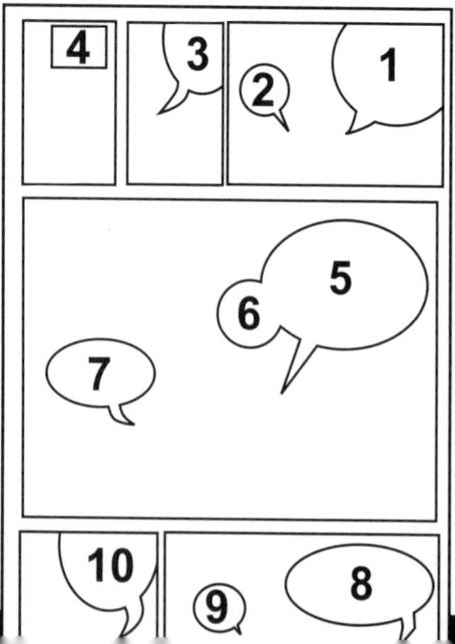
1
2
3
4
5
6
7
8
9
10

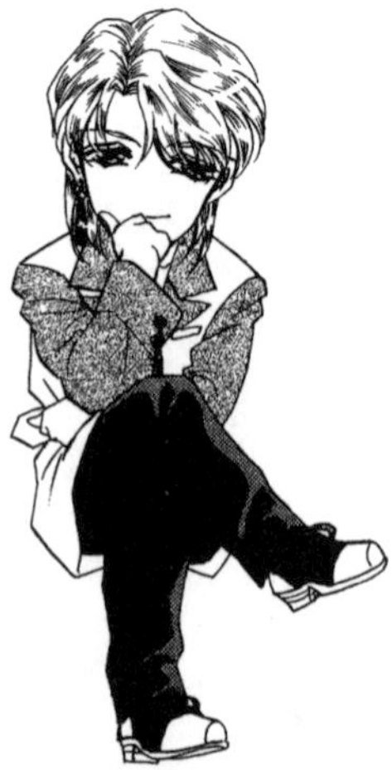

THIS QUESTIONNAIRE IS REDEEMABLE FOR:

Until the Full Moon Sticker

Broccoli Books Questionnaire

Fill out and return to Broccoli Books to receive an Until the Full Moon sticker!*

PLEASE MAIL THE COMPLETE FORM, ALONG WITH UNITED STATES POSTAGE STAMPS
WORTH $1.50 ENCLOSED IN THE ENVELOPE TO:**

> Broccoli International
> Attn: Broccoli Books Sticker Offer
> 12211 W Washington Blvd #110
> Los Angeles, CA 90066

(Please write legibly)

Name: _____

Address: _____

City, State, Zip: _____

E-mail: _____

Gender: ☐ Male ☐ Female **Age:** _____

(If you are under 13 years old, parental consent is required)

Parent/Guardian signature: _____

Occupation: _____

Where did you hear about this title?

☐ Magazine (Please specify): _____

☐ Flyer from: a store convention club other: _____

☐ Website (Please specify): _____

☐ At a store (Please specify): _____

☐ Word of Mouth

☐ Other (Please specify): _____

Where was this title purchased? (If known)

_____

Why did you buy this title?

_____
_____
_____

CUT ALONG HERE

How would you rate the following features of this manga?

	Excellent	Good	Satisfactory	Poor
Translation	☐	☐	☐	☐
Art quality	☐	☐	☐	☐
Cover	☐	☐	☐	☐
Extra/Bonus Material	☐	☐	☐	☐

What would you like to see improved in Broccoli Books manga?

___

Would you recommend this manga to someone else? ☐ Yes ☐ No

What related products would you be interested in?

☐ Posters ☐ Apparel Other: ___

Which magazines do you read on a regular basis?

___

What manga titles would you like to see in English?

___

Favorite manga titles: ___

Favorite manga artists: ___

What race/ethnicity do you consider yourself? (Please check one)

☐ Asian/Pacific Islander ☐ Native American/Alaskan Native

☐ Black/African American ☐ White/Caucasian

☐ Hispanic/Latino ☐ Other: ___

Final comments about this manga:

___

___

___

Thank you!

* While supplies last.

** For residents of Canada, please send an International Reply Coupon (IRC) of $3.00 US made out to "Broccoli International."

All information provided will be used for internal purposes only. We will not sell or otherwise divulge any of the information.

Requests not in compliance with all terms of this form will not be acknowledged or returned. All submissions are subject to verification and become the property of Broccoli International USA. Fraudulent submission, including use of multiple addresses or P.O. boxes to obtain additional Broccoli International USA information or offers may result in prosecution. Broccoli International USA reserves the right to withdraw or modify any terms of this form. Void where prohibited, taxed, or restricted by law. Broccoli International USA will not be liable for lost, misdirected, mutilated, illegible, incomplete, or postage-due mail. Sticker offer is only available to residents of the United States and Canada. For updates to the rules and regulations, please see www.bro-usa.com.

CUT ALONG HERE